DYNAMICS OF THE THIRD WORLD

Political and Social Change

EDITED BY

David E. Schmitt

Northeastern University

WINTHROP PUBLISHERS, INC.
Cambridge, Massachusetts

Library of Congress Cataloging in Publication Data

Schmitt, David E
Dynamics of the Third World

Includes bibliographical references.
1. Underdeveloped areas—Politics and government.
2. Underdeveloped areas—Social conditions. I. Title.
JF60.S33   320.9'172'4   73–22405
ISBN 0–87626–197–7
ISBN 0–87626–196–9 (pbk.)

Cover design by Joe Guertin

Copyright © 1974 by Winthrop Publishers, Inc.
17 Dunster Street, Cambridge, Massachusetts 02138

Contents

Preface

This book is an introductory text, not a treatise for advanced scholars. Its purpose is to provide an interesting, manageable introduction to Third World politics in Comparative Government courses as well as in political and social science courses dealing exclusively with Third World nations. Its concern with political change reflects the highly dynamic nature of Third World politics; a static description of present political structures would give students a quite inadequate understanding of political realities in the Third World.

Most of the countries chosen are large or quite important in their own right. Syria, however, was chosen because it is comparatively small, like many Third World countries, and because it constitutes a fascinating example of a country that has undergone nearly continual instability since independence, yet has made important economic, social and political strides. Also, it vividly illustrates the significance of international relations—in this case the crucial conflict with Israel. Chile was included not only because it represented successful or at least stable democratic development up to the fall of Allende, but also because it vividly illustrates problems of class conflict and the limitations of Third World political democracy. The countries represent a variety of types of political systems; they additionally represent all major Third World areas.

The book was student-tested at various stages in its development in Political Science courses at Northeastern University, an institution with a varied student body that is fairly representative of American university students. It became apparent that greater simplification was necessary, particularly in the introductory chapter and conclusion. As a result, a number of more sophisticated issues and concepts were omitted, and a simple, straightforward approach was adopted. This text thus represents a series of revisions aimed largely at making it more manageable and interesting for students. Of course, the comments of various scholars also proved quite helpful in revising initial drafts.

The central purpose of this text is to provide a useful tool for teaching courses in the social sciences. Instructors and students are invited to write to the editor at Northeastern University with suggestions on revisions. Though contributors were asked to employ a common framework and to deal with similar questions, each, of course, had freedom of interpretation with respect to his country of specialization.

The editor is grateful to the contributors for their willingness to make their chapters mutually comparative and to deal with common theoretical issues. The suggestions of the following scholars were of great help: Edward Friedman, University of Wisconsin; Robert L. Hardgrave, The University of Texas at Austin; Mary F. Katzenstein, University of Massachusetts, Boston; Arpad von Lazar, the Fletcher School of Law and Diplomacy; Fred R. von der Mehden, Rice University; Carl G. Rosberg, University of California, Berkeley; Abdul A. Said, American University; and Lois Wasserspring, Brandeis University. The research assistance of Christopher S. Allen and the excellent typing skills of Marilyn Zaslaw and Barbara Sladeck are appreciated. The comments of Northeastern University students on various drafts were of great benefit. As ever, the support of my wife, Gabrielle, proved to be a major source of inspiration for this undertaking. The editor, of course, is responsible and accountable for the conception of the book, the overall approach, and the choice of countries.

David E. Schmitt
Northeastern University
October, 1973

About the Contributors

David E. Schmitt, the editor, earned his Ph.D. at the University of Texas at Austin, and he currently teaches political science at Northeastern University. Dr. Schmitt is the author of *The Irony of Irish Democracy: The Impact of Political Culture on Administrative and Democratic Political Development in Ireland.* He has published several articles dealing with political change in Ireland and has travelled in Asia, Africa, and Latin America. He is currently engaged in research and writing on political change in Latin America.

Alan R. Balboni earned his Ph.D. at Brown University and teaches political science at Boston State College. Dr. Balboni is the author of "The American Zionist Lobby—Basic Patterns and Recent Trends," in the November-December 1972 issue of *Middle East Forum,* and he is presently engaged in further research on Middle East politics.

Victor C. Falkenheim earned his Ph.D. at Columbia and is currently an Assistant Professor in the Department of Political Economy at the University of Toronto. He has contributed articles on Chinese politics to *Asian Survey, Problems of Communism,* and to the book *Elites in the People's Republic of China,* edited by Robert A. Scalapino.

Minton F. Goldman earned his Ph.D. at the Fletcher School of Law and Diplomacy. He is currently an Associate Professor of Political Science at Northeastern University, where he offers courses on Western Europe, Communist political systems, and Africa. His most recent publication discusses colonial rivalry and was published in the *Journal of Southeast Asian Studies.*

Preston Lee Lawrence undertook his doctoral work at the University of Texas at Austin. He is currently teaching political science at Southwest Texas State University. With Fulbright support, he has conducted research in Chile. He is co-author of the book *Latin American Politics: A Functional Approach.*

Guy E. Poitras received his Ph.D. at the University of Texas at Austin and is currently Assistant Professor of Political Science at Trinity University, San Antonio. He was an Abraham Lincoln Scholar of the Mexican Government, and he has published articles on Mexican politics and administration. He is co-author of *Latin America: The Politics of Immobility.*

Walter L. Weisberg earned his Ph.D. in political science at the University of Texas at Austin. He has taught at Franklin and Marshall College as well as Kansas State University. Dr. Weisberg is currently engaged in further research on the politics of India.

To Alana and Michael

Introduction

DAVID E. SCHMITT

PURPOSE OF THE BOOK

This is an introductory text on political change in the Third World. Its purpose is to provide an understanding of some of the major problems confronting Third World nations and to give insight into the various tools and strategies that Third World political leaders can use in dealing with those problems. The book also will investigate some of the major avenues toward political development, and will briefly assess the costs and benefits of the approaches discussed.

Third World nations are poorer and less developed economically than nations such as the United States and the Soviet Union. Most of them are located in Asia, Africa, the Middle East, and Latin America. Indeed, with very few exceptions (such as Japan and Israel), Third World countries comprise most of the nations of these areas. In general, the modern capitalist democracies of Europe and North America (and, for practical purposes, such nations as Japan and Australia) can be considered "First World." The economically advanced Communist nations (the Soviet Union and much of Eastern Europe) can be termed "Second World." Although portions of modern nations, such as Appalachia and some American ghettos, may approximate Third World conditions, as a whole the modern First World and Second World nations are economically advanced and organizationally sophisticated.

1

Third World nations exist in a world seemingly dominated by giant economic powers. Indeed, many gained independence from the modern colonial powers only after the end of World War II. Third World nations see themselves as a distinct group of countries in competition with the more economically advanced nations. In fact, Third World countries have formed numerous international and regional conferences and associations to deal with common problems.[1]

However remote they may appear to Americans, the Third World nations have a direct, personal bearing on the security of citizens in modern countries. The Third World comprises most of the people and nations of this earth. Most of the warfare and political turbulence since World War II has involved Third World countries, and the most explosive international crises have usually centered on them.

ORGANIZATION OF THE BOOK

This first chapter discusses the patterns of Third World politics. It examines first some of the common pressures and forces on Third World nations that helped determine their present condition. Next it briefly examines some of the most important strategies and tools of political control, that is, the methods and techniques by which Third World leaders can deal with the profound problems confronting their countries. Finally, the introduction discusses various avenues of Third World political development. This discussion is brief and straightforward. A list of books for suggested further reading appears at the end of this introduction.

The chapters in the rest of the text provide concrete examples of some of the most important and interesting Third World nations on earth. *India,* a huge Asian nation, illustrates the democratic road to political development within the context of a traditional, fragmented culture. *Chile,* an important Latin American nation, represents a country that was one of the few seemingly successful cases of democratic political development in the Third World. Chile's political system was also an example of a Marxist government which came to power in a democratic nation; it additionally represents some of the problems of Third World democracies. On the other hand, *Mexico* is a major Latin American nation that illustrates the pattern of limited democracy, which it followed after its dramatic revolution in the early part of this century. *Nigeria,* with the largest population of any African nation, represents a country following an authoritarian avenue of development after being wracked by civil war. As much as any Third World nation, Nigeria vividly displays the significance of cultural fragmentation and the importance of national identity and institution building. *Syria* is an Arab state that is small, like many Third World countries, and subject to intense international pressures. It provides an example of left-wing authoritarian government and also of the problems of nearly continual political instability. Another Asian giant, *China,* will provide a fascinating example of the mobilization avenue toward political development. The examination of all six countries follows the format set out in this introduction and will deal with the questions raised herein. A concluding chapter will briefly compare the experiences of the six nations. Before turning to the studies of the six countries, it remains to discuss the analytical framework, the various pressures on Third World nations that help determine politics in those countries, the principal tools and strategies of political control, and different avenues toward political development.

FRAMEWORK FOR ANALYSIS

This text considers three principal concepts in relation to Third World nations: *dependent variable, independent variable* and *political development.* According to the concept of *dependent variable,* governments and political systems are viewed as products of their environment and as consequences of a variety of political, social, and economic forces. Yet it would be a great oversimplification to see a political system solely as a dependent variable, that is, solely as a response to its surroundings. A political system can be viewed also as an *independent variable* with other social systems responding (as dependent variables) to actions taken by government. Political leaders for example can exert many controls over society. As the study of Communist China will make clear, political leaders can sometimes wield an enormous control over social and economic systems.[2]

Political development means the processes by which political systems increase their ability to deal with the rising demands, increasing groups and participants, and expanding tasks required of governments confronting modernization. This involves the creation and maintenance of popular support and the building of effective political and administrative institutions such as political parties and modern administrative agencies. Traditional institutions such as tribal councils and bureaucratic empires are usually incapable of handling these burdens even though they may be quite sophisticated in coping with the problems and needs of earlier societies.[3]

One form of political development is political democracy, such as that of the United States and Britain. Another form of political development is the type of one-party system that evolved in the Soviet Union. Both patterns of development have, thus far, sufficiently coped with and managed modernization to survive. It should not be assumed that any one form of political development is automatically best or that the institutions of modern nations represent the only possible avenues of development. They may be quite inappropriate to many of the Third World nations which have their own cultural values and social conditions that present them with quite different patterns of modernization and goals than those of modern nations.

Furthermore, it is inaccurate to view the more modern nations as politically developed, for development refers to an ongoing process that can easily change into a decreased ability to cope with social change. For example, many argue that the centralized, bureaucratic systems of modern nations coupled with their seemingly insatiable thirst for material growth have nearly destroyed the environment and alienated the mass of citizens upon whom they depend for support. For these and other reasons some scholars such as Samuel Huntington have argued that the term "development" can be quite misleading.[4] Hence, it is important to keep in mind that the term political development, as we shall use it, refers to the *capacity* of political systems to manage and cope with change and the increasing tasks and problems associated with modernization. We must also remember that there are many possible approaches to acquiring this capacity, some of which may not even emphasize the importance of national government and the nation-state but might instead build on tribes or other configurations.

Additionally, the relationship between a political system and its environment is one of reciprocity. No government, for example, completely controls its environment, nor are many governments entirely at the mercy of the pressures and forces around them. For all nations there is a continual interplay of forces between political systems and other social configurations such as the cultural and economic systems. Nevertheless, many Third World governments seem virtually adrift in a sea of turbulent forces with which they are unable to cope. The following are some of the specific forces, both past and present, which contribute to this turbulence.

DETERMINANTS OF PRESENT-DAY POLITICS: THIRD WORLD POLITICAL
SYSTEMS AS DEPENDENT VARIABLES

Colonialism

The conquest by European nations of much of Asia, Africa, and Latin America shattered traditional political systems. The Incan and Aztec empires of Latin America, for example, were obliterated by the Spanish conquest, and the modernizing impact of today's Latin American governments is eroding the remaining Indian cultures. Tribal nations in Africa and traditional empires in Asia were permanently though not completely altered by their confrontation with Western imperialism. Of course, many earlier cultural values, if not the actual political systems, are still important.

The colonial powers introduced new methods of commercial, social, and political organization. The quest for profits transformed many agricultural communities into economies geared to the extraction of mineral wealth such as gold and silver. The Western emphasis upon science and modern administration challenged traditional cultural values. Missionary activity destroyed or modified many indigenous religions. Local social and political hierarchies were frequently molded to the wishes of the colonial rulers. Through military conquest, then, colonialism forever changed the character of Third World societies. It often violently set off forces of economic, social, and political change.

But colonialism is not in itself an adequate explanation of the rapid modernization in developing areas, for some nations such as Thailand and China were never under prolonged, direct colonial rule. Yet they are also facing the pressures of rapid economic and social transformation. Furthermore, the pace of change often increased after the departure of the colonial rulers. Forces other than direct colonial rule must therefore account for a substantial share of the pressures of change. In any event, old style colonialism is now virtually dead. Most of the nations of Latin America cast off the shackles of foreign rule during the last century, and since the end of World War II the countries of Asia and Africa have with few exceptions broken from the grasp of direct colonial rule. Between 1945 and 1973 over 70 new nations have emerged. Except for a few diehards such as Portugal, the Western powers have almost eagerly abandoned their political control of Third World societies. A variety of forces including the impact of World War II has made direct colonial rule nearly obsolete.

POLITICAL INSTABILITY. But chaos often followed independence. The turbulent politics of the new Asian and African nations bear witness to the shattered hopes of those in the West who envisioned orderly democratic political growth in these countries. The history of postwar Asia and Africa is littered with coups, civil wars, and rebellions. Nigeria represents one of the costliest illustrations of this instability. Most readers will remember the TV news coverage of starving Biafran children who were victims of the civil war in that country. The Nigerian experience, however, is not really unique despite its ferocity and destruction of human life. Between 1967 and 1973, for example, armed takeovers, attempted takeovers, or other major internal clashes occurred in over fifteen African nations.

Asian countries also have been plagued by chronic instability. Since World War II, major internal violence or the breakdown of constitutional politics has taken place in Burma, Cambodia, Ceylon (Sri Lanka), China, Indonesia, the Philippines, Laos, Malaysia, Pakistan, South Korea, Thailand, and Vietnam. Even in Latin America, where most countries have long been independent, few nations have avoided major political upheavals. Military takeovers have been especially commonplace. Revolutions in Cuba and Bolivia also illustrate the point that political violence has plagued our Third World neighbors to the south. In sum, chronic political turbulence has been a characteristic feature of Third World nations.

THE FAILURE OF WESTERN-TYPE DEMOCRACY. From the viewpoint of the United States and other modern democracies, politics in the Third World have been disastrous. Not only have developing nations been wracked by violence; they have also failed to create effective democratic governments. Authoritarian governments are the rule rather than the exception in Third World areas. In Africa, few if any Western-type democracies exist, and Asian authoritarian governments greatly outnumber the democratic governments in that area. There are a few noteworthy exceptions. India, a nation with more than 525 million people, has operated under democratic procedures since its independence in 1947. Despite poverty, overpopulation, and an archaic caste system, India has achieved a level of democracy to be found in few Third World nations. Democratic government in the Philippines survived the Japanese occupation of World War II and the violent Huk guerrilla rebellion of the 1950's, but now is threatened by the authoritarian measures of President Marcos.

In Latin America, stable democratic development has eluded the great majority of nations. Even formerly successful democracies have succumbed to authoritarian rule, Chile being a prime example. In other Latin American countries the success of democratic politics has been limited. As Professor Poitras demonstrates, for instance, Mexico is essentially a one-party state where the prospects are slim that the ruling party could be voted out of office.

But we have been using the term democracy in the traditional Western sense, namely as a type of political system or process characterized by honest elections, free speech, freedom of assembly, a free press, and the opportunity for open competition for control of government. A more meaningful interpretation of democracy for many in the Third World, however, refers to a system in which all citizens have a chance to partake of the fruits of economic advancement and in which there exists genuine social and economic opportunity for all. In other words, Westerners often see democracy as a *political* phenomenon characterized by a certain process of decision-making. Third World leaders and citizens, on the other hand, often emphasize *social* democracy. The significance of the distinction is that social democracy may sometimes be best achieved by authoritarian governments that do not permit oppositions and thus more easily implement major social and economic reforms. Similarly, Western-type political democracies can actually prevent social democracy and permit traditional elites to remain in power. Latin America's two-party systems have historically pitted sectors of the privileged classes against each other to the exclusion of the masses. In any event, as we shall see, democratic politics of the type found in the United States and Britain are probably impossible at present for most, though not all, Third World countries. Moreover, we shall see later that even some political violence, which most Westerners view with disfavor, may have positive consequences.

NEOCOLONIALISM. It was noted above that colonialism permanently altered the politics of the Third World, but that the old style, direct-rule colonialism is virtually dead. Yet some of the difficulties in the Third World result from the continuing economic and political involvement of modern nations in the affairs of Third World countries. This intervention is often called "neocolonialism." Indeed, some writers would argue that most of the changes and problems of the developing areas are the result of newer and subtle forms of domination by rich nations over poor. It is true that investments by corporations of modern nations in the economies of emerging countries sometimes lead to such problems as a quickened rate of social upheaval. This involvement sometimes additionally prevents reforms where investments help entrench conservative government in power. And there is little doubt that competition among the United States, the Soviet Union, and others for influence in the Third World may greatly shape the internal politics of these countries. Loans from economically advanced nations often specify how and where the borrowed money shall be spent, usually in the country doing the lending. These and other provisions restrict the options of Third World leaders in their quest for economic growth.

The study of Chile shows that meddling by modern nations in the domestic politics of Third World countries sometimes represents a real threat to their independence. In the case of Chile, a U. S. corporation apparently attempted to prevent the election of the Marxist President Allende, and the United States government brought a number of economic pressures to bear on Allende's government. Of course, Chile is more powerful and more economically advanced than most Third World countries. Intervention in weaker Third World nations by multinational corporations or modern governments is often less subtle, as in the U. S. military intervention in the Dominican Republic.

Yet for some of the developing nations the neocolonialist argument overstates the point. For example, foreign aid and investment sometimes have beneficial as well as harmful consequences; it depends on a variety of conditions, as we shall see. Perhaps the most important point about relations between modern and Third World nations is not merely that neocolonialism may exploit poorer and weaker nations but that it may impede more viable lines of economic growth and political development. In any case, there are other crucial pressures on Third World nations such as the impact of economic and technological change.

Economic Development and Technological Change

Virtually all Third World nations are struggling for economic growth. Whether or not they succeed, economic and technological change can profoundly alter their social structures. Economic and technological advances quicken the pace of life. For example, a developing economy requires efficient means of transportation to move workers, raw materials, and finished products. Changes in the pace of life produce great strain on citizen and government alike. Tight schedules, crowded busing, and hectic rushing help produce anxiety in persons accustomed to a less crowded and more leisurely life. Moreover, governments must take on the task of coordinating fast moving and complex economies, and they must somehow obtain the funds necessary to finance development programs.

The changes generated by economic development complicate the task of governing in other fundamental ways. Economic growth increases the number of professions and occupations and greatly specializes them. Automobile production, for instance, requires engineers, machinists, tool-and-die makers, shipping and supply clerks, and a host of other positions. This division of labor has important political consequences, for a specialized society is an interdependent society. Each part is important and therefore potentially politically powerful. For example, striking truck drivers can cripple an entire nation; technicians and managers are equally indispensable. Even unskilled workers in modernizing societies may sometimes be mobilized into important political forces. Governments in Third World nations must therefore balance the conflicting pressures of many diverse interests in a situation where they have little money and where they often lack institutions capable of handling the complex administrative and political problems associated with social and economic change.

Pressures of increasing demands are aggravated by the staggering population growth rates that often eat up real gains in Third World economic output. One of the consequences of modern technology has been the development of drugs, vaccines, and other medical advances that have greatly expanded the human life span and lowered death rates throughout the world. As yet, most efforts to institute widespread birth control programs have been unsuccessful. Population growth puts enormous burdens on governments lacking significant financial resources. It also aggravates problems associated with urbanization because of the increased number of Third World citizens living in mushrooming cities.

Urbanization

A variety of forces contributes to the rapid increase in the size of cities and towns. Population growth, changing agricultural techniques, and the hope for a better way of life are among the forces contributing to the problem of rapid urbanization. When people migrate from the country to the cities, they are more exposed to the value-shattering impact of mass media such as radio and television, even though they may retain traits of their traditional culture.

Urban dwellers require more government services than inhabitants of rural areas. Roads, sewage systems, fire departments, and enlarged police forces cost money and require sophisticated administrative systems to manage these and other necessary tasks well. Government itself is therefore compelled to modernize and specialize. Furthermore, people living in cities are more easily organized into a political force. When peoples of diverse ethnic groups and cultures are brought together in urban settings the potential for instability is great.

Furthermore, the economies of new urban centers in Third World nations cannot usually absorb the influx of workers; unemployment is rampant. Many who do work often hold marginal jobs such as the vendors described in the chapter on Chile. Moreover, the ties of city dwellers to relatives in the countryside contribute to the increasing political significance of rural citizens. Consumption patterns change when people flock to the cities. Not only do they require more government assistance, but they also put greater strain on the economy. All of their food must be purchased since none can usually be grown or gathered in cities. Also, urbanization raises consumer demands for such items as television sets. These and other pressures from urbanization place great strain on Third World governments.

The Worldwide Communications Revolution

Technological advances have produced a worldwide communications revolution that often creates serious problems for Third World leaders. Radio, television, movies, and magazines carry news of the materialistic products of the West to all corners of the world. American films, for example, have displayed a life of modern conveniences that erodes assumptions about the inevitability of economic poverty. Pictures of houses with indoor plumbing, refrigerators, electric lights, automatic stoves, and clothes washers are revolutionary to people who cook on open fires, walk to wells for water, and beat their garments clean with stones. Of course, not all Third World citizens have access to television or movies, and many are unable to read, but urbanization and other forces have eroded their former isolation.

Nations such as the United States certainly have not solved the problems of poverty, but the economic well-being of the majority of people in modern states is certainly higher. Furthermore, the modern nations can more easily meet needs for consumer goods while simultaneously investing in long-term projects. Poorer Third World countries often have difficulty doing either. Some citizens of modern nations criticize materialism in their own society, but people living in poverty view modern consumer goods as a means of freeing themselves from hard and heavy burdens. And most Third World citizens are economically poor.

Not only do the modern media carry messages of affluent materialism, they also increase awareness of the political system. News broadcasts inform citizens and groups of the government's central role in determining their economic opportunities. Word of public educational, agricultural, and welfare programs tells people that government is of increasing importance in their personal lives. Thus, the modern mass media increase the number of participants in the struggle for the rewards distributed by the political system, and they heighten the sense of urgency with which groups attempt to gain control of government.[5] All of the pressures noted thus far have contributed to one of the most disruptive forces of all: the shattering or alteration of traditional cultures.

Cultural Change

An extremely disruptive consequence of modernization is the shattering of old beliefs and values as modern ideas take their place. Tribal beliefs, for example, give way to scientific methods grudgingly. Traditional leaders often resist the encroachment of governments as political leaders assume control of education, economic development, and welfare. Towns, regions, or tribes must now compete with nation and government for the loyalty of citizens.[6]

The beliefs held by large numbers of citizens can determine whether governments stand or fall. Popular loyalty toward the nation and its institutions provides a foundation for the day-to-day strains of resolving political controversies. Indeed, national identity and popular support for government are basic to the development of a viable nation-state and effective political institutions. Where the state or political institutions have not acquired popular acceptance, ambitious politicians and military officers are less hesitant in overthrowing the government. Once a pattern of political instability is established, violence may be accepted as the norm by leaders and public alike. Latin American nations have witnessed so many revolts that they are accepted by many citizens as a way of life.

A principal task of Third World leaders is therefore to generate popular identification with the nation as well as with the government. Yet this is one of the most difficult goals to achieve in politics. It frequently means starting from scratch. Unlike people in the modern nations, many inhabitants of new states have never heard of their country and do not know what the word "nation" means. Nor can people simply be told that they are a citizen of "X" country. This would not in itself create public loyalty nor would it automatically infringe upon their other loyalties. When people have viewed themselves as belonging first to a particular tribe, community, or family, it is an enormous undertaking to instill a commitment to their state—the more so since the state may include peoples of diverse cultures, races, languages, and religions.

Cultural fragmentation greatly intensifies the problem of generating public commitment to the nation and its political institutions. Tribal, religious, and language diversities encourage disintegration rather than national unification. Few kinds of political conflict reach the levels of intensity and violence as those based upon ethnic rivalries and hatreds. Modernization itself can aggravate ethnic or tribal hostilities because the decisions of government become far more significant to citizens and groups. As Professor Goldman later demonstrates, the animosity between the principal tribes of Nigeria helped prevent the evolution of effective, democratic government and led eventually to civil war. Cultural fragmentation also has confronted India with serious though less devastating problems.

Even where the public identifies with the state and where there is little cultural diversity, popular beliefs and values may impede successful political development. Some of the most politically significant attitudes concern matters seemingly removed from politics. Do people, for instance, view one another as trustworthy in everyday life or do they expect others to cheat? Of course nobody trusts others completely. But when children are raised to distrust those outside the immediate family, tribe, or community, cooperation is more difficult to achieve.[7]

Workers in organizations cannot work harmoniously if they refuse to entrust others with delegated responsibilities. If fear makes employees adhere excessively to rules, organizations become inflexible and stagnate. Governments in rapidly modernizing nations need cooperative people in order to accomplish the complex administrative tasks of a rapidly changing society. The sudden value changes wrought by modernization, however, frequently breed insecurity and distrust, making all the more difficult the task of achieving cooperation.

Fatalism, or the belief that one's situation is determined by fate or by God's will, may also impede the rate at which nations develop economically and the success with which they develop politically. People will be reluctant to press for political or economic change if they feel that everything is predetermined. Also, they will be less likely to be personally ambitious and thus less likely to become dynamic business leaders, managers, or technicians. Yet fatalism is often merely a reflection of lack of opportunity, and no culture produces completely fatalistic people. Fatalism is therefore a matter of degree. Additionally, fatalism is clearly declining in the Third World. The mass media, urbanization, and other modernizing changes lead to rising expectations. Nevertheless, fatalism probably hinders economic growth in the Third World. While it may reduce political demands at a time when struggling governments can do with fewer pressures, it can also help perpetuate political stagnation and impede necessary political and economic change.

Personalism, a common feature of traditional cultures, may also impede economic and political development. In a highly personalistic society, loyalty to family, friends, or ethnic group almost always comes ahead of loyalty to government laws or bureaucratic rules. The government treasury may become a private fund for the person who holds public office. The ability to win a government contract depends not on submitting the lowest bid, but on having the "right" connections. Many citizens of the Third World, because of their cultural heritage, do not consider this kind of behavior immoral. Rather, they view decisions based on abstract rules and laws as heartless and cold. Also, personalism may provide a social cohesion of use in building organizations. But extreme personalism wastes government money, breeds inefficiency, and may very well prevent meaningful social reforms and hinder the development of effective political and administrative institutions.

Crises, Sequences and Rates of Change

Up to now we have talked about some of the specific forces and pressures that contribute to the instability of so many Third World nations. Our next task will be to review the pressures on Third World countries in terms of the crises they face. Also, we shall briefly discuss the critical problems of timing and pace of change. Among the problems or crises are the need to foster national identity and government legitimacy as well as to create institutions capable of handling the influx of new participants into the political system. Also, governments must establish organizations capable of authoritatively penetrating society, extracting resources such as taxes, and distributing or redistributing various benefits among groups and citizens. One of the most important requirements for any political system is to develop effective institutions capable of dealing with particular crisis areas. This component of political development will be termed *institutionalization*, which refers to the process by which structures and procedure (bureaucracies, legislatures, voting procedures, presidents, parties, etc.) acquire stability and public support.[8] In many of the modern nations the crises discussed above occurred at different times. For example, national identity and government institutions viewed as legitimate frequently emerged prior to the influx of new participants brought about by technological, political, and social change. It is usually important that national identity and the establishment of legitimacy precede mass participation if government leaders are to control it. In much of the Third World, however, fundamental crises are likely to occur simultaneously. The crises of creating a sense of national identity, legitimizing government, controlling participation, and penetrating the social and economic systems with the power to redistribute resources and otherwise govern effectively often occur together. Government leaders are often inexperienced and must acquire skills of leadership while attempting to build effective government and party structures. In brief, key problems of development tend to happen all at once. Above all, the rates of social, economic, and political changes are often so rapid that political disruption rather than political development ensues.

However, not all Third World nations confront identical crises in their sequences or identical rates of change. The timing of the above crises and pace of change is one of the most important factors explaining the politics of particular countries, and it will become apparent from the following chapters that the distinct sequences are crucial. India, for example, evolved adaptive political institutions prior to winning independence from Britain. Nigeria and Syria, on the other hand, lacked effective political and administrative structures at independence. Furthermore, Nigeria's citizens had no common sense of nationhood. The revolutions in China and Mexico confronted the new leaders of those nations with multiple crises. But as we shall see, the revolutions also served as a springboard to the development of popularly backed governments.

In sum, few Third World nations escape great pressure from rapid political, technological, and social change. The processes of profound change inevitably result in conflict between old and new values. They generate great demands and pressures upon governments that are often inexperienced and lacking in public support. They frequently foster conflict among different cultures, which now have a greater stake in government decisions. Above all, Third World countries frequently face simultaneous crises and an incredibly rapid pace of change—pressures which often result in political paralysis or violence.[9]

Revolution

A comparatively rare form of violence in developing nations is revolution. The term refers to fundamental and violent changes in the political, social, and economic systems. A simple overthrow of government is not enough to qualify as a revolution; the entire fabric of society must be radically modified. The violent overthrow of government coupled with the annihilation of the traditional ruling class and the creation of a new socialist economic system would constitute a revolution. In China, for instance, Mao won political control, destroyed the power of the middle and upper classes, and instituted a radically socialist economy. On the other hand, a series of government overthrows in Syria did not at first radically alter the economic and social system.

The rarity of revolutions may seem surprising in view of the chronic problems and rapid social changes in Third World nations. Their infrequency is explained in part by the consideration that they are not as likely to occur in traditional or in complex modern nations. Revolutions require the simultaneous alienation of several sectors of society and their willingness and ability to work together toward the destruction of the existing political and social order. Ordinarily, large sectors of the middle classes and peasants must be alienated from the regime at the same time. Not only must the current government be unwilling to admit new groups to the political system; there must be some perceived hope of successfully ousting the existing regime. Revolutions are more likely to occur when people's expectations are heightened by improving social and economic conditions.

Revolutions can break bottlenecks in the social, economic and political systems. They occur generally because political leaders are unwilling or unable to initiate reforms and allow new groups into the system or because the traditional government collapses. Therefore, revolutions, like other forms of instability, may lead to political development. If revolutionary leaders can build organizations capable of adapting to rapid change, the revolution may lead to long-term, viable evolution of both the economy and the political system as in the case of Mexico and China. On the other hand, revolutions offer no guarantee of political development. The Bolivian Revolution has been followed by a period of alternating coups between leftist and rightist military officers.[10]

Although revolutions are infrequent, the chronic problems and rapid changes occurring in the Third World suggest that others may take place. More common, however, will be the other forms of violence and instability discussed earlier: for example, military coups, civil wars, general strikes, riots, and assassinations. Prospects for stable, evolutionary political development in many Third World countries are therefore slim. Furthermore, rapid economic development, which can facilitate political development in spite of the strains it produces, is likely to elude most Third World nations.

But we must not lose our time perspective. Many Third World nations are new and inexperienced. Most are undergoing enormous strains, and instability sometimes provides a stepping stone to a better future. We should not forget the growing pains of modern nations such as the Civil War in the United States even with that country's slower, more sequential modernization and political evolution. Moreover, there are instances of viable political development in the Third World, as some cases in this book show. Of course, it would be equally naive to assume that all instability and violence is either helpful or necessary. Probably most is not. In guarding against being overly biased against stability, we should not forget that instability often produces great human suffering. The ultimate difficulty for students of contemporary politics is that it is often impossible at the moment to determine whether political turbulence is a component of greater modernization or political development or merely a result of breakdown.

Finally, however great the problems of Third World nations, we cannot assume that the political system is simply a dependent variable or a response to its environment and history. For leaders in political systems can help determine their own futures and indeed the rate and nature of social, economic and political change that has such a profound bearing on political development. In other words, we can view political change as dependent upon environmental forces. But we also need to ask ourselves to what extent the political system and its leaders can be an independent variable, helping to determine not only its own capacity to develop viable institutions but also the pace and nature of social, economic, and cultural change. It is to this task that we now turn.

TECHNIQUES AND STRUCTURES OF CONTROL: THE POLITICAL SYSTEM AS AN INDEPENDENT VARIABLE

The Use of Personality

The potential for great leaders to arise increases in times of crisis and in less institutionalized political systems. Thus, the chance of towering dominant leaders is probably greatest in Third World nations wracked by crisis and weakened by the lack of effective political organizations. In the modern nations, on the other hand, one more frequently finds bureaucratic types capable of manipulating complex administrative machinery. Richard Nixon of the United States, Leonid Brezhnev of the Soviet Union, and Edward Heath of Britain exemplify typical leaders of advanced nations. Even the few colorful and charismatic statesmen such as John F. Kennedy and Pierre Trudeau have usually not dominated the life of their governments. However shocked the American public was after the assassination of John F. Kennedy, the political system quite easily held together. In less institutionalized countries such a tragedy might easily tear the nation apart. This vulnerability suggests, of course, that dependence upon personal rule can be destabilizing if a leader is killed or where institutionalized means of choosing new leaders does not exist.

One of the most important uses of personality avails itself mainly to nations that won independence in wars of liberation or engaged in war with hostile neighbors. When heroes of these conflicts become leaders, they can bring an enormous advantage to the job. With strong public support for national leaders, the government has greater legitimacy and reforms are more easily accomplished.[11]

Public Bureaucracy

Successful governing in modernizing nations depends ultimately upon the development of effective public organizations. Governments must have the capacity to penetrate the society with regulatory mechanisms capable of extracting resources such as taxes and redistributing them in ways that facilitate the handling of new groups and goals. Few other tasks are so crucial as the need to develop institutions capable of controlling and coordinating economic and social change.

The principal coordinating and controlling mechanism in most modern societies is public bureaucracy. Complex, specialized societies require complex, specialized government agencies staffed by experts. Although the administrative systems of Third World countries need not necessarily follow the centralized models of Western countries, they clearly require organizations with the power to implement government policies.[12]

Some Third World nations have achieved effective bureaucracies. Scholars have pointed out that strong, effective administrations can even lessen the disruptive potential of ethnic conflict.[13] Typically, however, Third World political systems lack effective administrative systems. The reasons for this shortcoming are partly due to the policies of colonial powers, where colonial rulers often refused to recruit local persons into top administrative positions Thus, present government officials are frequently inexperienced.

The principal difficulty, however, is that traditional values have not caught up with modern structures. Family, ethnic and religious loyalties frequently take precedence over administrative rules so that government functions on a personalistic and unequal basis. Incompetent people are hired and promoted because of personal connections. This tendency is aggravated by the fact that with few other available jobs people clamor for positions in government. Corruption can sometimes help the development of viable government institutions by giving government leaders a means of building and controlling bureaucracy as well as a means of admitting new participants into politics. Yet much of the corruption and control of bureaucracy by outside groups does not produce institutionalization of effective structures and processes. It often merely impedes the admission of new groups into the political system and sidetracks money that might be used for economic and social purposes.

Unfortunately, politicians have few effective tools to overcome administrative incompetence and insubordination. Auditing and civil service procedures are usually inadequate because records can be faked and dual sets of books kept—one for the auditors and one with the real financial and administrative records. When people view corruption as the normal way of life, modern accounting and administrative techniques prove inadequate. Cultural divisions usually aggravate the problem of administrative control. Even in modern nations this problem has not been completely solved; one need only recall the difficulty American presidents have had enforcing equal opportunity for blacks in the U. S. federal bureaucracy. What is difficult to overcome in advanced nations is often nearly impossible to correct in Third World countries.

Political Parties

There are, however, circumstances and techniques that can help establish effective administrative systems. In several Third World nations such as India, the colonial powers helped create a core of trained administrators. Today, training programs can help, particularly in technical fields. But such programs cannot quickly alter cultural values; nor can they solve immediate problems of poverty and social turmoil that stifle effective administrative development. Strong cohesive political parties offer one possible method of control. In nations such as Mexico and China the party is an integral part of the administrative process and represents a principal means by which political leaders control bureaucracy.[14]

The principal role of parties, however, is to handle the participation crisis generated by modernization. Parties are the principal means of organizing and controlling the rapid influx of new people into the political system. Also, as societies modernize, many different groups come into being and exert demands on the political system. Political pressures

would soon inundate government were there not some means of grouping or simplifying them. Parties that bring together diverse interests
help accomplish this; they help balance the conflicting needs of groups
within the nation and present a unified voice to government leaders. In
one-party states most of the process of resolving conflicting demands
may be handled by the party.

We are, of course, speaking of effective party organizations. But in the
Third World, effective parties are the exception rather than the rule.
They are sometimes little more than personalistic cliques based on a
powerful leader and his immediate followers. Repeatedly one finds
parties that are merely fronts for narrow interests. Because parties fail
to bring together different interests, fragmented demands hit political
leaders who may find bargaining among them a nearly hopeless task.
Parties that fail to organize and simplify public pressures leave government leaders with few means of coping with complex demands. The
establishment of effective party organizations is therefore one of the
most important tasks confronting the leaders of Third World nations.
Those who succeed in establishing them have one of the potentially
most useful tools of contemporary politics.[15]

Ideology

An ideology is a system of ideas about politics that seeks to explain,
justify, and motivate. Through written and spoken word, leaders attempt to make people believe in the country, its leaders, and its policies.
The skill with which political leaders devise and employ ideologies
helps determine popular support. Naturally, leaders usually believe the
basic political ideas they promulgate, but they do have some latitude to
manipulate ideas, especially if the nation is new or if a revolution has
just occurred.

The most fundamental notion of Third World ideologies is national
independence. Most of the Third World nations won independence
during the last twenty-eight years and take great pride in their new
status as independent nations. But even long-independent nations of
the Third World stress national independence. The countries of Latin
America, for instance, are quite sensitive about their status as independent nations even though few face the threat of foreign invasion. Most
developing countries fear the economic dominance and control of the
modern nations of Europe, North America, and Japan. Latin Americans
sometimes refer to the United States as the colossus of the North, and
anti-Americanism is a central theme of Latin American ideologies. Nor
is the fear of the United States solely economic. The United States still
directly intervenes in Latin American politics. In the 1960's it invaded
the Dominican Republic and supported the abortive Bay of Pigs inva-

sion of Cuba. Interestingly, however, hostility toward modern nations can help build popular support. The United States economic boycott of Cuba, for instance, damaged Cuba's economy far less than Fidel Castro claimed. But the very existence of the boycott provided a rallying point for national sentiment and supplied a convenient scapegoat for Cuba's economic problems. We shall later see how this kind of nationalism has been an important tool in China's and Syria's quest for national unity.

Tradition often enables leaders to achieve remarkable successes in the use of ideology. Social and cultural behavior that emphasizes trust, obedience, and deference can sometimes be transferred to new leaders and institutions. Traditional symbols such as kings, emperors, and religious leaders may serve to legitimatize regimes even though these figures may have little power. Even such archaic institutions as caste systems may sometimes be a positive factor for political development.

In conclusion, ideologies of the developing nations typically stress national identity, independence, and economic development. As we have seen, however, ideologies do not automatically reflect reality; rather, they are one means of attempting to influence and control reality. Unfortunately, the cultural diversity, traditional loyalties, and the other myriad problems of Third World nations often keep ideologies in the realm of abstract ideas. In practice leaders often have great difficulty unifying their populations and establishing popular loyalty toward the government.

Additionally, we must remember that despite the common features of many Third World ideologies, they have important differences. Most significantly, they differ in their political approaches to economic and political development. The Communist, democratic, and various authoritarian roads to development have all been attempted, and at the conclusion of this chapter we shall discuss these different approaches in terms of their practical consequences for Third World nations.[16]

Mutual Cooperation and Self-Help

Third World nations want to free themselves of dependence on the economically powerful nations, and they want to achieve rapid economic growth. One strategy in achieving these goals is to help themselves by setting up regional economic unions, much on the pattern of the Common Market in Europe. A geographic economic union might not only increase markets for goods produced in each of the member countries; it might also help fend off domination by the economically advanced nations.

But the results of regional cooperation usually have fallen short of expectations. A principal reason for their limited success is that Third World nations possess very diverse characteristics despite their similar problems. Whereas the nations of the European Common Market all have democratic political systems and comparatively advanced economies, Third World nations do not. In Latin America, for instance, countries like Argentina, Brazil, Chile, and Mexico maintain fairly advanced economies while the economies of Paraguay and Bolivia remain economically backward. The political systems are equally diverse. In Latin America one can find Western-type democracies in Costa Rica and Venezuela; one-party limited democracy in Mexico; right-wing military dictatorship in Brazil; a left-wing, reformist regime in Peru; and the Marxist-Leninist regime of Fidel Castro in Cuba. These political and economic diversities have thus far helped preclude highly successful economic integration among modernizing nations.

Education

As a means of ideological indoctrination education is unsurpassed. Impressionable school children provide a captive audience. Even mathematics and the sciences can be taught with a political message. For example, a teacher can ask how many additional guerrillas are required to bring a band of fifteen heroic revolutionaries to its full strength of twenty. Reading, writing, history, and civics courses may also evoke loyalty toward the nation and its leaders.

Education is one of the easiest areas over which national leaders can exert substantial control, and the rewards for the skillful use of schools are great. Political education can also reach older citizens through adult education programs. In addition, literacy campaigns serve several purposes. They raise the number of literate people and therefore increase the available channels of political communication. Literate people can read and have access to more information. Adult education programs can be used to promote a sense of national identity or help stimulate an emotional attachment to a revolution or a new regime. A percentage increase in a nation's literacy can also be a source of national pride.

Education can also boost economic development. It can enable students to read instruction manuals and safety instructions. Moreover, organizations capable of planning and implementing developmental programs require thousands of literate employees. Furthermore, other abilities must be learned. Clerks must acquire bookkeeping skills, for example. Education in the Third World nations therefore requires multi-faceted programs covering technical and mechanical skills as well.

But education is no cure-all for the ills of emerging nations. Improperly handled it can even create more problems than it alleviates. When governments lavish huge expenditures on schools, less money is available for such crucial needs as port facilities, factories, roads, and hydroelectric plants. Such expenditures are particularly wasteful where money is spent on training excessive numbers of lawyers, poets, or other occupations that may not be economically or politically useful.

Education encourages greater participation in the political system. A literate public reads more and learns more. This may facilitate long-range economic growth and political development, but in the short run it increases the strain on governments that are already overloaded. It requires the development of political parties and other institutions capable of channeling mass participation in constructive ways. But this is beyond the capacity of many political systems. In fact, schools sometimes become the focus of conflict. When a nation has two principal languages, a decision to employ one of those languages in classrooms can produce a violent response from the losers.

In sum, education increases pressures on government. As a rule, the higher the level of education, the higher the expectations. High school and college graduates will not be satisfied with the menial jobs that all too often represent the only available positions in Third World nations. Education also creates economic pressures on Third World governments. Educated people expect higher standards of living, and demand more consumer goods than most modernizing nations can provide.

Education, then, is a two-edged sword. On the one hand, politicians can mold programs of instruction to help foster political and ideological commitment to the regime and to aid the acquisition of necessary skills for economic development. On the other hand, education can create more pressures on governments already undergoing the enormous stresses of rapid social and economic change.[17]

Economic Development

We have seen that rapid economic change can help produce social and political chaos. However, economic growth is also essential for long-term political development since public demands can only be met by a productive economy. Thus, economic development has both political costs and benefits. Almost without exception Third World leaders attempt to promote economic growth.

Economic development does more than just help meet rising public demands. It provides alternative channels of upward social mobility—avenues where ambitious people can get ahead. By opening up alternative levels of advancement a number of side benefits follow. For instance, there is less pressure on politicians to create unproductive jobs in the public service, and there is potentially reduced conflict among social groups over scarce government services. But whether or not conflict is actually reduced depends on a variety of circumstances such as the degree to which new wealth is redistributed to new participants in the political system.

The methods for economic development vary. The majority of development programs, however, do employ substantial public ownership, sometimes for ideological reasons but usually because there is not enough private investment to achieve rapid economic growth. Not only is there usually insufficient private money available; many of the necessary economic projects are also unprofitable for private investors. As a consequence governments must provide for such programs as transportation and hydroelectric schemes, develop basic industries, and provide banking facilities.

Large corporations in the modern nations are sometimes willing to provide capital, and many Third World nations are willing to accept foreign investment as a means of national development. These corporations provide money for new facilities, supply technical knowledge, and give jobs to people who might otherwise be unemployed. They may also contribute to the long-term economic growth of new nations by generating capital, through taxes and other means, for government-sponsored projects. Unfortunately, foreign investment may create serious problems. Extractive foreign operations such as copper mining sometimes hinder economic modernization by concentrating the developing of roads, electricity, and towns around mining operations, even though they may be more essential elsewhere. Although industries of this kind provide jobs and capital, they make Third World nations vulnerable to radically fluctuating world markets if too much of the economy is centered upon such production. The economic chaos produced by shifting prices of minerals or one-industry crops like sugar cane impedes long-range economic planning, fosters indebtedness, and aggravates political instability.

Politically, foreign investments can weaken public support for government. If foreign companies appear to dominate domestic politics, opposition leaders can charge that the regime in power is a servant of imperialistic nations. Certain kinds of investments are particularly damaging, for example, where large tracts of land are owned by foreigners. Citizens are prone to view their nation's soil as sacred. Similarly, monopoly industries owned by foreigners, such as telephone and bus companies, may also alienate the public. Rate increases or poor service would provoke hostility even if the companies were locally owned; how much more serious is discontent if they are owned by American or other foreign corporations.

Leaders of Third World nations who use foreign investments but want to avoid the political and economic disadvantages can attempt to mold foreign investment to their own requirements. Some nations, such as Mexico, accomplish this control more effectively than others. A nation's ability to attract and control foreign investment, however, depends upon a number of things. Consumer purchasing power, for example, makes it profitable for an automobile company to establish manufacturing plants in a Third World nation. Material resources and facilities to make investment worthwhile to profit-minded foreign corporations are desirable. It also helps if the political climate of the nation is stable so that investors feel that their property is safe.

Whether or not modernizing nations accept corporate foreign investment, most are willing to accept foreign aid. The bulk of aid funds comes directly from governments of individual donor countries, but some is available from international organizations such as the United Nations and the World Bank. Although their funds are quite limited, international organizations do provide assistance without the political and economic costs of bilateral aid, that is, direct aid from one country to another.

Politically, bilateral aid may carry with it some of the problems of corporate foreign investment; it may taint leaders, sometimes justifiably, with the suspicion that they are dominated by foreign governments, and it may limit their ability to plan flexible economic development programs where there are stipulations that aid money must be spent in the donor country.

To some extent it may be possible for leaders to play off one nation against another. For example, both the United States and the Soviet Union may give aid to the same country in an attempt to win political influence. Care may also be taken to insure that foreign aid projects visibly demonstrate that assistance comes from more than one source. Even if a nation receives most of its aid from the United States, for instance, it can attempt to secure Soviet backing for a large dam or other plainly visible program. In sum, foreign investment and foreign aid may assist economic development, but they may also create political and economic difficulties. It is the task of Third World leaders to balance skillfully the need for outside assistance with internal political realities.[18]

The Military

The military can be a helpful as well as harmful force in the Third World. Even military takeovers are sometimes followed by economic and political development. They are one means by which power can be wrested from unyielding aristocracies. The military is sometimes more effective than public agencies in carrying out development programs. Organized on a rigid chain-of-command principle, subordinates will normally obey orders more readily than their civilian counterparts. If instructed to build a road between two cities, the military may have a better chance of completing the task if it is less corrupt than the civilian agency. Additionally, the armed forces can help ease unemployment.

They provide secure jobs in unstable economic climates. When the military opens its officer corps to the middle and working classes, the avenues of social mobility are broadened. These opportunities ease the discontent created by job scarcity. Social democratization of the armed forces also reduces the likelihood of reactionary military coups against social and economic reforms, because middle and working class officers may be more willing to support reform programs which benefit their classes.

Military organizations may also accelerate national integration. Armies are by nature nationalistic, and they can teach their members the virtues of patriotism. As highly visible branches of government, their penetration of remote areas may speed the identification of isolated peoples with their state. To the extent that soldiers complete projects beneficial to the public, they can strengthen support for the government.

The above benefits of the military, however, often fail to materialize. Rather than serving as a tool of the government, the military often exploits its position as the most powerful force in society. The frequency of military takeovers in the Third World results more often from selfish goals rather than the desire for social and economic reforms. For example, when top ranks are filled and there is little opportunity for advancement, coups may be engineered by frustrated officers. In these cases political decline rather than political development may ensue. Furthermore, takeovers may be engineered by conservative or reactionary officers fearful of reforms.

Once in power, military leaders often lack the political skills necessary for the administration of a modernizing nation. One such political skill is conciliation, a quality not endemic to most military officers. Military leaders sometimes disdain the need for effective political parties and thereby limit their ability to control new participants in the political systems. While reformist military leaders may have the physical power to force economic reform, their chances of sustaining themselves in power are slim unless they also acquire political adroitness.

Armies are also expensive. Technologically sophisticated equipment and salaries are quite expensive. These costs may be defrayed in part by military assistance from modern nations, but this may bring meddling in the politics of the recipient nation. In any case, large expenditures for self-defense are unnecessary for most modernizing nations because there is remote threat of foreign invasion. Most of the soldiers of Latin America, for example, have never participated in a war. In short, despite the benefits discussed above, large armies can be an economic waste.

Should political leaders in such nations therefore cut back radically the size of their armies? Not necessarily. Politics is the art of the possible, and economic costs must be weighed against political realities. If the military will not tolerate a reduction in size or pay, then other worthwhile reforms might be needlessly sacrificed by provoking a military takeover.

Assuming that most nations require some level of military forces, how can a nation's leaders maintain control? The problem is delicate in Third World nations because strong beliefs against forced takeovers of government may not exist. Military officers will be less likely to turn out a popular leader who meets the demands of citizens, but politicians have difficulty maintaining popularity in part because of their inability to deal with chronic problems of modernization. The forced retirement of the more ambitious and dangerous officers may work. Rotating officers among different military bases helps prevent the development of strong personal followings. Paying officers well and bestowing social honors upon them may help retain their support. Bringing military officers into the decision-making process may commit them to government policies and eventually win their support for the nation's political institutions and procedures. The merits of various political techniques to control the armed forces will of course depend upon the particular circumstances of each nation. But so frequent is military intervention that this becomes one of the most important tasks facing the heads of modernizing nations.

Perhaps the most fundamental means of discouraging military intervention is the institutionalization of political and administrative organizations capable of sustaining the stresses of rapid social change. One of the principal causes of army takeovers is chronic political instability. Continual riots and general strikes may provoke coups simply because there seems no hope that civilian political institutions can cope with the situation. Military leaders often view themselves as guardians of their country, and prolonged political violence tempts them to "save" their country. Under such chronic political turmoil even moderates may support military takeovers. These conditions also provide a pretense for intervention by officers with less noble motives.

Since social, economic, and political turmoil is the rule rather than the exception in modernizing nations, the armed forces will in all probability continue their prominent role in the politics of the Third World. Fortunate indeed are those nations where the military represents a positive rather than a negative influence.[19]

AVENUES OF POLITICAL DEVELOPMENT

The techniques and structures of control just discussed are of use to leaders who follow a variety of different avenues of political development. For example, effective political parties and government bureaucracies are vital for both Communist and liberal-democratic modernizing nations of the Third World. Yet different avenues of development have different costs and benefits. Western-type democracies, for instance, tolerate more freedom of expression than Communist systems but normally have less capacity to impose tough reforms.

We shall now present a brief, simple scheme for classifying different patterns of development so that comparative costs and benefits can be more easily assessed. Of course, any such scheme oversimplifies. Categories can overlap, and we make no claim to cover all possible avenues. Some nations may exhibit features of more than one system either simultaneously or at different times. Nevertheless, the scheme is easy to grasp and covers some of the principal avenues attempted by Third World nations.[20]

Western Liberal Democracy

The system of Western liberal democracy involves free elections and open competition among political parties. It emphasizes procedures, such as vote counting in legislatures, and requires substantial mutual trust among competing political leaders. Bargaining among various interest groups frequently leads to compromise solutions. Of course, not all interests are necessarily equally or fairly represented.

In any event, for most of the Third World nations, stable democratic political development is probably impossible—at least during the initial phases of nation-building. A principal difficulty is that democratic leaders often lack the power to make firm decisions. The crises of Third World nations demand resolute action, yet political democracy actively seeks accommodation and compromise. Meaningful reforms and long-range investments may be impossible. Often wealthy interests will be able to manipulate the system to their advantage or at least block radical government reform policies.

Nevertheless, democracy has worked for some Third World nations even in the face of poverty. India is poor yet has maintained a democratic political system. What factors can help support democratic development in the face of comparatively low levels of economic development? Ironically, colonialism helped unify some of these societies and thereby eased the burdens of integration for future leaders. In a few countries, such as India, colonialism helped acquaint elites with democratic procedures—though certainly not through genuine democratic government since colonialism involved rule by foreigners.

Despite the limitations of democratic politics, there are some plusses. Because groups and individuals may more freely speak out, leaders may have more accurate information on the state of society and thus have more information on which to base decisions. Previously excluded groups might also find democratic political systems willing to allow them a new voice in the political process. For those valuing freedom of expression and limited government controls, political democracy has obvious advantages. But few Third World nations possess characteristics favorable to democratic politics. Most have had little previous experience with democratic politics. Moreover, the overwhelming nature of their problems suggests that hard and forceful decisions are required that often elude democratic politics, in which conciliation and compromise are paramount. Additionally, many groups in Third World nations would not abide by democratic rules, which have never been a part of their cultures and which might mean the loss of valued privileges if democratic procedures were followed.

LIMITED POLITICAL DEMOCRACY. One answer to the liabilities of democratic politics in Third World nations is limited democracy. The goal here is to guide societies under firm leadership through the necessary reforms and social changes so that democratic politics can be eventually established. Mass education, the eradication of poverty, and land reform are some of the changes often deemed essential by political leaders before a shift to democratic politics becomes possible.

As Professor Poitras shows, Mexico's political system is similar to the limited-democracy principle. Though elections are tolerated and a comparatively open system exists (free speech, free press, etc.), the nation is dominated by one party. The Mexicans claim that their system is democratic, but little chance exists that the ruling party could be voted out of office. In any case, Mexico has been one of the more successful nations of the Third World, at least as measured by the criteria of stability, institutionalization, and economic growth.

The limited or guided democracy approach, however, often precludes elections in the early stages of development. In this case, leaders promise to establish democratic procedures after necessary reforms have been implemented. Yet political leaders may promise eventual elections in order to placate uncooperative citizens and to deceive foreign nations such as the United States. Furthermore, to the extent that democratic participation is tolerated, social reform may be obstructed. Business interests, for example, may have greater power to block social legislation giving benefits to workers. Nevertheless, for many nations limited democracy constitutes a more realistic alternative than the more open and competitive democracies of the West.

AUTHORITARIANISM. Authoritarian governments rule by force and by coalition. Free elections and freedom of expression are prohibited, but various groups such as religious organizations, private business, and labor may retain substantial independence as long as they cooperate with the authoritarian leadership of the country. Although authoritarian governments base their rule on the cooperation of key groups in society, their power is ultimately based upon military and police power. Those who do not agree with government policies must either accept them as inevitable or rebel and risk annihilation. Government leaders cannot simply be voted out of office.

RIGHT-WING AUTHORITARIANISM. Right-wing authoritarian leaders normally seek to limit social change or to control it in such a way that new elite groups such as industrialists and traditional groups like the landed aristocracy, the military, and organized religion are protected. These groups in turn lend their support to the government. Usually student groups, democratic parties, and unions are repressed. After Allende was overthrown in Chile, the military regime that seized power appeared to be following a right-wing authoritarian approach.

LEFT-WING AUTHORITARIANISM. Left-wing authoritarian political systems seek to destroy components of the traditional order so that fundamental reforms may be accomplished. The present Ba'th Party of Syria represents this pattern of change. A frequent goal is the distribution of land to peasants. Leaders of these governments are committed to greater social and economic equality. Like the right-wing authoritarian governments, they also base their authority upon the support of comparatively independent groups and upon military and police power. But rather than allying with conservative interests they typically seek the cooperation of labor unions, student organizations, peasant leagues, and of course, sympathetic military officers.

Authoritarian regimes of both types usually have more power to make firm decisions than do democratic governments. They are less compelled to seek compromise and can employ more force in backing up their policies. However objectionable to some Westerners, political repression combined with progressive economic policies can be a viable method of economic development and even economic modernization. There is no inherent reason that these systems cannot also develop politically.

Yet violent opposition is a constant threat in systems where political office is based upon coercion rather than compromise. Those excluded from politics may seek admittance by force. The use of indiscriminate violence by the government often legitimizes its use by opponents. Nevertheless, authoritarian government may represent the only realistic option for some of the nations wracked by the turmoil of rapid social and economic change. For leaders who can retain popular support and stimulate stable economic growth, authoritarian politics may provide a viable alternative to more open systems. Also, the left-wing variety of authoritarian government may result in significant social democratization through the redistribution of wealth by major reform programs.

MOBILIZATION AND COMMUNIST SYSTEMS. Political systems of this type base their rule on extensive force, at least in the short run. The purest contemporary examples are Communist nations such as the People's Republic of China, but a few non-Communist systems approximate their characteristics. Reforms are not usually the result of cooperation and compromise among interested parties. Rather they occur by government decree. Land is simply taken away from landowners. Factories may be nationalized without compensating their owners, and resisters or counterrevolutionaries may be shot, imprisoned or deported. Even so, these systems require popular support if they are to survive. That leaders are aware of this fact is illustrated by their extensive use of ideology to maintain support.

The administrative burden on these systems is intense. Unlike the authoritarian systems, they do not usually base their rule upon a coalition of sympathetic groups; rather, they run the major organizations of society directly. The official political party dominates youth clubs, schools, factories, the state bureaucracy and the armed forces. In short, these systems seek to dominate all major political and social institutions and to mobilize public participation in support of government and its goals. No government, however, totally controls a complex society. Indeed, in the early stages of modernization under this pattern of development governments must often rely upon traditional institutions. Mao of China tolerated some private ownership and required the assistance of former capitalists.

The principal advantage of these political systems is their concentration and coordination of political power. Through sophisticated party organizations they can often remain in power and accomplish radical reforms. Unlike most nations of the developing areas, none of the Third World Communist regimes—North Vietnam, Communist China, or Cuba—have been overthrown.

On the other hand, governments of this type may have difficulty obtaining information because of their frequent reliance upon repression. People fear punishment if they criticize the system, so discontent is less readily detected. Administrators, fearful of harsh reprimands, more often withhold information thus making top-level decision making more difficult. Present generations must suffer for the long-term development of the nation since consumer goods take second place to capital investments in industry. Also, those who value liberal-democratic freedoms will normally find this avenue of development objectionable.[21]

In conclusion, each of these patterns of political development has advantages as well as disadvantages. Only a few of the costs and benefits have been mentioned. As you turn to the case studies of the six countries you will discover additional points. While reading the following chapters, try to discover why each country evolved in its particular fashion. Notice sequences and rates of change, the impact of colonialism and foreign relations, the pressures of urbanization, technological and economic advances, and the role of cultural conflict. Observe specific techniques and strategies of political control and how they have been employed in various settings.

Also, keep in mind that political development is not an ultimate condition. Crises come and go, and instability can be a necessary component of political development. From today's perspective most Third World nations appear to be experiencing political chaos rather than development, yet some of this turbulence is undoubtedly a prelude to eventual political development.

It is time now, however, to turn to the major task of this book—the analysis of representative and important Third World countries. When that task is completed, you will have taken a significant beginning step in understanding the politics of most of the peoples and nations of this earth—namely those of the Third World.

FOOTNOTES

1. For a further discussion of Third World characteristics see Irving L. Horowitz, *Three Worlds of Development: The Theory and Practice of International Stratification* (New York: Oxford University Press, 1966), ch. 1.

2. See the concluding chapter of Robert E. Ward and Dankwart A. Rustow, eds., *Political Modernization of Japan and Turkey* (Princeton, N. J.: Princeton University Press, 1964). This work helped stimulate the perspective of the introductory chapter and case studies. Though our framework, like all frameworks, is oversimplified, it provides a meaningful orientation for undergraduate students.

3. The definition of political development benefits from Alfred Diamant's "The Nature of Political Development," in Jason L. Finkle and Richard W. Gable, eds., *Political Development and Social Change* (New York: John Wiley & Sons, 1968), pp. 91–96. See also Leonard Binder, *et al.*, eds., *Crises and Sequences in Political Development* (Princeton: Princeton University Press, 1971).

4. For a useful discussion, see Samuel P. Huntington, "The Change to Change: Modernization, Development, and Politics," *Comparative Politics*, III (April, 1971).

5. For an important article that systematically discusses a number of pressures generated by modernization consult Karl W. Deutsch, "Social Mobilization and Political Development," *American Political Science Review*, LV (September, 1961), 463–515.

6. See Clifford Geertz, "The Integrative Revolution: Primordial Sentiments and Civil Politics in the New States," in Clifford Geertz, ed., *Old Societies and New States: The Quest for Modernity in Asia and Africa* (New York: The Free Press of Glencoe, 1963).

7. For a good discussion of some vital cultural factors affecting political development see Lucian W. Pye, *Politics, Personality, and Nation Building: Burma's Search for Identity* (New Haven: Yale University Press, 1962), pp. 195–207.

8. For a discussion see Samuel P. Huntington, *Political Order in Changing Societies* (New Haven: Yale University Press, 1968), p. 12 ff.

9. See Eric Nordlinger, "Political Development: Time Sequences and Rates of Change," *World Politics* (April, 1968), 494–520 and Brinder, *et al.* Crises and Sequences.

10. For a classic discussion of revolution consult Crane Brinton, *The Anatomy of Revolution* (New York: Vintage, 1958).

11. For an extended and useful discussion of leadership strategies read W. Howard Wriggins, *The Ruler's Imperative: Strategies for Political Survival in Asia and Africa* (New York: Columbia University Press, 1969). See also Taketsugu Tsurutani, *The Politics of National Development: Political Leadership in Transitional Societies* (New York: Chandler, 1973).

12. A discussion of the role of bureaucracy may be found in Joseph LaPalombara, ed., *Bureaucracy and Political Development* (Princeton, N. J.: Princeton University Press, 1963).

13. Milton J. Esman, *Administration and Development in Malaysia: Institution Building and Reform in a Plural Society* (Ithaca, N. Y.: Cornell University Press, 1972).

14. Huntington, "Political Order in Changing Societies," ch. vii provides a useful discussion of the role of political parties.

15. For a lengthy and useful treatment of political parties in Third World nations see Myron Weiner and Joseph LaPalombara, eds., *Political Parties and Political Development* (Princeton, N. J.: Princeton University Press, 1966).

16. A discussion of Third World ideologies together with statements of Third World leaders can be found in Paul Sigmund, ed., *The Ideologies of the Developing Nations*, rev. ed. (New York: Praeger, 1967).

17. For an analysis of the role of education in Third World areas consult James S. Coleman, ed., *Education and Political Development* (Princeton, N. J.: Princeton University Press, 1965).

18. A statement from a Western liberal viewpoint is contained in Lester B. Pearson, *Partners in Development: Report of the Commission on International Development* (New York: Praeger, 1969). See also Robert I. Rhodes, *Imperialism and Undevelopment: A Reader* (New York: Monthly Review Press, 1970).

19. Useful sources on the military include Eric A. Nordlinger, "Soldiers in Mufti: The Impact of Military Rule Upon Economic and Social Change in the Non-Western States," *American Political Science Review*, OXIV (December, 1970), 1131–48; Morris Janowitz, *The Military in the Political Development of New Nations* (Chicago: University of Chicago Press, 1964); and W. McWilliams, *Garrisons and Government* (Scranton, Pa.: Chandler Press, 1967).

20. A number of sophisticated typologies of developing nations can be found in the literature. For a more lengthy analysis see Edward A. Shils, *Political Development in the New State* (The Hague: Mouton & Co., 1960).

21. An interesting discussion of the comparative advantages and disadvantages of different political approaches toward modernization is found in David E. Apter's *The Politics of Modernization* (Chicago: University of Chicago Press, 1965).

FOR FURTHER READING

ALMOND, GABRIEL A. and POWELL, G. BINGHAM. *Comparative Politics: A Developmental Approach*. Boston: Little, Brown, 1966.

APTER, DAVID E. *Choice and the Politics of Allocation: A Developmental Theory*. New Haven: Yale University Press, 1971.

————. *The Politics of Modernization.* Chicago: University of Chicago Press, 1965.

BINDER, LEONARD et al. *Crises and Sequences in Political Development.* Princeton: Princeton University Press, 1971.

BLACK, CYRIL E. *The Dynamics of Modernization: A Study in Comparative History.* New York: Harper & Row, 1966.

EISENSTADT, SAMUEL N. *The Political Systems of Empires.* Glencoe, Ill.: The Free Press, 1963.

FINKLE, JASON L., and GABLE, RICHARD W. eds. *Political Development and Social Change.* New York: John Wiley & Sons, 1971.

GEERTZ, CLIFFORD, ed. *Old Societies and New States: The Quest for Modernity in Asia and Africa.* Glencoe, Ill.: The Free Press, 1963.

HALPERN, MANFRED. *The Politics of Social Change in the Middle East and North Africa.* Princeton: Princeton University Press, 1963.

HOROWITZ, IRVING L. *Three Worlds of Development: The Theory and Practice of International Stratification.* New York: Oxford University Press, 1972.

HUNTINGTON, SAMUEL P. *Political Order in Changing Societies.* New Haven: Yale University Press, 1968.

JAGUARIBE, HELIO. *Political Development: A General Theory and a Latin American Case Study.* New York: Harper & Row, 1973.

LERNER, DANIEL. *The Passing of Traditional Society: Modernizing in the Middle East.* Glencoe, Ill.: The Free Press, 1958.

NORDLINGER, ERIC. "Political Development: Time Sequences and Rates of Change." *World Politics,* XX (April, 1968), 494–520.

PYE, LUCIAN W. *Aspects of Political Development.* Boston: Little, Brown, 1966.

RUSTOW, DANKWART A. *A World of Nations: Problems of Political Modernization.* Washington, D. C.: The Brookings Institution, 1968.

TACHAU, FRANK, ed. *The Developing Nations: What Path to Modernization?* New York: Dodd, Mead, & Company, 1972.

VON DER MEHDEN, FRED R. *Politics of the Developing Nations.* Englewood Cliffs, N. J.: Prentice-Hall, 1964.

WELCH, CLAUDE E., JR., ed. *Political Modernization: A Reader in Comparative Political Change.* 2nd ed. Belmont, Calif.: Wadsworth Publishing Company, 1971.

INDIA

Democracy and Political Development

WALTER L. WEISBERG

India is the world's largest democracy. How did the system of constitutional democracy in India adapt to meet the stresses of political development? What were the costs of this road to political development in terms of economic development and rapid change in a society divided by religion, caste, class, region, and language coupled with widespread poverty and illiteracy? Why didn't a Communist regime develop as in China? Or political fragmentation, civil war, and military rule as in Nigeria? How and why is the Indian brand of democratic development different from that of Mexico? How and why did political democracy in India help maintain the stability and unity of the political system and still allow for relatively peaceful, albeit gradual, change?

This chapter shall argue that democratic institutions, i.e., political parties with a mass organization and base, a modern bureaucracy based on merit, parliaments, and elections developed in India long before the Indian masses began to make greater demands for economic goods and services. Political participation preceded economic development. The Indian political structures gained legitimacy and were institutionalized before independence in 1947 and before wide-scale economic development disrupted rural India. Given this legitimacy, demands from different strata of the population could be met within the existing parliamentary framework. In addition the traditional society, which was culturally fragmented, authoritarian, and lacking the values of constitutionalism that developed in Great Britain and the United States, could and did adapt to new values and sustain new organizations.

34

Colonialism, Nationalism, and the Rise of Gandhi

Traditionally, India was the home of many great civilizations, religions and empires. Nevertheless, no stable political order evolved and no empire ever ruled the entire Indian sub-continent until the British arrived. The last great empire, the Mughal, was Muslim, not Hindu, and was in a period of decline when the British began to make serious inroads into the sub-continent during the eighteenth century. The British had to contend with a variety of authoritarian princely regimes: Hindu, Muslim, and Sikh. The Indian masses, illiterate and largely settled in thousands of villages, had little political participation under these regimes.

Nevertheless, unlike Africa, the British presence in India was of long duration, dating from the seventeenth century. It was also broad in scope and multi-faceted. During their presence, the British trained an elite corps of civil servants, the Indian Civil Service (ICS), which became the Indian Administrative Service after independence. Furthermore, the British responded, however reluctantly and half-heartedly, to demands for greater participation in governmental decision-making on the part of the educated elite. Since the late nineteenth century, a series of policies were implemented to secure better representation of important Indian interests, involve more and more Indians in the legislative process at local, provincial, and national levels, and introduce an Indian element into the executive. In fact, the Government of India Act of 1935 provided for greater provincial autonomy. It expanded the electorate from six to thirty million, offered a basis for the present Indian Constitution, and trained large numbers of the native elite in parliamentary democracy. Nearly one-sixth of India's adult population, women included, were enfranchised. Furthermore, Indian chief ministers, responsible to a popularly elected assembly, became effective heads of provincial administration.[1]

The British also provided structural unity and a strong degree of administrative cohesion in a country formerly divided into various princely regimes and regions with different languages and traditions. Railroads and roads connected the scattered parts of British India and increased communications between the regions. After the failure of the Sepoy Mutiny in 1857, the traditional rulers never again attempted a revolt of such a widespread nature. The military defeat of the traditional, authoritarian elite, including many of the aristocracy and large landlords, prevented them from becoming a serious stumbling block to democratic political development as they were in Latin America.

Under the peace enforced by the British *raj* (rule, or government) interregional trade developed and with it a new middle class. This middle class provided the British with middle level administrators and lawyers to enable the colonial power to impose Western concepts of law on traditional Indian society. This new middle class was educated in English with English ideas of parliamentary democracy. Percival Spear, a noted historian, argues:

> Not only was the middle class stimulated and expanded by the new opportunities; it was drawn together as never before. The new education gave it a common language and common stock of ideas and knowledge to be held side by side with its various sectional traditions. The new press continued their contact with the new mental world and enabled their own reactions to it to circulate. The new communications enabled Madras to talk to Delhi and Bombay to meet with Calcutta.[2]

Many members of the middle class, trained in Western ideas, began to make serious demands for reform. They formed the kernel of what was to become a growing nationalist movement.

Unfortunately, the British encouraged, knowingly or otherwise, severe social and political fragmentation by playing off prince against prince, Hindu against Muslim, and caste against caste in the familiar tactics of divide and rule. Many British administrators were only too willing to rely on the support of the princes and traditional elites in order to stymie the growing nationalist movement that increasingly threatened their right to rule.[3] British policy sometimes led to exploitation of the peasant masses by the creation of tenancy systems encouraging absentee landlords.

In any case, a series of nationalist movements developed by the latter part of the nineteenth century. A number of terrorist organizations arose in response to the more exploitive and repressive aspects of British rule. However, most of the rising middle classes found it possible to press their demands within the institutions established by the British. Their major organization was the Indian National Congress, an organization composed largely of lawyers, journalists, and schoolmasters. From this narrow urban elite, the Congress was to develop into a mass political party. The Indian National Congress was founded in 1885 to press for greater representation for Indians in the civil service and legislative councils as well as for liberal reform. The Congress grew rapidly among the middle classes. Finding the British unwilling to meet their demands, they assumed a stance of constitutional opposition, confined to the rules of the game recognized by the British in the early 1900's, e.g., petitions, votes in councils. When these methods failed to influence the British, large numbers of the Congress elite became frustrated. A rift developed between two groups—moderates, who stressed gradualism, and extremists, who attempted to reach the masses through boycotts, advocating violence and a return to the days of Hindu glory, and *Swaraj* (self-rule).[4]

The British responded with half-hearted reforms and repression, culminating in the Amritsar massacre of 1919 which left 379 Indians dead and about 1200 wounded. The new Congress leader, Mohandas K. Gandhi, proclaimed that "cooperation in any shape or form with this satanic government is sinful."[5] Largely due to Gandhi's efforts, the predominantly urban middle class Congress was changed into an organization capable of arousing the Indian masses. At the same time that the Congress party became a mass organization under Gandhi's leadership however, a split occurred between India's Hindus and Muslims. All these developments were interconnected. How and why did they happen?

A leader of charismatic proportions, Gandhi developed a system of *satyagraha* (soul force) or non-violent resistance resulting in a wave of fasts, peaceful marches and demonstrations, and boycotts. All these methods are still widely used in Indian politics.[6] In order to reach the masses, he evoked concepts of the Hindu religion like the sacred cow and symbols familiar to the Indian peasant, for example, the hand-operated spinning wheel with which villagers would make most of their clothing. However, at the same time that the use of traditional Hindu symbols attracted large numbers of the Hindu masses to the nationalist movement, it antagonized many Muslims who understandably could not identify with the cow. Hinduism and Islam were different faiths with different symbols and beliefs, and the cow is not sacred to Muslims.

Of course, Hindu-Muslim differences went far deeper than a mere religious symbol. The subject of Hindu-Muslim rivalry will be treated in more detail later in this chapter. The point remains that the cow did not serve as a unifying nationalist symbol to the millions of Indian Muslims. Furthermore, the use of Hindu religious symbols by the Nationalist movement increased the Muslim's fear of Hindu domination, although many Muslims joined and gained positions of leadership in the Congress party. The Congress leaders, Gandhi included, claimed that their party alone spoke for the Indian people of all religions and classes.

Development of the Congress and the Winning of Independence

By the early 1920's, the Congress had organized thousands of local units. Delegates were elected and Provincial Congress committees conducted their deliberations in the local languages, not English, the language of the urban elite. More and more peasants were drawn into a Congress which, quite literally, spoke their languages. The importance of these occurrences for democratic political development have been succinctly indicated by the political scientist, Gopal Krishna:

> By accident rather than design the Congress did not develop a party bureaucracy, with its attendant loss in efficiency. The amorphousness of the organization was, however, also a safeguard. Given the diversity of its people, the intractability of its economic and political problems, the low level of social integration and the essentially authoritarian political tradition of India, the temptation to impose uniformity through the instrumentality of the state apparatus and a highly bureaucratized party, might have been irresistible. The democratic process of nation-making through participation in political life required a relatively open party organization; this was also perhaps a necessary condition for political liberty.[7]

As a result, the Congress developed into an organization in which accommodation and bargaining were stressed in order to maintain its unity. Like the British *raj*, the Nationalist movement was too fragmented to rely entirely on coercion. Just as the British needed to reach an understanding with various groups in order to govern, so the Congress had to hold the backing of a multitude of groups in order to gain independence. With the notable exception of the Communists, almost all major Indian party leaders of Gandhi's generation were at one time associated with the Congress.[8] Nevertheless, as in any large organization composed of diverse interests, all groups could not be accommodated and some leaders were deprived of power.

The failure of the politics of accommodation to satisfy all politicians had two major results. One consequence was the formation of more radical parties like the Communists and Forward Bloc that could not tolerate Gandhi's non-violent resistance and the pursuance of independence and social change through parliamentary means.[9] Another was the defection of large numbers of Muslims to the Muslim League. This latter occurrence resulted in the dismemberment of the British India into India and Pakistan in 1947.

When India gained independence from the British in 1947, Gandhi wanted the Congress to become a service organization since its goal had already been achieved. After Gandhi's assassination at the hands of a Hindu religious fanatic in 1948, the Congress leaders, the only party leaders with an all-India organization, carried on the task of writing the Constitution and forming the government. The Congress leaders were very careful to include non-Congress or opposition politicians in the task of framing the Constitution and all political views were aired. The outcome was two-fold. First, the Constitution was adopted with the general support of the delegates who represented most shades of political opinion in India. Second, the democratic process of freedom of opinion and bargaining was sustained. The prospects of both national unity and democracy were increased by the unanimous adoption of the Indian Constitution.[10] Of course, the Congress party was opposed by the princes, the traditional elite. However, they posed few problems to the Congress leadership.

The princes, who ruled or merely reigned in a variety of princely states under the British, were not united and were easily absorbed into the Indian Union with the promise of an annual salary from the new government. Force or the threat of force was used to integrate some of the larger states, notably Kashmir and Hyderabad. The acquisition of Kashmir involved an armed conflict between India and Pakistan. Hyderabad was in no position to challenge the Indian Army.[11] Today princes run for office on various party labels, especially Congress and the right-wing Swatantra and Jana Sangh.[12] Although the princes rarely act as a unit, individual princes can be very powerful in their home areas. This is partially due to the traditional respect for "our maharajah" but mostly due to their economic power. When asked whether the Maharajah of Gwalior helped the populace, a guide answered, "Oh yes, he employs many people." Today, princely areas are as wealthy (or poor) as the non-princely areas in their respective regions. As a rule, the traditional aristocracy was deprived of its power by the British, unlike the emirs in Northern Nigeria. Unlike Chile and much of Latin America, the middle classes in the Nationalist movement did not aspire to be members of the aristocracy and hence did not unite with them against the lower classes.

Nevertheless, the threat of internal violence remained. India was still a country of vast poverty and discontent. A peasant revolt, supported by the Communists, took place in the Telengana region of what is now the state of Andhra Pradesh.[13]

The revolt was squelched, but the conditions of poverty, grave inequality of land distribution, and general economic backwardness leading to the revolt are still present in many areas, including Telengana. Poverty in some regions of India is nowadays made more obvious by the relative prosperity of neighboring areas. For example, some of Telengana's people look with envy and hatred on the richer sections of their own state of Andhra Pradesh. Needless to say, poverty and land inequality remain severe problems, leading to disaffection and even revolt. Although the preceding questions will be treated in more detail toward the conclusion of this chapter, they must be mentioned here to suggest the difficulties that faced the Congress leaders at the time of independence (1947).

Moreover, the Congress party contained several characteristics that seriously hampered its effectiveness in solving social and economic problems. Officially pledged to democratic socialism and a secular state

in which no religion was to be given special favors, many of its supporters included rural landlords and urban businessmen who did not agree
with these goals. The Congress party also operated in a society in which
the hold of religion and traditional political values was still strong.
Under a system of universal adult suffrage, elected politicians, like their
counterparts in other nations, had to reach an accord with their constituents. Finally, the problem of economic development had yet to be
solved.

Economic Development

The chief success of the British in India was in political, not economic,
development. They established institutions, provided structural and
administrative unity, and trained an Indian political elite. They did not
provide an infrastructure conducive to rapid economic development.
Most of their economic measures were meant to ensure stability and
order, not change, because rapid change would upset the traditional
society and raise new demands that they would not be able to handle.

The British economic policies were not unusual for rulers. Elites like
the British may neglect economic development in the interests of national unity and stability. In India, as in other British colonies like
Nigeria, order was maintained at the cost of limited economic development.

India was blessed with huge mineral reserves of iron and coal, but the
countryside remained largely underdeveloped. The average farm holding was small, often fragmented, and the poor farmer was dependent on
the vagaries of the monsoon rains. Although most of the arable land had
been depleted by centuries of harvests, it was usable and could be
developed further with proper agricultural methods. The peasants were
largely ignorant of these methods but the potential for improvement
was there.[14]

In many parts of the country, the British misunderstood the nature
of traditional systems of land tenure and introduced Western concepts
that benefited large landlords at the expense of the small peasants and
tenant farmers. For example:

> The introduction of new systems of land tenure, particularly the *zamindar*
> (landlord) system in Bengal and in eastern India, regularized the collection
> of land taxes and ensured a continuous and substantial revenue for the
> East India Company. The creation of this prosperous intermediary class
> of *zamindars* between the tillers and the state caused capital that might
> have been invested elsewhere to be put into the purchase (not the devel-
> opment) of land. Fragmentation of holdings, the introduction of cash
> crops dependent upon a world market, the growing power of a money-
> lending class, and increase in tenancy all contributed to the deterioration

in the position of the peasant, particularly during the world economic crisis in the early 1920's. It was no accident that at this time the peasantry in India joined in the national movement for independence.[15]

The British also developed an economic system where raw materials such as cotton, jute, oilseeds, and minerals were extracted from India, processed in Great Britain, and the finished product resold to India. Many English firms were willing to employ and train Indians only for subordinate positions, and the British refused to provide protections for Indian industries, forcing them into open competition with more established British businesses. In this way, Indian-owned manufacturing enterprises were discriminated against and discouraged. Like the peasants in the countryside, many Indian businessmen were attracted to the Nationalist movement by British economic policies.

Ironically, British policies encouraged the Nationalist movement by antagonizing so many different classes and by making them more willing to join the Congress. Of course, the landlords and princes largely opposed the Congress, but these classes were too few and disorganized to stem the tide of a rising mass movement centered in a democratically organized party with a democratic elite.

Nevertheless, at independence (1947), the industrial revolution had still not come to India. A small working class had developed in urban areas, but its divisions of skilled, semi-skilled, and unskilled workers were not united. Workers did make greater demands, but unions were also weak and collective bargaining was not recognized as a firm principle by businessmen. Many businessmen had power in the Congress party through their connection with the nationalist movement. Consequently, Congress labor leaders were faced with strong opposition to labor reform within their own party.

Fortunately, the Congress party and its leaders had the support and legitimacy to frame a democratic constitution and maintain order. The institutionalization of the mass party and political participation before independence was helpful for both India's democracy and stability. How did it deal with new demands caused by economic development and cultural fragmentation?

Cultural Fragmentation: the Problem

There are many divisive tendencies in Indian society. Some critics have denied that India is one nation.[16] More optimistic observers claim that India possesses "unity in diversity," but distinctions in fable and folklore are only too readily apparent.[17] In fact, as people become more socially mobilized and begin to compete for the benefits that economic development offers, they may seek the support of their own group, caste, religion, or region against the others. The unity projected by the nationalist movement against the colonial power, as in Nigeria and India, or a foreign enemy as in China, may dissolve once the enemy leaves the scene. A Muslim guide told some Hindu tourists: "I used to be an Indian. Today I am a Muslim. Now there are no Indians, only Gujaratis, Punjabis, Bengalis." A democracy like India allows for the representation of diverse groups, but diversity involves conflict. Too much conflict may lead to instability in the political system.

Regarding region and religion, it is said that when three Gujaratis get together, you have a stock exchange, three Bengalis, an association, three Muslims, a feast, and three tribesmen, a blood feud.[18] The martial "races" in North India are given recognition in the saying: "When the North sharpens its sword, the South sharpens its pen." The Sikhs, a "martial race" whose adherents are prominent in driving buses and taxis in the North, are the butt of many jokes. When asked what a Sikh has inside his turban, a Hindu may say, "Nothing."

Differences exist, but differences in people do not necessarily lead to disunity as in Nigeria. Our concern is with the political implications of these differences. A further topic involves the degree and directions of change in Indian society.

The Western impact mobilized a large proportion of the Indian people. What is questionable is whether that impact has basically changed the traditional society or whether the social and political institutions and values of that society have persisted despite the professed modernizing values of the elite. Indeed, change has occurred and traditional structures like caste have adapted in response to the challenge of modernization. On the other hand, the elite have adapted to and absorbed some of the elements of traditional society. As the following discussion indicates, the process of change is neither one-dimensional nor unidirectional.[19]

Cultural Fragmentation: Caste

The caste system is "the most characteristic institution in the social life of the Hindus."[20] It divides Hindus (and in some cases Indian Muslims) into thousands of sub-groups that marry only within their own caste and are ranked in a status hierarchy of ritual purity. According to the sacred texts, there are four caste divisions: Brahmins (priests), Kshatriyas (warriors), Vaisyas (merchants) and Sudras (common people). The lowest social caste is the untouchables, who serve as scavengers and sweepers, the lowest of the low whose shadow could be a source of contamination to the higher castes.

In reality, the main working unit of caste was the *jati,* or sub-caste. Its particular area of power was the village or group of villages. Very rarely did a sub-caste extend beyond the confines of a region. Villages were often headed by a dominant caste who gained their position through economic power, a grant from a local king or prince, or outright conquest.[21] Except for the Brahmins, the highest, and the untouchables, the lowest, castes could rise in the status hierarchy by gaining economic and/or political power. Within a few generations, a lower caste would receive the status to which its newly acquired wealth and political power entitled it. The important point is that an individual remained a member of the caste in which he or she was born, no matter what changes occurred in his life style and occupation. His rise in the status hierarchy depended on the rise of his caste in economic and/or political power.[22]

Under the Western impact, the political and economic aspects of the caste system changed. The peace enforced by the British allowed castes from outside the village and region to move into a particular area and build an economic base. Trading castes like the *Banias* and *Marwaris* began to usurp the economic power of the local dominant caste or notable.[23] With the movement to the cities, the hold of the *jatis* (local or regional sub-caste) upon their caste members weakened. Caste associations formed to press demands on the British rulers; unlike the *jatis,* these were voluntary associations that did not contain all the members of the caste. Moreover, as members of a caste moved into different occupations and became differentiated by class, their former political solidarity diminished.[24] For example, the Rajputs, a dominant landowning caste in the state of Rajasthan, split on the issue of land reform in the early 1950's. The large Rajput landholders were understandably against the reform, while the peasant Rajputs were for it. Different Rajput classes joined different parties that fought each other tooth and nail.[25]

Furthermore, new employment opportunities opened by the Western impact outside the village gave avenues of social mobility to individuals within specific caste groups. Naturally, wealthier people were more able to afford the advantages of a Western education. Given the fact that many of the poorer castes were also the ritually lower ones, Western education and employment was only a partial solution to the problem. Due to this fact, upper castes still predominate in leadership positions, and the problem of integrating the untouchables, or *Harijans* (Children of God) as Gandhi called them, remains.

Technically, untouchability is against the law. In order to ensure representation to the Harijans, a number of parliamentary and state legislative assembly constituencies have been reserved for them, the scheduled castes. Openings are also guaranteed in the civil services and colleges, and Harijans are increasingly taking advantage of these opportunities. Although there is a party, the Republican, that claims to represent the interests of the Harijans, it remains small. Most Harijans vote for and receive leadership positions within the larger parties. Socially, they still remain the dregs of society to orthodox Hindus, and their economic gains are slow and intermittent.[26]

As more Harijans become educated, they become increasingly dissatisfied with their lot. Nevertheless, their low ritual status is compounded by their precarious economic position. A large proportion of Harijans are landless laborers, and clashes with their higher caste, wealthier neighbors have become more frequent. In Tamilnadu state, a Harijan village containing largely landless laborers was burned because they dared to challenge the landlords regarding distribution of the harvest. Since most Harijans live in rural areas, they are divided by subcastes *(jati)* like other Hindus, and are geographically spread over India, unified action on their part has been lacking. As elsewhere, attempts at social mobility by one group causes conflict with others. Modernizing forces like education may increase caste conflict.

Due to the diversity and large numbers of castes as well as the fact that status and class conflicts do not necessarily coincide, the impact of these caste conflicts has not been cumulative. An Iyengar Brahmin may not want his daughter to marry an Ahir but he may join lower caste trade union workers in a strike against a factory owner of his own caste. More significantly, the parliamentary framework and mass party organizations allow different caste groups to pursue their goals through institutions which are already legitimized.

In seeking to win elections, it is not surprising that many politicians use the traditional caste groups as bases of support. However, the task of organizing all-India caste parties is difficult because these *jatis* are scattered geographically. The electoral system also changed the hierarchical and authoritarian nature of the traditional caste system. In some constituencies on the local level, people from one village would unite with their caste fellows in other villages in order to secure an electoral constituency, and, at the state level, a few ministerial posts. Due to factional struggles among the leaders, these new and wider caste groups emerged divided. In many other constituencies, no caste predominated and a candidate's electoral fortunes also depended upon his securing the support of a variety of castes. In those constituencies where one caste did predominate, most major parties would nominate candidates from that caste, further destroying any effort at caste solidarity.

As a result, no major party relies solely on the support of one or even a few castes. Most of these parties, like the Congress, contain members with diverse caste backgrounds and are able to absorb new caste groups as they emerge. Regardless of the low ritual status of a caste, its numbers might gain it more political power in a party than members of a higher caste. For example:

When Sudras or Brahmins organize themselves into separate groups to win elections, they are using the system in a way the original Aryan settlers did not intend. This change in purpose really means the creation of a new system while retaining the outer shell of the earlier one. In any case, when caste groups negotiate among themselves over the sharing of power, they do so with a sense of equality that negates the basic assumption of caste.[27]

In summary, caste is still an important factor, particularly in village politics. However, recent studies have suggested that it is not the major determinant of Indian political behavior.[28] Rather, economic and political power gained either on a local level or through a place in the party or government hierarchy is far more significant than caste in the Indian political process. It is through these means that a politician can provide services to his constituents in the form of patronage, a road for a village, the granting of a permit, and other amenities.

Cultural Fragmentation: Religion

India contains followers of almost every major world religion, but the great majority of Indians are Hindus (85 percent). The major religious division in India is between Hindus and Muslims, who comprise about 10 percent of the population. Sikhs have also been politically important, particularly in the state of Punjab. Under the Mughals, the Muslims ruled much of India until their defeat at the hands of the British, who replaced the Muslim elite with their own countrymen in the nineteenth century. In the areas most strongly affected by the British system of law and education, the presidencies of Bombay, Bengal, and Madras, the Muslims were economically and politically weak. Consequently, the Hindus benefited most from Western education and were trained in large numbers to administer the needs of the British rulers. The rising Muslim middle class as well as the more traditional rulers in the "backward" provinces suffered the most discrimination.[29]

The Nationalist movement, in which adherents of the majority religion (Hinduism) predominated, failed to prevent the breakup of British India into India and Pakistan, and the partition took place in an atmosphere of communal (religious) violence. The circumstances leading to this development were long and complex.

Realizing that modernization was largely benefiting the Hindus, a number of leading Muslims founded the Muslim League in the early 1900's. Their strategy was to align with the British and demand separate Muslim representation to prevent the Muslims from being submerged by a Hindu majority; the British granted their request.

Originally, the League was not a mass organization. As the Congress party began to appeal to the symbols of Hindu nationalism in order to reach the masses, more Muslim leaders began to feel that they would lose their power in a predominantly Hindu country. Unfortunately, Muslim fears of Hindu oppression had some basis in reality. Only highly educated and Westernized Muslims had continuous social relations with Hindus. In both villages and cities, the Muslim masses lived in separate quarters. The situation was analogous to cities in Northern Nigeria, where non-Muslims were confined to sections called *sabon gari* (strangers' quarters). Monotheistic Islam and polytheistic Hinduism were not only separate faiths, but their adherents also lived under separate laws and customs. Unlike many areas in the West, with their long tradition of separation of church and state, Hinduism and Islam were also separate social systems that regulated the personal affairs of their respective believers in different ways.

These differences led to mutual suspicions, hostility, and violence in the form of communal (religious) riots. If a Hindu saw a Muslim beating a Hindu, he would search for a Hindu policeman, knowing that a Muslim policeman might turn his back.

Under Mohammed Ali Jinnah, the Muslim League turned into a mass organization by the late 1930's. Despite its mass character and openness to all groups, the Congress party could not hold the majority of Muslims. Hindu-Muslim differences were too salient, and the League's appeal to Muslim fears was successful. During the partition into India and Pakistan, large numbers of Hindus and Sikhs fled from Pakistan into India, creating a huge refugee problem in the border areas.

The costs of the partition were very high. In addition to the thousands killed and displaced, a great deal of bitterness exists between Hindus and the millions of Muslims still in India. Communal riots still occur, particularly in the north where Muslim rule had been strongly entrenched and its impact on the Hindus more exploitive in nature. As one journalist explains, "between 1960 and 1970, the number of communal incidents rose from 700 to 3,000, and according to official figures as many as 3,508 persons lost their lives."[30] This does not augur well for integration and stability.

The benefits of the partition, if less obvious, are also important. The most numerous separatist movement, the nationalist Muslims, were removed from the scene by the division of British India. Had they remained, the legitimacy of the Congress party would have been effectively challenged by a Muslim League with the support of India's most numerous minority. Since Jinnah's Muslim League was also far more heavily dominated by wealthy landlords than the Congress, its continuing presence in the new India would have placed a severe brake on economic development and constitutional democracy. It is no accident that India's rather limited land reforms have been more successful than Pakistan's. Furthermore, unlike Nigeria and many of the Third World nations, this major source of secession and instability was removed before independence.

Since those Muslims who demanded separation the most had already left India in 1947 and the Congress party remained open to Muslim influence, most Muslims remaining in India have chosen to advance their demands within the major parties. Many top Congress leaders, including a past president of the Indian Union, have been Muslims. Nevertheless, at least one major party, the Jana Sangh, is Hindu and quasi-communal and has attempted to inculcate all non-Hindus with their own ideas of Indian culture.[31] At times, this party has been associated with religious riots and its growing strength is a cause of concern to Indian Muslims. The Sangh opposes Pakistan and does not recognize religious minorities. Finally, the number of Muslims in lower government and party positions in India is not known, but their representation is probably not proportional to their numerical strength.

The Sikhs also have a long anti-Muslim tradition. Today, this group constitutes a majority in the Punjab. Nevertheless, the Akali Dal, a Sikh separatist movement, has failed to capture a majority in the state legislature and has had to rely on coalitions with non-communal parties, even the Congress, which has often been willing to satisfy Sikh demands for the sake of unity, including the establishment of a separate Punjabi state. Religion, then, like caste, has not proven a firm basis for unity if it is not supported by political and economic factors. For example, the Akali Dal has split into two main political factions and does not have the support of the majority of the Sikh population.[32]

Finally, a word should be said about the majority religion, Hinduism, and its impact on political change. Unlike the Catholic Church in many Latin American countries and the *ulema,* a traditional Muslim religious elite in both the Middle East and India, there is no organized Hindu church that could act as a deterrent to a modernizing elite. Under the British impact in the nineteenth century, organizations like the Brahmo Samaj and Arya Samaj formed to reform Hinduism. Although not directly measurable, their influence on the Nationalist movement was considerable. At the grass roots level, *bhakti* (devotion) movements brought Hinduism to the people in their own regional languages. Since the division of India and Pakistan in 1947, language has been a more divisive force than religion, as we shall see.[33]

Cultural Fragmentation: Language and Region

During the 1950's, the growing demands of linguistic and regional groups threatened the stability of the Indian Union. There are at least fourteen major language groups in India. Hindi, an Aryan tongue, is native only to northern India. In the south, the major languages were

Dravidian in origin. The British introduced English as the medium for administration all over India, but this language is still spoken by only a small elite. Furthermore, Dravidian languages like Tamil are completely unrelated to Hindi and possess a long literary tradition. Like Switzerland, a country can have four languages, but can its people communicate with each other in fourteen? A story is told of two Indians from different regions who met in Germany and had to converse in German in order to understand each other.

Language differences in India involve the struggle for political, economic, and social power for a wide variety of individuals and groups. For example, if Hindi were made the only official language, politicians who did not speak Hindi would be at a disadvantage. Even within a single state, there are often large linguistic minorities who feel disgruntled when their political leaders cannot understand the legislative proceedings because they cannot understand what the speaker is saying. In Andhra Pradesh, those Muslim legislators who speak only Urdu are often unable to converse with their Hindu colleagues who may speak only Telegu. In this case, language differences become transformed into political and religious issues.

As the people in different regions became socially mobilized, they began to make demands for greater autonomy for their home areas and for the use of their native languages for government purposes. They claimed, not without foundation, that requiring an administrator to be fluent in English and Hindi discriminated against native speakers of other languages in securing government posts. Regional and linguistic groups used every means, fasts, demonstrations, even violence, to assert their demands. The Indian Congress leaders reacted in the 1950's by redrawing state boundaries to create states on a largely linguistic basis. As a result, the official language of Andhra Pradesh is now Telegu, Tamilnadu (formerly Madras) Tamil, etc.

An important consequence of this act was to transform most regional movements from avowed enemies of the Indian Union, arguing for separatism as well as autonomy, into groups willing to work within the framework of Indian constitutional democracy. The development of the Dravida Munnetra Kazhagam (Dravidian Progressive Federation) in Tamilnadu (Madras) is a case in point.[34]

Under the British, the upper caste Brahmins, a minute proportion of the population, filled most of the important government posts in Madras. Not surprisingly, sections of the Dravidian movement, consisting of middle and lower caste groups seeking more influence in the government, that developed in the first half of this century, were anti-Brahmin and even anti-Hindu. After all, it was the Hindu religion that designated Brahmins as the highest caste! Certain participants in the movement gladly proclaimed: "If you see a Brahmin and a snake, kill the Brahmin first."

In its early stages, the Dravida Munnetra Kazhagam (DMK) was a communal party containing members of most important caste and religious groups in the Madras region, aligned against the Brahmin caste and the domination of the Hindi-speaking Aryan north. Its leaders vociferously advocated Tamil nationalism, and demands were made for a separate "Dravidisthan"—a state for the Dravidian people of South India. When the DMK decided to contest elections, however, its leaders found that they needed the support of others to defeat the Congress party. Alliances were made with the Muslim League and Swatantra, led by the Brahmin "Rajaji" and members of all castes were welcomed into the DMK.

As the DMK gained in electoral and legislative strength in their home state, and advocacy of separatism became illegal under the Indian constitution, they revoked all their past stances except Tamil nationalism. They won an absolute majority in Tamilnadu in 1967. At the death of their founder-leader, C. N. Annadorai, the Indian government issued a stamp in his honor, and the DMK contested the 1971 elections in coalition with Indira Gandhi's Congress party (R) and the Communist party of India. Although autonomy and local control is occasionally demanded, the DMK leadership is unwilling to sacrifice its political and economic gains for the goal of separatism.

Although other regional demands crop up from time to time, the major problem seems to have been solved by the reorganization of states in the 1950's and the willingness of the Congress leadership to accommodate various groups. Nevertheless, two difficulties remain. First, the number of possible separatist movements in India is so large that any number of new states might be established on a linguistic basis. Since the 1950's, Punjab was divided into Punjabi Suba with a Sikh majority and Haryana with a Hindi-speaking majority. The Nagas, former headhunters, were also granted a separate state after an armed struggle with the Indian army. At present, demands are being made for a separate Telegana state in an economically impoverished section of Andhra Pradesh.[35]

Second, the satisfaction of regional demands by the government may lead to a gross waste of economic resources in a country that cannot afford it. A prime example was the Assam oil refinery controversy. The government of India placed an oil refinery in Assam state of India to avoid continued controversy and the possibility of violence by the region's elite should the refinery not be placed in their state. For the sake of peace, a plan involving less expense but location in a different region was abandoned. Support for the political system is gained at the cost of economic rationality.[36]

In any case, many regional demands are met. Without government imposition, the Hindi language is spreading throughout the country at a rapid rate, and many inhabitants in particular states or regions speak more than one language. Increased communications and inter-regional trade, building on the base left by the British, led to this development and helped prevent the predicted breakdown of the Indian political system. The spectre of disintegration that haunted the 1950's remains a spectre, despite regional tensions.[37]

Urbanization

Professor Schmitt has noted in the introduction that growth and urbanization can upset established values and thwart advances gained through economic development. Nevertheless, a degree of stability has been maintained in India by the comparatively gradual migration to the cities. From 1951 to 1961, the urban population changed from 17.2 percent to 19.05 percent of the people. This slow rate of migration to urban centers has not placed undue overloads on the political system.[38] Existing organizations, whether political parties, trade unions, caste organizations, etc., have been able to absorb many of the urban immigrants.

Population Growth

Population growth is a serious matter in India. The Indian government encouraged birth control with only limited success, especially in rural areas where the hold of tradition is still strong. Signs in Delhi advise, "Make love, not babies." The annual net increase in population of 2.5 percent may nullify food production, despite the fact food production has grown by almost 90 percent. From 1950–1967, industrial production rose by 7 percent annually, power generation increased sevenfold, and school enrollment tripled.[39]

In India the rate of population increase and urban growth to date has been gradual and has not posed a threat to the democratic system. Whether this situation will continue is another question. In any case, democratic regimes like India are not alone in facing this problem.

Crises, Sequences, and Rate of Change

Finally, the sequences and rate of change in India have been important determinants of India's avenue to democratic development. In a suggestive article,[40] the scholar Eric A. Nordlinger has argued that a stable, effective, and representative democratic government will form if political development follows four stages with gradual rates of change. These are:

1. Formation of national identity.

2. Institutionalization of a central authority subordinate to an executive and legislature.

3. Founding of mass parties, representative of wide and varied segments of the population rather than merely local notables and aristocrats.

4. Mass suffrage.

India has been fortunate in that the British institutionalized a central government and gave the country structural unity in a process that lasted for about a century and a half before India's independence. Legislative councils in which Indians played an important role were set up before the nationalist movement assumed a mass character. As the nationalist movement, spearheaded by the Congress party, achieved a mass base, its leaders were able to use their mass support to coerce the British into granting further powers to Indians. Naturally, the British kept most of the central authority in their own hands, but the powers of Indians in both provincial and local governments were very real. Legislative positions, as well as the training of substantial numbers of Indians in the administration, helped prepare India to govern itself.

Although complete adult suffrage did not come until independence (1947), at least one-sixth of the adult population, male and female, could vote by 1935. The Congress party had become a mass organization in the early 1920's and had learned to gear itself to winning elections in competition with other parties. At independence, the Congress was the only party with an all-India organization that represented the wide variety of classes, castes, religions, and regions in Indian society.

Nevertheless, India faced two severe crises of national identity, the Muslim break which culminated in the foundation of Pakistan in 1947 and the language and regional crisis after independence. The formation of national identity did not precede the creation of institutions, mass party, and suffrage. Instead, it had to be created along with them. In this process, a rapid rate of social mobilization of the masses in the 1920's with Gandhian appeals to Hindu symbols accentuated Muslim fears of Hindu domination. Only the strength and adaptability of the Congress party, the legitimacy of the central authority, and the growing commitment of the masses to the use of the ballot prevented further splits on regional and linguistic grounds in the 1950's and 1960's.

Nordlinger suggests that the establishment of mass suffrage before the creation of national identity may lead to widespread violence among groups rather than against a central authority.[41] This is especially true in a country as culturally fragmented by caste, religion, language, and region as India. Why didn't these crises in national identity lead to greater instability in the Indian political system with a subsequent overthrow of constitutional democracy? The answer lies in the ability of the

Indian political system to act as a control over forces that would otherwise lead to political as well as social fragmentation.

STRUCTURES AND STRATEGIES OF CONTROL: THE POLITICAL SYSTEM AS AN INDEPENDENT VARIABLE

We have noted that the political system is not merely a reflection of social and economic forces but indeed shapes and even changes the nature of these forces. The institutions of government, formal and informal, channel and adapt themselves to demands. The political system also acts as an independent variable to which the social system, as dependent variable, responds. For example, as we mentioned earlier, legislation organizing Indian states according to linguistic criteria in the 1950's assimilated regional elites into the political process. If these regional elites had been excluded, they would have provoked even greater tension and unrest. Likewise, caste was integrated into the political system by the electoral and parliamentary system.

I shall specifically be concerned with parliamentary democracy, federalism, the bureaucracy, the military and police, and the party system and electoral politics, and how they have provided arenas in which different groups may compete within a democratic framework. The Indian political system contains a judicious blend of a strong central authority and a distribution of important powers (for example, collection of land revenue) to the states. The party system and the federal framework have adapted to forces of change in Indian society.

Parties, Parliamentary Democracy, and the Electoral System

At the national level, India has a Parliament consisting of two houses. The lower house, the *Lok Sabha* (House of the People) is more important and is elected by universal adult suffrage. A prime minister is chosen by the majority party in the lower house as in Great Britain.[42] On the state level, the Legislative Assembly is again the most important, and a chief minister is selected by the majority in the assembly.

Power resides largely with the prime minister, Cabinet, and high party officers, and with their counterparts on the state level. If they are skillful, and they generally are, they can use their governmental or party powers to enforce discipline on their relatively loose, open, and undisciplined party organization.[43] In order to reach the top, a person has to exhibit some skill in uniting disparate groups, and Congress party leaders have had to deal with this problem long before independence. Most Congress politicians have, in recent years, been willing to follow the prime minister on questions of national unity, although there are strong differences on economic questions.

Except for a brief period (1969–71), the Congress has held an absolute majority in the *Lok Sabha*. This phenomenon led some observers to christen India as a one-party dominant system, characterized by "inter-party competition but no alteration of power."[44] The Congress acted as an umbrella, open to diverse groups connected by a variety of links: caste, economic power, religion, personality, etc. Factionalism pervaded the Congress organization at every level, and political bosses, on whom the party was dependent for votes, established their own fiefdoms in many districts and states.[45]

The Congress was able to use its government position to strengthen the party by allocation of resources to actual or potential supporters. The opposition parties, representing all hues of the ideological spectrum, were at a disadvantage in this regard. Nevertheless, they were not without a voice. In 1966, the scholar Gopal Krishna argued:

> The ruling party, though it enjoys secure dominance, is subjected to unfettered organized opposition, making it responsive to currents of opinion and interests expressed through the instrumentality of the latter. The numerically weak opposition is not only permitted to exist but is looked upon as a legitimate and necessary part of the system, often consulted on matters of public policy and allowed to exercise influence far in excess of its strength in Parliament and the State Legislatures.[46]

In some states, Congress leaders would make deals with opposition party leaders to unseat Congress leaders of other factions. This only increased party instability. Following a period of severe public dissatisfaction with the Congress over the deteriorating economic and law-and-order situation, coalition governments took over many states in the 1967 elections. Due to inter-party rivalry and the same factionalism that plagued the Congress, most of these coalition governments were short-lived.[47] But they did have an impact on the Congress party.

First, many of the old Congress bosses with strong systems of patronage and power in the states lost to the opposition parties. The Congress split into Indira Gandhi's Congress (R) and the Congress (O) in 1969, and most of the old bosses joined the much weaker Congress (O). The doors were thrown open to new men in Indira Gandhi's party who had previously been deprived of power by the bosses.[48] For example, in the state of Bihar, most of the Congress leaders and all of the chief ministers prior to 1967 represented the higher castes. Since the Congress split, leaders from lower castes have been able to gain that office. As a result, these electoral politics and shifting factions provide means of political, as well as social and economic mobility.

Second, the Congress (R), with only a plurality in the *Lok Sabha*, had to rule at the center (Union Government) with the aid of the DMK and Communist Party in India (CPI). In order to satisfy its allies and outmaneuver its more radical opponents, e.g., the Communist party of India-Marxist, the Congress (R) turned to the left. In coalition with the CPI and some other parties, Mrs. Gandhi's party won an absolute majority in the 1971 parliamentary elections and 71 percent of the seats in the 1972 state assembly elections. Electoral competition forces the Congress party to take account of opposition opinions and groups and to be sensitive to shifts in the electorate. When the Indian electorate moved to the left, making more demands for economic security and government action, the Congress (R) likewise moved to the left. Indira Gandhi, the Prime Minister, exclaimed, "If I don't do anything to take the wind out of the sails of the Communists, the entire country would go red."[49]

We have noted to what extent the Indian parties, both Congress and opposition, do represent wide varieties of people and are open, in varying degrees, to changes in leadership. They also serve as effective links between the government and the people. Since independence, all parties, particularly the Congress, have taken in more leaders and cadres from the rural areas. As a result, the party elites are not isolated from the mass of the people. On the one hand, these rural leaders help create and maintain stronger links with the constituencies through a variety of local networks based on caste, economic interests, kinship, common party membership, and, increasingly, issues. On the other hand, national and state party leaders are more subject to local influences whose support they need in order to win elections.

Of course, the system of democratic electoral politics has its costs, particularly regarding the development of wide-ranging policies. Most people serving in the state legislatures, and to a lesser extent the *Lok Sabha*, are very attuned to the needs and demands of articulate groups in their constituencies, for politicians are judged by their service to their electorates. In plain terms, they are liked if they provide goods and services to their constituents and frowned upon if they do not. P. C. Ghosh, once a prominent West Bengali politician, was called the "Arambag Gandhi" more because of what he did for Arambag than for any saintliness. Before elections, politicians are apt to promise anything concrete, like a water pump, in order to get votes. A cartoon in an Indian journal of political opinion pictured a politician addressing a family in front of their hut: "I promise to build a hospital, a university, a railway station, a steel plant, and an atomic reactor in your village."[50]

These "bread and butter" issues important to the electorate, have a decided impact on the behavior of Indian legislators. Indian legislatures, including the *Lok Sabha*, are more like the fragmented and factionalized American House of Representatives and the French National Assembly than the British Parliament, upon which model they were created. Bargaining and accommodation is the key political style in these legislatures. As a result, many compromises are made to the benefit of many groups and individuals. But groups without sufficient representation can suffer and broad range plans are often difficult to formulate. In many cases, opposition groups, frustrated in their attempt to gain power, use the legislature to stage demonstrations and embarrass the government. Sometimes violence ensues in the form of clashes between individual legislators and rival party members.

Federalism, Decentralization, and Democracy

The division of India into different states with elected legislatures and chief ministers with wide realms of authority in both economic matters and law-and-order situations implies a sharing of power peculiar to democratic governments. The language controversies that threatened to destroy India's unity in the 1950's was met by dividing the states on a linguistic basis. The open party system allowed leaders from different regions speaking different languages to share power within the system.

The states also serve as basis of support for opposition parties that could not hope to defeat the Congress party at the national level. The Communists are strong in Kerala and West Bengal, the DMK in Tamilnadu, and the right-wing, communal Jana Sangh in the Hindi-speaking regions. If a viable and vocal opposition is conducive to democracy, then the states aid in maintaining this end.

The cost of this system of federalism, however, is national economic development. Often wealthy states refuse to share food with their poorer neighbors, and many state politicians bicker over who is to derive the benefits of economic plans formulated by the national government. One cartoon showed the grinning state chief ministers descending on the Planning Commission like a pack of vultures and leaving with bits and pieces of a Five Year Plan. Since the state leaders are more dependent on local interests, including wealthy peasants and landlords, they are generally less likely to implement land reforms.

Bureaucracy and President's Rule: A Check on Federalism

Therefore, it is not surprising that Indians rely on other means than parliament, parties, and elections to hold the diverse federal system together. They have a unified civil service that controls the greater part of both national and state public administration, the military and police, and the threat of President's Rule. The President of the Indian Union, chosen through a complex system of election by members of the state legislative assemblies and Parliament, appoints a governor in each state.[51]

In normal times, the governor's main duties are to appoint the chief minister with the approval of the majority in the Legislative Assembly.

President's Rule, by which the Union government rules directly through the governor, was designed to meet emergencies like "a threat to security by external aggression or internal disturbances; a breakdown of constitution in a state; financial crisis."[52] The president announces the emergency in a proclamation that requires parliamentary (national) approval within two months. The state Legislative Assembly is usually adjourned and the governor rules under the president's direction. President's Rule has been used frequently since the 1967 elections when the political parties failed to form a stable government. The ruling Congress leaders have often been accused of using President's Rule to topple state governments controlled by their opponents. In any case, the knowledge that the central government can and has intervened provides an important constraint on a state's internal politics.[53]

The bureaucracy also has a unifying influence. We have mentioned how the British trained an elite corps of civil servants that became the basis for the Indian Administrative Service (IAS) after 1947. The IAS men possessed a strong *esprit de corps* and sense of dedication. However, top bureaucrats in British India, even the native Indians, were not responsive nor responsible to political parties and were distrusted by the Nationalist movement. Their sense of superiority to any organization purporting to represent the will of the people borders on arrogance and persists even today. Despite this fact, the IAS has adjusted to the new democratic framework and has become more representative of the diverse caste, regional, and class groups in India.

Originally, the higher echelons of the bureaucracy were Western-educated, often in an exclusive Indian "public school" modeled in the English image of Eton. Social graces and poise were important. Merit, not caste, was the major basis for promotion, and the elite shared a cosmopolitan, all-India outlook. English was the main language of communications.

However, increased educational opportunities offered by the Indian government since independence, including instruction in English, has made it possible for more middle- and lower-middle class people to pass the examinations required for entrance into the IAS. The bureaucracy has also been expanded to admit people with a stronger sense of regional culture, and entrance requirements have been altered in favor of those whose main language is regional, not Hindi. The demands for representation by the variety of castes, languages, and regions in India has been accommodated by the bureaucracy as well as the political parties. The costs of greater democraticization in the bureaucracy and the wider influence of electoral politicians in administrative matters have largely been in areas of policy implementation.

At lower levels, civil servants are pressured by state and local political groups, including party factions. In order to get anything done at the village level, bureaucrats have to reach an understanding with local powers. This may stifle broad developmental plans made by the Union government. Bureaucrats are also burdened with paper work and red tape that prevents them from efficiently implementing their alleged goals. Although the bureaucracy has largely succeeded in keeping order and maintaining a continuous system of authority when political parties have failed to do so, its authoritarian structure and vulnerability to pressure by vested interests works against the implementation of policies aimed at economic development and changing the status quo.[54]

Bureaucratic corruption is also a problem.[55] Most civil servants are underpaid, and the temptation to increase gains by granting favors to those willing to pay for them is always present. On the one hand, corruption helps the stability of society by allowing many individuals access to an otherwise impersonal bureaucratic machine. Greasing the wheels of the machine helps it to work more quickly and smoothly. The force of tradition is also accommodated. Many Indians feel that such things as "bribery" and "nepotism" are not wrong. A man who wants a favor has to pay for it, and family and caste loyalty demands that you use your influence to help your relatives and caste fellows.

On the other hand, corruption leads to public loss of confidence in the bureaucracy. Politicians from different parties and factions use the charge of corruption against their opponents, and demands for legislative or judicial enquiries into the workings of various agencies clouds an already murky political atmosphere.

The Military and Police

The military is not subject to the same problems as the bureaucracy, although charges of corruption and malpractice are often leveled at the police. Regarding the army, Hugh Tinker argues:

> Under British rule the army was genuinely intercommunal, despite its organization upon the basis of caste and religion, with emphasis upon the kshatriya or warrior tradition of the 'martial races' of North India. Before Independence, Congress leaders had termed this an army of mercenaries and insisted that India did not require such a massive military machine for its defense. However, tentative plans for reductions in the armed forces were soon halted as events in Kashmir, Hyderabad, and Goa and on the border with Tibet, demonstrated how vital the army was to India's national interests. The regimental traditions preserved for a hundred years or more assumed a new significance, and the jawan, the enlisted man, became an honoured symbol of India's determination to preserve national security. When war with Pakistan came in September, 1965, and the armed forces stoutly battled for the nation's cause, enthusiasm for the Sikh, the Rajput, and the Gurkha, as fighters for India, created an emotional bond bringing together the middle classes and the mass, the city and the countryside.[56]

The officers' professional training has made them loyal and subservient to the government representing the will of the people. Some officers have been extremely critical of the law and order situation, but few have challenged the concept of parliamentary democracy and none has attempted a *coup d' état*. The division of the armed forces into five regional commands also mitigates against a unified military conspiracy against the government. In the extremely unlikely event of a coup, the military would be faced by organized opposition of such proportions that the stability of any regime they might establish would be precarious. Brecher argues:

> To hold together a country of 470 million people with fourteen major languages and cultures is difficult enough for a deeply rooted Congress machine and Civil Service extending to the village; for the Army alone to do it is inconceivable, though it might succeed with the total cooperation of the Civil Service. There is no evidence of such an alignment at present; nor is it likely in the near future.[57]

Finally, the strength of the Indian civilian institutions, the *esprit de corps* of a military with traditions of subordination to a civil authority, and the openness of the armed services to men of all castes, languages, and regions functions to prevent a takeover by a narrow military elite. The military was able to exercise more influence in countries like Syria and Nigeria because, unlike India, either the parliamentary tradition was lacking or the legitimacy of the mass parties was weak. People respect the armed forces in India. Since their victories over Pakistan in 1965 and 1971, the Indian officers also respect themselves and the civilian government that produced the materiel and granted the funds to make these victories possible. A self-satisfied military generally sees no reason to revolt.

The police are a different matter.[58] Public respect for them is often low, and many villagers fear the policeman as an outside agent which enforces the will of *Sarkar* (government). Although there is a Central Reserve Police, most police are state, not national, officials under the control of the Home Ministry or its equivalent in a state Cabinet. Unlike the army, the police are primarily concerned with internal order, and are often accused of unduly persecuting any opposition to the state governments. Naturally the Home Ministry is a much sought after prize among politicians.[59] A struggle for control of it was an important bone of contention in some of the coalition governments formed since 1967. Lack of any unified command prevents any type of police takeover of the government, but charges of corruption and political pressure indicate that the police are subject to some of the same maladies as the civil service.

Ideology

Unlike China, Syria, and, to a less extent, Chile and Mexico, India's leaders have generally not relied on an ideological enemy in the form of imperialists and revisionists, Zionists, or Yankee imperialists to strengthen national identity. The extent of foreign capital controlling economic enterprises in India is much smaller, proportional to India's gross GNP, than in the Latin American countries. The desire of most of India's leaders to pacify India's large Muslim minority militates against a rabid anti-Pakistan stance. The Chinese presence, confined to remote border areas, is not felt to be a continual threat.

Likewise, the ideology of the Congress party is pragmatic, not rigid. The Congress brand of democratic socialism leaves a substantial area of operations open to private enterprise. The benefits of this type of socialism are that the competitive private sector is allowed to advance despite government regulations that are often too rigid, and that more burdens are not placed on a government lacking the capacity to bear them.

The costs are that socialism, adhered to by most Indian parties, often becomes an empty slogan, devoid of content and an insufficient instrument of economic change.[60] At the most, Indian socialism allows for limited and gradual reform.

AVENUES TOWARD DEVELOPMENT

Does India provide a model of political development for the emerging Third World nations? In a large sense, it does. Professor Schmitt earlier argued that a poor country can be democratic, and the Indian case illustrates this point rather well. India's example also indicates how modern organizations like mass parties, legislatures, and bureaucracies can absorb the traditional elements of cultural fragmentation like caste, language, region, and, to some extent religion, and channel them in a democratic direction without an overdose of political suppression as in the Soviet Union in an earlier era or Nigeria recently.

In another sense, however, the representation of large landholders, businessmen, and local elites in Indian parties and governmental institutions have blocked or slowed down efforts at genuine reform. This may be the burden of a democracy whose leaders have to give representation to increasing numbers of groups in order to maintain stability. The fact that lower caste and class groups can use democratic institutions as a means of economic, political, and social mobility does provide some measure of hope. More Harijans (untouchables) in the civil services and greater efforts at land reform by the national government are signs that the pressure of numbers, since numbers can be translated into votes, can at least obtain limited reforms and benefits for groups that would otherwise be alienated from the political system.

Advantages and Costs of Democracy: Limited Reform

The major advantage of a democracy is representation of diverse groups. The cost is limited and gradual reform. Economic and political development plans, originating at the Center (Union Government) and implemented by the states, have not resulted in enough material advancement to match the population growth. These plans have been massive and broad in scope: land reform and new agricultural methods, *panchayati raj,* five year plans, and mass education. Yet their success has only been partial and some of their results unintended. Why?

Land reform has helped break up some of the larger landholdings and innovations in agriculture, including the "Green Revolution" with its new seeds and fertilizers, has increased productivity. However, the beneficiaries have largely been the middle and upper class peasants who had the capital to invest in new techniques. The poor could not afford to risk trying new methods because they would face economic annihilation if their meager crop failed. In fact, land reform has had the dual impact of creating a middle class of peasants and maintaining a class of landless laborers unable to compete with their wealthier compatriots. Some landless laborers and poor peasants move to the cities, aggravating the unemployment problems in urban areas. The vast majority remains on the land, discontented and impoverished.[61]

Panchayati raj (government by local council), a pet project of Nehru's that aimed at augmenting economic development by expanding democratic participation at the grass roots level, has also had mixed results. Nehru's idea was to have locally elected officials decide and implement plans for community development. These plans would be coordinated at higher levels, largely elected. The officials would meet together in a *panchayat,* discuss matters like irrigation, road building, and farming, and make plans for their village or group of villages. In some cases, *panchayat* elections have widened the nature of the local elites as low-caste and high-caste villagers sit together on the same council. Progressive leaders have come to the fore. In other cases, factionalism has weakened village solidarity and has led to a stalemate. Another effect has been that traditional leaders and castes relying on wealth and status have used the elections to entrench themselves further.[62]

Panchayats cannot be written off as a failure. They tend to create support for the Indian political system by bringing government to the people in a language and idiom that they understand. Villagers may not understand the decisions of distant courts, but they do comprehend the decisions of their local *panchayats.* To the extent that *panchayats* increase political participation, the chances of a stable democracy in India also increase.

The Indian government has also developed a series of Five-Year Plans, aimed at stimulating its economy.[63] They have had some impact, but many times economic growth would be gained at the expense of a more equitable distribution of resources. As in land reform, the wealthy benefited at the expense of the poor. The Five-Year Plans have shifted in their emphasis regarding the relationship of industry to agriculture, but basic social changes such as those implemented in Stalin's early five-year plans in transforming the Soviet Union have not been forthcoming. The refusal of India's leaders to use coercive methods like Stalin and Mao that would result in repression of the opposition and destruction of the wealthy peasants and landlords preserves the democratic character of the state and its openness to changes in political leadership. New men offer the chance for new policies, or at least may voice demands for previously unrepresented groups. For example, a shakeup in the older Congress party leadership of West Bengal resulted in preponderant numbers of younger congressmen in the state legislature.[64] In any case, India has not chosen a Stalinist or Maoist road to development. Given the vast decentralization of power and the commitment of many Indians to democracy, it is doubtful that it could.

Nevertheless, some have opted for the Maoist alternative of violent revolution. The situation in sections of the countryside is not peaceful. In rural areas of severe population concentration and economic exploitation, poor peasants have waged civil wars against the wealthy landholders. The more radical factions in the Communist parties have played a role in some of these uprisings, but the discontent did not originate with any outside agitators.[65]

The circumstances leading to the above development are interesting and require a brief examination. In 1967, a group of landless laborers led by extremist Communists rebelled against landlords and police in the Naxalbari region of West Bengal. The rebellion was crushed by the Indian government. A group of younger members of the Communist party of India-Marxist, kept in subordinate positions by the older leaders, bolted their party on the grounds that it had betrayed its revolutionary goals by not supporting the rebellion. A new Communist party was formed in 1969, and the movement spread to different parts of India. Split into various Maoist groups, the movement became known as the "Naxalites." In 1969, the Indian Home Ministry reported:

> Certain political parties have succeeded in organizing effectively landless workers, poor peasants and others with insecure tenancies in some pockets. . . .
> Although the peasant political organizations in most parts of the country are still organizationally weak, and their capacity for launching sustained

agitations is limited, the tensions in the rural areas, resulting from a widening gap between the relatively few affluent farmers [and] landless agricultural workers, may increase in the coming months and years. A bad agricultural season could lead to an explosive situation in rural areas.[66]

Weakened by factional splits and opposed by all major political parties, including the Communist party of India-Marxist, the Naxalites were defeated. Their major leaders are in prison or dead. The major parties, even the Communists, had built up organizational as well as legislative strength under Indian parliamentary democracy. They were unwilling to risk their gains in a revolution. By allocating shares of power to different groups, even with diverse ideologies, a political system can subsequently gain their support by giving them a stake in its preservation. This is an advantage of a multi-ethnic, culturally fragmented, multi-party democracy. The cost is lack of radical social and economic change and its consequence in increasing discontent in the form of mass protests and abortive revolutions.

In addition, mass education has produced more qualified candidates than jobs.[67] Addressing a group of sixteen hopeful applicants, a businessman exclaimed, "It is a race not to feed yourself but to take food out of the other person's mouth to feed yourself."

Due to frustrations caused by their precarious economic position, students often turn to mass demonstrations and political violence. For example, some of the young in Calcutta have become assassins for various political groups. A noted political scientist argues that "the fact that student protests in India, given the general condition of competing for scarce opportunities, aim more at finding a place in the establishment than at challenging its legitimacy is further likely to keep the challenge of youth within manageable limits."[68] This is largely true and indicates the strong degree of legitimacy that the Indian political system has gained in the British period as well as after 1947.

Despite the inequalities that have characterized the Indian form of democratic political development, a combination of political democracy and economic development has further increased opportunities for rapid individual advancement:

Power has also become independent of class to a greater extent than in the past. Ownership of land is no longer the decisive factor in acquiring power. Numerical support and a strategic position in the party machinery play an important part. Adult franchise and Panchayati Raj have introduced new processes into village society. The struggle for power has become a pervasive phenomenon. This may partly be due to the fact that today much more power is accessible to the common man than was ever the case in the past. Mobility in the caste system has always been an extremely slow and gradual process. To acquire land and move up in the hierarchy of class also takes a generation or two. Shifts in the distribution of power under the new set-up are by comparison, quick and radical in nature.[69]

Indian Democracy in Comparative Perspective

Indian democracy has succeeded due to four factors:

1. A lengthy and broad colonial period in which large numbers of Indians were trained in democratic government and administration.
2. Institutionalization of a mass party organization and political competition before independence.
3. Institutionalization of legislatures and bureaucracy before independence.
4. Charismatic leaders like Gandhi and Nehru who believed in democracy in its original meaning—rule by the people.

The fact that the Congress party actually functioned on an all-India basis left it open to wide varieties of influence from caste, regional, and linguistic groups who could press their demands within the mass party. The failure of the Congress to integrate the Muslims and the split into India and Pakistan in 1947 indicates that even the most open organizations may not be able to deal with severe cultural fragmentation.

In this regard, India is often compared to Nigeria, where strong tribalism and an Ibo separatist movement led to a bloody civil war and the downfall of parliamentary democracy. The situation, however, was quite different. The British presence in Nigeria was comparatively short and narrow, and relatively few Nigerians were trained for either the bureaucracy or the legislature. While the British effectively destroyed the power of the aristocracy in India, they bolstered it in Northern Nigeria by ruling through the traditional elite, which later became a stumbling block to democracy in Nigeria.

Unlike India, there was no Nationalist movement and no national charismatic leader to unite the country. The movements and parties that developed, largely after World War II, were regional and tended to represent the three largest tribal groups, the Ibo, Yoruba, and Hausa-Fulani. While India had a strong central government, the central government of independent Nigeria was weak. Cultural fragmentation was reinforced in Nigeria by the political system. In India, due to the presence and scope of the bureaucracy, mass parties, and legislatures in which diverse groups could bargain and be represented, severe cultural fragmentation was mitigated.

Mexico pursued a different course of democratic development. There, a form of limited democracy developed with a single mass party in control. No colonial regime like the British set up and legitimated democratic institutions. The aristocracy and wealthy landlords, always a stumbling block to democracy, were destroyed by a popular revolution, 1911–1924. Faced with political but not cultural fragmentation, different groups in the revolutionary elite united to form the Institutionalized Revolutionary Party (PRI) which has monopolized the government ever since.

The PRI used the revolution to legitimize its own role in politically developing Mexico. The popular revolution and destruction of the aristocracy gave it mass roots and it developed into a mass organization. Like the Congress party in India, the PRI serves as an arena in which different groups can bargain and press demands. In addition, the position of the Congress as a dominant party is similar to that of the PRI, with the qualification that other political parties in India have a greater voice and can win at least on the local and state levels. India's cultural fragmentation and diversity are more conducive to a multi-party system. Moreover, party competition and the British colonial power before independence prevented the Congress from completely depriving the other parties of power. In a revolution like the Mexican and Chinese it is easier to repress alternatives.

Since independence (1947), the Indian electorate has demonstrated a greater awareness of national problems and a willingness to use votes rationally.[70] In order to win success at the polls, Indian parties have had to correctly gauge the mood of the electorate and change their strategies accordingly. Sensing the greater demands of many Indians for stability and economic improvement, Mrs. Gandhi's Congress (R) moved to the left, nationalized the banks, deprived the aristocracy (princes) of their annual salaries, and began to push for more meaningful land reform measures. The knowledge that the Congress can lose, as in 1967, makes it more responsive to both the electorate and other parties.

Indian democracy and the relative openness of the party system to "new blood" has also achieved a transfer of power to the middle and lower class without a revolution:

In India, power has passed in twenty years from princes and the Western-educated urban elite to the lower middle classes—and now seems within reach of the factory worker and the peasant. The caste system and other social structures that had remained unchanged for several thousand years have developed serious cracks since independence. That India should be manufacturing its own supersonic fighter aircraft while the bullock cart, the traditional symbol of its backwardness, is nowhere near obsolescence yet characterizes the size of the task before India as well as the measure of success it has so far achieved.[71]

India's problem is not that its elite has failed to adapt to political demands but that it has adapted too well. In gaining and maintaining the support of diverse groups, including many vested interests, and nurturing a political system that stresses bargaining, accommodation, and incremental change, the leaders have sacrificed broad range rapid change that would seriously upset the status quo. India's problem is that of a democratic government working in an area of scarce resources. As in other democracies, there is a vocal and well organized opposition on both the left and right to criticize the government and to ensure some change, however slow.

FOOTNOTES

1. Robert L. Hardgrave, Jr., *India: Government and Politics in a Developing Nation* (New York: Harcourt, Brace and World, Inc., 1970), p. 35; Percival Spear, *The Oxford History of Modern India; 1740–1947* (London: Oxford University Press, 1965), pp. 330, 367.

2. *India, Pakistan, and the West*, 4th ed. (New York: Oxford University Press, 1967), p. 103; Spear, *Oxford History*, p. 291.

3. Percival Spear, *A History of India*, Vol. 2. (Baltimore: Penguin, 1969), p. 153.

4. Hardgrave, *India*, pp. 26–27.

5. *Ibid.*, p. 31.

6. A good selection of Gandhi's writings is found in Homer Jack, ed., *The Gandhi Reader: A Source Book of his Life and Writings* (Bloomington: Indiana University Press, 1956).See Erik H. Erikson, *Gandhi's Truth* (New York: Norton, 1969). An overview of the variety of Indian political ideas and methods is found in Myron Weiner, "India's Two Political Cultures," in Lucian Pye and Sidney Verba, eds., *Political Culture and Political Development* (Princeton: Princeton University Press, 1965) and *The Politics of Scarcity* (Chicago: University of Chicago Press, 1962), ch. 8.

7. Gopal Krishna, "The Development of the Indian National Congress as a Mass Organization, 1918–1923," in Thomas Metcalf, ed., *Modern India: An Interpretive Anthology* (London: Macmillan, 1971), p. 272.

8. Gopal Krishna, "One Party Dominance—Development and Trends," in Rajni Kothari, ed., *Party System and Election Studies* (New Delhi: Allied Publishers, 1967), p. 44.

9. The development of the leftist parties is treated in Myron Weiner, *Party Politics in India* (Princeton: Princeton University Press, 1957), chs. 6–7. On Pakistan, see, Khalid Bin Sayeed, *Pakistan: The Formative Phase* (Karachi: Pakistan Publishing House, 1960). The transfer of power from the British to the Indians and Pakistanis is discussed in V. P. Menon, *The Transfer of Power* (Princeton: Princeton University Press, 1957).

10. Granville Austin, *The Indian Constitution* (London: Oxford University Press, 1966), ch. 1.

11. V. P. Menon, *The Story of the Integration of the Indian States*, 3rd ed., (Bombay: Orient Longmans, 1961).

12. See William L. Richter, "Princes in Indian Politics," *Economic and Political Weekly* (February 27, 1971); Howard L. Erdman, "Conservative Politics in India," *Asian Survey*, VI:6 (June, 1966); *Link*, 3 (January 8, 1967).

13. A fictional account is given in Zahir Ahmed, *Dusk and Dawn in Village India* (New York: Praeger, 1966).

14. Krishan Bhatia, *The Ordeal of Nationhood* (New York: Atheneum, 1971), pp. 239–241.

15. Myron Weiner, "The Politics of South Asia," in Gabriel Almond and James S. Coleman, eds., *The Politics of the Developing Areas* (Princeton: Princeton University Press, 1960), p. 165.

16. See Hugh Tinker, "Is There an Indian Nation?" in Philip Mason, ed., *India and Ceylon: Unity and Diversity* (New York: Oxford University Press, 1967), pp. 279–281.

17. Jawaharlal Nehru, *The Discovery of India* (Garden City: Doubleday, 1959).

18. Spear, *India, Pakistan, and the West,* ch. 1.

19. David J. Elkins, "Social Mobilization, Social Structure, and Politics: Evidence and Qualifications," paper delivered before the American Political Science Association, Chicago, (Sept. 7–11, 1971) pp. 18–19.

20. Sachchidananda Bhattacharya, *A Dictionary of Indian History* (New York: George Braziller, 1967), p. 199.

21. The great variety of caste relationships in different areas is indicated in N. M. Srinivas, ed., *India's Villages,* 2nd ed., (London: Asia Publishing House, 1960), and several fine monographs exist. See Alan Beals, *Gopalpur: A South Indian Village* (New York: Holt, Rinehart & Winston, 1963); Oscar Lewis, *Village Life in Northern India* (Urbana: University of Illinois Press, 1958); A. C. Mayer, *Caste and Kinship in Central India* (London: Kegan Paul, 1960); on politics, see F. G. Bailey, *Politics and Social Change: Orissa in 1959* (Berkeley: University of California Press, 1963).

22. See N. M. Srinivas, *Social Change in Modern India* (Berkeley: University of California Press, 1966), ch. 1.

23. Selig Harrison, *India: The Most Dangerous Decades* (Princeton: Princeton University Press, 1961).

24. Hardgrave, *The Nadars of Tamilnad: The Political Culture of a Community in Change* (Berkeley: University of California Press, 1969).

25. Lloyd and Susanne Rudolph, *The Modernity of Tradition* (Chicago: The University of Chicago Press, 1967), pp. 91–92.

26. Harold Isaacs, *India's ex-Untouchables* (New York: John Day Co., 1965).

27. Bhatia, *The Ordeal of Nationhood,* p. 193. See Richard G. Fox, "Resiliency and Change in the Indian Caste System: The Umar of U.P.," *The Journal of Asian Studies,* XXVI: 4 (August, 1967); Rajni Kothari and Rushikesh Maru, "Caste and Secularism in India," *The Journal of Asian Studies,* V: 1 (November, 1965); Lloyd and Susanne Rudolph, *The Modernity of Tradition: Political Development in India* (Chicago: University of Chicago Press, 1967), part 1.

28. See O. P. Goyal "Caste and Politics: A Conceptual Framework," *Asian Survey,* V: 10 (October, 1965); Rajni Kothari, "Voting Behavior in a Developing Society," in Kothari, ed., *Party System and Election Studies,* p. 265; Iqbal Narain, "Democratic Politics and Political Development in India," *Asian Survey,* X: 26 (February, 1970), p. 91.

29. See Anil Seal, *The Emergence of Indian Nationalism* (Cambridge: Cambridge University Press, 1971).

30. Kuldip Nayar, *India: The Critical Years,* rev. ed., (Delhi: Vikas Publications, 1971), p. 327.

31. The Jana Sangh is treated in Craig Baxter, *The Jana Sangh: A Biography of an Indian Political Party* (Philadelphia: University of Pennsylvania Press, 1969).

32. See Baldev Raj Nayar, *Minority Politics in the Punjab* (Princeton: Princeton University Press, 1966).

33. On religion and Indian politics, see Donald Eugene Smith, *India as a Secular State* (Princeton: Princeton University Press, 1963); Donald Eugene Smith, ed., *South Asian Politics and Religion* (Princeton: Princeton University Press, 1966), part II.

34. The Dravidian Movement and emergence of the DMK is discussed in Hardgrave, *The Dravidian Movement* (Bombay: Popular Prakashan, 1965) and K. S. Ramanujam, *The Big Change* (Madras: Higginbothams, Ltd., 1967).

35. Hugh Gray, "The Demand for A Separate Telengana State in India," *Asian Survey*, XI:5 (May, 1971).

36. James A. Steintrager, "The Politics of Planning in an Underdeveloped Area: The Case of the Assam Oil Refinery Controversy," Unpublished MA Thesis, University of Chicago, 1960.

37. On tensions and regional hatred in Bombay, see Ram Joshi, "The Shiv Sena: A Movement in Search of Legitimacy," *Asian Survey*, 11 (November, 1970).

38. Rajni Kothari, *Politics in India* (Boston: Little, Brown and Company, 1970), p. 356.

39. Bhatia, *The Ordeal of Nationhood*, p. 252.

40. Eric A. Nordlinger, "Political Development: Time Sequences and Rates of Change," *World Politics*, XX:3 (April, 1968), p. 498.

41. *Ibid.*, p. 499.

42. A good introduction to India's institutions is found in W. H. Morris-Jones, *The Government and Politics of India*, 1st ed., (London: Hutchinson University Library, 1969).

43. See Morris-Jones, *Parliament in India* (London: Longmans, Green, 1957).

44. Paul R. Brass, "Coalition Politics in North India," *The American Political Science Review* LXII: 4 (December, 1968), p. 1174. See Kothari, "The Congress 'System' in India," *Asian Survey*, IV: 12 (December, 1964) and Morris-Jones, "Dominance and Dissent: Their Inter-relations in the Indian Party System," *Government and Opposition* I: 4 (August, 1966). The development of the party is considered in Stanley Kochanek, *The Congress Party of India* (Princeton: Princeton University Press, 1968).

45. On state politics, see Myron Weiner, *Party Building in a New Nation* (Chicago: University of Chicago Press, 1967) and Myron Weiner, ed., *State Politics in India* (Princeton: Princeton University Press, 1968).

46. "The Indian National Congress" in Betty Burch and Allan Cole, eds., *Asian Political Systems* (New York: D. Van Nostrand Company, Inc., 1968), p. 282.

47. See articles by Brass; Marcus F. Franda, "Electoral Politics in West Bengal; The Growth of the United Front," *Pacific Affairs*, XLII: 3 (Fall, 1969); Morris-Jones, "India Elects for Change and Stability" *Asian Survey*, XI: 8 (August, 1971); Subhas C. Kashyap, *The Politics of Defection* (Delhi: National Publishing House, 1969).

48. Narain, "Ideology and Political Development: Battle for Issues in Indian Politics," *Asian Survey*, XI: 2 (February, 1971), p. 195.

49. Nayar, *Minority Politics in the Punjab*, p. 81.

50. The cartoon, along with many others, is reproduced in R. Chandidas, *et al.*, *India Votes* (Bombay: Popular Prakashan, 1968), p. 227.

51. On the role of the President and Governor, see Granville Austin, *The Indian Constitution* (Oxford: Oxford University Press, 1966), p. 117; Vishwanath Prasad Varma, "Forum: The Role of the State Governors in India," *The Indian Political Science Review*, II: 3 & 4 (April–September, 1968).

52. Morris-Jones, *The Government and Politics of India*, p. 83.

53. Weiner, *State Politics in India*, p. 20.

54. These problems are discussed in David C. Potter, *Government in Rural India* (London: London School of Economics and Political Science, 1964); Richard Taubs, *Bureaucrats Under Stress* (Berkeley: University of California Press, 1969). See Ralph Braibanti, ed., *Asian Bureaucratic Systems Emergent from the British Tradition* (Durham: Duke University Press, 1966). See Andre Beteille, "Elites, Status Groups, and Caste in Modern India," in Mason, *India and Ceylon*, pp. 223–43.

55. See John B. Monteiro, *Corruption: Control of Mal-administration* (Bombay: Manaktalas, 1966).

56. Tinker in Mason, *India and Ceylon*, p. 288. Today Muslims, prominent in the army under the British, are only "sparingly accepted." *Ibid.*, p. 292.

57. Michael Brecher, *Nehru's Mantle: The Politics of Succession in India* (New York: Praeger, 1966), p. 170.

58. See David H. Bayley, *The Police and Political Development in India* (Princeton: Princeton University Press, 1969).

59. Duncan Forrester, "Indian State Ministers and Their Roles," *Asian Survey*, X: 6 (June, 1970), p. 476.

60. See Francine Frankel, "Ideology and Politics in Economic Planning: The Problem of Indian Agricultural Development Strategy," *World Politics*, XIX: 4 (July, 1967), pp. 621–645.

61. Kothari, *Politics in India*, ch. 9. An excellent discussion and bibliography of the "green revolution" is given in T. J. Byres, "The Dialectic of India's Green Revolution," *South Asian Review*, V: 2 (January, 1972).

62. Hardgrave, *India: Government and Politics in a Developing Nation*, pp. 91–100; Kothari, *Politics in India*, pp. 132–136.

63. On the impact of the plans, see George Rosen, *Democracy and Economic Change in India* (Berkeley: University of California Press, 1967).

64. All-India Congress Committee (AICC), *Peoples Victory—Second Phase* (New Delhi, 1972), p. 28.

65. Recent developments in Indian Communism are discussed in Marcus F. Franda, "India's Third Communist Party," *Asian Survey*, IX: 11 (November, 1969); Mohan Ram, *Indian Communism: Split Within a Split* (New Delhi: Vikas Publications, 1969); Donald S. Zagoria, "The Ecology of Peasant Communism in India," *American Political Science Review* LXI: 1 (March, 1971). For further views on the possibility of revolution in India, see Kathleen Gough, "The South Asian Revolutionary Potential" and Mytholy Shivaraman, "Thanjavur: Rumblings in Tamil Nadu," *Bulletin of Concerned Asia Scholars*, IV:1 (Winter, 1972).

66. Cited in Nayar, *Minority Politics in the Punjab*, pp. 126–7.

67. Cf. Warren F. Ilchman and Trilok V. Dhar, "Optimal Ignorance and Excessive Education: Education and Inflation in India," *Asian Survey* XI: 6 (June, 1971).

68. Kothari, *Politics in India*, p. 373.

69. Andre Beteille, *Caste, Class, and Power* (Berkeley: University of California Press, 1965), p. 221.

70. Rajni Kothari, "Continuity and Change in India's Party System," *Asian Survey*, X: 11 (November, 1970), pp. 937–948.

71. Bhatia, *The Ordeal of Nationhood*, p. 369.

CHILE

Radicalization and the Breakdown of Democracy

PRESTON LEE LAWRENCE

In September 1970, in a free election in which nearly 90 percent of the eligible population (virtually everyone over 20) voted, the people of Chile selected an avowed Marxist as president of their country. This life-long member of the Socialist Party, the most radical major group in Chile, campaigned on a platform which promised a complete, unequivocal overhaul of the Chilean economic and social systems. The figures, largely members of the Socialist and Communist parties, who assumed the executive leadership positions in November, 1970 promised to achieve the goals of the Cuban Revolution, in a democratic context. The road to socialism, according to the new leaders, would be initiated.

As might be expected, American foreign policy leaders reacted to this situation with incredulity, then dismay, and finally anger. One major voice of the American Establishment, *The New York Times,* in a September 6, 1970 editorial reasoned that this was a "heavy blow at liberal democracy." The United States government quickly responded by cancelling the previously scheduled stop in Chile of the carrier *Enterprise,* then on a South American good-will trip, and by threatening that any financial losses sustained by US investors in Chile would need to be immediately compensated in full by the new government. Some interesting documents revealed by the columnist Jack Anderson in mid-summer, 1972, suggest that one of the American investors, International Telephone and

Telegraph, together with an agency of the US government, thought the situation serious enough to merit an attempt to create short-term economic chaos (and possibly other actions), to facilitate collapse of the regime and/or intervention by the Chilean military.

How, wondered many, including some academic observers, could a country with a long and durable respect for democratic forms, with a basically privately-owned economic base, with a higher standard of living for most of its population than 90 percent of the Third World countries, opt for such a radical alternative in free elections? The situation is especially puzzling since the country has most of the trappings usually associated with nations of the politically developed world. In 1970 Chile had strong, effective political parties; numerous, well-organized and active functional interest associations; a long history of popular elections with binding results; a professional, career bureaucracy; probably the most politically powerful legislature in Latin America; a relatively independent judiciary, and several other characteristics usually associated with the "developed" countries. More specifically, in terms of the definition used in this volume, Chile would have been evaluated as relatively politically developed. The Chilean system has been remarkably successful over the years in sustaining new organizations, supporting new values and goals, incorporating emergent social groups into the system, and coping with socio-economic change.

In the post-World War II period, however, the political system of Chile was increasingly unable to handle the social and economic pressures it faced. By the mid-1960's the system's inability to deal with the rising tide of demands became so evident that almost all elements of the national leadership were calling for basic changes in the prevailing political as well as social and economic arrangements. Chilean politics of the last decade has been dominated by those proposing a "revolution in liberty," which translated, in practice, into a serious reform-orientation. Others advocated even more basic restructuring of the existing institutions.

The election of Salvador Allende in late 1970 and the Allende Administration's commitment to massive changes in Chilean society increased both the volume and intensity of pressures on the system. The polarization increasingly evident in Chilean politics since the 1950's reached the point of near-open warfare. A society previously characterized by moderation and temperance in its politics witnessed political assassinations, street riots, economic lockouts, and strikes. Propertied interests resorted to terror, violence, and lawlessness at least as often as the propertyless.

The Allende Administration's indecisiveness along with growing evidence that there would be no constitutional means of removing the government (if anything, the Left may have been gaining popular support) increased the resolve of the business community and white-collar allies to end the socialist experiment in any way possible. Pressures on the military to intervene, ranging from economic disruptions (such as lockouts), production halts, and refusals to pay employees, to public appeals by former presidents Frei and Alessandri for the military to save the country from chaos and Communism finally proved too much. On September 11, 1973, a bloody coup d'etat occurred, in which President Allende was either murdered or committed suicide. Thousands of his supporters were killed, and tens of thousands more were imprisoned, many held for several weeks in the country's largest open-air stadium, with hundreds of party leaders and former ministers in the government imprisoned on an air force base in the icy, barren southern tip of the country.

THE SIGNIFICANCE OF THE CHILEAN CASE

The recent events in Chile rendered a number of lessons about Third World politics. Recent presidential and congressional elections in Chile clearly show strong popular disapproval of traditional solutions to Chile's current problems and willingness to turn to the left—even to the Communists—as a viable alternative.

What kinds of changes have occurred in Chile to create a political climate so conducive to radical alternatives? What social, economic, and/or political conditions prevailed to encourage this new pattern of political conflict? Why have the traditional Chilean patterns of response to socio-economic change, especially in recent years, resulted in increased support for a *Marxist* left instead of other reform-oriented alternatives?

The Chilean political scene provides an excellent case study of how a radical alternative can function in a relatively democratic setting in a Third World country. How was real and rapid transformation of social institutions pursued in a system which fosters compromise and stability? What explicitly political conditions encouraged, or at least tolerated, the emergence of the Left as a political choice for governing the country? What kinds of restraints, formal and informal, presented themselves in this setting? How did the Left attempt to overcome them, in an effort to pursue serious change?

The case of Chile is of interest to students of the Third World for reasons other than those immediately raised by the electoral success of the radical Left. With a population of about 10 million, Chile is the second smallest of the countries surveyed in this volume. At the same time, Russet, *et al.*, report that only fifteen of the more than 100 economically underdeveloped countries have substantially larger populations and/or area, including such giants of Asia as India, China, and Indonesia.[1]

More important for comparative purposes, Chile shares similar socio-economic and political problems with other Third World countries. Like virtually all of the Third World, Chile faces staggeringly high rates of urbanization, an unevenly developed and stagnating economy (with its concomitant problems of high rates of unemployment, imbalance of payments, importation of food products, uncontrolled inflation), elements of both internal and external colonialism, and widespread political mobilization, among other conditions. An examination of Chilean politics reveals, therefore, how conditions found in the vast majority of the Third World countries have affected the development of a political system and how that system has tried to cope with and manipulate those conditions.

There are significant similarities between the Chilean situation and that of Latin American countries in general. Despite important differences within the area, similarities in historical development, cultural background, ideological influences, social structure, and basic political patterns are shared widely.

However, the case of Chile is also unique. While almost literally surrounded by countries in which political turmoil and resort to extra-constitutional processes have been the norm, the political system of Chile has experienced relatively little violence and only one period of non-constitutional government in this century, up to this current period of turmoil. While it has been far from a model democracy, Chile's stability and the widespread adherence to formal democratic procedures separate it from other Third World nations.

Among the countries examined in this volume, Chile's political evolution is somewhat unusual, especially insofar as it has exhibited a *mass-based* formal democracy, the most recent product of which was the free election of a Marxist government committed to restructuring the country's economic and social institutions. In a number of other respects, too, Chile's evolution differs from the nations considered in this book.

The unique flavor of Chilean politics is in substantial part a derivation of the differences in social and economic conditions which separate Chile from most other Third World nations. None come close to Chile's level of literacy (over 90 percent, compared to 75 percent for Mexico, the closest competitor), percentage of school enrollment (94 percent, compared to 65 percent for the closest competition, again Mexico), health care (Chile's doctor per capita, hospital bed per capita, etc.—is considerably better than the other cases in this study), and national income (Chile's $600+ per capita income is rivaled, again, only by Mexico, with a slightly lower figure). Chile has far fewer of its people working in agriculture (28 percent compared to Mexico's 47, Syria's 62, India's 73, Nigeria's 80, and China's 85) with about half the population living in cities of 50,000 or more. The printed and audio media extend to virtually all parts of the nation, the population is quite homogeneous racially, Spanish is universally spoken. Chile is a real *nation,* a fact that again separates it to some extent from most other Third World nations.

THE DETERMINANTS OF POLITICS: THE POLITICAL SYSTEM AS A DEPENDENT VARIABLE

Chile is a nation of ten million people, with an area slightly larger than the state of Texas. The country is a geographical absurdity, being 2,600 miles long and averaging about 100 miles wide. Located on the southwestern coast of South America, it borders Peru, Bolivia, and Argentina but is essentially isolated from its neighbors by desert in the north and a particularly rugged section of the Andes in the east. Largely because of climatic conditions, the population is concentrated in the temperate central valley area, especially in the Santiago and Valparaíso-Viña del Mar region. The northern third of the country is an increasingly arid sector. In certain parts of this area no rain has ever been recorded. The southern third of Chile is a region of cold rain forests, fjords, and glaciers, not unlike the northern regions of the Scandinavian countries.

Colonialism and External Linkage Patterns

Being geographically isolated, with no obvious mineral enticements, and inhabited by particularly hostile Indians, Chile was overrun quite late in the process of European conquest of the Americas. The original enticements to Chile were gold panning, which was never a major activity and became a lost cause by the late 1500's, and the Mediterranean-like climate and rich soil of the Central Valley. Livestock raising and wheat farming became the primary economic activities. Thus, the European settlers of Chile, like their counterparts in North America, came to stay, as considerably more stable, less exploitative conquerers than their brothers in the other Spanish colonies.

Also, as in North America, the Indians were not particularly needed as a source of cheap labor, and when they objected more seriously to European domination than had their counterparts in the other colonies, they were largely exterminated. Not, however, before causing the Spanish more loss of life than in all other Indian wars in Latin America combined. Thus, while there is a racial mixture in most of the Chilean population, it is clearly a white-dominated mix. Indeed, although Mexico and Chile are both *mestizo* countries, the visible physical contrast between the peoples of these nations is striking.

Indians are found in significant numbers only in the southern provinces of Chile, where they were driven in wars with the Spanish. In the two most "Indian" provinces they account for only 25 and 12 percent, respectively, of the population, and constitute probably no more than 5 percent of the total population. At the same time, skin darkening is readily apparent as the social ladder is viewed from top to bottom. European features, especially white skin pigmentation, are highly valued social characteristics.

Physical isolation and lack of easily exploitable wealth contributed greatly to the somewhat unique early development of the country. Largely because of these two factors the Chileans were allowed a long period of relative independence even in the colonial era. The capital of the Spanish vice-royalty of which Chile was a part, Lima, is nearly 2,500 miles from Santiago. It is close to 8,000 miles to most European trade and political centers, with those distances much greater before the Panama Canal was opened in the early 1900's. Contrast this situation to that of Mexico, which was first the object of Spanish exploitation of mineral wealth and later faced a strong and aggressive United States (losing half its territory to the United States during the period 1835–1846). These foreign pressures have contributed substantially to social and political instability and inhibited the peaceful resolution of social, economic, and political conflicts. In Chile, foreign domination was delayed, and a spirit of independence and national identity developed rather early in the history of the nation.

The "isolation" argument should not be carried too far, however. By no means was Chile without contact with the rest of the world. Valparaíso, Chile's major port, was the key stopover point on the Western South American coast in pre-Panama Canal times. However, it was the dominant sea power, Britain, that took greatest advantage of the harbor, bringing in ideas, products, and settlers from *northern* Europe. Also, Chile did have an extensive wheat and fiber trade with other Latin American areas, as well as with the Western European states, and the United States. At the same time, none of the major world powers perceived Chile as a potential object of domination, political or otherwise.

Independence from Spain came almost by accident to Chile. In short, Chile was not high on the list of Spanish priorities. With rebellion occurring all over the South and Central American regions, the Spanish were forced to try saving the more valuable of the overseas possessions. About the only objections to the independence movement (which itself was not too strong) came from local governors, other *peninsulares,* and their allies, who saw their positions of social and political domination being jeopardized. The conflict between *peninsulares*—Spaniards born in Spain—and *criollos*—Spaniards born in the New World who, because of their place of birth, were excluded from social and political positions of rank—was the most serious intra-elite division. Probably of equal importance in generating support for independence, however, was the perception of many local notables that their economic interests, already tied to the international capitalist system (primarily through Great Britain), would suffer if Spain reasserted active domination in a mercantilist context.

Independence came after a relatively short struggle and without major social disruption. The basic social structures were left intact. While part of the colonial elite lost its position in the independence conflicts, the pre-independence aristocracy for the most part maintained its position of supremacy. The basic economic patterns remained undisturbed. The mass of the population was left in the same social, economic, and political status in the new republic as in the colonial monarchy.

This is not to suggest that the colonial experience had no impact in Chile. Spanish governors ruled in Santiago and Spanish law was enforced (if somewhat sporadically). We would emphasize, however, that Chile's colonial ties with Spain were quite loose during much of the pre-1817 period. Insofar as Spanish domination existed, it was primarily cultural; the political ties normally involved little more than formal acquiescence to Spanish authority, again not too different from the pre-1780 relationship between the North American colonies and Great Britain. In fact, a substantial part of the Spanish migration to Chile consisted of the Basque, a minority which had a firm tradition of opposition to rule from Madrid even when they were living in Spain.

Chile's colonial experience has been mostly indirect and occurred largely during the twentieth century. As Andre Gunder Frank notes, Chile since Spanish discovery has been tied to the "metropolitan" centers (first Lima, then European capitals, and finally the United States.)[2] Yet only in the past 100 years has this tie become a virtual economic umbilical cord.

This recent "colonial" experience in Chile is a direct product of the discovery of mineral resources, especially nitrates and copper in the northern desert region. The mining of silver in the first half and nitrates during the last half of the 1800's brought enormous wealth to sectors of the upper class of Chilean society and contributed to the expansion of the urban white collar sector. It also brought foreign capital and investors in abundance. After the discovery of artificial substitutes for nitrates in the early 1900's, copper was discovered in the same area. These mineral resources have been almost entirely owned and exploited by foreigners, particularly North American and British investors. US companies owned virtually all the copper and iron mines, the two contemporary basic resources, until their nationalization during the past decade. Furthermore, the Huachipato steel and chemical complex came to be dominated by US capital, mainly through the copper companies. Huachipato supplies all of Chile's domestic steel and chemical needs as well as exporting substantial quantities of basic steel materials. The Huachipato complex was originally established with government funds and management, but controlling interest was sold to the private sector after it became a profitable enterprise.

Investment in Chile by private US firms reached almost one billion dollars in 1968, ranking fifth among Latin American countries in cumulative dollar totals. In addition, Chile owes more than two billion dollars in external public debt, that total more than doubling in the 1960's, with most of it being owed to the United States. Over one-third of Chile's imports are from the United States, with an additional one-quarter coming from three European countries—Great Britain, West Germany, and France. Over three-fourths of Chile's exports go to the United States and Western Europe.

Perhaps most importantly, Chile has been sold, loaned, and given (through the US military aid programs) virtually its entire store of weaponry, almost exclusively by the United States. The United States also gives "assistance" to Chile by alleviating the burden and expense of training officers by bringing them to bases in the Panama Canal zone and the United States.

The various financial interests—investments (especially as they are concentrated in the key economic activities), trade, loans—of the major powers have caused these powers to take an active interest in Chilean politics. Since the late 1800's the United States, through actions of both private citizens and government officials, has competed actively with England, France, and Germany for political and economic advantages. Since the 1930's the United States has dominated the field, displaying often heavy-handed "expressions of interest" in the affairs of our hemispheric sister state.

With the exception of United States ownership of its copper industry, the most objectionable aspect of foreign influence for the Chileans in recent years has been the cultural penetration of the country. While this type of "colonialism" is difficult to verify empirically, the evidences of such penetration are abundant. Almost regardless of discipline but particularly in the sciences, foreign, usually North American, texts are used in Chilean universities and some high schools. Even in the social sciences the basic texts are often North American, although occasionally there are Spanish editions. North American and European novels, magazines *(Reader's Digest, Time, Newsweek)*, music, and especially movies and television programs dominate the Chilean scene.

Political Culture

The patterns of authoritarianism inherited from the colonial era and reinforced during the early independence period have persisted in Chilean political culture. After a decade of post-independence instability in the early 1800's, the threatened elites reunited behind Chile's answer to

Alexander Hamilton—Diego Portales—and reimposed a highly ordered and centralized system, ensuring upper class dominance and authoritarian, paternalistic, political order. The habits of mass obedience and respect for authority resulting from this regime have had much to do with the lack of overt social conflict and the apparent decorum that has characterized Chilean politics, at least until recently. An acute observer of Chilean political and social life, Frederick Pike, comments:

> To almost every political predicament except dictatorship they respond with patience and forbearance. In spite of their refreshing individualism, Chileans possess a deeply ingrained acceptance of authority and devotion to stability . . .[3]

Still another important inheritance from this early post-independence period is a pattern of strong civilian leadership. For a variety of reasons, including the concentration of the country's population in the fertile Central Valley, integration of the elite, lack of major conflicts within that group, and the establishment of the precedent of a strong, centralized, and civilian government during the Portales era, the *caudillo* tradition did not take hold in Chile. As is detailed in the chapter on Mexico, most of the factors mentioned above were lacking in the development, especially in the nineteenth century and before, of that country. In addition, the external pressures so evident in Mexican history have contributed to the military interventionist tendency, particularly by creating conditions of insecurity and instability. The pattern of the "man on horseback," riding in to save the country from chaos and ruin, largely absent in Chile, so characterized Mexican development as to make that country's history prototypical of the *caudillo* phenomenon. In contrast, Chileans have tended to regard military involvement in their neighboring countries as indications of political immaturity.

One should not conclude from the above that personalism is an inconsequential factor in the country's political culture. To the contrary, the attachment of political loyalties to an individual rather than a party, movement, or group, usually with overtones of a paternalistic relationship, is clearly a prominent element in the attitudes of most Chileans. Perhaps the most vivid illustration of its impact in more recent Chilean affairs is in the career of Carlos Ibáñez. An obscure military officer with political ambitions, Ibáñez in the turmoil of the late 1920's organized a military coup and in the period 1927–1931 ran Chile's only military dictatorship prior to the present regime. Less than a decade after his dictatorship collapsed, Ibáñez re-entered the political arena and in 1952 was overwhelmingly elected to the presidency, without major party support (in fact running an anti-politics campaign) and essentially on the basis of his personal "I'll take hold of the mess and clean things up" appeals. Other recent presidents, including Frei and Jorge Alessandri, have also been able to take advantage of the continuing strength of *personalismo,* especially in consolidating their political base once in office and being able to establish themselves as the real *jefe* or *patrón.*

As noted earlier, Chile, Mexico, and most other Latin American countries have engaged in extensive "borrowing" from abroad, including the borrowing of social and political philosophies. The "demonstration effect" of the United States has been particularly important, beginning with the immediate post-independence period when the United States presented a successful model of colonial overthrow. A dominant theme among liberal thinkers in both the United States and Western Europe during the nineteenth and twentieth centuries has been the importance of individual freedoms and political democracy. These ideas had a considerable impact in Chile. While there was little socio-cultural foundation for operational democracy in early post-independence years, a strong commitment to democratic ideals has persisted among some sectors of the Chilean social and political elite. With the emergence of an urban middle sector and a numerically strong and partially organized working class in this century, political leaders have felt political as well as philosophical compulsion to extend political freedoms. A gradual liberalization occurred, especially since the 1930's, to the point that by mid-century freedoms of speech, press, assembly, and petition were exercised in forms tolerated in few countries of any part of the world. Furthermore, by 1964, the system had become a genuine mass-based democracy, with much higher voting rates than were found in the United States.

The influence of the arguments concerning personal freedom and political liberties as well as the moderation of the Chilean political temperament is perhaps best illustrated by the tolerance of political opposition traditionally shown by Chilean elites. While not encouraged, serious opposition, even from representatives of the masses, has rarely been overtly suppressed. To say the least, this kind of tolerance is not characteristic of the Third World countries. Even when carried beyond bounds tolerable to the ruling groups, exile has usually been the most severe punishment administered. Even in the very unstable years of the 1920's and 1930's the prevailing pattern of punishment for "uncooperative" leftist leaders was exile to the southern provinces for short periods, where their tempers might be cooled by the Antarctic breezes.

This is not to ignore the incidents of violence that have occurred. The army in particular has been quick and deadly in response to perceived threats to the established order. The army was requested to maintain order in the mining areas during strikes in the 1880–1910 period. On numerous occasions miner-military confrontations resulted in the slaughter of miners, including a half dozen encounters which resulted in several thousand deaths. In 1907 a crowd of 10,000 striking nitrate miners was machine-gunned, with 2,000 killed.

The regionalism that has plagued other Third World countries, such as India, Mexico, and especially Nigeria, never developed on any wide scale in Chile, even though the distances from Santiago to the northern and southern provinces are more than 1,000 miles in either direction. Under pressure from their parties political leaders in the "outer" regions rarely have made regional identity a major issue. The feelings of abandonment and isolation in these areas have taken the expression of strong support for leftist causes and candidates. Recent pressures have resulted in major efforts by the government in Santiago to upgrade public facilities and services, grant special privileges such as free ports, and attempt to integrate the regions into the national economy, efforts that have been reasonably successful.

As mentioned earlier, the indigenous element in Chile's population was given a treatment quite familiar to students of North American history. Furthermore, there has been extensive later borrowing of European philosophies, social customs, and economic patterns. Unlike the other countries surveyed in this text, Chile is not simply heavily influenced by European and North American influences but for practical purposes *is* a European country, in much the same way that the United States is European. Unlike Mexico and most of the other Latin American and Third World countries, Chile has no significant indigenous sociopolitical component. Basic ideas concerning property ownership, the scope of civil liberties, the proper role of the state in economic affairs, to mention only a few examples, are in very large part transplanted from Western Europe, although from a variety of European sources. While the Allende Administration made efforts to revive indigenous elements, the president and virtually all his colleagues in political and social leadership were European, not just in racial or ethnic background but more importantly in terms of their social and political values.

Chile is not only European but Catholic European. The Church, primarily influenced by the Catholicism of Spain and France, and the Low Countries in the contemporary era, has been an important factor in shaping basic values and beliefs, including political values and beliefs. Especially in the pre-twentieth century period the Church exercised a powerful role in the development of attitudes toward authority, hierarchy, social relations and social status, and even the appropriate role and scope of government activities.

The influence of the Church is derived not just from the moral authority accruing from its religious functions, but from its key position in the educational system of the country. While there has been semi-official church-state separation since the 1890's, most of the private schools in the country are run by the Church. And, until the 1940's, there was officially-sanctioned religious instruction in the public schools. In Chile as elsewhere in Latin America, private education is the cornerstone of later success in virtually any aspect of social and/or business life; most of the nation's leadership class has received Church-directed education.

As in Mexico the Catholic Church in Chile finds itself in a declining position with little direct influence over nonreligious issues. However, there can be little doubt that the Church doctrines, as well as informal preachments, have reinforced the patterns of respect for authority, obedience, acceptance of one's "station in life" that underpinned the stable, orderly, and autocratic system dominant in Chile well into the twentieth century.

The acquisition, discovery, and development of mineral wealth shortly after independence have also been important in the formation of Chilean political culture. For the middle and upper social sectors it made access to education, jobs, and ultimately political power much easier than would have been otherwise possible. While this may have had the short-run effect of relieving political and social pressures, it also contributed to an unjustified image of prosperity and economic wealth. When the nitrate bubble burst in the 1920's some of the more farsighted recognized this, but the copper boom that replaced nitrates undercut those who argued that the mining wealth was not an unmixed blessing.

The mineral wealth thus contributed to the enlargement and satisfaction of urban middle groups but did not lay any solid foundation for future economic development. It did not improve significantly the conditions of the masses, especially since much of the mining base was foreign-owned, and the profits were sent back to the foreign country. The unrealistic euphoria among the white-collar sectors has been frustrated by the failure of the economy to continue expanding (and during some recent decades it has even contracted). The economic stagnation has had the effect not only of undermining the position of some middle sector groups but also has kept aspiring members of the lower social sectors, especially the marginal white-collar groups and the organized and better paid workers, from moving up the social ladder. The political effect has been that more and more people have lost faith in the private economy as a means of improving their conditions and have turned to overtly political means to gain their objectives.

Social and Economic Modernization

The population of Chile more than doubled during the period from 1900–1960 from 3 to 7.4 million and is expected to nearly double again by the year 2000, reaching approximately 17 million. Even more striking has been the urbanization trend. (See Table 1.) In 1900, 12 percent of the population lived in the three cities of 50,000 or more. By 1940, 28 percent lived in the six cities of 50,000 or more. By 1970, 25 cities of

TABLE 1

URBANIZATION AND POPULATION GROWTH RATES

Country	Annual Urban Growth Rate (1969–70)	Population Growth Rate (1960–70)	(1968–69)	Percent Urban
Dominican Republic	6.7	2.8	3.4	40.0[a]
Venezuela	5.6	3.5	3.5	74.9[b]
Honduras	5.2	3.4	3.4	32.2[b]
Mexico	5.2	3.3	3.5	58.7[b]
Colombia	5.0	3.2	3.2	57.7[a]
Guatemala	4.9	3.1	2.9	30.8[a]
Ecuador	4.7	3.4	3.4	45.7[a]
Nicaragua	4.6	3.5	3.2	39.7[b]
Brazil	4.6	2.8	3.0	47.6[a]
Panama	4.4	2.8	3.3	47.1[b]
Costa Rica	4.3	3.5	3.4	49.0[b]
Peru	4.2	3.1	3.1	51.9[b]
El Salvador	4.0	3.7	3.4	38.8[c]
Haiti	3.8	2.0	2.4	17.3[a]
Paraguay	3.5	3.1	3.1	36.0[a]
Chile	3.4	1.3	1.9	74.2[b]
Uruguay	2.9	1.3	1.3	79.9[a]
Argentina	2.4	1.6	1.5	78.9[a]
Bolivia	2.4	2.6	2.4	29.3[d]
Latin America	4.7	2.8	2.9	

a. Data for 1970.
b. Data for 1969.
c. Data for 1968.
d. Data for 1967.

Source: Annual Growth Rates from *América en Cifras* (Washington, D.C.: Pan American Union, 1970), pp. 42–43. Population Growth Rates, 1960–70, and Percent Urban from *Socio-Economic Progress in Latin America: Social Progress Trust Fund Tenth Annual Report, 1970* (Washington, D.C.: Inter-American Development Bank, 1970), Part II. Population Growth Rates, 1968–69, from *The Statistical Abstract of Latin America, 1969*, edited by K. Ruddle and M. Hamour Los Angeles: (UCLA Latin American Center, 1971) pp. 74–75.

approximately 50,000 or more contained almost 50 percent of the population, and two urban complexes, Santiago and Valparaíso-Viña del Mar, contained nearly 45 percent. The city of Santiago grew from 300,000 in 1900 to over 2.5 million in 1970 (about the size of Greater Boston); Valparaíso-Viña went from less than 200,000 to 400,000. The third most populous area, Concepción, went from just over 50,000 to nearly 200,000 (See Table 2.)

About 70 percent of the population lives in urban areas of 20,000 or more. The annual urban growth rate is near 4 percent, placing an enormous strain on urban resources and contributing to creation of pressures that will continue to have grave consequences for the political future of the country. Comparatively, however, only five of the Latin American countries (including only one major country—Argentina) have lower rates of urbanization, suggesting the Chilean situation to be considerably less critical than it could be.

TABLE 2

URBAN GROWTH—CITIES, 50,000 OR MORE, 1970

City	1907	1930	1940	1960	1970
Santiago—Metro*	350.0	735.0	1,050.0	2,482.0	3,335.0
Santiago	332.7	696.2	953.0	1,907.4	
San Bernardo	7.7	14.5	20.7	45.2	
Puente Alto	.9	4.1	10.1	43.6	
Valparaíso—Metro*	205.0	265.0	310.0	440.0	
Valparaíso	162.4	193.2	209.9	252.9	
Viña del Mar	26.3	49.5	65.9	115.5	
Quillota	11.4	14.9	17.2	29.4	
Quilpué	4.1	6.3	9.2	26.6	
Concepción—Metro*	100.0	150.0	190.0	330.0	
Concepción	55.3	77.6	85.8	148.1	
Talcahuano	15.6	27.6	35.8	83.6	
Coronel	5.3	9.0	14.8	33.9	
Lota	10.4	25.0	31.1	27.7	
Tomé	4.7	5.0	10.7	26.9	
Antofagasta	32.5	53.6	49.0	87.9	
Temuco	16.0	35.8	42.0	72.1	
Talca	38.0	45.0	50.5	68.1	
Chillán	34.3	39.5	42.8	65.1	
Valdivia	15.2	34.3	34.5	61.3	
Osorno	7.4	16.2	26.0	55.1	
Rancagua	10.4	23.3	31.0	53.3	
Iquique	40.2	46.2	38.1	50.7	
Punta Arenas	12.2	24.3	29.9	49.5	
Arica	4.9	13.1	14.1	43.3	
Total Population Total Cities	3,231.0	4,287.4	5,023.5	7,375.2	

*The figures for the three major metropolitan areas are estimations derived from totaling the populations of the core city and the smaller towns immediately surrounding the core city. In the case of Concepción the cities of Coronel, Lota, and Tomé are included in the metro area because of their close economic and political ties with the core city, even though they are up to 25 miles from Concepción itself. The figures are undoubtedly underestimations, since they include only the larger urban areas surrounding the cities.

Source: Figures are taken from the national censuses of the respective years, excepting the 1960 and 1970 Santiago—Metro figures, which are data from the Centro Interdiciplinario de Desarréllo Urbano y Regional of the Universidad Católica de Chile.

Unlike urbanization in North America and Northern Europe the migration to the cities in Chile and most of the economically underdeveloped areas is not primarily due to the lure of urban employment in industry and manufacturing. Many observers argue, in fact, that the "pull" of the cities (better jobs, improved living conditions, more opportunity for children) has been less important in producing the migration than the "push" of the conditions in the rural areas. Clearly, there has been little real economic development accompanying urbanization in Chile.

New developments in communication and transportation have also contributed to socio-political mobilization in Chile. While not equivalent to urbanization in its impact, the introduction of the transistor has brought a new dimension to the life of both urban and especially the rural poor. The messages of the mass media clarify and emphasize the rich-poor and urban-rural differences (especially since an idealized view of urban life is presented), as well as exposing the poor to the possibilities of improvement of conditions through political action. This is especially true in Chile with its long history of relative freedom of press and highly politicized mass media. While the situation may be changed under the military regime, radio stations have been owned and/or dominated by groups with definite political positions and few scruples about using the air waves for political "education" and advantages. The newspapers have been similarly partisan, and over the past decade even the leftist papers, formerly almost exclusively big-city in distribution, became active competitors in the villages and countryside.

More and better transportation into the rural and small town areas has further increased exposure to urban influences, including political alternatives not previously considered. In their explanation of "agrarian radicalism" Petras and Zeitlin give special attention to the return of urban migrants to the rural areas, either for visits or sometimes permanently, as a source of change in attitudes and actions.[4]

Economic Development

By virtually any standard used, Chile ranks with Argentina, Venezuela, and Uruguay among the most economically advanced Latin American states, and Latin America is easily the most economically advanced area in the Third World. A per capita gross national product of $600 and 33 percent of the economically active population employed in commerce and manufacturing[5] places Chile relatively high among Third World countries in terms of its economic development. By the end of World War II, a substantial light industry was established, although the economic base of the country remained its mining sector.

As is the case for all the countries considered in this volume, with the possible exception of contemporary Mexico, and for Third World countries generally, the economy of Chile has been based on agriculture, and since the 1800's on mining. Even though just more than one in four economically active workers are employed in agriculture, mining still remains by far the largest single economic activity, and its current weaknesses have undercut the determined efforts of recent governments to strengthen other aspects of economic activity.

While accurate, dependable data are not available, most observers seem to agree that the current problems in agriculture (e.g., while 28 percent of the economically active are employed in that sector, it contributes less than 10 percent of gross domestic product) stem from changes that occurred in the early nineteenth century. Reasons for the decline vary, but a representative sample includes the concentration of estates in the hands of those interested in land ownership for other than commercial reasons, the decline of foreign markets both in other Latin American states and in Europe, for Chilean agricultural products, especially wheat, and a general de-emphasis of agriculture, especially after the discovery of nitrates in the mid-1800's. Little governmental attention was paid to the development of the agriculture sector. Infrastructural supports such as road systems and irrigation systems were left undeveloped. In more recent years, the equipment needed to modernize the rural agricultural areas has been absent. Since it must be imported, it is very expensive (remember that the costs of machinery have been one of the primary factors driving people off the farms in the United States), the country has lacked foreign exchange and the available exchange has been used to import other items. In more recent years the landowners have argued that government price controls on some food products have contributed to lack of agricultural productivity.

Efforts by political leaders to meet the landholders' complaints of lack of incentives and unavailability of mechanical equipment have largely been counter-productive. Government subsidies have proved largely unsuccessful in inducing any major output increases, and have only drained government budgets. Mechanization, commercialization, and corporate ownership of estates have also had the effect of reducing the need for labor, continuing the urbanization tide, and "proletarianizing" the remaining rural workers.

Especially in recent years the situation in the countryside has deteriorated significantly. The available data suggest a *decline* in agricultural and stock production from the late 1930's to the late 1960's. Per capita food production declined from a base of 100 in 1935–39 to 88 in the late 1950's and may have gone lower after the severe drought of the late 1960's; using a base of 100 for 1951–53, by 1965 this index registered 95. During the last decade imports of food exceeded $100 million in value annually; the net imbalance of agricultural trade for the 14-year period 1949–1963 was $1,000 million. Since World War II about one-third of Chile's foreign exchange has been used for food imports. Wheat imports doubled and milk imports more than doubled from 1961 to 1966.[6] Doctors working in the shanty towns surrounding the major cities estimate that close to half of the thousands of children living in these areas are permanently retarded before school age because of lack of basic food items.

Tragically, like most of the other Latin American countries, Chile should be exporting, not importing foodstuffs, considering the amount of its fertile land relative to its population. This importation only makes worse an already bad balance-of-payments situation; instead of being able to use their dollars for importation of vitally needed products of the advanced technology of the United States and Western Europe, including tractors, reapers, and so on, the foreign exchange must be spent on importing milk and meat.

Of the causes that have been noted for the persistent weakness of the agricultural sector, probably the most frequently mentioned is the concentration of land ownership, at least until the mid-1960's. A comprehensive study of seven Latin American countries in the early 1960's determined that in Chile less than 7 percent of the owners held over 80 percent of the land and 10 percent held over 90 percent of the usable property.[7] It has been long observed that the landed elites in contemporary Latin America hold land for a variety of reasons—for prestige, to beat inflation, for speculation, and so on—that have nothing to do with production. Many of the Chilean landed gentry are absentee owners, and virtually all have urban business interests which are their real sources of income. With relatively little mechanization on most great estates, effective utilization of the land has not been possible. Much fertile soil has been given over to pasture land, which has the advantages of requiring fewer hired laborers and little of the extremely expensive equipment required by farming. (Also, much of the best land is devoted to wine vineyards in Chile.) Thus, land concentration has two main impacts: it has contributed to the shortage of foodstuffs, and it has provided a strong political base for a very small stratum of owners, because they controlled vast amounts of property, and large numbers of farm workers, as well as many of the farm-related businesses in the villages and towns in the rural areas.

The other basic economic activity in Chile is mining. Like agriculture, over the long run the way the mining resources have been developed has probably had more negative than positive impact, in both economic and political terms. Since the early 1800's the mining and exporting of silver, nitrates, and finally copper has been the basic source of foreign exchange—since World War II averaging about 75–80 percent of all foreign exchange—and the largest single source of government revenue —since World War II about 25 percent of the governmental budget.[8] Since the mines have been largely owned and developed by foreigners and foreign capital, and the profits taken "home," the wealth generated in that sector has rarely benefited the rest of the economy, especially developmental activities. Instead, capital has been siphoned off from other economic sectors, further retarding development and creating even more serious economic imbalances. Until very recently even the taxation on mining was minimal, ensuring that even this potential benefit was lost.

Largely because of the enormous dependence on the mining sector, Chile's economic history since independence has been a classic boom-bust cycle. The discovery of artificial substitutes for nitrates in the early part of this century sent the economy into a tailspin. The discovery and development of the copper resources shortly brought on another boom period in the 1920's. The Chileans suffered with the United States (even more than the United States) during the Depression. As in the United States, World War II brought back Chile's economy, largely because of high prices for copper, but also because of the import substitution policies of a "popular front" government. The period of the 1940's was one of virtually unprecedented prosperity in Chile. The prosperity of the 1940's proved to be ephemeral, however. With the availability of foreign products again after the war and the exhaustion of the easy areas of substitution, and especially with the decline in copper prices, economic conditions rapidly deteriorated, and stagnation has continued with only minor interruption since 1950. While the decade of the 1960's showed some improvement, Chile still demonstrated one of the lowest per capita gross national product increases of any of the Third World countries, an under two percent per annum increase since 1955. Per capita real growth in the recent period 1965–1969 was 1.8 percent.

This stagnant economic situation has cultural as well as political and economic roots. For example Chileans exhibit strong cultural preference for immediate satisfaction of material desires, preferences that have been reinforced by economic conditions (e.g., boom-bust economic cycles, rampant inflation) that have historically made buy-now-pay-later a rational economic strategy. The lack of investment resulting from this pattern of values seriously inhibits development. Also, Chileans have a well-developed taste for imported consumer goods, again behavior inhibiting long-term development of the country.

An additional long-term characteristic of the Chilean economic picture is a phenomenal inflation. Over the past two decades inflation has rarely fallen below 20 percent per annum and has often gone over 40 percent. One of the main effects of inflation, of course, is to erode the economic position of those on fixed incomes and salaries, while those in stronger economic positions are able to beat the game in various ways (e.g., buying land, converting Chilean *escudos* to "safer" currency and sending it abroad, raising prices of goods and services, and so on).

Another important factor in understanding the socio-economic base of political change in recent years is the distribution of income. While reliable figures are rare, the available data strongly suggest that in the last two decades all social sectors except owners and proprietors have suffered relative declines in income—e.g., income inequalities have increased. The lowest social strata—the urban and rural workers—have felt the greatest relative loss. In fact, the income of workers showed an apparent absolute decline during the period. One probably conservative estimate in the mid-1960's indicated that about 80 percent of the population received only 25 percent of the national income. Another source provides similar data—the bottom half of the income-earning population received 16 percent of the total personal income; the top 5 percent received 25 percent. Borón uses figures indicating that the per capita income for the upper 5 percent of the population in 1960 was $2300, while that of the lower 50 percent was $140.[9]

It is the human aspect of the economic stagnation that is of most concern to us here. The weakness of the industrial-manufacturing sector in the past two decades is reflected in the employment picture for that sector. There has been a decline in the percentage of economically active in that sector, during a period of spectacular increases in the urban population. Between 1952–1960 the manufacturing sector had an average annual employment growth of 473 persons. The only sector experiencing substantial expansion in employment has been the personal service sector. Not only is this the urban sector with the lowest per capita income by far but it has experienced an apparent *decline* in income received as well.[10]

Unemployment during the 1960's approximated 10 percent of the labor force, although no really accurate figures are available. *Underemployment* is a much more serious problem than unemployment, if numbers of persons involved and wasted man-hours are the criteria of comparison. On virtually every street corner one sees the magazine stands, the boot blacks, the balloon salesman, the hawkers of pencils, razor blades, and a near infinite variety of items the selling of which can sustain the individual for another day. The widespread use of household servants, especially men of all ages (gardeners, chauffeurs, general handymen), further evidences the problem.

One social impact of the weaknesses of the agricultural sector is the generation of seemingly endless streams of ill-educated, unskilled, poorly fed, clothed and housed urban migrants, who remain in those same conditions because the rural sector is unable to generate enough food and fiber to make available cheap food and clothing.

The lack of adequate food supplies has a differential impact on the various social sectors. For example, in 1970 strict meat rationing was implemented; meat could be purchased only on certain days of the month. This ostensibly nondiscriminatory measure in fact has a very discriminatory impact; those with refrigerators and freezers buy large quantities of meat on the prescribed days and store it. The overwhelming bulk of the population, without these appliances, buys for the short term and does without the rest of the time.

The distribution system works in much this same fashion even without legislation such as the meat rationing. Realizing the shortages, suppliers send their goods to the higher income areas where higher prices can be asked. Even in the face of a complex set of government price controls on basic food products, working class areas have been literally forced into changes in consumption patterns, patterns which include low protein intakes and heavy emphasis on cheap breads, beans, and sometimes corn.

Social Conditions

The quality of life in Chile reflects the meaning of these statistics. In housing, there is a backlog of nearly 750,000 units, with close to 70 percent of working class families currently living in one-room dwellings. In education, despite a strong effect by the Frei government (1964–1970) that raised literacy to near 90 percent, the problems of functional illiteracy and early dropouts persist. A study completed in the late 1950's found that 50 percent of working class children did not finish the third grade; 85 percent dropped out after the sixth grade. The lack of facilities in some urban slums and rural areas, the poor quality of facilities where they exist, the lack of well-trained instructional personnel, as well as the general conditions of poverty which force youth to seek work at the earliest possible time ensure a continuation of the stream of badly educated unskilled youth.[11] Even Ministry of Education officials agree that these conditions have changed little in the past decade.

Overall national figures may not be as important as differences within Chile.[12] For example, the national infant mortality rate for 1967 was 98 per 1000 live births, the highest in Latin America excepting Haiti. More important, however, in terms of political impact is the fact that for workers in Chile the rate of infant mortality is 98 per 1000, but for salaried and self-employed (no-obreros), the figure is 67 per 1000. In housing, in Santiago (where 35 percent of the nation's people live) four times the percentage of workers' homes need to be replaced compared to homes of middle sector groups.

Class Structure

Chilean society manifests serious, politically important class distinctions. One long-time observer of Chilean affairs, Federico Gil, argues that there are "three universally recognized groups or categories: an upper class, a middle or 'employee' class, and a lower class."[13] Awareness of class distinctions is heightened by a number of factors, in addition to the objective differences in living conditions. Chilean law provides for differential treatment of workers, *empleados* (employees), and self-employed (managers and owners), in everything from the Social Security program to health insurance. Different sets of regulations apply for each category mentioned. Also, Chilean intellectuals have long interpreted Chilean development in terms of class-related variables. For nearly a century political clubs, groups, and parties have propagated class-based explanations for the condition of the masses. Furthermore, "proletarianization" of substantial sectors of the working class, especially in mining and the export-related farm activities (e.g., wheat raising, vineyards), occurred quite early in Chilean development, creating fertile ground for class identification and awareness of distinctions. The existence of a salaried working class in a nonpaternalistic work setting in the most vital national economic activities paved the way for an early unionization of industrial workers and further encouraged class awareness.

The Chilean aristocracy dominated the life of the country, including its politics, well into this century. One of the major factors facilitating this relatively easy, almost undisputed control was the flexibility and permeability of the traditional elites. By 1900 this upper class was not only a mix of national origins but also a mix of bourgeois and aristocratic elements. Successful mining, industrial, and business figures who were willing to accept the values of the upper class were allowed entrance into the "correct" social circles and political decision-making positions. Once initiated, the pattern of cooptation of the particularly successful developed a momentum of its own. Once some representatives of the urban bourgeoisie were accepted, the pressures both within and outside the upper class for further "softening" of the barriers to entrance were increased.

This is not to say that there has been widespread social mobility in Chile. On the contrary, upward mobility has never been experienced by anything more than a very small percentage of the population and movement into elite circles has been even more tightly controlled. At the same time, Chile's social structure has been considerably less rigid than that of most other Latin American countries. Chile's upper and middle social sectors are larger and more diverse, relative to population, than any in Latin America, perhaps excluding Argentina and Uruguay.

Adequate explanation of this phenomenon is quite difficult. One factor might be Chile's relative independence from Spain during the pre-1817 period. The resident Spanish aristocracy was apparently quite small and found alliance with the rising urban business class necessary to secure continued control of the situation. In addition, and to the significant advantage of Chile's later development, much of the immigration in the eighteenth and nineteenth centuries consisted of groups from northern Spain, France, and Germany, and Great Britain. While the motives of the different immigrant groups varied, most did not come as illiterate, impoverished workers. Most apparently had some education, rather well developed entrepreneurial instincts, and even in some cases available monetary resources. Moreover, they tended to reflect more egalitarian, individualistic, independent attitudes than immigrants to other Latin American states.

The immigrants of the nineteenth century came to Chile during a period in which a relatively fluid economic situation prevailed. Fortunes were being made in mining. Even in the countryside the rigid estate system had not yet solidified. There was available land, and with a strong market for Chilean cattle, sheep, and other agricultural products, there was money to be made. In the cities, too, the mining and agricultural boom meant new jobs and commercial opportunities. It was, in sum, a most propitious time for enterprising Europeans with some education and ability to arrive on the scene.

An early coalescing of the rural and urban elites is also relevant. The large estates in Chile grew up around Santiago, meaning that physical propinquity if nothing else threw the two groups together, especially since most large landholders maintained homes in Santiago. The small size of the country further encouraged amalgamation of both urban and rural elites as it meant that the elites joined the same clubs, sent their children to the same private schools, intermarried, and so on.

Another factor is the social as well as economic effects of the boom-bust post-independence economic cycle. The Chilean economist, Osvaldo Sunkel, notes that the periodic recessions and depressions served to weaken the economic and political power of especially the land owning aristocracy.[14] This made possible the acquisition of land by new rising social groups, usually with urban economic interests and often non-Spanish background, under conditions which encouraged their acceptance by traditional elites.

Largely as a result of economic development, by 1925 there had developed in Chile an educated, middle group of clerks, small businessmen, teachers, bureaucrats, and other white-collar workers. Until recently, social and political observers have tended to view this diverse "middle sector" as a middle *class*. However, this "new middle class" does not form a true class in any meaningful sense of the term. Most particularly, it does not exhibit an identification and interests separating it from other social groupings. "Almost the only clear middle-class trait has been the tendency to shun the lower mass and to embrace the aristocracy."[15] This tendency of the white-collar group to emulate the life style and accept the values of the upper class has been developed to the point that a name, *siútico*, has been originated for the type. In political office the representatives of the "new middle class" have rarely failed to forget their working class allies and to remember their shared interests with the upper social groups.

For purposes of political analysis, in fact, a strong argument can be made for viewing the class structure in Chile, as well as most of Latin America, as a simple two-tiered system—an upper, prestige sector, in which the acquisition of status and/or power is the standard, and a lower, work-wage sector in which acquisition of economic resources is the primary goal. Important distinctions are present within the classes, but the basic divisions in values, behavior, and attitudes are between these two major groupings.[16]

As is characteristic of the Third World countries in general, the bulk of the population in Chile consists of rural and urban working class poor. The 1960 census data suggest that 80 percent of the economically active population could be classified as laborers. Preliminary 1970 figures indicate only slight change over the decade. The most conservative estimates place more than two-thirds of the population in the working class.

Until recently, however, this working class majority has been characterized by lack of socio-political organization and apathy. As in most of Latin America, a labor elite of organized, relatively privileged workers is found in the key industries, such as mining, steel, and construction. However, even in the mid-1960's only about 12 percent of the active population was organized, and before 1965 virtually no agricultural workers were organized.[17] The relative lack of development of heavy industry and generally low levels of economic growth have contributed to difficulties in organizing workers. Most of the workers are employed in the service sector (23 percent) and agriculture (29 percent.)[18] But even the manufacturing sector is dominated by the traditional, "soft" manufactures in which organization has been difficult and leftist political activity uncommon. One of the results of all this is that as late as 1961 less than 20 percent of the population voted, even though voting was a legal requirement.

During the past decade this picture has changed substantially. Major organization efforts in both urban and rural areas were undertaken by center and left groups. During the Frei Administration, laws facilitating the organization of rural workers were passed, and the countryside became a veritable hotbed of political activity. Analysis by this observer of the 1970 voting data leaves little doubt that the victory of the Left coalition was possible only through a marked change in rural voting patterns—both in terms of widespread high turnouts as well as much stronger support among rural workers for the Marxist candidate than the Left had ever received from that sector.

Organized Interests

In any society it is the politically organized interests that prevail in terms of having their voices heard by political decision-makers. Perhaps even more than in the industrialized states of the West, the organized sector of Chilean society has been the upper social stratum. An early coalescing of potentially competitive urban and rural elites reinforced the position of the upper class relative to other social groups. As early as the independence period there was striking overlap of landowners and business-mining interests.

An extreme concentration of resources, urban and rural, has given the owner-manager class even greater pressures to apply in the political arena. Ricardo Lagos argues that four percent of Chilean corporations control 60 percent of all corporate capital, and that the use of interlocking directorates hides even greater concentration.[19] Petras suggests that over 60 percent of all firms are monopolistic, being dominant firms in industries having no effective competitors.[20] As noted earlier, until the past half-decade there has existed tremendous concentration of agricultural resources.

To better understand the meaning of this concentration of resources, the observer should remember the extent to which "private government" prevails in the Third World systems. In these contexts of stratified societies, private educational systems for the privileged, close social ties among the elite, and scarce and concentrated resources, decisions are as often made in the country club, exclusive restaurant, or drawing room as in the legislative chamber or cabinet minister's office. Open bargaining among competing forces becomes unnecessary when elites are small in number, cohesive, and share views on most policy questions and/or when possible competition is unable to present any viable challenge. While modern Chile has had a much more open system of decision-making than many of its neighbors, the existence of the above mentioned characteristics plus a system of widespread intermarriages within the upper social sectors and the concentration of elite groups in one location—the capital, Santiago—have contributed to an exclusion of the vast bulk of the population from any meaningful influence on policy making.

The informal ties among social elites, including governing elites, are supplemented by well organized formal economic interest groups. The

National Agricultural Society and the Society for Industrial Development have origins in the last century and remain as important spokesmen for their memberships. Organizations of more specialized interests are also active and effective. Dairymen's associations, textile manufacturer's associations, leather and shoe industry associations, and so forth are all politically organized.

Quite typical of the business community's strength and the relationship between the economic elites and government is the policy of turning over government-initiated or subsidized projects to private hands. Petras's data show 35 percent of the large enterprises in his sample were established with substantial state aid, a kind of "socialism for the rich."[21]

Similarly, the "decentralized agencies" in Chile (semi-autonomous government agencies designed to guide, supervise and/or encourage economic activity in particular areas) are strongly influenced by the private economic interests in the agencies' relevant area of activity. According to one observer, a typical situation is that of the Chilean Development Corporation's Agricultural Division, with four of its ten members representing the government and the others representing large landholders' associations. Sunkel says that the Development Corporation (CORFO) has become little more than a banking institution for the larger economic interests.[22]

Much of the middle sector, too, is organized in Chile. Government bureaucrats and public school teachers, for example, have formed what amount to unions. Smaller organizations representing other white-collar groups also exist. A substantial part of the middle sector is directly organized into overtly political associations. The Radical Party, the largest party and key to the system from 1935 to 1960, was organized into local community units, led and composed largely of middle sector groups. Similarly, the party that replaced the Radicals as the dominant grouping, the Christian Democratic Party (PDC), is well organized locally, with its leadership and rank-and-file activists mainly professionals, intellectuals, and white-collar elements.

Associations representing workers appeared very early in Chile, although organizations were concentrated in the mines. Strikes in mining areas were not uncommon in the 1860's and 1870's. In the years 1911–1920 there were almost 300 strikes involving 150,000 workers, yet it was another 20 years before even the most basic and largely symbolic demands of labor were won. In fact, from the 1920's until about 1960 (with the exception of a brief period 1943–1946) the labor movement declined relative to population and labor force growth, representing about 10 percent of the labor force in recent years.[23]

Three important characteristics of Chilean unions should be noted, characteristics that are shared by organized labor in most of Latin America and much of the Third World. First, and perhaps most important, the unions have been essentially the "captives" of either the government in some periods or the political parties at other times. This has substantially reduced their flexibility and freedom. Furthermore, the high levels of partisanship within the labor ranks with labor leaders taking their cues from the political party to which they are tied, has divided and weakened the movement.

Secondly, effective organization has been restricted to the company, rather than the industry or national level. While several loose national confederations have been operative in the past, they have been somewhat ineffective devices, at least until recently, for coordinating union efforts and for securing benefits for the working class.

Third, labor union strength has been concentrated in a few areas of the Chilean economy. Mining related industries still account for about 25 percent of all union members. Perhaps one-third, and possibly more, belong to professional unions (public employees, teachers, etc.) which are obviously likely to have very different, usually more moderate, views than members in mining, manufacturing, and industry.[24] Also most enterprises remain small. The 1965 Industrial Census found only 52 manufacturing industries in the country with more than 500 employees, only 367 with more than 100 employees, of course with a number of these in white-collar or middle level positions. Furthermore, the lack of heavy industry in the Chilean economy means that much unionization must occur in the "traditional" manufacturing sector—textiles, food production, shoe manufacture, and similar activities where unskilled, easily replaced, labor is the rule.

The decade of the 1960's witnessed new initiatives in organization. With both formal and informal barriers to working class participation breaking down, the parties were forced to compete fiercely for working class adherents. Of particular importance was legislation passed in 1965 by the Christian Democrats which for the first time allowed widespread unionization in the rural areas. By 1969 100,000 peasants had been organized, and undoubtedly that figure will inflate with later data.

Even the leftist parties had hesitated to agitate and organize in the countryside. Petras and Zeitlin attribute this to lack of access to the peasantry and the "backward" attitudes of the rural workers.[25] Others have suggested that additional factors should be considered, noting the willingness of the leftist leadership to play by the rules set by the prestige sector interests as long as minimal allocations of resources have been provided their constituents and their own status was assured. The conjunction of events strongly suggests that the Left's effort among the rural work forces was at least partially spurred by the Christian Democrats' initiatives in that area and their fear of losing the rural electorates.

Two other major organized forces in Chilean social and political life —students and representatives of the Church—deserve brief mention at this point. Both continue to exercise political influence across a rather broad spectrum of issues, although the role of the Church has been reduced from its predominance of past decades.

As children of the prestige class and future leaders of virtually every aspect of Chilean society, students in Chile as in the rest of Latin America are given some deference. A history of political involvement, usually with an anti-establishment orientation, includes the initiation of the overthrow of the Ibáñez dictatorship in 1930 and leadership of the contemporary MIR (Revolutionary Leftist Movement), the activities of which have been a painful thorn in the side of the recent Chilean governments. As vocal spokesmen for reform, students have been especially important in educating other relatively privileged groups to prevailing conditions as well as raising hopes of the relatively oppressed.

Perhaps no group in Chile has experienced such a remarkable change in political role as has the Church. For a variety of reasons, including consistent past support of the interests of the elites, the Church lost substantial prestige and support in recent years, especially among the lower social groups. Efforts to regain support among the masses and the renewal of clergy ranks with younger, more reform-minded priests have contributed to a change in Church policy in the past 10 to 15 years. With the added push of recent progressive encyclicals and papal pronouncements, the Catholic Church in Chile moved dramatically to the left. By the late 1960's, the dominant, though by no means unanimous, view of Church leaders supported basic structural change in Chilean society. Thus, the Church leadership finds itself in opposition to the traditional allies and in fact instrumental in legitimizing some of the more serious demands of the masses.

CRISES, SEQUENCES, AND RATES OF CHANGE

Several recent contributions to the literature of the social sciences have pointed out the importance of "timing" of issues and/or crises and "rates of change" as independent variables affecting the way a system develops or fails to do so.[26] This discussion will attempt to elaborate the primary issues and crises that have faced the Chilean system—for example the timing of those issues and/or crises. Did they occur before, during, or after the institutionalization of the decision-making process? Did they occur when physical resources were available for their solution? Did several issues arise together, in rapid sequence, or separated over long periods of time? Rates of social and political change were also significant. Did creation of a national identity occur rapidly, or over a long period? Did democratic politics evolve in a decade, a generation, or a century? Did socio-political mobilization occur over a short or extended period of time? An examination of these variables should enable us not only to better explain the particular development process of Chile but should also suggest considerations relevant to the analysis of the process in other countries as well.

The pre-independence period in Chile was characterized by a relatively slow process of European immigration, a relatively complete racial homogenization in a socially stratified, hierarchical system in which a quite small elite dominated the decision-making process. There were relatively few major social and/or political conflicts, with the politically relevant population being very limited and privileged. Consequently, the pressures on the political system were not significant.

The most important early cleavage was settled by the break with Spain in 1817. The division between those of Spanish descent but born in Chile and largely excluded from positions of authority during Spanish rule and the colonial governors was settled when the former took control of the system after independence.

The pattern of Chilean development was also strongly affected by the early development of feelings of independence, perhaps even national identity, at least among the more educated and affluent groups, largely for reasons cited earlier. In addition the conjunction of a number of factors, including a relatively small population base, substantial unsettled and usable land, the slow but steady influx of colonists from a variety of social origins and national backgrounds, and, later, opportunities for wealth in the mining sector, contributed to the development of a relatively permeable social structure, at least insofar as the traditional aristocracy proved willing to accept, more correctly coopt, the leading members of the urban bourgeoisie and successful landowners. All these factors enabled the Chilean system to more effectively cope with the immediate strains of independence, while maintaining sociopolitical stability and continued domination by the traditional aristocracy.

As noted earlier Chilean separation from Spain came without disturbing the basic pre-independence social and economic structures. The subordination of the masses remained in the new regime as in the old. In this fashion the Chilean system passed through the crisis of independence. This pattern of limited intra-elite conflict and limited social violence has prevailed, with one exception, to the current period.

As might be expected, the immediate post-separation era witnessed a political domination by the military, as the only well-organized social force. However, when the military attempted to initiate social reforms designed to lay a foundation for a genuine republican form of government, the Chilean upper class re-united in solid opposition. The military leaders resigned without precipitating serious conflict when this pressure was applied, establishing a precedent of civilian supremacy that was only once abandoned, until late 1973.

Usually referred to as the "autocratic republic," the period 1830–1870 was in most respects a continuation of the colonial political patterns, a monarchy without the monarch. During this period the Chilean upper class re-established and reinforced a strong, civilian, centralized political system, emphasizing stability, even if at the expense of innovation and political democracy. In fact, Gil argues that Chile has experienced stability precisely because of the lack of break with the colonial past.[27]

While the rate of political change was slow and a stable social and political order was maintained during this period, there was not a complete lack of political conflict, even within the upper social sector. By the 1850's some reasonably important divisions appeared, including conflict over separation of church and state, expansion of public education, and the widening of political liberties. Two general political tendencies coalesced around these issues. The *pelucones* (bigwigs), dominated by the most conservative social elements, governed until the 1870's. The *pipiolos* (novices) were equally upper class but favored a greater separation of church and state, a lessened role of the Church in the education system, a broader-based public education system, and particularly an extension of political freedoms.

By mid-century these tendencies were organized into competing political parties, although competing for a very restricted electorate in an exceedingly hierarchical system. This rather early development of organized political forces has profoundly influenced the development of Chilean politics. Most particularly, the organized party system *institutionalized* political decision-making, even in a system with a strong president. After 1870, party support became a crucial factor in the ability of governments to maintain themselves in power. Division by parties also facilitated the organization of the legislature, almost undoubtedly strengthening that body as a viable institution of political decision-making.

Furthermore, the party system (by more or less openly competing for popular support) lent an aura of democracy to the system that would have been lacking otherwise. In the twentieth century, party competition broadened the system substantially by encouraging the participation of previously excluded social groups.

The level of popular awareness of political issues in Chile, given the low levels of social and economic development of the country, has been a regular source of amazement for foreign observers. At least partially, this phenomenon must be attributed to the political socialization and mobilization activities of a strong party system institutionalized over the past 130 years.

Early development of the party system also facilitated political control by the president and the legislature over the bureaucracy and the military, the two institutions presently exercising such dominance in most of the Third World. Obviously, neither the bureaucracy nor the military has been inert in Chilean political decision-making, but the degree of independence from the elected political forces has been considerably less than in most other systems lacking competing, organized parties.

The substantial economic development after 1850 contributed to the downfall of the *pelucones'* autocratic republic. The desire of the urban bourgeoisie and professionals to gain access to the system's rewards encouraged first an alignment with the *pipiolos* in the Liberal Party (PL), and then formation of a separate organization, the Radical Party (PR). A loose coalition of Liberals and Radicals governed from 1870–1890.

The continued economic and political power of the more conservative forces provided ample challenge to the new leadership. Only the outbreak of the War of the Pacific (1879–1883), a struggle with Bolivia and Peru over the mineral-rich Atacama Desert, forestalled the civil conflict that occurred in 1891. Chile's military success had the effect of reinforcing and expanding the feelings of national identity and pride, even among the lower social sectors, as well as increasing its mineral wealth.

As suggested earlier, this mineral wealth has been the foundation of the Chilean economy to the present time. It also enticed a substantial entourage of foreigners to add to an already significant non-Spanish population component. Foreign capital came to dominate the vital national economic activities over the next three decades, a situation which prevailed until the early 1970's.

To call the conflict of 1891 a civil war is something of misnomer, since the struggle was basically a culmination of six to seven decades of dissension *within* the upper class. Two consequences of the conflict have had lasting impact, however. Both sides in the war appealed to the masses of the population for support, encouraging the already increasing awareness among the masses of their potential role in the political process. Of more immediate importance, victory by the more conservative elements in the legislature assured that the system would not be quickly opened to the growing white-collar and organized working class groups and that the paternalistic social and political order would be retained and if possible strengthened. The victory of the legislature also destroyed, temporarily, the strong executive system dominant in Chile since pre-independence times.

The period 1891–1932 is best viewed as a deviation from the normal pattern of Chilean politics. In general, it was a period of personal and public corruption, political stalemate, and near chaos. The political party system broke down, the legislature, without executive leadership, divided into an incredible array of virtually warring factions, the public bureaucracy floundered, vote-buying was common, bribery of public servants became an accepted practice.

This rapid deterioration suggests that the strong presidency fulfilled a vital role in the Chilean system. The centuries of strong executive leadership instilled a psychological dependency on the single dominant leader, the absence of which invited lack of organization and discipline on a wide scale. The importance of personalism as a cultural characteristic should also be remembered in this context. Additionally, the ease by which many in the prestige sector were enriched by the mineral wealth of the time encouraged corruption, lack of discipline, and personal greed (not unlike what happened in the boom years of the late nineteenth century in the United States).

Of more immediate political importance was the development during this same era of a numerically important white-collar sector. Professionals, government employees, clerks, and small businessmen grew steadily in numbers from the turn of the century but were systematically excluded from political influence until the 1920's and in practice excluded from serious political impact until 1938.

Finally, the increasing external orientation of the Chilean economy should be mentioned. The overwhelming majority of Chile's exports since the late 1800's have been mineral products, most of them owned and exported by foreign nationals and bound for either the United States or two or three Western European countries. The dependence on the United States was such that by 1931 the economic depression hit Chile probably more seriously than any Latin American country.

The unwillingness of the politically dominant groups in the Chilean upper class to recognize the urban middle sectors and the organized working class as legitimate contenders in the political arena resulted in an impasse resolved finally by overt military intervention. The difficulties the military encountered and lack of success it achieved may partially explain the reluctance of the military to engage in a repeat performance. While the military regime did pursue some social and political reforms, designed largely to meet the most insistent demands of the middle groups, the major function of the intervention was to allow a cooling-off period during which the differing political forces reassessed their positions and alternatives. By 1931, when the military regime collapsed (largely due to the consequences of the economic depression), the propertied interests, although still very much in control of matters, indicated a willingness to extend formal political democracy to other organized groups. It should be remembered, however, that the groups entering the system largely accepted the prevailing system and the values underlying its existence. These were not forces interested in depriving the traditional propertied interests of their advantages. They only wanted access to some of the advantages for themselves.

The resolution of the conflict over extension of political democracy is illustrative of how crises have been confronted by the Chilean system. Even though a major point in the debate within the upper class in the nineteenth century was this very issue, the franchise as late as 1920 was exercised by a very small part of the population (4.5 percent). On the other hand, even that small percentage apparently included much of the politically aware population desiring the franchise. Furthermore, formal extension of the franchise without other changes is basically a symbolic gesture.

The relatively slow, at least until recently, process of incorporating middle and lower class populations was accomplished peacefully, without enduring social conflict. By allowing new groups to enter over rather long time spans, Chile's political leaders largely escaped the systemic "overloading" so often found among Third World countries. The Chilean system was able to incorporate, at least partially, each new group before adding other groups and their demands to the political arena.

The slowness of the process has also facilitated the cooptation of the representatives of the lower sectors into the prevailing value system, including their acceptance of the existing political arrangements. As suggested in the earlier section on social classes, the representatives of even the working class groups accepted the existing rules of the game. In fact, the only period (1947–1957) when one group, the Communist Party, threatened the stability of the prevailing system that group was banned from political competition and its leaders exiled.

In an earlier section it was argued that real external domination in Chile is a twentieth century phenomenon. In effect, the foreign influence has been greatest in a period in which a mass-based democracy has been developing. Foreign capital in Chile has also been concentrated in the country's basic economic activities, making the foreign presence even more visible. Even if there was no substance at all to any of the charges, North American "exploitation" would still be an important issue in Chilean politics. It is simply too tempting a target for parties having to appeal to a mass-based electorate.

The timing of the arrival of genuine foreign economic influence has also had the effect of increasing further the already significant polarization within Chilean society. The traditional parties have had a particularly hard time dealing with the charge that they have been collaborators with the North Americans. The parties most dependent on working class support have recognized the issue as an easy means of demonstrating the "sell-out" of the political opposition. Newly mobilized working class citizens cannot be expected to discriminate between these elements of the middle and upper sectors with close ties to the foreign sector and the larger part of the upper social groups that has vigorously opposed, especially in recent years, the foreign domination.

In this analysis we have argued that until the last three decades the timing of the major issues and the rate of social change has worked to benefit the Chilean system in its efforts to handle the demands placed upon it. Social and economic changes have been relatively slow and orderly. By and large, social divisions have been few, and they have not been cumulative. The particular colonial experience, the easy break with Spain, the propitious discovery of valuable mineral resources are among the factors that have facilitated the subordination of socio-political conflict and the easy resolution of those conflicts not subordinated. Strong national political institutions, including effective political parties and interest groups, have also been valuable in organizing social conflict and stabilizing the process of reaching decisions on major social questions.

Since World War II, however, the rate of social and political change has accelerated dramatically and the system has been strained to the breaking point. In 1940 just over 50 percent of the population was urban and less than 30 percent lived in cities over 50,000. In 1970 over 70 percent was urban and about half the population lived in major cities. The literacy rate has gone from near 60 percent to near 90 percent in the same period. In other words, the conditions conducive to mass mobilization are present as never before, and that mobilization has clearly occurred. Probably the best evidence is the increase in the electorate noted earlier. In 1970 almost 30 percent of the population voted in the presidential election. Between the presidential election of 1958 and the election of 1964 the number of votes cast doubled, from 1.25 to 2.53 million. By 1970 the number reached nearly 3 million and by 1973, in a nonpresidential election, the figure jumped dramatically again to 3.6 million. (See Table 3.) That kind of change would put a strain on any system, regardless of the available resources. Other similar evidences of widespread socio-political mobilization are detailed in a later section.

These rapid social and political changes have occurred during a long period of economic stagnation in Chile. As one might imagine, one result has been tremendous pressure placed on government to expand by whatever means possible the number of jobs and economic opportunities. In addition, the spokesmen for the working class groups have taken the opportunity to fasten the blame for the unsatisfactory conditions on the propertied class and their political representatives who have been governing the country until recently. The continued incapacity of governments dominated by middle and upper sector representatives has considerably improved the political positions of those groups with an interest in basic social and economic changes. In social origin the overwhelming majority of the new voters are from the most deprived sectors of the population. As political awareness increases these groups very naturally become the most interested in *any* kind of change that promises to improve their life conditions.

STRATEGIES AND STRUCTURES OF CONTROL: THE POLITICAL SYSTEM AS AN INDEPENDENT VARIABLE

The Constitutional Framework

As mentioned earlier, the framers of Chile's Constitution were strongly influenced by the model of the United States. Chilean constitutions (only two have been promulgated since 1833) established a strong,

TABLE 3
VOTING, REGISTRATION, AND TURNOUT PATTERNS, 1920–70

Year	Popu-lation*	Poten-tial Voters*	Regis-tered Voters*	Votes Cast*	% Poten. Voters Regis.	% Pop. Regis.	% Pop. Voting	% Regis. Voting	% Poten. Voters Voting
1920	3,785	898	370	167	41.6	9.9	4.5	45.1	18.6
1932	4,495	1,110	430	344	38.7	9.5	7.3	86.2	29.5
1938	4,914	1,219	504	444	41.3	10.3	9.0	88.1	36.4
1946	5,643	1,394	632	479	45.3	11.2	8.5	75.9	34.4
1952[a]	6,295	3,267	1,105	957	33.8	17.6	15.2	86.6	29.3
1958	7,298	3,697	1,498	1,250	40.6	20.5	17.1	83.5	33.9
1961[b]	7,802	3,881	1,859	1,386	47.9	23.8	17.8	74.5	35.7
1964	8,369	4,176	2,915	2,531	69.8	34.8	30.2	87.4	60.6
1969[b]	9,092[c]	4,523[c]	3,245	2,406	71.6	35.7	26.5	74.1	53.1[d]
1970	9,297[c]	-----[d]	3,540	2,955	----[d]	38.1	31.7	83.5	----

*In thousands.

a. The 1952 election was the first presidential contest in which female suffrage was present. About 30 percent of the vote in that year was cast by women. However, registration and turnout was lowered by the application of a law that outlawed the Communist party and struck its members from voting lists. Between 1952 and 1970 registration for women rose 507 percent, for men, 241 percent.

b. Congressional elections. Turnouts are usually somewhat, though not significantly, lower than in presidential contests.

c. Preliminary 1970 census figures suggest these population totals to be lower than indicated here and thus the percentages in columns 6, 7, 8, and 10 for 1969 and 1970 would be larger than those presented.

d. Figures not available.

Sources: All figures except for 1969 and 1970 are from Atilio Borón, "Political Mobilization and Political Crisis in Chile, 1920–1970," a paper presented to the Eighth World Congress of the International Political Science Association, 1970. The original data sources are the Dirección del Registro Electoral, Santiago, Chile; R. Cruz Coke, *Geografía Electoral de Chile,* Editorial del Pacífico, 1952, p. 12; Instituto Latinoamericano de Planification Económica y Social, *Antecedentes Cuantitativos Referentes al Desarrollo de América Latina,* Santiago 1966, pp. 32–44. Figures for 1969 and 1970 are from the Dirección del Registro Electoral.

independent executive, a bi-cameral (two-house) legislature, and a relatively independent court system early in the country's history.

The most significant differences between the Chilean and US constitutional arrangements have been the rejection in Chile of federalism in favor of a unitary system and the much stronger formal position of the president. Since the Portales era of the 1830's, republican Chile has been a presidential system with very broad powers delegated to the executive. The only period of parliamentary dominance (1891–1925) proved so chaotic and unpopular that the 1926 Constitution even *increased* executive powers.

The 1833 Constitution was a faithful representation of political realities of the time. It established an oligarchic republic—the franchise was sharply limited to the upper social groups (in 1864 the total number of qualified voters was 22,261, in a population of 2.5 million). A highly centralized system with virtually all political power residing with the Santiago government was established, and the executive was given broad discretionary authority. Gil flatly states that no candidate could win an election during the period 1830–71 without government (presidential) acquiescence.

The 1925 Constitution democratized the system considerably, establishing near-universal male suffrage (women were given the vote in the early 1950's; illiterates in 1970), proportional representation in the Congress, and direct election of the president. It also made constitutional change easier, defined property as a social function (which has given later governments the basis for forcing propertied interests to use their holdings for more "public-regarding," socially beneficial purposes), and included a number of welfare functions for the state.

The 1925 document, composed in a climate of reaction to almost unrestrained oligarchical rule and social disorders, thus provided the basis for the development of meaningful democracy in Chile. Direct election of the strong president, at a separate date from the legislature, has served to focus popular attention on the office and by the late 1950's truly make that office-holder dependent on a mass base. A proportional representation system in the legislature further "democratized" the system by ensuring that almost all significant popular views were given a voice.

The popularly elected legislature, which was composed of the Senate and Chamber of Deputies, has been strong enough that virtually all recent presidents have tried to reform the legislature structure to restrain what both Presidents Frei and Allende have called "parliamentary irresponsibility." In addition to the customary legislative powers, including the budget, taxes, power to create and abolish public offices and agencies—the Congress could also impeach Cabinet ministers by majority vote, (which it did regularly), refuse to allow the president to leave the country, and, in general, make life miserable for any executive who had a weak congressional base.

Recent Constitutional changes during the Frei Administration enabled the president to call for popular referenda on issues stalled in recalcitrant legislatures and to call one special election to renew an opposition Congress. However, the legislature is still the customary focal point for organized opposition to the executive.

Thus, while clearly not the central political decision-making institution, the legislature ensured that the executive was not the "constitutional dictator," the position has become in countries such as Mexico.

At the same time, the presidency has been the key institution in the system. Especially important are its decree and administrative powers. Perhaps the best illustration of this point is to note the extent to which President Allende reshaped the Chilean economy, including nationalization of many of the basic enterprises, in the face of a hostile majority in both chambers of the legislature. Only a violent and extra-Constitutional counterrevolution was capable of reversing Allende's actions.

The Military

Textbook treatments of Latin American politics have almost inevitably put Costa Rica, Uruguay, and Chile together as the countries with subordinated militaries. The fact that both Uruguay and Chile are currently being governed directly by military regimes may tell us much about the current social and political conditions in at least the Latin American region. It is very true that the Chilean military has virtually no history of overt intervention into the political arena—the only exception since the independence period being the Ibáñez dictatorship of the late 1920's. At the same time, the military has almost always been a potent political force.

Officers are well-paid and receive extensive fringe benefits. Defense spending as a percentage of GNP in Chile for 1971 was third highest in the Latin American area, excluding Cuba. During the first months of the Allende Administration one observer argued in a not atypical position regarding the military, "the brake and check on the present popular front government in Chile is the military."[28] This opinion was given further substance in late 1972 when President Allende was forced to include three high-ranking officers in key Cabinet posts during a period of particularly serious agitation and threats of disorder. Under Allende, the military was given a number of important and sensitive duties (e.g., the administration of a food rationing program). A variety of subtle and occasionally not-too-subtle pressures were applied to the government which many military leaders clearly regarded as a potential threat to their positions long before the coup. However, it should be remembered that the military refused to intervene under circumstances which would surely have promoted a coup in other Third World states.

Various explanations of the lack of military intervention can be noted. Huntington, among others, has suggested that military intervention is a product of few countervailing political forces.[29] Thus, in Chile the presence of a strong and cohesive upper class, allied with significant segments of an expanding middle sector, has, until recently, served to effectively counter other potential power contenders. The presence of well-organized political parties may also have deterred military intervention.

More importantly, the forces and pressures that have encouraged military intervention elsewhere have largely been absent from Chilean politics, at least until recently. The only prior intervention of this century (in 1925–31) followed one of the few periods of Chilean history when weak leadership, division within elites, and social instability combined to present a serious threat to the established order.

There is also a lack of precedent for military intervention. In contrast to most of the Third World countries, intervention is simply a violation of the rules of the game in Chile. For example, during the bitter presidential election of 1970, I was quite surprised to note the extent and intensity of sympathy for intervention among certain sectors. Many shopkeepers, larger property owners, even professionals, openly supported intervention to deal with problems such as inflation, lower-class agitation, and especially the possibility of Marxist victory in the election. After that victory even greater pressures were applied, reaching a climax in the assassination of the Army Chief-of-Staff by a pro-interventionist group in apparent hope of precipitating a coup.

In June, 1973, an army unit attempted to precipitate a general revolt by an open attack on the president's offices in downtown Santiago, with several civilian and military fatalities. What was most striking about the incident, however, was its failure. No additional military units joined the revolt, even though the very seat of Chilean government was under seige for several hours. In fact, when the military was asked to put down the revolt, it did so.

Many observers have maintained that professionalization tends to reduce interventionism, although the argument has been subjected to considerable dispute (many "professional" militaries in Latin America have records of interventionism). The Chilean military has traditionally been a highly professional force. There are national military academies of repute in which officers receive their training, and a military career is regarded as a prestigious occupation.

In addition, the officer corps is recruited from the prestige class (though not from the traditional elites), and many of the higher officer corps have close social ties with the economic and social elite of this century.[30] Secondly, like virtually all military establishments there are sharp divisions among the different forces (the navy and air force think of themselves, and are generally regarded by other observers, as more prestigious than the army) and within the individual forces themselves. The army, especially, has apparently been seriously divided in recent years, a conflict deepened by the potential threats raised by the actions of the socialist government of Allende.

The international ties of the Chilean military are also important to its role. In the early part of this century the Chilean government brought in German military advisors to train the military forces of the country. Since World War II, however, the external linkage has been with the United States. Through grants (the Military Assistance Program), loans, and extensive training programs, the United States has built strong ties with the ranking figures in the Chilean armed forces. The United States provides substantial grants, of up to 30 percent (in 1963), of the Chilean defense budget. It has made available surplus equipment at bargain prices, and has provided loans for purchase of more sophisticated weaponry. Chilean officers are trained for lengthy periods at United States military bases where they are instructed in the uses of equipment and the virtues of democracy.

The extent to which these linkages are important is reflected in an incident which occurred during the second year of Allende's term. The administration wanted to reduce the dependency on US military supplies and made deals for supplying armaments with several East European countries. The military officers of Chile refused to accept the already completed arrangements. Interestingly enough, the only type of assistance continued by the United States during the Allende Administration was extensive military assistance, which apparently even exceeded past levels of aid during the Allende years.

The Bureaucracy

The bureaucracy increasingly has set national policies in Chile. Petras maintains that the public bureaucracy is *the* problem-solving institution in Chile.[31] Latin Americans have not opposed government action in economic and social development as a matter of principle. Especially since the rise to political dominance of the white-collar groups in the 1940's government has been given a broad and expanding role in economic planning, in particular, but in some social welfare activities as well. The center-left Christian Democratic government of 1964–70, and especially the socialist government of Allende, have accelerated this trend.

The Chilean Development Corporation (CORFO), formed in 1939, was one of the first semi-autonomous government agencies of its kind in any non-socialist country. The model has been used extensively in other countries, such as Mexico and India. CORFO and sister agencies engage in a wide range of economic activities, usually either in development and encouragement of economic infrastructural activities (hydroelectric systems, irrigation projects, transportation systems, steel mills) or high risk, capital intensive activities (e.g., tourism—a nationwide system of government financed hotels is superb).

One practical impact of the substantial state role has been the creation of a large and growing government payroll. The number of persons employed in government service has risen nearly 75 percent since 1940. Indeed, the bureaucracy has become the means of social mobility for large numbers of the lower sectors of the prestige class and the means for providing jobs for the sons and daughters of the prestige class, thereby contributing to social stability.

The inability of the traditional political forces to solve basic social and economic problems, especially in the last two decades, has heightened the importance of bureaucracy. Because of its skills and control over, or at least access to, key national decision-making posts, the bureaucracy has political significance far beyond its numerical strength and the status positions of its members. The bureaucracy will almost surely remain the stabilizing force in future Chilean politics that it has been, as its size and role can be expected to increase.

At the same time the bureaucracy cannot be viewed as a dynamic repository for change-oriented policies, especially reforms directed toward aiding the masses. Higher level public administrators and professionals clearly identify with the middle and upper social sector. Largely because of an obvious stake in continued state intervention, top bureaucrats tend to be somewhat reform-oriented, but on a very narrow spectrum of issues. A recent survey of high-level bureaucrats showed that only slightly more than one of ten considered agrarian reform and housing issues of prime importance, even though the incumbent administration was giving these two issues top priority. Stability and security, rather than structural change, were the primary interests expressed.[32]

The future of the bureaucracy as a policy-making institution is in some doubt under the new military government, although there will clearly continue to be considerable dependence on the career civil servants. The military may give a great deal of independence to the bureaucrats and rely on bureaucratic initiative, given their lack of experience in day-to-day governing. This seems unlikely, however, given the fascist orientations of the current set of military leaders and the collaboration of the bureaucracy with the socialist regime of Allende. More likely is the lopping off of a good part of the bureaucracy, especially those agencies and programs developed under the Allende and Frei governments, and a heavy supervision of the bureaucracy with the purpose of ferreting out so-called Marxists. It is even possible that the military may use the armed services themselves as a kind of alternative bureaucracy, like Peru, but with a rightist orientation.

Political Parties

In Chile the political parties have been key institutions in a true multi-party system. While it remains unclear what importance the current military regime intends to relegate to political competition and party activities, there is some evidence that it intends to take its cues from the Brazilian neo-Fascist regime and organize a government-sponsored (and controlled) party. The leaders of the National Party, the representative of the propertied interests, have been publicly proclaiming the virtues of this system, seeing their organization as the logical nucleus of such a party. Whatever choice is made for future action it seems unlikely that the current set of military leaders will tolerate genuine party competition, given the clear popular preference for leftist alternatives. Thus, political parties may not be of great relevance in future Chilean politics. At the same time, they have been crucial in the development of Chilean politics to this point and are likely to remain of some consequence as organizers of opinion, even under this most violent and repressive of military governments. They therefore deserve serious attention.

Of the five major parties in Chile, all but one were active by the early 1900's. The Christian Democratic Party (PDC) developed in the late 1930's from a split of the youth from the Conservative Party—the oldest in Chile. The multi-party system in Chile has roots in basic social divisions, already briefly examined. It has been reinforced by the use of a complex, proportional representation system that assured more accurate representation of varied interests than most systems but also virtually assured coalition governments and the lack of legislative majorities.

Parties in Chile have had a number of important functions. They have had very wide discretion over who could run as party candidates for public offices; as a general rule, only candidates with party identification have had a chance for victory. Furthermore, party discipline has been maintained to a considerable degree. This means that parties have served the function of offering real alternatives to the electorate. Fragmentation of parties has been common, however. Parties have been the major politicizing agents for much of the population. Parties have organized and directed labor unions, published and distributed newspapers, owned or in other ways significantly influenced radio stations, distributed pamphlets, run social service agencies, and in general engaged in a wide range of activities that seemed to politically "educate" substantial sectors of the population. In a country where intermediate linkages are weak-to-nonexistent for much of the population, political parties, especially well-organized units such as the Communists and Christian Democrats, served as the major and sometimes only really effective politicizing agents. Considering that the number of actual voters went from 0.95 million in 1952 to 3.66 million in 1973, the importance (and magnitude) of the political socialization effort is evident.

The parties in Chile are arrayed into three identifiable, if not too neat, tendencies—a pattern made increasingly explicit since the mid-1950's. The Right is represented by the National Party (PN). Its plea for order, stability, and a basically privately-owned economic system has most appeal to the privileged groups. Democratization of the system has hurt the Right badly. In only one national legislative election, from 1932 through 1961, did the Right fail to get at least one-third of the vote total. However, in an expanded electorate, its percentage of support has declined sharply. The 1969, 1971, and 1973 election results suggest a stabilization of the Right's vote at about 20 percent of the electorate. (In fact, the recent polarization of the electorate has probably benefited the PN, as many frightened white-collar, non-property holders have joined ranks.)

Until the late 1950's the Center was dominated by the Radical Party (PR) a grouping of disparate forces that has been described as having only one interest in common—control of political office and the accompanying spoils. Previously viewed as the party of the white-collar worker and the bureaucrat, Ayres' analysis emphasizes the rural and small town base of the party.[33] With origins in the 1870's and having during its history swung from one end of the ideological spectrum to the other, it is not surprising that the party has received support from practically every sector of the population.

The Radicals have never had enough strength to dominate national politics alone, but in coalitions, with the Left from 1937 to 1947 and with the Right until the mid-1960's, they were able to dominate or at least strongly influence national politics for more than two decades. The PR has consistently drawn from 18 to 23 percent of the ballot in national elections (until 1965), distributed so that it has almost always been overrepresented in the legislature.

Like the Right, the PR has been hurt by recent socio-political change and democratization. Its vote dropped from 21.4 (1961) to 6.0 (1973). In 1969 the party split internally, which accented its problems, as indicated by the very weak showing in the 1971 municipal elections and the 1973 congressional elections.

One of the Radical's biggest problems has been the rise of the Christian Democratic Party (PDC), the dominant party during the 1960's. With a strong reformist pitch, the PDC has had strong appeal not only to white-collar professionals, executives, and technicians, but has been very active in seeking support in both urban and rural working class areas.

The electoral rise of the PDC has been phenomenal, from 9.4 in 1957 to 42.3 percent in 1965. So, too, has been the decline, down to 30 percent in the congressional elections in 1969 and 1973 and finishing last in a three man contest in the 1970 presidential race, with 27 percent. The party's success has apparently been based, to some extent, on the personal appeal of its longtime leader, Eduardo Frei. Beset by major internal disagreements and defections, the vigor of the party has been seriously affected and its future as a serious agent of reform seems dim.

Although the Left in Chile has included a variety of groups, it has been dominated by the Socialist (PS) and Communist (PC) parties, both with Chilean origins in the early part of this century. Both are basically urban, working-class movements, although the PS has a history of support in some rural areas. Recent electoral patterns suggest that both parties, but especially the Communists, are getting much greater support from newly organized rural workers.

The combined strength of the Left has been sufficient to threaten the bourgeois parties for three decades. The early proletarianization of a substantial sector of the working class and especially the importance of mining in the economy provided a solid base for moderate leftist activities. In the 1940's they could count on about a quarter of the vote total. But when the Communists became too strong and immoderate in the late 1940's, the PC was banned and did not legally participate again until 1958.

Since 1961 the Left's position has consistently improved from 23 to 43.4 percent in congressional elections. In presidential contests the Left candidate (the same man in all cases) received 29 percent of the vote in 1958 (four man race), 39 percent in 1964 (two man race), and 37 percent in 1970 (three man race). (See Table 4.) What makes the 1970 figure more impressive is the fact that one of Allende's opponents was running a campaign that was on most issues at least as reform-oriented as his own. One could argue that nearly two of every three votes in that election was for a candidate supporting major structural change.

In its efforts to ensure its future friendly ties with the United States and eliminate any possibilities of threats to the position of the military or its prestige sector allies, the current military regime has killed most of the leadership of the Left and imprisoned the remainder. In the most emphatic terms possible, the military leaders have made clear their intention of outlawing the Left insofar as Chilean political competition is concerned. The demonstrated ability of the Left to gain and hold political power and at the same time improve their base of support will undoubtedly provide a rationale for the Christian Democrats and *nacionales* to support this disenfranchisement of the working class.

Perspectives of Political Leadership

In societies characterized by low levels of education, subsistence level living standards, and only the most indirect access to decision-makers, the nature of political leadership is a crucial variable. This is particularly the case where the public sector is increasingly emphasized as the means of increasing the quantity of resources as well as more equitably distributing available resources. The development over centuries of a patron-peon dependency relationship as a cultural characteristic reinforces the tendency to look to government as the ultimate benefactor and problem solver, as the masses transfer their allegiance to this patron-of-last-resort. In societies where class barriers are high and economic opportunities few, politics becomes one of the very few arenas in which the deprived can hope to improve their lot.

TABLE 4

RECENT ELECTORAL PATTERNS

Congressional Elections Year	The Right	Radicals	The Center Christian Democrats	The Left
1937	42.0	18.6	----	15.3
1957	29.1	21.4	9.4	10.7[a]
1961	31.4	22.5	15.9	22.9
1965	12.8	13.7	43.6	23.3
1969	20.8	13.6	31.1	29.4
1973	23.5	3.6	29.0	43.4[d]
Presidential Elections				
1952[b]	27.8	20.0	----	5.5[a]
1958	31.6	15.6	20.7	28.9
1964	----	5.0	56.1	38.9
1970	35.1[c]	----	28.1	36.4

a. The Communist party and its supporters were barred from participating in elections during the period 1947-1957.

b. An independent candidate, former dictator General Carlos Ibáñez, was elected in 1952, with 46 percent of the vote.

c. The candidate of the Right in 1970 was former President Jorge Alessandri, a figure whose support transcended traditional party and ideological lines, accounting for his near-victory. He very likely would have won, except for his age (he was in his mid-70s).

d. Including the Radicals, who aligned with the Left in this election.

Source: Direccion del Registro Electoral, Santiago, Chile.

Political leaders in Chile have been recruited largely from the upper social strata, almost regardless of party or ideological outlook, or have held elitist attitudes toward governing. As a result, political leadership in Chile has been characterized by the continuity of basically moderate-to-conservative policy orientations. The more conservative administrations, like that of Alessandri (1958, 1964), have not attempted large-scale pullbacks from welfare-state programs initiated by the Popular Front governments. On the other hand, the Frei Administration (1964-1970), after campaigning on a strongly reformist platform, was very careful in attempting to maintain the prevailing equilibrium. While there was a commitment to improving conditions for the masses, the improvement was not to come at major expense to the privileged groups. As a consequence, the major contributions of Frei's Christian Democratic government were in the area of upgrading and expanding public education, at the expense of the much more socially sensitive and potentially disruptive areas of land reform and control and direction of economic activity.

The underlying consensus among elites concerning the necessity of limits on social changes within a stable social order has profoundly influenced the flow of Chilean politics, especially as it affected the leadership of the Left. The basis for a strong radical leftist movement has been present in Chile since the early part of this century. The electoral support of Socialists, Communists, and leftist Radicals has been consistently high and nationwide. At the same time the leadership, in both public and party offices, of the leftist groups has been almost without exception accommodating and conciliatory in its interaction with the leaders of the more privileged groups. Zeitlin suggests that this is a continuing bargain worked out between the Left and other political forces, in which the "revolutionary" groups trade their support and containment of working class demands for "policies of national development" desired by both Left and the bourgeois groups.[34] The Left has become bureaucratized (especially the Communists), with the leaders given the prestige and status they desired in return for not "rocking the boat." Furthermore, the Left has been met in the past with solid opposition and severe sanctions in cases where the ill-defined boundaries between acceptable and unacceptable behavior have been breached.

It is with this background that one can better understand the hesitancy of the Socialists and Communists to actively proselytize among rural workers, the policy of largely ignoring the urban slum dwellers, and the other accommodations made in the interests of stability and status at the apparent expense of interests of the working masses.

THE DEMOCRATIC APPROACH TO POLITICAL DEVELOPMENT

Stability and continuity have been, until quite recently, the overriding characteristics of the Chilean political process, in an area where instability has generally prevailed. Until the 1950's new groups were incorporated into the political arena in a controlled, slow process, as they accepted the prevailing "rules of the game," which were set up by the elite.

The authoritarian, oligarchical system of the early 1800's was not immune to the dominant philosophical currents of European life, however, currents which emphasized liberalism, republicanism, and democracy since the mid-1700's. The fact that the independence movement came into conflict with the autocratic Spanish monarchy reinforced the "liberal" tendencies. One of the justifications for independence was the establishment of a more "republican" form of government, although this verbal commitment to republican government and to political democracy was a most inaccurate reflection of reality for much of the country's history. However, an ideal was established toward which the country has moved, especially in the twentieth century.

Nor could increasingly numerous and self-conscious middle sectors, generated largely by urbanization and economic differentiation, be easily ignored. For a variety of reasons the traditional Chilean leadership has maintained a more moderate stance vis-à-vis sharing political power with rising elements in the urban middle sector than elites in other Latin American countries. In addition, economic development and urbanization in Chile was experienced rather early, under conditions of relative prosperity in which resources could be shared without serious deprivation to the traditional elites. The chances for democracy in Chile were enhanced by some other early factors, such as the particular sources of immigration, the relative independence of the colonial period, and the lack of mineral riches in the early years of European conquest.

The trauma of opening the system to new groups was softened by the discovery and development of mining riches during a critical historical period. In general, this largely mineral-based wealth provided the resources for a relatively easy satisfaction of the basic demands of the newly organized and politically mobilized social groups. Most particularly it supported the growth of the public bureaucracy and expanded public services, especially education.

At the same time, the ease and rapidity with which the money flowed and economic growth occurred had serious consequences. The new economic growth brought very little improvement to the working class population, excepting the very small "labor elite" in the mines. By making possible the cooptation of leading elements of the urban white-collar and even emergent working class groups, the somewhat artificial economic growth increased the social and economic gap between the working class and the middle and upper groups. The political reflection of this has been the strong tendency of the middle sectors to support the maintenance of the existing order, at the expense of their occasional electoral allies in the working class. Instead of a coalition of white collar and urban workers pressing for a more egalitarian society and political democratization, the real coalition that developed worked to inhibit genuine working class participation and significant social change.

It should be remembered that by the late nineteenth century there existed constitutional provisions and legislation providing for virtually the same political freedoms and personal liberties as were found in the democracies of Western Europe and the United States. Few *formal* restraints existed on the exercise of most basic democratic freedoms. Informal restraints kept the system free from any serious influence by the masses, however. While economic development in the late 1800's provided more comforts for the tiny upper and small middle sectors, the masses (probably at least 75 percent of the population) remained at a subsistence level. The lack of access to education for both urban and rural working class also meant a fatalistic acceptance of subsistence conditions as justified and inalterable on the part of the masses. Other factors which kept worker participation in the political process to a minimum were: the lack of decent transportation and communication systems; the pattern of cooptation of potential mass leadership; the unwillingness of the parties, even of the Left, to proselytize among the lower classes, especially in the countryside; the concomitant lack of organization of the masses; and even overt governmental denials (and government condoning of private denials) of political freedoms and civil liberties to those not willing to accept the prevailing conditions and political arrangements.

The kind of quasi-democracy, or perhaps pseudo-democracy, that prevailed in Chile until the past two decades excluded most potential sources of serious dissent. By limiting real participation to those with some education and at least modest income and status, but at the same time tolerating token activity by and representation of the organized sectors of the working class, the Chilean political elites maintained a system, which featured remarkable stability and continuity. The only major political violence, due to strikes by miners and efforts to put them down (in the early 1900's), resulted in recognition of the miners as political participants. It should be noted that other working class groups were not actively trying to enter the political arena. At least partially because of political decisions, most urban workers were not organized, and virtually no rural organization existed. Thus, as long as the leaders of the Left could be placated there was little pressure on elites to open the system to the great masses of the population.

A number of major disadvantages of this pattern of development are readily apparent. While the system has satisfied most of the demands of the more advantaged and reinforced their positions vis-à-vis the rest of society, the exclusion of the working class majority even while maintaining the democratic facade has created a great potential for polarization and instability, one which has been exacerbated by the growing political awareness of the Chilean masses over the past several decades, combined with the presence of relative political freedoms of press, speech, assembly.

These limitations also undermined some of the support for the democratic system itself. The equilibrium of Chilean politics became increasingly unsteady after 1950 when the economic development altered. The hopes of those believing that economic development even without access to political power would improve conditions for the masses were frustrated. Even some white-collar workers saw their positions threatened unless quick remedies were found. The political consequence was an increased willingness of some middle sector groups to endorse major reforms, providing the base for the quick rise of the center-left Christian Democratic Party.

As mentioned earlier, a wide array of relative political freedoms essential to the functioning of a mass democracy have been present in Chile long before other conditions favorable to real democratic action have been present. The existence of these relative political freedoms has introduced some problems. Clearly, dissidents, usually the representatives of lower social status groups, have had a much easier task in organizing support, thus introducing pressures that might have been subordinated and more easily ignored in a less open system. On the other hand, it is quite possible that the presence of these political freedoms has also contributed to socio-political stability. By maintaining democratic forms, Chilean elites have been able to create an identity with the system among the masses. There is considerable evidence that the openness of the system has generated more support than opposition.

RECENT POLITICAL CHANGE—BREAKDOWN OF DEMOCRACY

One major theme of this essay has been that major socio-economic changes in Chile, particularly over the past two decades, have brought new pressures to bear on the traditional political institutions and political processes. The impact of these changes has been shaped by the particular historical framework, the style of political leadership, as well as the kind and amount of resources available for public distribution. The changes detailed here serve as excellent illustration of the point that basic patterns of political action are developed in response to a variety of pressures. In Chile, as elsewhere in the economically underdeveloped world, the twentieth century has witnessed the pressures of modernization and rising public expectations.

While no effort is made here to present an inclusive list of the various political impacts of recent developments, the major changes from the past patterns can be noted. Perhaps the most important and fundamental change in Chilean politics has been a sharply increased politicization of the population (e.g., the decision by party leaders to open the countryside to political agitation). The most visible indicator of this change is the increase in number of voters. As Table 3 shows, the electorate tripled in size in the period 1960–1973 and was eight times larger in 1973 than in 1938. In addition, the percent of the potential electorate casting ballots has tripled since 1920 and doubled since 1952. At present the percentage of Chilean voting age population casting ballots is about the same as for the United States; the Chilean voting record for congressional races is much better than that of the United States.

Another objective indicator of the same phenomenon is the sharply rising number of politically relevant strikes and work stoppages in the past few years. The growing disenchantment and better national organization of workers has been compounded by a much greater awareness of their political powers the result has been a rapid rate of shop takeovers, work stoppages, and strikes. Some of these are related to economic grievance, especially since 1971. Many, however, have little or no relationship to specific employer-worker grievances. For the first time in the history of the country, a national strike of farm workers took place in 1970; perhaps one-third of the nation's rural workers took part.

Another important change in the Chilean political climate is the polarization of the electorate and the political leadership. This polarization can be seen in a variety of ways; in the inflamed political rhetoric of the 1960's, the serious increase in political violence, the platforms of the major competing parties, and the results of recent elections.

The rhetoric of the past decade marks a clear departure from previous years. While Chileans are justly proud of a long tradition of relatively free speech and press, the brutality of the public debate, especially in the presidential campaigns of 1964 and 1970 and the congressional races of 1973, and the charges made by the different parties so inflamed the atmosphere, that middle ground has become increasingly tenuous. Even the leadership participated in the intemperance. The increase in violence, especially politically related violence has shaken the more privileged sectors of Chilean society. In the last six months of 1970 three assassinations of significant public figures occurred, including the killing of the army's chief-of-staff by a group of militant rightwingers. With a tradition of civil peace, moderation, and compromise of political disputes, this series of acts shocked most elitist Chileans. Since Allende's election the right wing groups have also organized their own urban terrorist organizations. The often-violent actions of these groups on both left and right convinced many, especially those with some stake in the maintenance of the traditional institutions and social relationships, that the system was breaking apart and that drastic action was necessary.

The physical take-overs of land and factories, the lockouts and production cutbacks, the physical attacks and threats on persons all represent serious violations of both the formal and informal "rules of the game" in Chilean politics. There has been a kind of internal momentum to the process in which one action generates a number of responses, which in turn prompts increasing counterattacks, in a vicious cycle of action and reaction, resulting in further polarization, distrust, and erosion of faith in normal democratic processes.

The drift and in some cases full-fledged flight to the Left by political leaders has a sound electoral rationale. The new voters in Chile and apparently some of the older ones as well, have found little to entice them toward the traditional parties of the Center and Right. The traditional parties of Right and Center before the mid-1960's could virtually always count on dividing more than half the electorate among their forces. They can now count on less than a half that percentage in a vastly larger electorate.

As late as the 1940's and 1950's the parties of the Right were not considering serious social change and were sending to high public office wealthy businessmen and large landholders. In the early 1960's these same forces initiated modest agrarian reforms to better conditions for rural laborers and colonize undeveloped lands. By the 1970 presidential campaign the most conservative candidate, actively supported by the parties of the Right, promised if elected to essentially consolidate the reforms of the Frei administration, reforms that in 1940 would have been viewed as communistic at best.

Even the Left moved leftward. From active cooperation with the representatives of small property and white collar groups in the 1940's, the Socialists, for example, moved to a point in 1970 where a significant body of support among party leaders was gathered for a doctrinal position favoring the "violent way" to revolution and rejection of democratic means of change. While more conservative than the Socialists, the Communist Party, too, moved to support positions regarded previously as too radical for the Chilean situation.

Equally interesting is what has happened to the middle of the spectrum. The Radical Party, which for decades claimed this ground, and the Christian Democrats, with center-left aspirations, have both been ripped asunder by splits between left and rightist factions. The Radicals were virtually wiped out, electorally, by the early 1970's. And while the PDC remained the largest party in Chile its candidate finished last in the three-man presidential race of 1970 and its regular 30 percent of the electorate is divided in congressional races between radical Social Christians and supporters of former President Frei, who wants alliance with the Right and who encouraged the military coup of September, 1973. (Frei, current spokesman for the party, has aggressively defended the coup and supported its goal of wiping out the political Left.)

In 1964, in a head-to-head contest between a moderate reformer and a Marxist opponent, Chileans opted for the former. To be sure, both candidates called for basic change in the socio-political order, but clearly the socialist, the late president Salvador Allende, was the more radical of the two. The campaign was intensely fought, with the Christian Democratic Party spending enormous sums of money in the successful effort. The candidate of the Left could not shake the charge that he was a Latin Stalin, and toward its end the campaign became little more than an effort by Allende to disclaim any "communist" ties. (The extraordinary personal popularity of Eduardo Frei, Allende's opponent, was another feature of the election.)

Frei's election was hailed in the United States as democracy's greatest hour in Latin America. His ideology and personality constituted a virtual prototype of what US policy-makers wanted for Latin America. Frei's victory in 1964 was followed by congressional elections in 1965 which gave him an unprecedented majority in the lower house and a near majority in the Senate.

That, however, was the last of his good fortune. The period 1965–70 witnessed a disastrous four-year drought in Chile, so bad that many farmers were forced to slaughter breeding stock. Agricultural production collapsed. The high hopes aroused by both sides in the 1964 election produced strong demands for a wide range of actions and benefits. These demands could not be met, especially since the PDC was unwilling to launch any major attack on the privileges and wealth of the upper social sectors. To make matters worse, the Frei Administration met unremitting hostility to their reform efforts in the Senate—from the Left because they wanted more basic changes, from the Right because of opposition to any serious changes at all.

By 1970 the PDC failure to fulfill their major reform promises had antagonized and alienated much of their support in the working class, both rural and urban. On the other hand, the more privileged recognized that a bona fide effort at serious change in some areas had been made and that even more was planned for the future.

Internally, the PDC itself was being torn apart over the extent and rate of change to be pursued. By 1969 a wing of the party had left to join the Left in dissatisfaction over the failure of the Frei government to more aggressively push for major changes. Other leaders in the party openly suggested a shift to the right in preparing the 1970 campaign, and many of these refused to work for the PDC when a spokesman for those advocating more rapid reform was selected as PDC candidate for president.

CHANGE AND PRESSURES UNDER MARXIST SOCIALISM

The processes of social and political change in Chile detailed in this essay came to their first climax in the election of 1970. The contest was extremely close, with Allende receiving just over one percent more of the vote than his closest opponent. What should be remembered, though, is that the vote for fundamental change was split between Allende and the Christian Democratic candidate, Radomiro Tomic, who often sounded more radical than Allende. The combined vote for Allende and Tomic was almost 65 percent of the total.

Usually reasonable men were forecasting anything from the development of a Stalinist dictatorship to the new utopia after the election of 1970. Clearly, the Left coalition brought the country close to neither alternative. In fact, the policies pursued were almost exactly what most acute observers were predicting even before Allende's election—given the context of comtemporary Chilean politics, recent trends, and the "personality" of the new leadership, and Allende's own policy statements concerning his intentions.

As expected, the new government was very serious about economic and ultimately social change. Extensive land reforms, including the apparent breakup of most of the large estates and in fact many fairly modest holdings as well, were pursued. Under heavy pressure from organized peasants and a leftist guerrilla force, the government almost haphazardly took land from previous owners and transferred it to the rural laborers, with a minimum of compensation. Nationalization of the banks and basic industries, especially those owned by foreigners (including copper mines, iron mines, auto assembly plants), reached the point that a recent observer estimated that close to 50 percent of the manufacturing and industrial sector came under direct government control. Through a complex set (and really strikingly clever use) of credit controls and general fiscal policies the new government secured a more direct control over even those economic enterprises not nationalized. In fact, government control of the banks and the extensive fiscal powers of the Chilean presidency were perhaps the most powerful weapons the Allende Administration was able to bring to bear on understandably reluctant owners and managers.

This reshaping of the Chilean economy is made more striking by the fact that it took the opposition largely by surprise. Opposition leaders clearly felt that Allende's weak electoral position and his minority support in both chambers of the legislature minimized his chances of any serious efforts to carry out his programs. Instead, the administration used presidential administrative and decree powers, very extensive under any circumstances, to even greater advantage than former president Frei (and he spared few efforts in this regard), bypassing the legislature on issues of considerable substance. Perhaps even more importantly, the administration dusted off a whole series of old laws, dating to the 1930's and beyond, that have served to justify moves desired by the new set of leaders. The opposition, without the necessary two-thirds majority needed to repeal the old legislation, was again helpless in watching continued change.

On the other hand, the government refused to bother most smaller businesses and even some larger ones in the face of worker pressure favoring intervention. Leading representatives of the Communist Party even publicly advocated "retiring" back to the private sector some of the "intervened" firms that were losing money under government control.

Although some had feared otherwise, Allende's commitment to political democracy remained firm. In the face of enormous domestic pressure from both foreign and domestic propertied interests, the new government pursued its objectives without changing the basic formal rules. Several serious charges were made by the opposition groups, however. First, it was feared the newspapers were to be subjected to at least informal censorship. The well-known hostility between Allende and the major newspaper chain in the country and several indiscreet statements by administration figures fueled this fear. Another charge was that the "worker's control" in the nationalized industries amounted to a not-too-subtle effort by the government to monopolize access to the unions and workers, cutting out the competitors for working class support. In addition, the opposition argued that the worker takeovers of numerous factories and hundreds of large and medium-sized farms were not only illegal but were actively encouraged by the government itself. Similarly, businessmen charged that they were the constant objects of harassment from government authorities, being asked to comply with absolute fidelity with laws that had never before been enforced, and which were being enforced in ways never intended by their authors.

These charges are difficult to evaluate in the absence of much solid evidence to support either side. Of the charges, the censorship issue seems to have least merit—the opposition press functioned openly and vitriolically under Allende. The second issue appears to have only slightly more substance. While there is every indication that the government actively proselytized among all workers, including those in the nationalized industries, there is little indication that political competitors were being unfairly squeezed. The same seems true for activity in the rural areas. During the nearly three years of the "popular unity" government there were nationwide municipal elections (1971), national congressional elections (March, 1973) and numerous special elections, with candidates of the Left winning some and losing some, with no more complaints of election irregularities than is normally the case.

The fact that political freedoms were so assiduously respected, even though the leaders of the Left recognized the minority status of their national support, raises questions concerning the other charges brought by Allende's opponents. Without doubt there were actions by the government that exceeded accepted political custom and procedure. The new regime included many, especially in the sub-Cabinet level positions, who had never held authoritative decision-making positions previously. These persons found themselves in positions which allowed them to punish those individuals and groups they held responsible for the country's problems—members of the class which had for centuries "exploited" the people represented by the new government. Especially in the face of overt hostility and efforts to subvert the programs of the new government, some of the officials in the new administration undoubtedly exceeded the accepted boundaries.

This is especially true in the area of economic relationships—the main target of change in the Allende years. There may well have been some official encouragement of factory and farm takeovers, but it is unlikely there was much, given the administration's efforts to minimize unnecessary conflict with the business classes and their allies in the military. The serious pressures for property takeovers came from the workers themselves, who often believed that government intervention as a result of worker takeovers would result in better wages, in the case of factory takeovers, or recognition of the *fait accompli,* in the case of land takeovers. Also, some pressure for takeovers came from the unions, which the Allende Administration was unwilling to confront in fear of losing any of its fragile base of support, and some radical leftists, such as the Revolutionary Leftist Movement (MIR) which apparently led some land invasions in the southern part of the country.

It seems clear that many of the most objectionable governmental restraints on the private sector were largely predicable responses to the well-organized opposition of other elite groups, especially economic elites. Every conceivable obstacle was placed in Allende's path. Businessmen discontinued operations rather than meet government demands for higher wages for workers or increased production. Large quantities of money was exported from the country. Investments were delayed. In the legislature, the combination of Christian Democratic and rightist groups formed a consistent majority in opposition to government initiatives. Even beyond that, there were constant references to the "constitutional duty" of the military to keep things from getting out of hand.

On the international scene, the expected opposition from Washington quickly developed, although the extent of United States obstructionism was surprising. Not content with stopping only American aid (with the significant exception of military assistance) and sharply cutting trade as well, the US leadership put apparently heavy pressure on friendly European governments and international monetary agencies to curtail assistance and purchasing of Chilean copper, with some measure of success in several instances. In addition, pressure was put on Chile's Latin neighbors to take actions essentially isolating the "Marxist sore," like Cuba. Given the potential impact of the Chilean socialist experiment for their own systems, the Latin Americans' unwillingness to respond to US pressures was surprising. For example, Venezuela, normally a devout disciple of Washington, joined the Andean Common Market (consisting of Chile, Colombia, Ecuador, Peru, and Bolivia), a grouping the US government has conspicuously opposed, given the strong restrictions on foreign investments included in its charter.

In general, the first steps on the "road to socialism" were strewn with obstacles. To achieve the proposed reforms, the country was asked to give much greater authority to the executive, vis-à-vis the legislature, and in terms of some personal freedoms. It was also asked to tolerate what amounted to near-confiscation of some forms of private property, and to support a much larger role for government in a wide variety of social and economic activities, among other changes. At the same time, the Allende government's actions followed almost precisely a path charted by previous administrations, especially the Frei government (1964–70). The "economic nationalism," the land redistribution program, the nationalization of certain larger business enterprises and most of the financial institutions, like most other major efforts of the socialist government, were merely extensions, although in many cases sharp extensions, of trends established 10 to 30 years prior to Allende's election to the presidency. For example, Sunkel notes that 20 percent of the GNP consisted of contributions made by state-run enterprises five years before Allende.[35] A greater government role in directing economic development was not unpopular among the masses of Chileans, given the levels of unemployment and underemployment, inflation, and small economic growth rates. The demands for greater "social consciousness" in the use of property were not considered unreasonable by most, given the pressures of the day.

Breakdown of Democracy

On September 11, 1973, almost exactly three years after Allende's election to the presidency, the military intervention that both Allende's supporters and opponents had been expecting since his election finally occurred. Very generally, the breakdown of Chilean democracy can be described as a result of overwhelming pressures on a weakened system at one particular point in time. The political opposition perceived its interests to be in the most serious jeopardy, with no recourse within the accepted rules of the game. And, finally, some elements of the military, the ultimate arbiter, proved willing to support the opposition even if it meant violation of historical and constitutional norms. Without question, the social and economic pressures on the Allende government were enormous.

When faced with the crucial choice of major change versus confrontation with established economic and social elites, the Frei Administration usually chose to respect the economic and political muscle of the propertied interests and their white-collar and military allies. The Left, ideologically commited to basic change and politically supported by the working class, had little choice in the matter, without betrayal of both ideology and political support.

The restraints of a democratic system, indecisiveness at the highest governmental levels, and lack of discipline among its supporters plagued the Allende administration, compounding its problems. Instead of establishing ground rules at the beginning, the administration was forced—by the rules of the Chilean system and by splits in the governing coalition—to make and remake the rules as they went along, especially in the area of economic policy. No owner of property felt safe from government action; virtually no saving and/or investment activities could be encouraged when the rules were constantly changing.

In addition, the government was unable to control its own supporters. An orderly redistribution of land, which would have assisted in maintaining reasonable levels of agricultural production, was disrupted by land seizures. In the cities, production was disrupted by work stoppages and plant takeovers. Perhaps most important, the crucial copper production was badly reduced by strikes and slowdowns, as the traditionally leftist miners feared losing their privileged "labor elite" status under the new regime.

The economic problems made even more difficult the process of improving conditions in the short run for the working class. Instead of having enough goods to allow a relatively painless redistribution of rewards to aid the less privileged, there were fewer, making the perceived losses of the middle sectors even greater than might have been the case, with the attendant intensification of opposition to government efforts.

It has often been said that democratic action is usually slow and inefficient. With an opposition majority in both chambers of the legislature, a vocal opposition press, and a weak electoral base, the Allende Administration discovered the disadvantages of the system. And when efforts were made to avoid the hostile congress or to punish recalcitrant businessmen, the result was predictable cries of "Communist dictatorship" and "breaking the rules." With the stakes so high, the polarization so complete, the pressures from all sides so intense, there was little surprise when the system collapsed. What circumstances prompted intervention at this point, and not before or later? At this point any answer is highly speculative.

My impression is that intervention came because of the success, rather than the failures, of the Allende government. By mid-1973, especially after the congressional elections of March, 1973, it became very clear to all that, barring intervention, the administration was going to survive, and perhaps even flourish, even in the face of enormous problems, intense opposition from a substantial sector of the population, and its own ineptitude. The assumption of many observers, especially Allende's opponents, was that his government would be tied from the very beginning by its several weaknesses. The economic disruption that quickly followed Allende into office only added to the conviction that even if the government maintained the executive offices, little serious action could be taken. This line of reasoning persisted in the face of successful administration efforts in restructuring some significant areas of national life. The enormous inflation, food shortages, continuing high unemployment, and housing shortages, led many to believe that the government was faltering and that it would lose even its base of support among workers.

The outcome of the congressional elections of March 1973 were crucial to the fall of the Allende regime. With all the social, economic, and political problems the government faced, the opponents of Allende, led by Frei, felt they could win a majority. The results stunned the opposition. The governing coalition significantly improved on their plurality of 1970 and surpassed even their share of the vote in the 1971 municipal elections. The message: even in the face of some of the worst social and economic conditions to face the country in modern history the government's strategy of shifting the pattern of rewards and punishments was paying off, politically. The support of the Left was growing, not declining. The administration's efforts were not going to be cut short but were instead likely to be redoubled.

Thus, the ingredients for extra-constitutional action consisted of the following elements. On the one hand, the executive branch could be accused of violating the fundamental rules of the political game, by encouraging and even initiating property takeovers, by stimulating class warfare, by punishing the propertied interests and even the white-collar groups through formal and informal government action. Economic disorder prevailed, with inflation virtually out of control, agricultural production reduced, many of the factories not producing, or on reduced production, even the copper mines periodically shut down. On the other hand, even this scene of domestic disorder was not eroding the Left's base of popular support. In fact, the conditions for much of the working class were improving, as the government forced wage increases, better work conditions, redirected food distribution to the working class neighborhoods, and in rural areas redistributed land to the workers. It became more evident daily that the government was not going to fall or be forced to cease its efforts to achieve major change in social and economic institutions and relationships.

Little is known at this point about the details of the intervention. Probably most important, it is known that the military acted under great pressure from the more privileged social sectors. In the weeks immediately preceding the intervention the major opposition political figures repeated with increasing frequency and intensity the traditional arguments used to justify military rule—the military must protect the society from disorder and a government which had broken the rules and is threatening to deprive some groups of their political and economic positions of influence.

The ferocity of the reaction to the socialist experiment was unexpected, both by foreign observers as well as by many Chileans. With the open support of the conservative political groups and the major wing of the Christian Democratic Party, the military undertook the "patriotic duty" of physically destroying the forces of the Left. Thousands of former government officials, union leaders, journalists, students, and apparently random selections of workers in their homes, have been executed. At least 100,000, and almost surely more, have been imprisoned. Massive book burnings have taken place, and even the more prestigious districts of the cities have not been immune to the arbitrary searches and seizures the military thinks necessary to eliminate the Left as a political force. The numerous political refugees from the dictatorships in Bolivia, Brazil, Paraguay, and elsewhere have either been executed or, more often, sent back to the governments of their native country, where they can meet the same fate but at another government's hand.

Again, it is too early to tell what policy direction the military will take, but the evidence suggests that the model will be the neo-fascist regime of Brazil. Already, the party representing the enthusiastic propertied interests has expressed an interest in forming the nucleus for a government-controlled political party, as in Brazil. The new governors have also indicated that the "nationalized" industries are going to be returned to their prior owners, and that even the previously foreign-owned enterprises are probably going to be returned to their original owners. (Two days after the coup, the copper market went up 5 cents a pound in London, and 8 cents in the United States.) Also, a scheduled pay increase for the nation's workers was cancelled, with the military explaining that it would be inflationary. Strangely enough, the lines for bread, meat, and other staples no longer are being formed in middle class neighborhoods, with the shortages being shifted to the working class neighborhoods. There seems little doubt that the new regime knows the source of its support base and will be working closely with the pre-Allende social and economic elites.

It would be dangerous to speak very definitively about the current situation, as of late 1973. There is simply not enough solid evidence available. In addition, the military faces numerous challenges to its current predominance. Probably the most serious threat to the current set of leaders is dissension within the military. There can be little doubt that the government's systematic campaign of terror, executions, and political repression is opposed by many in positions of influence within the military ranks. Whether the objectors can or will make their voices heard cannot be ascertained at this time, but the threat is definitely a real one.

Furthermore, there will be strong pressure from some sources, especially those groups represented by the Christian Democratic Party, the largest grouping in the country, to return the country to civilian rule, although without the "corrupting" influence of the Left—now banned and leaderless. The logical civilian leader would be the former president, Eduardo Frei, probably the only figure that might offer a faint hope for a return to the previous constitutional arrangements, but who would almost certainly have the military at his back to "guide" him in this critical period.

FOOTNOTES

1. Bruce Russet, H. Alker, Jr., K. Deutsch, H. Lasswell, *World Handbook of Political and Social Indicators* (New Haven: Yale University Press, 1964), pp. 18–20.

2. Andre Gunder Frank, *Capitalism and Underdevelopment in Latin America: Historical Studies of Chile and Brazil* (New York: Monthly Review Press, 1969).

3. *Chile and the United States, 1880–1962* (University of Notre Dame Press, 1963), p. xx, quoting from Pike and Donald Bray, "A Vista of Catastrophe: The Future of United States-Chilean Relations," *The Review of Politics,* XXII; 3 (July, 1960), pp. 393–418.

4. James Petras and Maurice Zeitlin, "Agrarian Radicalism in Chile," *British Journal of Sociology,* XIX; (August, 1967), pp. 578–586.

5. Inter-American Development Bank, *Socio-Economic Progress in Latin America: Social Progress Trust Fund, Tenth Annual Report,* 1970 (Washington, 1971), p. 147, AID, *Latin America Economic Growth Trends* (Washington: US Government Printing Office, December, 1969), p. 14.

6. The above data are from Comité Interamerican de Desarrollo Agrícola, *Chile: tenancia de la tierra y desarrollo socio-economico del sector agricola* (Santiago, 1966) p. 204 and Merwin Bokan, Morton Pomeranz, *Investment in Chile* (United States Department of Commerce) (Washington: US Government Printing Office, 1969), p. 53.

7. The study was conducted by CIDA (see note 6), with the findings summarized in "Agrarian Structure in Seven Latin American Countries," by Solon Barraclough and Arthur L. Domike, in *Land Economics,* XLII; 4 (November, 1966), pp. 391–424.

8. From a speech by President Salvador Allende, October, 1971, quoted in Norman Gall, "Copper is the Wage of Chile," in American Universities Field Staff, *West Coast South American,* XIX; 3 (August, 1972), p. 1.

9. The above data are from an excellent discussion in James Petras, *Politics and Social Forces in Chilean Development* (Berkeley: University of California Press, 1969), pp. 27–34; from

the United Nations Economic Commission for Latin America, *The Economic Development of Latin America in the Post War Period* (Santiago, 1963); and from Atilio Borón, "Political Mobilization and Political Crisis in Chile, 1920–1970," a paper presented to the Eighth World Congress of the International Political Science Association, 1970, p. 28.

10. Petras, *Politics and Social Forces*, p. 16. *El desarrollo industrial de Chile*, paper presented by the Chilean government to the Latin American symposium on Industrial Development sponsored by the United Nations Economic and Social Council (ST/ECLA Conf. 23/L. 46, February, 1966); similarly, a nine country ECLA study of 1961, which included most of the population of Latin America, suggested that the share of the manufacturing employment in all urban employment declined from 32.5 to 27 percent. "The Demographic Situation in Latin America," *Economic Bulletin for Latin America*, VI; 2 (October, 1969), p. 74.

11. Eduardo Hamuy, *et al., Educación elemental, analfabetismo y desarrollo económico* (Santiago: Editorial Universitaria, 1960), p. 10.

12. Robert L. Ayres, "Economic Stagnation and the Emergence of the Political Ideology of Chilean Underdevelopment," in *World Politics*, XXV; 1 (October, 1972), pp. 37–38, quoting Pan American Union, *Statistical Compendium of the Americas* (Washington, D.C., 1969).

13. *The Political System of Chile* (Boston: Houghton Mifflin Co., 1966), p. 23.

14. "Change and Frustration in Chile," in Claudio Veliz, ed., *Obstacles to Change in Latin America,* (London: Oxford University Press, 1965), p. 110.

15. Pike, "A Vista of Catastrophe", p. 284.

16. For an elaboration and justification for using this basic model, see Richard N. Adams, *The Second Sowing* (Scranton: Chandler Publishing Company, 1967) and Adams, "Political Power and Social Structures," in Claudio Veliz, ed., *The Politics of Conformity in Latin America* (London: Oxford University Press, 1967), pp. 15–42.

17. Petras, *Politics and Social Forces*, pp. 168–174.

18. Figures are from 1960 census data; "service sector" refers to personal services.

19. Lagos, *La concentración del poder económica* (Santiago: Editorial del Pacífico, 1965), p. 23; Petras, *Politics and Social Forces*, p. 53; Comité Interamericano de Desarrollo Agrícola (CIDA) *Chile: Reforma de la tierra y desarrollo socio-económico del sector agrícola* (Santiago: Hispano-Suiza Ltda., 1966).

20. Petras, *Politics and Social Forces*, p. 289.

21. *Ibid*, p. 50.

22. Gilberto Flores, "Bureaucracy and Political Stability: The Chilean Case," (unpublished M.A. thesis, University of California, Berkeley, 1968), p. 26, quoted in note 31 of Ayres, "Economic Stagnation", p. 44.

23. See the study of Chilean labor unions by James Morris, *et. al., Afiliación y finanzas sindicales en Chile,* Instituto de Organización y Administración (Santiago: Editorial Universitaria, 1962).

24. *Ibid.*

25. Petras and Zeitlin, "Agrarian Radicalism in Chile."

26. Note especially the following: Eric A. Nordlinger, "Political Development: Time Sequences and Rates of Change," in *World Politics* (April, 1968), pp. 494–521; Leonard Binder, *et al., Crises and Sequences in Political Development* (Princeton: Princeton University Press, 1971).

27. Gil, *op. cit.,* p. 39.

28. Francisco José Moreno, review of Ben G. Burnett, *Political Groups in Chile: The Dialogue Between Order and Change,* in the *American Political Science Review,* LXV; 4 (December, 1971), p. 1199. Figures on defense spending are from Agency for International Development, p. 39.

29. Samuel P. Huntington, *Political Order In Changing Societies* (New Haven: Yale University Press, 1968), p. 4.

30. Alain Joxe, *Las Fuerzas Armadas en el sistema político de Chile* (Santiago: Editorial Universitaria, S.A., 1970), translated from the French by Narciso Zamanillo, Section B, Part III.

31. Petras, *Politics and Social Forces,* pp. 288–289.

32. *Ibid.,* pp. 291–292.

33. Robert L. Ayres, "Some System-Level Implications of Elections in the Communes and Provinces of Chile, 1957–1967," (unpublished Ph.D. thesis, University of North Carolina at Chapel Hill, 1970), chapter 2, section D, pp. 135–154.

34. James Petras and Maurice Zeitlin, "Miners and Agrarian Radicalism," in Petras and Zeitlin, *Latin America: Reform or Revolution?* pp. 242–247.

MEXICO

Continuity and Change in an Institutionalized Revolution

GUY E. POITRAS

Mexico has developmental problems like most of the
Third World, but unlike some Third World nations it
has taken dramatic steps to come to grips with its
problems. The Mexican Revolution left an indelible
stamp on contemporary Mexican politics and
development; it brought political stability and economic
growth to Mexico at the expense of ideals concerning
political democracy and social justice.

Schmitt views Mexican politics as an example of
limited democracy in a developing nation. The mixed
outcome of the Revolution is that effective and stable
political institutions were created without allowing
independent popular involvement. The Mexican
political system is led from the top and, because it may
do things for the people rather than with them, it has
not turned out to be as responsive to popular pressures
as many had hoped. In contrast to India and Chile
until 1973, Mexico has followed an authoritarian
variant of democratic political development.

DETERMINANTS OF MEXICAN POLITICAL CHANGE:
POLITICS AS A DEPENDENT VARIABLE

The Revolution was a landmark for Mexican politics.
It not only led to new political institutions; it also
established the autonomy of these institutions from
social forces within Mexico and to a lesser extent from
military and economic control outside Mexico's
borders.[1] These new institutions were able to chart the
course of events and not just reflect them as they had
during the pre-Revolutionary period. Politics became a

means to harness social forces to new goals. The military, the church, the large landowners and the foreign businessmen all came to feel the force of a vigorous and independent political order. Indeed, critics of contemporary Mexican politics bemoan what they view as an emergence of the old pattern—politics subordinated to the more powerful social and economic interests in Mexican society.

As Schmitt suggests, revolutions are infrequent. More to the point, however, is that no one knows for sure why a few nations are buffeted by revolutions but why most are not. Although there is little agreement on how best to understand such complex and fast-moving events, it can be suggested that a revolution, in its most ideal sense, is a major and radical transformation of politics and society, probably through violent means. Whatever their unique features, revolutions indicate that existing political institutions are unable to cope with intense crises of equality, complexity, participation, and heightened expectations.[2]

In Mexico, the pre-Revolutionary system sowed the seeds of its own demise by fostering imbalanced development. Rapid economic growth, increasing inequality, and political repression could not be contained within a political order that was subservient to narrow and unyielding interests. The political order of pre-Revolutionary Mexico was, despite outward appearances, really quite weak and unable to adapt to growing pressures that it had precipitated. Even with the Revolution, however, not everything changed. New elites, new institutions, and new goals did not mean the end of authoritarian paternalism in the exercise of this increased power of political institutions. Nor did inequalities disappear by revolutionary edict. Control and stability in post-Revolutionary Mexico depended on maintaining some of the continuities of the old regime.

Colonialism

Colonialism was one of several factors which helped to determine the course of the Revolution and subsequent political development of the nation. Like India, Nigeria, Syria, and Chile, Mexico was once a colony of a European power. Mexico's legal independence came long before its economic or political independence. The persistence of this limited neo-colonialism may have had much to do with the growth of antiforeign nationalism in Mexico that fueled revolutionary inclinations.[3]

The Spanish were late-comers to Mexico. Before Hernando Cortes set foot on what is now Mexico, an assortment of diverse Indian civilizations such as the Aztecs, Mayas, Zapotecs, and Toltecs forged intricate empires. Much to their astonishment, the Spanish conquerors found elaborate cities, impressive structures, and systems of writing.

The Colonial period lasted about three centuries, from the early 1500's to the early 1800's. During this time, the Spanish replaced the Indian empires with their own, based on a state bureaucracy and the church. Large estates called *haciendas* came under the control of an oligarchy of the church, the large landowners, and colonial officials including the military. The Indians were not systematically killed off as they were in North America. They were needed as slaves and workers on the large estates. As much as anything else, this fostered a dual society of colonial rulers and Indian slaves. Despite their lowly position, the Indians and their cultures survived. The colonial domination of Mexico never meant cultural extinction for the Indian. Instead, a racial and cultural mixing took place over many years. The result was a *mestizo* culture, an uneven blend of different cultures and races that exists to this day.

Things changed slowly if at all in colonial Mexico. But things were happening in Europe that had important consequences for Mexico. Embroiled in European politics and pushed to the wall by a waning economy, Spain could do little to prevent Latin America from drifting toward independence. Mexico, like many of its colonial neighbors in Latin America, gained its legal independence in 1821.

The struggle in Mexico for independence was not a social revolution. The expulsion of the colonial elite by *creoles* (Spaniards raised in Mexico) was a power play more than a genuine rearrangement of Mexico's internal situation. True, *creole* leaders of the independence movement like Father Miguel Hidalgo had more in mind for Mexico than just independence from Spain. Hidalgo sought also to activate the Indian and *mestizo* (mixed-blood) poor into a fanatical force against Spain and the elites. Hidalgo failed because he also attacked the *creoles* instead of aligning with them against Spain. Somewhat more conciliatory toward the *creoles* was the strategy of José María Morelos who tried to unite all Mexicans against colonialism in Mexico. Despite the eventual failure of both Hidalgo and Morelos, the continued resistance of other leaders as well as the rise of constitutionalist forces in Spain combined to bring independence to Mexico. In 1821, Mexico began its legal independence under the treacherous leadership of Augustín de Iturbide as "emperor." The social and economic system had not changed. And for the next fifty years, Mexico suffered from political decay, foreign intervention and the loss of much of its best territory.

Political Decay and the Search for a Nation

Mexico gained its independence before it was able to govern itself wisely. For much of the nineteenth century, Mexico was unable to develop effective national institutions, to construct a consensus to which all groups would adhere or to fend off neo-colonial domination over its internal affairs. Throughout this turbulent period, one man— Antonio López de Santa Anna—ruled over this uncertain country or waited in the wings for his next try at it. Santa Anna and an array of other leaders preyed on the national treasury for individual gain. Governments, but not policy directions, were overturned with predictable regularity. Internal weakness invited external intervention during these unsettled years.

Santa Anna's first major external challenge came over the Texas question. In the early 1830's, the influx of Americans into Texas put great pressure on Mexico. To head off an independence movement in Texas which threatened to deprive Mexico of valuable lands, Santa Anna led his troops north in 1836. His celebrated victory at the Alamo in San Antonio was offset by his conclusive defeat at San Jacinto. Texas won her independence.

A decade later Mexico again sought to defend its northern territories against an expansionist United States. The United States wanted not just the annexation of Texas but of California as well. In 1846 the United States went to war against Mexico. Only two years later, when the Treaty of Guadalupe Hidalgo was signed, Mexico had lost more than half of its territory in the north. Several years later, Santa Anna, back in power but in need of money, sold what is now southern Arizona to the United States. Internal decay and foreign domination demonstrated that Mexico was not truly a nation capable of internal order or of defense against external threat.

Eventually, the plight of Mexico provoked the opposition of bourgeois liberals like Benito Juarez. With the goals of Morelos in mind, the liberals promulgated the 1857 Constitution which embodied many classical democratic views. But to implement their reforms, the liberals had to fight for three years against the Church and its oligarchic allies. In 1861, Juarez and his army marched triumphantly into Mexico City.

The triumph was short-lived. After the War of the Reform and the years of chaos, European nations were demanding reparations for economic losses suffered by their nationals. But unlike Britain and Spain, France under Napoleon III wanted more than just reparations—Napoleon also wanted to build an empire in Mexico. In early 1864, Napoleon sent Maximilian and Carlotta to preside over the empire. Maximilian entertained the illusion that Mexicans wanted him to reign as emperor. But reverses for Napoleon in Europe and a waning interest in empire in the Americas left Maximilian and Carlotta amidst a hostile population led by the Liberal opposition. In 1867, the dream of empire evaporated. Maximilian, Napoleon's naive tool, was executed in Queretaro and his wife Carlotta fled to Europe where she died many years later, hopelessly insane.

Benito Juarez, a full blooded Zapotec Indian, tried to put together the pieces of a nation. He sought to build roads, communications, and other elements of infrastructure. He tried to run the government on the Liberal tenets of classical democracy. Mexico was unprepared for democracy. The death of Juarez in 1872 left a vacuum which neither weak institutions nor other Liberal leaders were able to fill. Economic stagnation and political incoherence became more prevalent. Finally, in 1876 Mexico's experiment with classical democracy came to an end with a military coup led by General Porfirio Diaz. The rise of Diaz was to loom large for Mexico's future.

The Porfirian Era of Right-Wing Authoritarianism

The next 34 years of personalistic, paternalistic and authoritarian rule under Porfirio Diaz was a prelude to the Mexican Revolution. As a conservative reaction to the doomed experiment of the Liberals and the Reform of 1857, the Porfirian era substituted law and order for chaos, economic development for stagnation, stability for the political game of "musical chairs," and repressive authoritarianism for the ideals of constitutional democracy.

To be sure, the Porfirian dictatorship contributed to Mexico's economic development and to the Mexican Revolution. Commercial, industrial and mineral development surged forward with high rates of growth, benefiting a small elite within Mexico as well as large foreign interests. Repression of Liberal opposition and of popular demands for justice imposed a kind of artificial tranquility which heartened those looking for a secure investment climate. Diaz's rural police repressed both the political discontent of the Liberals, who abhorred the dictatorship, and the simpler and more fundamental needs of the peasants. Industrialization and scientific progress promoted by a few were the goals of the government. Justice, democracy, and equality were denigrated.

This pursuit of uneven and inequitable development was sustained by an assortment of groups which had much to gain from Diaz's policies. Diaz formed a network of loyal military governors and local political chiefs who served the arbitrary will of the system throughout the country. They were suitably rewarded for their services. Diaz also relied upon the support of rural potentates whose large estates (*latifundas*) were as large as one million square acres. This concentration of land in a few hands was accentuated rather than reduced in the Diaz period. Also, during this time, the role of the foreign investor flourished with new importance in the areas of land, mining, utilities, and the like. Finally, a staff of close advisors armed themselves with an inhumane and ruthless philosophy of survival of the fittest to justify their policies of peace and prosperity for the few at any price.

The policies of the Diaz dictatorship eventually hastened the collapse of the system. Uneven economic development in which a few gained enormously and the many suffered led to discontinuities which could not be reversed within such a rigid system. The growth of the economy at this time mobilized enough workers into national life to make them aware that they were not being justly dealt with. Land tenure patterns held back productivity and made life harder for the peasant. Repression of the middle-class Liberals only stiffened their resolve to fight Diaz by any means at hand. Intellectuals rallied the small middle class and Liberals throughout the country to the political and economic grievances held by many against the Diaz government. Opposition from bourgeois Liberals who demanded democracy, not to mention growing dissension of the workers and the peasants who were becoming more aware of the inequalities of the system, gained force at the turn of the century. But the unintended effects of Diaz's policies provided the opposition with the weapons to fight the government. By partially mobilizing Mexicans within a system of uneven development that did not hold out hope for the many, the Diaz government did much to guarantee its own fate. Its rigidity, its subservience to vindictive and narrow elites and its policies of selective development mobilized the intellectuals and the peasants against a system which excluded them politically and economically.

Economic Change

As Schmitt suggests in the introductory chapter, economic change in the developing world may have profound consequences for the politics of countries like Mexico. With industrialization, technology, investment, and education, pressures build up in the political system. In Mexico's case, economics became one of the major pressures for the Revolution.

The basic failure of the Diaz regime was not only that it had little regard for democracy, but that it strove for economic growth without economic modernization. The distinction between economic development and economic modernization is useful here. The former involves high growth rates with increasing productivity, investment, and consumption. But economic development tells us little about who gets the benefits of this growth. Economic modernization means that the benefits of development are being distributed to all segments of society—a process that failed under the Diaz regime. The benefits accrued to the small oligarchy and to foreigners. These groups saw little if any need in catering to the rising expectations of the masses for a more just distribution of the benefits of economic development. Diaz used police and military repression to put a lid on mass discontent over visibly unfair policies. By pursuing limited economic development without economic modernization, and by using political repression to serve the interests of rigid elites, Diaz unintentionally forged an alliance between the poor who wanted economic justice and the middle class who wanted political democracy. As Schmitt points out, economic development can lead to political instability. In Mexico, it did this, and more: it led to a major overhaul of the entire system, changing not only the people in power, but the system of power.

Cultural Change

Economic change may have been more important than cultural change in setting the scene for the Mexican Revolution. And yet the changing patterns of culture in the developing nations help shape their politics. At the time of the Revolution, and even today, Mexico's culture is different from that of the other nations discussed in this book. As a mixture of Hispanic and Indian culture, it is not as ancient as China's; not as fragmented as India's or Nigeria's; and not as unified as Chile's. But like all these, Mexico's culture played a part in the shaping of the Revolution and in the contemporary politics of Mexico as well.

Mexico in the late nineteenth century was a mixture of cultures and races. The few pure-blooded Spanish descendants sat at the top of the system. Their ideas and attitudes owed more to Europe than to the Americas. At the bottom of this dual society were the Indians. They were from many different tribes and civilizations; they spoke many different languages. The term "Indian," then as now, is not just a biological one. It is also a cultural description involving loyalty to certain cultural traits that were alien to the non-Indian elite.

As Indians became integrated into the economy as laborers they became more aware of their position in the national culture, and their resentment grew. The rise of the *mestizo* (or mixed-blood) signalled the gradual nationalization of the culture. Racial mixing led to an amalgamation of attitudes. Moreover, and largely on an individual basis, Indians started to speak Spanish as well as their own tongue, to wear shoes, to eat flour, and to take on the cultural traits of a small *mestizo* middle class. These changes were significant, but they should not be exaggerated. Most Mexicans were Mexican in name only; most were rural peasants who remained outside the mainstream of national life. They only became part of the nation at the peak of revolutionary fury which gripped Mexico decades later.

The Diaz regime lasted as long as it did perhaps just because of the Indian cultural fragmentation. The Indians of Mexico were not culturally unified. They were isolated in rural areas either as rural laborers or as virtual slaves. Divided since the Spanish Conquest, they could not have provided a united front against the Diaz government even if they had wanted to.

As Schmitt notes in the introduction, a lack of trust among a nation's citizens makes political development more difficult. This lack of trust was also characteristic of the vast number of Mexicans at this point in history. Indians have always been suspicious of strangers. Strangers have been the conquerors and the exploiters, so this seemed to be a reasonable response by the powerless. But Indians also had only limited trust among themselves, and this greatly restrained their efforts to make them a powerful political force. Even today rural peasants in Mexico greatly distrust strangers as well as their national government in Mexico City.

Fatalism is also a force in traditional cultures, and was present in the different sub-cultures of Mexico at this time. After years of domination and perhaps as a consequence of Indian culture itself, most Mexicans during the pre-Revolutionary period were quite fatalistic. At most, they hoped just to be left alone. They had no concept of the nation or their active role in its political life. This served the status quo quite nicely. Fatalism and repression helped the old oligarchy who ran things. Clearly, the revolution was an extraordinary event if for no other reason than that it gave hope that the powerless could bring about change, whether in land reform, democracy, or whatever. Despite the cultural disposition to accept their lot in life, the Revolutionary leaders mobilized millions of Mexicans, who finally saw that there was more to gain than to lose by challenging the Diaz dictatorship.

Personalism has long been associated with Latin American culture. In countries like Mexico at this time, loyalty to a person took precedence over loyalty to the nation or its institutions. People were loyal to Benito Juarez or Porfirio Diaz, not so much to what they might have stood for. Anyone with great personal dynamism might have a political following; those without it did not. Mexicans followed personalities, not causes. In Mexico, this simply indicated the weak loyalty most Mexicans invested in their government or in their nation. Madero, the leader of the Mexican Revolution in 1910, had a certain personal attractiveness. Even Pancho Villa in the north and Emiliano Zapata in the south were revolutionary leaders with large personal followings.

Related to personalism in Mexico was the idea that, in a closed, hierarchical society, a *patron*, or boss, would take care of his *peon*, or worker, in exchange for the latter's loyalty and service. This is simply called the *patron* system, and it permeated much of Mexican society and politics then as it does even today. This relationship of unequals served the status quo for many years because it helped the elites to control the masses. But, again, the Revolution did not abolish personalism and the *patron* system. It just set up a variant of this system under a new political order.

Cultures change much more slowly than economics. This was the case in pre- and post-Revolutionary Mexico. But it is easier to see now why things did not change very rapidly before the Revolution. And yet one can also see the possibility of this cultural setting disintegrating under unusual strains, especially from the economic sector.

The Sequences of the Mexican Revolution

How rapidly a political system copes with certain crises in a particular sequence has a lot to do with how the system will develop and how democratically it does so. Gradual change makes democratic development more likely. As will be seen later, although Mexico's Revolution was not a complete break with the past, neither was it a gradual political evolution. As an abrupt and violent circumvention of old institutions and elites, the Revolution was uninspired by any coherent ideology of democracy and development. The Revolution itself was carried on between regional leaders, who had little regard for national identity and did not sincerely care about pluralist democracy. Mexican followers of revolutionary leaders were loyal to charismatic leaders, not to a unified system of democratic beliefs. They were fighting for private gain more than a preconceived view of what Mexico should be.

The sequences of the Revolution also undercut the chances of gradual democratic evolution such as that of India and Chile. According to Leonard Binder, democratic political development for the most part follows these sequences: a national identity emerges between the people and their government; legitimate and effective institutions are set up to cope with problems; a party system is then constructed to link the government and its people; the people finally are allowed to participate in running the government through elections.[4] In Mexico, this sequence was not generally followed. First, violent, unstructured participation of growing numbers of Mexicans came before any sense of national identity. Nationalism was not the same as loyalty to institutions and processes for coping with Mexico's problems. National identity emerged about the same time as, or a little later than, viable political institutions during the 1920's and 1930's. The party system, organized from the top down, was organized in the late 1920's. Popular participation in the party came in the late 1930's, but this was more a case of manipulation from above than genuine power wielded from below. Things are done *for* the people rather than *by* them. Still, this sequence of events did not completely rule out a more limited brand of political democracy.

The Revolution itself began meekly enough. Francisco I. Madero, a classical democrat from the landed elite, led a political revolt of the middle classes against Diaz's heavy-handed tampering with the 1910 presidential elections. With surprising ease, Madero's forces took over the government. As far as the classical bourgeois democrats were concerned, the Revolution should have stopped there. All they really wanted was more responsive democratic government. But for nearly a decade, Mexico had no national government; it became an expanding arena of violence between quarreling and ambitious revolutionary leaders throughout regions of the country. As the conflict broadened and deepened, new demands for social and economic reform became more prominent. Men like Pancho Villa and Emiliano Zapata, different as they were, wanted power or land for themselves and their *peones*. But few saw, during this violent period, that Mexico would have to be reconstructed on new terms if these popular demands were to be met.

After one out of every seventeenth Mexican had been killed, the Revolution passed through a different stage in 1917, with the drafting of the Constitution. This marked the beginning of the end of anarchistic violence and unstructured participation. The quarreling elites and their followers apparently concluded that they had more to gain than to lose by agreeing on some common rules by which the new order should be governed. The 1917 Constitution, for all its promises and ideals about Mexico's new future, was most important for making the president the *patron* of a new order. It set in motion a painful process of stabilizing the country and institutionalizing its politics. As Schmitt warned earlier, revolution may help a country to develop politically and economically or it may result in unreconstructed chaos and decay. With the Constitution, Mexico's course was by no means predictable, but it was an important stage in the development of Mexican politics. Although its problems were by no means vanquished, Mexico was now to undergo a period of sustained development.

STRATEGIES OF CONTROL: POLITICS AS AN INDEPENDENT VARIABLE

Whatever their differences, the Chinese and Mexican Revolutions both signalled the supremacy of politics. More specifically, both led to the building of power in autonomous institutions. The drama of the supremacy of politics is still quite vivid in China today. In Mexico, powerful and autonomous institutions play an indispensable role in promoting broadly supported goals of economic and social development. Nevertheless, the Mexican government since 1940 appears to be less radical and more cautious than it once was. The course of Mexican policy has been to cooperate with, rather than to subordinate, larger economic forces. The development of stable, legitimate institutions has resulted in some gains and liabilities of the new political order.

Personality of Leaders

Schmitt emphasizes the importance of individuals in molding the politics in developing nations. The absence of strong institutions in the immediate post-Revolutionary war period threw the burden of building a new political order onto several key generals who ascended to the office of the presidency. Each general as president had his own ambitions and views of post-Revolutionary Mexico. And yet each also accepted the assumption that Mexico badly needed to create legitimate political institutions with a firm power base.

Following Carranza, under whose administration Revolutionary factions hammered out the 1917 Constitution, Obregon left his own distinctive mark on Mexico and the presidency. Between 1920 and 1924, Obregon had very little to work with. The country was economically prostrate; old elites continued to lurk as potentially dangerous enemies of the tentative Revolution. Without strong institutions to curtail Revolutionary generals, Obregon had few resources for reform. He was concerned mostly with consolidating gains, restoring economic normalcy and nurturing a sense of national identity.[5]

Elias Calles followed Obregon as president. Like Obregon, he was able to leave his own imprint on the emerging political order. Calles adhered to his own personal views of what should be done, but he was able to do what he did because Obregon left government institutions on a firmer base. One of Calles' personal preoccupations during his time in office was the virulent persecution of the Church. As one of the three anti-Revolutionary elites, the Church was the target of many provisions of the 1917 Constitution. It was Calles' personal inclination to implement these provisions in a ruthless and direct way. He expelled foreign priests, seized Church property, forbade clerical activity in politics and attacked parochial education. Sensing a battle for survival, the Church struck back. But as the Cristero rebellion in the late 1920's demonstrated, the Church and its supporters could not effectively challenge the dictates of a more powerful and autonomous political order.

More than any other single revolutionary leader, Calles was personally responsible for creating the one-party system.[6] His personal motives behind this important step were not completely altruistic. To perpetuate his control over Mexican politics regardless of who was president, Calles patched together a Revolutionary alliance of regional military commanders, peasant leaders, businessmen and the like. What Calles did not foresee, however, was that the party he forged would take on an autonomous life of its own. Power in the system was not a matter of who institutionalized the party but who occupied the presidency within the party structure. When Calles sought to institutionalize the party, his own personal power was doomed.

The political weight of such personalities as Obregon and Calles is undeniable during this period. But one should not ignore or underestimate the importance of President Lázaro Cárdenas (1934–1940) as an illustration of personal power. While Calles left his personal stamp on Mexico as a conservative of the Revolutionary tradition, Cárdenas made his personality felt as a radical improviser within a political order that Calles had begun to institutionalize. Cárdenas was a unique and vigorous leader who took seriously the Revolutionary rhetoric about nationalism, social justice, the rights of the downtrodden, and political involvement. Although Cárdenas could not do it alone, he was personally responsible for initiating the process by which the military's political role was radically reduced. Moreover, he launched the largest land reform program in history and sealed the fate of the traditional large estate owner. He created the mechanism by which workers and peasants were politicized by their leaders. And he boldly struck at the foreign domination of key national industries like oil production. For all his personal impact on Mexico at this time, Cárdenas was careful to refine and elaborate national institutions. His was not just a case of one-man, charismatic rule. Due to his personal power and that of his predecessors, Cárdenas helped to make the dominance of personalism less important in an increasingly institutionalized political system.

Ideology

If one accepts the notion of ideology as "a set of ideas about politics that seeks to explain, justify and motivate," then the Revolution produced an ideology, although not as coherent as China's, to account for and gain support for what had transpired and what was about to take place in Mexico. Much of the fighting came out of pragmatic rather than abstract desires of the participants. The revolutionary leaders often used slogans and ideas to rally support for their own interests. But with the drafting of the Constitution in 1917, the revolutionary ideology became "codified" myth. It sought to suggest why the Revolution happened and to justify what was going to happen.

With pragmatism came some lack of coherency in the revolutionary ideology, but its slogans, (such as "Mexico for the Mexicans," "Land and Liberty," "Universal Suffrage, No Re-Election") evoke powerful feelings for many Mexicans. The ideology of the Revolution embraces many sentiments, but strongly emphasizes nationalism, democracy, land reform, economic modernization, and welfare.

The 1917 Constitution is a modern constitution that embodies these ideas. This means that the Constitution guarantees not just political, but economic and social rights. As Schmitt notes, ideology can diverge quite a bit from reality in many cases and the Mexican ideology, embodied in the Constitution, is no exception. But the ideology of the Revolution gives a legitimacy to the system which it would otherwise lack. Moreover, the ideology, slogans, and myths of the Revolution receive unwavering support from Mexicans. This is an important source of regime support, but most Mexicans view their leaders and their policies with cynicism.

It is easier to say that the Revolutionary ideology has aided the legitimacy of the government in the eyes of most Mexicans than it is to account for how the ideology has affected the policies of the Mexican government since 1920. Unlike China, there is no spokesman for the ideology. Unlike China, the revolutionary ideology of Mexico is not totalitarian or puritanical. It is an amalgamation of pragmatic alternatives. It permits free enterprise as long as it is accountable to public goals. It permits party competition, but the revolutionary party wraps itself in the flag as the true spokesman of the Revolution. Nearly every president has been able to justify what he has done within the scope of the Revolutionary ideology, even though some of their policies have contradicted the ideology. The Mexican Revolutionary ideology, then, does not spell out what the government is to do and how the people are going to relate to it; rather it legitimizes the system in the eyes of most Mexicans even though they may not always be very happy with those in power.

Bureaucracy and Political Parties

Political institutions capable of coping with new problems and new participants are essential for the political development of changing societies. Demands on government that outrun the capacity to meet them hold forth the dark possibility of political decay or chaos.[7] How Mexico went about building its political institutions is probably one of the most important stories of the post-Revolutionary period.

Unfortunately, it is easier to discuss democracy in general terms than it is to evaluate Mexican political democracy in particular. In fact, outsiders have a hard time fitting Mexico into preconceived political classifications. Besides Schmitt's "limited political democracy," one may find such terms as "semi-authoritarian" or "one party dominant, semi-competitive" as cumbersome attempts to take into account Mexico's unique political set-up. Strong criticisms levelled against Mexico's bureaucracy and party system call into question how democratic Mexico really is.[8] Given this ambivalence, let us examine how the Mexican political system took shape and how its major institutions—the government bureaucracy and party—evolved.

In the first place, the government and the revolutionary party are sometimes indistinguishable: at the highest levels, they are virtually one and the same. The president of the Republic is always the head of the government; he is also the head of the Institutional Revolutionary Party (PRI). This blending of government and party should be kept in mind as we look at the formation of Mexican politics between 1920 and 1940.

The Revolution left Mexico damaged politically and economically. The old political system was unable to satisfy the demands of new groups seeking power. Unrestrained participation by many led to wide-ranging violence. There were no institutions that could cope with this revolutionary wave, and revolutionary leaders were forced to overlook their differences and to organize sufficiently to start building a viable institutional framework.

As Obregon, Calles and later Cárdenas fashioned the political institutions of Mexico, control and stability slowly gained the upper hand over unstructured participation and regional autonomy. In other words, viable national institutions gradually took hold and began to establish control from above rather than to leave unchecked wide open participation from below. The post-Revolutionary leadership felt that chaos had to be replaced by an institutional base that could bring together different and sometimes opposing factions within the Revolutionary movement.

The Revolutionary party to be a successful institution had to combine the powerful and the powerless; it had to bring together those the government could not antagonize and those who had little to lose. In 1928, Calles forged an alliance of military leaders, who had considerable residual power from the Revolution. It took time before this very loose and decentralized alliance could be brought under the more centralized control of the national *patron*—President Calles.

Under Cárdenas, the party was reorganized, but the trend of centralizing the power under the presidency was reinforced by Cárdenas. To secure his own power against Calles and his followers, Cárdenas ran off Calles' supporters in the party, as well as in the military and the state governments, if they were reluctant to fall in step behind the new president. He also carried one step further what Calles had done in the area of group representation within the party. He set up the political party with four major sectors, each covering a broad functional area. The military sector, the popular sector (made up of the middle class), the peasant sector, and the worker sector were all for the first time represented within the party. Unlike Calles, who catered to the middle classes, Cárdenas sought to bring into the evolving system the participation of the lower-class peasants and workers. Until then, there had been no systematic way of representing them within the new institutions born of the Revolution itself. But Cárdenas was careful not to slight the sensitivities of the military, whose support was crucial. Instead, by including the military as one of four sectors within an institutional setup, Cárdenas set in motion the process by which the Mexican military would be gradually eased from a position of political power. The military was no longer the most important force in Mexican politics; it was simply one of several competing groups. Moreover, Cárdenas took steps to curb the political ambitions of the military by professionalizing them. He retired the old revolutionary generals who wanted to play power politics under the old rules and he gained the loyalty of the younger officers. Promotions became based on merit, not political maneuvering. Unlike Syria, where the military plays a role as partner with the Ba'thist Party, the Mexican military today concerns itself with community development and relatively nonpolitical matters. Its budget has shrunk from 40 percent of the total government budget in the 1920's to 7 percent in recent years.[9] As the system gained legitimacy and became more effective, the role of the Mexican military declined. By 1940, the military sector had been phased out of the party's organization. Strong civilian institutions had filled the vacuum.[10]

During the 1920's and 1930's, the presidency became the mainspring of power between the government and the party. Like much of Latin America, the Mexican executive branch under the president was the government. The legislature was easily dominated and the courts were not very independent. But unlike many developing countries, the president and the presidency in Mexico were not the same thing. The presidency was the most powerful institution in the Mexican government. A president like Calles could be powerful, but his power was grounded in the office, as his run-in with Cárdenas in 1934 proved. Starting with Obregon, the presidency came to rely on a growing number of agencies and ministries, as well as the party apparatus. Today there are over a dozen ministries and over 400 semi-autonomous agencies charged with some role in the development of the country.

The presidency, the PRI, and the bureaucracy all share the exercise of public power. But despite the generally recognized fact that the Mexican system emphasizes control and stability directed from the top, it is not exactly clear which of the three—presidency, party and bureaucracy—runs the show. Let us look at each of these divisions briefly and outline the diverging opinions about each.

The PRI inspires contradictory views. One is that the role of the PRI serves mainly to bring different power groups together. By integrating important groups such as laborers, the middle class sectors and the peasants, it helps to stabilize and harmonize Mexican politics. In return, these groups get out the votes for the PRI. This view sees the PRI as an arena of trade-offs where power "trickles down" from the elite but also "bubbles up" from the masses.[11] A less charitable view of Mexico's one-party system is that it is an authoritarian tool of the president. As an extension of the government, the party is used by the president to control various groups.[12] The third view is something of a compromise; it holds that the president makes the final decisions but that the party and its three sectors (the workers, peasants and the middle classes) make demands and provide support.[13] Whichever view one finds most attractive, the PRI lies at the center of controversy about who rules Mexico and who does not.

Since it is somewhat unusual, the organization of the party calls for more inspection. Each sector of the party must be officially recognized by party leaders. It is hard to be sure if official recognition is a source of power alone or if the power of the various groups—measured by their size—gains the recognition. In any event, the sectors—popular, peasant and labor—are creations from above. Each sector has its own recognized confederations of smaller interest groups. For example, the main labor confederation is the Mexican Workers' Confederation (CTM) which Cárdenas virtually created in the 1930's.[14] Today the CTM represents about 44 percent of all unionized workers, although only 10 percent of all workers belong to any organization, whether it is the CTM or something else. Like the other sectors, however, it is not the rank-and-file who are directly represented in the councils of the party, but rather the leaders of these organizations.

The one thing that has not changed since the Revolution is the *patron*-like organization in politics. In other words, labor leaders tell their followers what is best for them. The leaders owe their jobs to the party not to their followers. Organizational democracy is a rare virtue, especially in Mexican politics.

For the most part, the organization of the peasant sector follows the same pattern.[15] Again, the peasants, or more accurately their leaders, who rarely are peasants themselves, gained political importance under Cárdenas' reorganization of the party. Of the sector organizations within the party today which claim to represent the peasant, the National Peasant Confederation, or CNC, is the largest. As a collection of smaller peasant organizations from semi-collective farms and rural workers, the CNC gives voice to peasant demands. And the peasant is better off now than he was before the Revolution. But most peasants do not belong to any sector organization. Moreover, peasant leaders rather than peasants themselves are influential with the government. Due to the nature of the peasantry, its isolation, poverty and ignorance, peasant leaders are more likely to do things for the peasants rather than with them. As it has turned out, leaders of peasant organizations within the PRI are the tools of governmental control over peasants rather than independent and militant representatives of their interests.

In contrast to these two sectors, the third party sector, the "popular sector," is largely made up of middle class bureaucrats, and business-men.[16] Representing as it does a more economically potent class, the National Confederation of Popular Organizations (CNOP) is politically and numerically stronger than the other two sectors. It also has a conservative view of the Revolution. It is likely to favor political stability and economic growth rather than social change and greater lower class political involvement.

The Mexican party organization best serves stability and control. It evolved from the days of Calles and Cárdenas as a device to bring about popular consensus. In Mexico, consensus is a preoccupation of the elites from within the government and from the various sector groups. Consequently, the party must seek, if not always find, unanimity before it can take any new path. Such caution, unless overridden by a bold president like Cárdenas, gives a conservative tinge to Mexican politics.

What about the voters in this one-party system? Do they have any say about "their" party? About 14 million voters, or 64 percent of those eligible to vote and about one out of every four Mexicans, cast ballots for the 1970 presidential election in which the PRI's Luis Echeverría won as expected.[17] But elections in Mexico are not used to decide who will win, since most voters go for the PRI which wins national offices almost without fail. The people do not actively make decisions about politics and government in such contests. Instead, they participate in a way that helps them reaffirm that the PRI is their party and that, by implication, the Revolution is theirs as well. Elections are for reaffirmation of the faith, whatever the actual failures of the system to give the common folk what they want; they are a ritual for renewing the system's legitimacy.

Of course, a voter who feels that the PRI is not "his" party may turn elsewhere. But the choices are not very compelling. He may defect to the National Action Party (PAN), made up of conservatives and pro-clergy sympathizers, or to the Socialist Party (PPS), a sort of leftist satellite of the PRI itself. It is only in a few local races that these parties can hope to challenge the hegemony of the PRI. As long as the PRI can sustain the illusion that it does things for the people (if not with them), then the individual voter, however powerless he may really be, may find more reason than not for sticking with symbolic reaffirmation of the Revolution by supporting the PRI.

Aside from the sector organizations, who supports the PRI at the polls? The party draws its strength from all segments of Mexican society. But it does best with the lower classes.[18] This at first may seem odd.

The middle classes have benefited most from the government's policies while the lower classes have received substantially less. Why, then, do they vote for the PRI? Again, the answer may lie with the symbols rather than the substance of the Revolution. The PRI has fostered the image among the masses that it virtually is Mexico and the Revolution. The loyal supporters of the PRI are not voting on the performance of the regime, but on their approval of the idea of the Revolution and its promises for them. It is the more affluent such as the urban businessmen who are less likely to show unwavering loyalty to the PRI.

The Presidency

We have noted that the President of the Republic is head of the party and head of the government. Combining the institution for achieving power and the institution for ruling brings to the president unchallenged authority in Mexican politics. Even more than the President of the United States, the Mexican president is the *patron* of his people, the father of his country for a six-year term. Despite the 1917 Constitution's adherence to the separation of powers, federalism and other institutional formalities found in the United States, presidential dominance was encouraged by constitutional provisions and indeed flourished in the post-Revolutionary construction of the new political order. And yet there is some difference of opinion about the real power of the president.[19]

One view holds that the president is nearly all-powerful, although not equivalent to a Nasser or a Castro. But this view claims that the president and his closest associates are not accountable to the party or the people. The president does things on their behalf but without their meaningful involvement. Despite this uncompromising view of the Mexican presidency, there is something to be said for it. The president clearly has the last if not the first word about the basic decisions in Mexican national politics. No one dares to defy him publicly although it may be possible behind the scenes to delay matters or circumvent some of his preferences.

A contrary view of the presidency as an all powerful institution maintains that the presidency is stalemated by the party and the bureaucracy. The presidency, in this view, tries to hammer out policies which please the major contending groups. This view sees the presidency as an arbiter in the political machinery that presidents created before 1940. The president cannot do anything he wants; rather he must maintain a delicate alliance of opposing interests.

Another perspective views the president as not restrained from bold action by his role as a balancer of interests but by a large and ponderous public bureaucracy. For those who advocate this view, the paradox for the presidency is that the more powerful he becomes and the more things he wants to accomplish, the more he must surrender his power to the bureaucracy if anything is to get done. It is not so much that the bureaucracy dictates to the president the major outlines of public policy. It is more likely that the power of the bureaucracy lies in its ability to fill in all important details of a public policy. In this respect, Mexican bureaucracy is not all that different from the political and perhaps corrupt bureaucracy in other developing countries. The president's chances for controlling the bureaucracy are going to be greatest in ministries and top level positions in semi-autonomous agencies. They will be less likely in the day-to-day realm of applying policy. This view holds, then, that the Mexican presidency is caught in the common trap of bureaucratic power.

Finally, the president is seen as simply an administrator—the head technocrat. Although personalism has not died in Mexican politics, there seems to be a noticeable difference between the charismatic presidents before 1940 and the rather faceless bureaucrats and technicians who have dominated the office since then. Ruiz Cortínes perhaps best typified the new breed, but most of the other presidents since 1940 have been of the same mold.

Whether we like it or not, the precise relationship between the Mexican presidency, the PRI, and the public bureaucracy is unclear. What is clear is that these three institutions share power. Growing as they did from a legitimate overhaul of the system, and doing things in the name of the people if not with their close participation, these basic institutions have shown remarkable stability. That these institutions have not forsaken elitist control is their most glaring contradiction with Revolutionary ideology.

Education

The institutionalization of Mexican politics brought with it an elite consensus and control from above. Although Mexico prizes stability over democracy in its institutional arrangements, it has generally been regarded as a benevolent government which does things for people but with only their limited participation. The tradeoffs of a bureaucratic party and a political bureaucracy have been important for the achievements of the system and the way in which it is developing Mexico. Recalling that education is one of the devices of political control in developing countries, let us turn briefly to the role that education has played in Mexico since 1920.

Schmitt notes that the educational policies of governments in developing countries like Mexico may have a mixed impact on society. Education is not just the development of skills; it is the learning of attitudes about politics and other things. By properly training young people and indoctrinating them with new ideas, education not only cultivates human resources but has direct results on the politics and development of countries.

Before the Revolution, Mexican education was the privilege of a handful who attended parochial schools. The Church had always been a major institution for educating the elite. But it was a traditional and elitist enterprise that contributed little to Mexico's development. Most Mexicans were uneducated. Their apathy served the country's underdevelopment.

The Revolution changed all this, much to the chagrin and outright opposition of the Church. In the 1920's, the government made its first move by setting up a Ministry of Education. The government replaced the doctrines of the Church with the doctrines of the Revolution in the curriculum of the public schools. They had to start from scratch. Children had to learn loyalty to the national government, patriotism, nationalism, faith in the precepts of the Revolution. As in China, but with less intensity, the government leaders correctly saw the crucial nature of starting with the attitudes of the young. With this would come support for what the government was trying to do. Uncle Sam became a convenient villain, and xenophobic nationalism became commonplace. Slogans and symbols were systematically ingrained.

The secularization of the schools and the political indoctrination that came with it were perhaps inevitable. But the government knew that it could not stop there. Aroused and aware young people could cause trouble for a government unable to meet their rising expectations. The government had to develop skills that could directly help Mexico develop economically. The Mexican government therefore established compulsory education, set up a system of technical and vocational schools and a number of state universities in addition to the large National University of Mexico just outside Mexico City. The Mexican government claims to spend about one-fourth of its federal budget on education of all kinds. But education beyond the sixth grade is still restricted to a few and a college education is all but beyond reach except for the sons and daughters of the Establishment. Large, poor families find it necessary for their children to drop out of school before achieving functional literacy so that they can bring in some income or help the family in some way. However, it is hard to learn while hungry, and despite earnest government efforts to the contrary, education is hard to bring to the rural people, the lower classes, and the great mass of Mexicans.

Mexican education is striving to modernize its curriculum. For the most part, it has been too bound to the traditional and humanistic disciplines which had little to do with training citizens for productive jobs. Even today, there are too many lawyers being graduated and not enough agronomists. Moreover, the role of education in shaping attitudes has left some things largely unmodified, especially cultural values that have survived since the Revolution.

Education has been able to stir loyalty to the nation among the middle classes, but it has not yet been able to improve the attitude of most Mexicans toward their government. The most highly educated, the college students, are prone to sometimes violent opposition to the government and its policies. But most uneducated Mexicans have the attitude that they cannot influence the paternalistic government. These attitudes and the failure of the government to modify them in its education program have aided the stability of the system but are testimony of the failure of the Revolution. Fondness for the Revolution but mistrust of its leaders is common among most Mexicans.[20]

Mexican education does little to reverse other values as well. Submission to authority of a *patron* is as basic to Mexico today as it was earlier, except that the *patrons* have changed. This attitude that the *patron* is one's protector and provider can but reinforce paternalistic government. *Machismo* is another value that dies hard. A man who is *macho* is one whose claims to dominance are unquestioned in sexual, social, and political matters. He is likely to be flamboyant, aggressive, sensitive to insult, quick to take revenge, and prone to violence. *Machismo* and its close relative, *personalismo,* provide continuity to Mexican attitudes about authority.

Mexico invests much hope and many resources in its education. Although not as doctrinaire as China's, Mexico's system of education hopes to bring forth the new Mexican. Although not as puritanical and moralistic as China's, Mexico's educational system does try to bring a sense of one's duty to the nation. The failure of this Revolutionary goal is unfortunate. Education has been important in Mexico's strategy for development. It is more practical, more broadly based, and more purposive than that of some developing countries. Since it has by no means closed the gap between the rich and the poor, its redistributive qualities are quite modest.

Economic Development

We will now turn to the broader economic aspects of the Mexican Revolution. Economic development lies at the center of contemporary Mexico.[21]

The pre-Revolutionary economy rested on agricultural subsistence for most Mexicans and large estates for a few. In this traditional and closed system, the old oligarchy pretty much ran things. But during the years of Porfirio Diaz, another kind of economy was superimposed on this one: a colonial economy based on extractive products and geared to rapid but limited development. As the limited modern sector and the broad primitive sector went their own ways, the economy grew out of alignment. Greater and more obvious disparities began to surface. The submission of Mexico's resources to foreign interests and to a narrow band of the privileged became a point of contention among the nationalists. Growth was not bad; however, unbalanced growth became untenable.

From what has been said earlier and from what others have argued elsewhere, the economic causes of the Revolution loom large in any retrospective of Mexican development. More to the point in this respect is an examination of the economic aspects of the Revolution after the violence had subsided and the building of a new system began to unfold. And although the economy has never been far from the central concerns of the revolutionary leaders, other problems have vied for its limited resources. For example, Wilkie sees Mexican history since 1920 in four parts.[22] First the "political revolution" occupied the government leaders from 1910 to 1930. During this time, the government used the resources at hand to propagate new institutional life. Later, in the 1930's, Cárdenas led a "social revolution" the goal of which was to use the institutions already set up to foster social change among the peasants and urban workers. Social justice and equality came to the forefront of government policy. With the end of major political change in Mexico and Cárdenas' exit from office in 1940, the "economic revolution" gained preeminence. The main priority from this time on was not equality but growth, and the Revolution entered its conservative phase.

The "economic revolution" was nothing more than a gradual shift in public policy, but its impact has been dramatic and controversial. Its most dedicated advocates were the presidents who followed Cárdenas into office—President Avila Camacho (1940–1946) and President Miguel Almeán (1946–1952). Together, they lured Mexico away from the radicalism and collectivism of the Cárdenas years. They sought and got a larger and more pampered place for business, both domestic and foreign, in Mexico's development while slimming down the government's commitment of large expenditures for the lower classes.

The policy of catering to business and the demands of investors brought with it some economic bright spots in Mexico's recent development:[23] growth rates since 1940 have been, on the whole, quite high, hovering around 7 percent in recent years.[24] Booming with a 3.5 percent annual population growth rate, income per capita is not the highest in Latin America, but it is above average ($765 at current prices) for the region. Unlike Chile since 1970, Mexico has been for some time an attractive place to invest capital. Government leaders rely quite heavily on the private sector for capital, investment, manpower, and ingenuity.

Unlike some Latin American countries, Mexico especially since 1940, looks quite favorably toward private enterprise. Business and the private sector spur the nation's growth. On the other hand, public leaders are quick to note the faults of private business in a developing country. So, today, the public sector in Mexico tries to make up for the timidity or short-run goals of the private sector with an involvement that is vigorous but not overriding.

From the time that the post-Revolutionary picture began to stabilize, the public sector was expected to take the lead. Its job was not just to manage and guide the economy, but in some cases, such as oil and transportation, to own some of it as well. The Revolution struck at the foreign domination of the economy that Porfirio Diaz encouraged. And while Obregon and Calles sought to bring about the financial stability and national monetary system Mexico had lacked for many years, it was not until Cárdenas that a frontal assault was made upon foreign ownership in Mexico.

By the time of Cárdenas' term of office in the 1930's, the national government was confident enough of its own power to attempt nationalization of key resource industries such as oil. Under the 1917 Constitution, oil was owned by the government. With Calles, who was for foreign investors, this provision went unenforced. Cárdenas was hardly inclined to go so lightly on these groups. But to defy the United States would take courage. Cárdenas felt the national identity of the people and the legitimacy of the government would give him the support he needed to make such a dramatic move. Behind the question of the seizure of foreign-owned oil industries in 1938 was really a broader one: Mexico could only develop economically if it had control over its own basic resources. Nationalism, independence and development all came together in Cárdenas' controversial seizure of the oil industry. By doing this, Mexico did not intend to say to foreign investors that their help was unwanted or unneeded. What it did say was that Mexican development was to be in the hands of Mexicans and that foreign investors had to accept the conditions laid down by the government if they wished to do business in Mexico.

The nationalization and Mexicanization of the economy was an important step in the development of the country. But under the more growth-minded governments since 1940, it also became clear that the government was not hostile to foreign business. True, many businesses had to be owned on a 51 percent basis by Mexican nationals. But others were not so restricted and there were and are ways of getting around such restrictions. Today one can find such ironies as "American Airlines de Mexico" on billboards in Mexico City. Clearly, an accommodation of the public sector and the private, both domestic and foreign, has led to the economic growth Mexico has enjoyed for many years. Even so, foreign businesses must justify their investments by how they will help Mexico.

For better or worse, the Mexican leaders see economic development in terms of industrialization. It is not surprising then to note the tremendous growth of the manufacturing segment of the economy and the relative stagnation of the agricultural sector. With movement from light to heavy industries such as steel, the disparity between urban, industrialized Mexico and rural, primitive Mexico becomes harder to overlook. The government has done more for the modern sector too. Its policies on taxation, tariffs, banking regulations and direct investments have helped promote high growth rates. The government has also met the modern private sector more than halfway by creating "mixed enterprises" with both public and private participation. According to some Mexican intellectuals, such policies have enthroned the business middle class and their foreign counterparts as the new elite.

The rise of the government-business elite was quite at odds with the tendencies of the Cárdenas years. Between 1934 and 1940, Cárdenas showed more interest in agriculture than in business. Little land had been distributed to the landless until Cárdenas came to power. During his term in office, Cárdenas seized and distributed more uncompensated land to the peasants than any president has since that time. He distributed 45 million acres to 750,000 families in some 12,000 settlements.[25] Cárdenas pursued land redistribution in two ways: first, he parcelled out land to individual peasants to work and to eke out an existence; second, he preferred to distribute land through a system of collective farms called *ejidos.* Under this system, the land of the *ejido* could not be sold, only used, by the collective members. In fact, the government owned the land. Although the *ejido* went back to Indian communal traditions and was supposed to encourage grass roots democracy among the peasants, this program, a uniquely Mexican creation, served to augment the government's control of the peasants.[26]Moreover, the *ejido* has never been an economic success: productivity has lagged; credit is still scarce, and the peasant is as dependent as before on the blessings bestowed by the government.

At the time, Cárdenas' agrarian policies broke the old-style, hacienda system and provided a way by which the peasants could become involved in the new national system, directive and authoritarian as it was. By pursuing land reform the way he did, Cárdenas could strike at his enemies and enhance the power of the new *patron* in the countryside. Since this period, the peasant's status has declined. His more affluent urban compatriot has been blessed with economic abundance compared with his own fortunes. The middle class of the modern sector is a different world from the peasant's. Moreover, although agrarian reform (meaning land redistribution) continues to this day, the peasants get smaller plots of the least desirable land. The large tracts of good land have not been divided up into smaller plots. This might be inefficient anyway. They have instead fallen under the growing power of large, efficient agri-businesses run on modern precepts. So, today in Mexico, 5 percent of all farms occupy half of all the land.[27] Official representation of their leaders within the PRI has not appreciably helped the peasant. It has not brought the peasant the land he wants or the education and resources he needs.

For all the growth and development of the modern sector, the most glaring deficiency has been and continues to be the neglect of the rural situation. The Mexican economy is more dynamic than Chile's; it is more advanced than Syria's and more industrialized than China's. Yet, Mexico has been unable to reverse the trend of inequality, and the rural problem has become more acute.

The rural poor, by far Mexico's largest and most important problem, are "marginal" to the urban modern sector in both a political and economic sense. The "marginal" Mexican is without power and without the benefits of economic growth. He is illiterate, ill-fed, and ill-housed. His situation is as desperate as it is perennial. He is part of the primitive and underdeveloped hinterland of Mexico which is exploited by a form of internal colonialism. Urban and rural Mexico are not separated, despite their gross inequalities. One preys on the other. This internal colonialism perpetuates the inequality and uneven development that originally impelled Mexico toward its Revolution.[28] Just as Mexico was and still is in some ways an economic colony of the United States, internal colonialism benefits the affluent urban Mexican at the expense of the rural poor, thereby perpetuating inequities and underdevelopment.

Recent figures show that about 30 percent of the work force is unemployed or underemployed in some temporary, "make-work" job.[29] People flock to the cities from the countryside to find a better life, but one-fourth of the unemployed live in Mexico's largest metropolitan area, Mexico City. Unemployment and underemployment are related parts of a larger whole. Mexican developmental policy has been more wrapped up in growth and capital accumulation than it has been in justice and human resources. The Mexican Revolution set the targets of development, but the system has not yet been able to achieve all of its goals consistently.

The Mexican government is aware of, if not always willing to discuss openly, its problems of economic development and modernization. Imbalanced development, growth without redistribution, paternalistic policies set from above, the urban-rural cleavage, continued dependence on foreign markets all sound like the same problems Mexico had before the Revolution. Certainly, Mexico has made advances. But the Revolution has not wiped out the economic problems which provoked it, nor has the government unlocked the gates of comprehensive political and economic development. Building the system and using it for new purposes have brought political stability and economic growth, and to a lesser extent a better life for more Mexicans than ever before. But unless Mexico can more effectively grapple with its economic problems, and especially the question of uneven development, economic growth could bring forth severe political and social problems that could threaten the system.

THE ONE-PARTY, LIMITED-DEMOCRACY APPROACH TO DEVELOPMENT

The Mexican Revolution, its institutions and policies, have had their costs and benefits. One of the things that the Mexican Revolution and its institutionalization have brought about was a very rapid break with the initial obstacles to national development. The Revolution curbed foreign domination, set up a more benevolent and broad-based government, helped more Mexicans have something better or at least hope, and brought political stability and economic growth to Mexico. This required that old enemies be eliminated or "de-fanged;" that new groups be created and coddled; that new demands be recognized and acted upon. In other words, the Revolution lowered the barriers to political and economic development.

But revolutions and their development always have a price that has to be paid later. In Mexico's case, the extremes of revolution led to a reaction in which control from above through a party and government bureaucracy took precedence over spontaneous participation and instability. The institutions were set up before the masses were given some approved participation. Although Mexico's system is not quite as mobilized as China's, political participation by the masses is still ritualistic. The PRI and the government bureaucracy are operationally remote from most Mexicans. Doing for the people what they cannot do for themselves is the attitude of the government leaders. It is better than the attitude of the pre-Revolutionary period, but it ill-serves the revolutionary political ideals of Mexico.

By embracing all major groups, formally or informally, the system has a kind of superficial cohesion. As long as not too many want to get involved or want to change the rules, groups with opposing interests can agree to take less than they might want. But elite consensus between government, president, party, and sector leaders does not solve problems of those who are not in this elite. The capacity of the government to reach out to those who lie beyond this inner circle is surprisingly feeble. The stability of such a system has also depended a great deal on the frailty of human character. Political opposition outside the inner circle has often sold out its principles in exchange for the largesse of the system.

University students have become a hard core base for opponents of the regime. In 1968, violence between the government and students flared up in the headlines of the world press around the time of the Mexico City Olympics. Some of the student leaders are still in jail. With the carrot of cooptation and the stick of not-so-subtle repression, the opposition, if indeed it exists at all, is limited to bandits, guerrillas, militants, students, and the young. The system is not about to collapse under their weak resistance, but all this is symptomatic of the failures of the Revolution.[30]

In summary, the Mexican path of one-party development spawned by social revolution has gained political stability and economic growth at the price of democracy and social justice. It would be preferable if Mexico could accommodate all of these goals. With its scarce resources and impressive problems, the Mexican system serves better some of those goals than it does others.

Does the peculiar path of Mexican development harbor ominous warnings for the future? Again, we must fall back on speculation. The ruling elite in Mexico admits that some problems are harder to solve than others. But they do not seem very troubled at all about the choices they have made or the priorities they have established. The orthodox view accepts in a satisfied way the basic assumptions of government policy. That is, the elite sees Mexico's development best served by economic growth and political stability. In recent years, Wilkie finds in government spending a more "balanced" revolution in which the government tries to pay more attention to pressing social problems. But the basic faith in growth and stability remains unshaken. Diaz Ordaz (1964–1970) was particularly fond of the prevailing orthodoxy. He turned back attempts to democratize the PRI led by Madrazo and pursued unswervingly the goal of economic growth. Luis Echeverría, his successor, seems less dogmatic but still finds nothing wrong with the basic strategy of development that the Mexican government has pursued in recent years.

Less sanguine about Mexico's persistent problems are the views of the regime's critics. They point to the growing alienation of the young and the intellectuals. They do not fail to note the corruption and privacy of government run for the few and by the few. They denounce the repression of radical alternatives by such methods as cutting off the supply of newsprint to dissenting newspapers or taking sometimes brutal efforts to suppress radicals. They are forever harping on the clear failures of the system to greatly expand the benefits of growing productivity (which more than doubled between 1940 and 1965) to the "marginal" lower classes whose real income actually declined in the 1950's.[31]

Decades after Cárdenas' efforts on behalf of social change, the income of Mexico remains grossly maldistributed. The top 10 percent gains about 40 percent of all income while the bottom 10 percent gets about 2 percent. About 70 percent of all Mexican families earn only about 30 percent of the national income.[32] Despite Wilkie's claim that the government is seeking more balance between spending on growth and spending on justice, he concludes that ". . . [p]er capita expenditure for social change . . . has ranked much less importantly than economic administrative expenditures since 1940."[33] Until 1970, the government on the average invested about 66 percent of its capital in manufacturing, transportation and communications and only about 36 percent in social welfare and agriculture.[34]

Such failures to uplift those in poor circumstances has not led to widespread and active resistance to the government. For one thing, those in power have effective ways to control such activities. For another, people may be cynical about what happens, but this may encourage apathy and a feeling of powerlessness. Moreover, whatever the failures of the Revolution, the Mexican people do not question the basic legitimacy of the Revolution or its institutions. Although it doesn't meet everyone's expectations, the economy's growth and the slight improvement in real income for urban dwellers is hopeful. Although opportunities are limited, they still exist.[35]

CONCLUSION

The politics and development of Mexico have followed a unique course. Like China, revolution in Mexico broke down the inadequate institutions of the old regime. But unlike China, Mexico's Revolution is not totalitarian. In China, where political participation is not voluntary, there has not been the pragmatic compromise within the party that one can find in the PRI and in India's Congress Party. There is nothing quite like the Chinese Cultural Revolution in Mexican history.

With the Mexican Revolution long established, there are still many Mexicos. But the political centralization and institutionalization in Mexico stands starkly against the earlier chaos of Nigerian politics and the ethnic tribalism which lay at its root.

Like Syria, Mexico was at the mercy of events outside its borders. But unlike Syria, Mexico pursues modernization and independence without an important military establishment. Unlike Chile, Mexico has not yet confronted the problems of participation and justice within the system. On the other hand, Mexico is not going through the trauma of instability and radical change that Chile has since 1970: Mexico went through this in its own way during the 1920's and 1930's. Moreover, democratic political development in Chile did little toward bringing about high economic growth rates. In Mexico, with a one-party system and with favored position for business, the economy has grown consistently since 1940. In India, the price of a decentralized, democratic and stable political system has been to give up the hope of broad and sweeping economic changes. In Mexico, with its radical change apparently behind it, the government has sought growth and stability before democracy and justice. Revolutionary politics has been diluted under an institutionalized system.

Mexico's path of development has its advantages and disadvantages. However, even measured by its own standards, the success of Mexico's approach is limited. Perhaps it would be unwise to expect much more. Problems of elite rule, external dependency on the United States, internal colonialism, uneven economic development, and social injustice plague Mexico, although perhaps to a lesser extent than other developing countries. The Revolution will not soon alleviate these problems, but it has provided a unique strategy for coping with them.

FOOTNOTES

1. Samuel P. Huntington, *Political Order in Changing Societies* (New Haven: Yale University Press, 1968), pp. 315–324.

2. Leonard Binder *et al., Crises and Sequences in Political Development* (Princeton, N.J.: Princeton University Press, 1971), p. 74; Eric Nordlinger also develops this analysis in his "Political Development: Time Sequences and Rates of Change," *World Politics*, XX; 3 (April, 1968), pp. 494–520.

3. For a brief discussion of historical background to the Mexican Revolution, see Frank Brandenburg, *The Making of Modern Mexico* (Englewood Cliffs, N.J.: Prentice-Hall, Inc., 1964), ch. 2.

4. Leonard Binder *et al., Crises and Sequences.*

5. Frank Brandenburg, *Modern Mexico,* p. 67.

6. Calles' efforts to build a party system are recounted in Robert E. Scott, *Mexican Government in Transition* (Urbana, Ill.: University of Illinois Press, 1964). A very critical analysis of the party system today may be found in Kenneth F. Johnson, *Mexican Democracy: A Critical View* (Boston: Allyn and Bacon, 1971).

7. Samuel P. Huntington, *Political Order,* ch. 1.

8. Kenneth F. Johnson, *Mexican Democracy,* ch. 3.

9. Edwin Lieuwin, *Mexican Militarism* (Albuquerque, N.M.: University of New Mexico Press, 1968).

10. For further reading on military politics in developing countries, see Samuel P. Huntington, *Political Order* and Eric A. Nordlinger, "Soldiers in Mufti: The Impact of Military Rule upon Economic and Social Change in Non-Western Societies," *American Political Science Review,* LXIV; 4 (December, 1970).

11. Robert Scott, *Mexican Government in Transition.*

12. Frank Brandenburg, *Modern Mexico.*

13. L. Vincent Padgett, *The Mexican Political System* (Boston: Houghton Mifflin Company, 1966).

14. L. Vincent Padgett, *Ibid.*, especially ch. 3; Joe C. Ashby, *Organized Labor and the Mexican Revolution Under Cárdenas* (Chapel Hill: University of North Carolina Press, 1967).

15. L. Vincent Padgett, *The Mexican Political System*, ch. 4.

16. L. Vincent Padgett, *Ibid.*, ch. 5.

17. Martin C. Needler, *Society and Politics in Mexico* (Albuquerque, N.M.: University of New Mexico Press, 1971), p. 97.

18. Barry Ames, "Bases of Support for Mexico's Dominant Party," *American Political Science Review*, LXIV; 1 (March, 1970).

19. The following discussion on presidential power relies greatly on the synthesis of views found in Carolyn and Martin Needleman, "Who Rules Mexico? A Critique of Some Current Views on the Mexican Political Process," *Journal of Politics*, 31; 4 (November, 1969).

20. Gabriel Almond and Sidney Verba, *Civic Culture* (Boston: Little, Brown and Company, 1963), p. 72.

21. From an ample and growing literature on Mexican economics, see Raymond Vernon, *The Dilemma of Mexico's Development* (Cambridge: Harvard University Press, 1963); Clark W. Reynolds, *The Mexican Economy* (New Haven: Yale University Press, 1970); Morris Singer, *Growth, Equality and the Mexican Experience* (Austin: University of Texas Press, 1969).

22. James W. Wilkie, *The Mexican Revolution*, (Berkeley: University of California Press, 1970), ch. 4.

23. Raymond Vernon, *The Dilemma of Mexico's Development*. See especially his comments on relations between the public and private sectors, *passim*.

24. Inter-American Development Bank, *Socio-Economic Progress in Latin America* (Washington, D.C.: Tenth Annual Report, 1970), p. 272.

25. Julio A. Fernandez, *Political Administration in Mexico* (Boulder: Bureau of Governmental Research and Service, University of Colorado, 1969), p. 190.

26. Frank Brandenburg, *Modern Mexico*, p. 84.

27. Kenneth F. Johnson, *Mexican Democracy*, p. 89.

28. Rodolfo Stavenhagen, "Seven Erroneous Theses About Latin America" in John D. Martz, ed., *The Dynamics of Change in Latin America* (Englewood Cliffs, N.J.: Prentice-Hall, Inc., 1971), pp. 47–59; Pablo González-Casanova, "Internal Colonialism and National Development," in Irving Louis Horowitz, Josue de Castro and John Gerassi, eds., *Latin American Radicalism* (New York: Vintage Books, 1969), pp. 118–139; Pablo González-Casanova, *Democracy in Mexico* (New York: Oxford University Press, 1970).

29. "Unemployment Worries Mexican Government," *Dallas Morning News* (June 3, 1973).

30. Kenneth F. Johnson, *Mexican Democracy*, ch. 5.

31. Ifigenia de Navarrette, *La Distribución del Ingreso y el Desarrollo Económico de México* (Mexico:UNAM, 1960).

32. Clark W. Reynolds, *The Mexican Economy*, p. 76.

33. James W. Wilkie, *The Mexican Revolution*, p. 269.

34. Inter-American Development Bank, p. 277; for the "effective" budget for 1970, see Gustavo Diaz Ordaz, *Sexto Informe que rinde al H. Congreso de la Union el C. Presidente de la República,* No. 10 (Septiembre, 1970).

35. Wayne A. Cornelius, "Urbanization as an Agent in Latin American Political Instability: The Case of Mexico," *American Political Science Review,* LXIII; 3 (September, 1969), p. 855.

NIGERIA

Political Change in a Multi-National Setting

MINTON F. GOLDMAN

Nigeria is a creation of the British.[1] Before they arrived
the area that today comprises the state of Nigeria
consisted of a multiplicity of mutually antagonistic
ethnic groups and independent tribal kingdoms. In the
latter half of the nineteenth century, British
missionaries, explorers, and traders entered Nigeria, and
in the next twenty years British influence penetrated
deeply from a foothold at Lagos into the hinterland of
the country. The boundaries of the modern state of
Nigeria were drawn in this period in agreements
between British, French, and German statesmen with
little, if any, reference to traditional frontiers. The
entire area of what is today the Nigerian state was
brought under British control and became a British
dependency in 1899. Britain administered Nigeria for
the next sixty years. In 1960 Nigeria became
independent under a constitution that provided for a
parliamentary democracy. Democratic government
lasted until 1966, when the government was struck by
a military coup. Today Nigeria is administered by a
military dictatorship led by General Yakubu Gowon.[2]

In the administration of Nigeria, the British
confronted a problem which was to confound the
governmental leadership of Nigeria right up to the
present. They were never able to resolve the country's
acute ethnic and cultural fragmentation which
prevented Nigeria from developing a stable and
effective political system. The purpose of this study is
to examine why the British, and later, indigenous,
leadership failed to overcome this problem. Alter all,
other Third World countries with a similar

164

environment, like India, had succeeded, after independence, in developing stable and effective political systems.

There are four parts of this analysis of Nigerian political development: (1) the determinants of politics (ethnic and cultural fragmentation, colonial rule, nationalism, and political parties, especially their role in the ethno-centered political crises of the 1950's and their failure to promote political integration and national unity on the eve of independence; (2) the failure of politics to achieve control (the extent to which the independent political system was unable to promote national unity and stable government); (3) the consequences of political failure (the end of civilian representative government and the establishment of a military dictatorship, the outbreak of civil war); and (4) reunification and reconciliation, and prospects of a return to popular government (the emergence of the political system as an independent variable).

DETERMINANTS OF NIGERIAN POLITICS: THE POLITICAL SYSTEM AS A DEPENDENT VARIABLE

Ethnic and Cultural Fragmentation

IN THE NORTH

In the northern part of the country, there are five major ethnic tribal groups, each with its own separate cultural, historical, and political traditions: Hausa, Fulani, Nupe, Kanuri, and Tiv.[3] The Hausa and Fulani are the largest group comprising 11.8 million people. The Hausa were politically and culturally dominant in the northwestern region until the nineteenth century when the Fulani, who were Muslim, defeated the pagan Hausa in a holy war and forced them to accept a Fulani overlordship.

The Fulani empire in northwestern Nigeria was governed on principles very similar to medieval European feudalism. Fulani sultans ruled supreme, commanding the loyalty of lesser princes called emirs who were the administrators of smaller population centers. Emirs paid tribute and owed allegiance to the sultans. The emirs in turn ruled over village leaders who paid them tribute and allegiance.

The Fulani conquest of Hausaland brought a measure of unity and cohesion as well as stability and security to a huge geographic area and, by strengthening Islam, provided the conquered area with a common bond which considerably reduced inter-tribal conflict. The cultural, religious, and political unity the Fulani brought to the Northern Region in the nineteenth century goes far toward explaining its political cohesion in the twentieth century. Finally, Fulani rule inspired a kind of pride and confidence in the Islamic peoples of the north which strengthened them in their dealings with the peoples of the south whom they suspected and disliked because of their very different culture and way of life.

There are, however, several negative aspects of the Fulani impact on northwestern Nigeria. The Fulani-Hausa society was very provincial and suspicious of the non-Islamic peoples elsewhere in the country, especially in the south where European influence and change were greatest. Northern suspicion, stemming from the practice of Islam as well as the geographic distance that separated the two sections of the country, complicated and obstructed political development in the transition to self-rule and independence after World War II. The Hausa and Fulani political leaders initially were not sympathetic to the creation of a united Nigerian state. They did not want to participate with southerners in national politics. They preferred to be left alone—an impossibility because the Northern Region was the largest region in Nigeria and therefore the obvious source of leadership of the new country. Their Islamic culture and their conservative political tradition set the Hausa and Fulani people apart from and against not only the other non-Moslem peoples of the Northern Region, but also the people of the south.

Other important minority ethnic groups in the north are the Tiv, Kanuri, Illorin and Yoruba. The Tiv, in the central "middle belt" of Nigeria, adopted Christianity and accepted western ideas and institutions far more eagerly than their Hausa-Fulani neighbors. In contrast with the centralized Hausa-Fulani political and societal organization, the Tiv were individualistic and independent and had no distinctive administrative tradition. The Tiv had never been conquered by the Fulani and resented inclusion in the Northern Region in the colonial period. Because of repressive and corrupt government by Hausa-Fulani officials, the Tiv aspired to have their own middle belt region in which they would predominate. In the 1950's and early 1960's they supported a political party, the United Middle Belt Congress, that was committed to the creation of a Tiv region.

The Kanuri are another people in the north who live mostly in the area known as Bornu. Like the Tiv, the Kanuri of Bornu had never been conquered by the Fulani, enjoyed a separate cultural and historical tradition, and resented having to live in a region dominated by the Fulani and Hausa. The Kanuri people had been converted to Islam in the eleventh century and had cultural ties with Egypt and the northeast coast of Africa rather than, as the Hausa, with the kingdoms of the western Sudan and Morocco. Like the Tiv, the Kanuri agitated for a separate region in the 1950's, and the Bornu Youth Movement, a Kanuri political organization, championed this goal.

Also living in the northern part of the country and administered by the Northern Regional government in the 1950's and 1960's were the Illorin Yoruba. In the early nineteenth century the Illorin Yoruba broke away from the large Yoruba nation in the western part of Nigeria and sought the protection of Fulani emirs. Thereafter the Illorin Yoruba were governed by the Fulani and in the 1950's and early 1960's they supported the Hausa-Fulani political party, the Northern Peoples' Congress, thus antagonizing the Yoruba in the Western Region.

IN THE SOUTH

An equivalent ethnic diversity prevails in the southern part of Nigeria.[4] In the southeast there are three large ethnic groups: the Ibo, who predominate, the Ibibio, and the Ijaw. These groups are much more cosmopolitan than the northern groups primarily because of their early involvement in trade and commerce with the Europeans. Educated in the ways and ideas of the West, the Ibo produced ambitious, competent, articulate spokesmen like Nnamdi Azikiwe who played an important role in the political development of Nigeria in the twentieth century. The Ibo people easily embraced Western ideas and values partly because they were not encumbered by the kind of religious and cultural conservatism found in the north. The Ibo and other groups in the east are either animist or Christian.

For a time the Ibo, more than any other ethnic group, believed in one Nigeria. Many Ibo took residence in northern cities in the 1950's because of the need of the Northern Regional government for trained administrators. Their economic interest, which spread over much of Nigeria, made them strong advocates of unity. But in the mid-1960's, after Nigeria became independent, Ibo sentiment changed. They began to harbor separatist ambitions that led to the 1967 secession of the Eastern region from the Federation and the establishment of an independent Ibo state, Biafra.

In the southwest, the large Yoruba nation predominated. The traditional political system of the Yoruba was very different from that of the Hausa and Fulani in the north. There were many separate Yoruba tribal kingdoms. A Yoruba king was chosen by a council of chiefs or kingmakers who were heads of small tribal groups. If the council found fault with the king they could cause his replacement, indeed his demise, which suggests a substantial restraint upon monarchical power not found in the somewhat despotic emirate system in the north. But, of greater importance is the fact that in spite of the existence of what seemed to be a sovereign overlord, real power in Yorubaland lay with local chiefs who were closer to the people and exercised greater authority over them than the king, who was only a figurehead.

The Yoruba in the west and the Ibo in the east always found it very difficult to get along with one another and almost impossible to cooperate politically against the northern dominance of national politics in the late 1950's and early 1960's. The Ibo, coming from a fragmented, decentralized, and individualistically oriented society, were ambitious and aggressive, eager for material success. The Yoruba, on the other hand, were less ambitious, less aggressive than the Ibo, and very resentful of their pushiness, especially at Lagos, the national capital, where they met in competition for employment in government, business, and education. Their different cultural backgrounds and perspectives and their mutual jealousies and rivalry constitute an important source of ethnic conflict in the south.

The dimensions of this ethnic and linguistic diversity are obviously extraordinary and explain why Nigeria did not really have a common national history like other countries in Africa. That this diversity profoundly influenced the emergence and development of the modern Nigerian state in the mid-twentieth century is an understatement. It is, perhaps, one of the most important characteristics of the country's political environment and a cause of many of its governmental and political difficulties during and after the period of colonial control. Indeed, in this respect, Nigeria was very like India where linguistic and cultural diversity also influenced political development. The conflict between Moslems, Hindus, and Sikhs in India was no less profound than that between the Hausa-Fulani societies of northern Nigeria and the Yoruba and Ibo in the south. For reasons discussed in the India chapter, however, cultural fragmentation in that country was far less harmful for political development.

British Colonial Rule

Positive Contributions to Political Development

Certain aspects of British colonial policy undoubtedly contributed positively to Nigerian political development, particularly self-rule, political unity, and economic growth and development. British accomplishments in this regard can be divided into two broad categories: socio-economic and administrative.[5]

In the socio-economic category the British may be credited with three major accomplishments: (1) the creation of a communications and transportation infrastructure; (2) the development of a money economy and the introduction of direct and general taxation; and (3) the expansion of Nigeria's exports which, though it enriched the European entrepreneurs at the expense of Nigerian interests in the short run, broadened the economic base of the country and increased national wealth in the long run.

Another positive contribution of British colonial policy to the development of the Nigerian nation-state lay in administration. The British developed over a period of sixty years (1899–1959) an administrative system that knit the country together politically and at the same time provided Nigerians with valuable experience in self-government. In 1900 the British govenment divided the country into two protectorates, one in the north and the other in the south, each under a High Commissioner. There was also the colony of Lagos on the coast.

The British administered the protectorates indirectly through local tribal authorities. This system of indirect rule was a cheap and an effective means of ensuring British interests. The colony of Lagos on the other hand was administered directly by a British governor mainly because it consisted of a relatively small area confined virtually to the port of Lagos and possessed no indigenous governmental system prior to the arrival of the British. In each case the administrative apparatus was authoritarian; there were no representative institutions and no visible restraints on the exercise of political power by British and Nigerian authorities except traditional tribal limits such as those that prevailed in the Yoruba kingdoms.

After 1900 the British tried various means to foster unity but their basic belief about the best way to govern the country was that its ethnic diversity had to be respected. Governor Clifford, in a speech to the Nigerian Council on December 29, 1920, articulated this concept when he declared:

> Assuming . . . that the impossible were feasible—that this collection of self-contained and mutually independent native states, separated from one another, as many of them are, by great distances, by differences of history and traditions, by ethnological, racial, tribal, political, social, and religious barriers, were indeed capable of being welded into a single, homogeneous nation—a deadly blow would thereby be struck at the very root of national self-government in Nigeria, which secures to each separate people the right to maintain its identity, its individuality and its nationality, its own chosen form of government. . . . [6]

Within this framework the British did try to achieve a meaningful broadening of the representative character of their Nigerian administration and therefore, after some experimentation, established Nigeria's first real legislative body in 1922. Although few Nigerians had the right to vote, reputable and capable spokesmen for provincial interests were elected, and the new council was given authority to pass on financial legislation to make laws for the country.

The British may rightly be blamed for doing things intentionally or unintentionally to perpetuate the country's profound ethnic diversity. For example, the British policy of indirect rule tended to strengthen indigenous political systems, values, and loyalties. It perpetuated tribal differences and favored tribal aristocracy rather than the new groups of educated, urbanized Nigerians who were ready for self-government. Also, indirect rule, especially in the feudal north, retarded the development of self-government and to that extent encouraged a susceptibility to authoritarianism and exacerbated the cultural isolation of north and south.

The divisive effects of indirect rule were aggravated by British educational and landowning policies. In the area of education they cooperated with the northern emirs in limiting the development of Christian mission schools in the north. By thus discouraging the spread of Western ideas, they retarded the development of a modernized elite on the local level, assuring thereby the future dependence of the North on alien experts from other parts of the country, notably the more progressive, westernized, and better educated Ibo from the east, who in increasing numbers settled in the north in the post World War II period.

British policy toward landownership was also a liability for political development, especially national unity and cohesion. The British recognized and supported the traditional form of landownership in which land was held by the tribe and administered by tribal authorities. During the colonial period Nigerians lived on the land but did not have title to it and therefore could not dispose of it. As long as Nigerians could not own land and could not sell it, they were dependent on the tribe for their economic survival and this in turn restricted their freedom of movement. Finally, restriction on freedom to move intensified regional differences and separateness, which, though welcomed by the exclusivist Islamic north, was detrimental to the country as a whole in terms of undermining tendencies toward national unification.

A final criticism of British colonial policy in Nigeria has to do with the fact that in the interwar and post-World War II years the British were in no rush to promote a strong central government that could conceivably have knit the different tribal groups into a cohesive nation. They believed that tribal differences were too strong to permit a central government to administer the country effectively and peacefully and therefore preferred to introduce self-government on the regional level. Also, the British feared that a strong central government run by the Nigerians themselves would inevitably be dominated by the educated and progressive southerners whom the British disliked because they were too aggressive in their efforts to emulate and achieve equality with Europeans.

The British rather hoped for and contrived to have the northerners succeed to the leadership of the country if for no other reason than that they were in a majority and deserved the position of dominance. But the British preferred the northerners to run Nigeria for still another reason. The northerners were more conservative and less pushy about nationalism, self-rule, and independence than the southerners.

Finally, as in India, it would appear that the positive aspects of British colonial policy, such as development of the indigenous economic and administrative infrastructure, were outweighed by its negative aspects, notably the practice of divide and rule. In both Nigeria and India the British policy of preserving the autonomy of traditional politics and either intentionally or unintentionally playing them against one another for the purpose of keeping them weak and subservient, hindered the development of tendencies toward national integration, unity, and cohesion.

Nationalism

Along with ethnic diversity and British colonial policies, a third important determinant of Nigerian political development is the growth and development of nationalism.[7] Nigerian nationalism consisted of racial identification and political awareness that ultimately produced drives for self-rule and national unity, especially in the southern, more Europeanized parts of the country.

CAUSES

European urbanization, which occurred more in the south than in the north in the pre-independence preiod, may be considered a first cause of nationalism in Nigeria. James Coleman writes in his *Nigeria: Background to Nationalism* that the new Western-style centers of population were ". . . the breeding and training grounds . . . of Nigerian nationalism."[8] Nigerians who came to work and live in the cities to obtain money, status, personal independence of traditional tribal authority, and Western gadgetry and dress, became dependent on and victims of the impersonal, European dominated, capitalist-oriented urban economy and society. They also became vulnerable to the appeal of assertive nationalists who, though sympathetic to the problem of adjustment to the new Europeanized environment, exploited Nigerians for their own political purposes.

The evangelical activities of Christian missionaries from Europe also fostered the growth of nationalism by arousing a common national resentment, although their activity was more prominent in the south than in the north. Missionaries were condescending and patronizing. They fancied themselves rescuing "the natives" from a cruel and irrational cultural environment. Nigerians also resented the biases and blindness of the missionaries, especially their silence on such offensive features of colonial rule as inequality and exploitation. European evangelism in Nigeria provoked Nigerian nationalist writers in the 1920's and 1930's to articulate resentment against the European order imposed on their country. Also, by detaching the Nigerians whom they Christianized from their traditional culture, without really providing them with a satisfactory alternative, the missionaries in their evangelical zeal rendered their protegés susceptible to an integrating philosophy that did have appeal—namely nationalism.

Economic grievance, caused mainly by British domination and exploitation of the Nigerian economy, also aroused national sentiment and produced a desire for self-rule. A large source of grievance was concentration of economic power in the hands of British firms like the United Africa Company, which in the 1930's exercised a dominant role in the economy, particularly over the country's foreign trade. The United Africa Company and other firms effectively excluded Nigerians from participation as entrepreneurs in their country's economic life, ostensibly because they lacked capital and competence. When Nigerians tried to obtain capital from the only available source—British controlled banks—they were usually turned down, a situation that began to change only after World War II, when a Nigerian controlled banking institution emerged that received support from newly formed Nigerian governments. Finally, British economic concentration centered on the south. Thus, anti-British sentiment arising out of economic grievances was stronger among southern Nigerians than northerners.

A fourth cause of Nigerian nationalism was the Western educational system. At its best Western education endowed Nigerians who received it with the knowledge, skills, and ambitions that enabled them to challenge the British colonial regime, to compel its "Nigerianization," and ultimately to achieve complete emancipation from British tutelage. But, Western education was also a good target for nationalist leaders who, ironically, were the beneficiaries of this system. They leveled grave but very justifiable criticisms against it. Azikiwe, for example, stated that the British "miseducated" the Nigerians who were de-Africanized in the English schools of their country. Nigerians educated in English schools were taught little if anything about their own culture and history. There was also the feeling that Western education was calculated to perpetuate Nigerians as "heavers of wood and haulers of water," and thus unable to challenge their subservience to the Europeans.[9]

Furthermore, Western education offended and antagonized Nigerians because of its narrow application. Educated and articulate Nigerians, especially in the south, resented the unwillingness of the colonial regime to establish compulsory, universal and free education. It was not difficult for Nigerian nationalists to see in this policy of neglect an intentional effort on the part of the race conscious British elite "to keep the African down." What bothered Nigerian nationalists perhaps the most was the awareness that the schools, because of an overly British orientation in goals and methods, did not inculcate the youth of the country with a sense of racial and national identification. Still another facet of Western education important for the development of nationalism was the disparity between school facilities in the north and those in the south. As a result of the policy of the emirs and the British, schools offering a European type education on the primary and secondary levels were much less numerous in the north than in the south. In 1947, students from the Northern Region constituted only 2.5 percent of the Nigerian school population.

A fifth and decisive factor that encouraged the growth of nationalistic and anti-British sentiments was British racial prejudice. British hostility to the Nigerian black was only thinly disguised and surfaced for all to see in attitudes of contempt, amusement, condescension, and sometimes downright hostility toward those who had become Westernized. Typical of British feeling was the sentiment expressed by Joyce Cary, a writer who had some administrative experience in Nigeria as a district officer in the Northern Region. Cary once wrote that northern Nigeria was a paradise because it was "without the hybrids (Westernized Nigerians) we see in the coast towns." The educated elite, those Nigerians who embraced British culture, were alienated by this prejudice, which provided an important stimulus to the development of Nigerian nationalist sentiment and action. It is not surprising that the earliest manifestation of Nigerian nationalism was racial in character and that it occurred in the south, particularly at Lagos, where contact between Nigerians and the British was greatest and where a wealthy, educated, and cultured professional class began to articulate ideas and sentiments of negritude and contemplated mild resistance to and protest against the British colonial regime.

IMPACT OF WORLD WAR II ON NIGERIAN NATIONALISM

The Second World War greatly encouraged the development of nationalism in the south.[10] It was at this time that Nigerians began to think of the Nigerian community not so much in broad racial terms but rather in a narrower political sense. Several factors during the war fostered this thinking. The Japanese victories over the English and their allies dealt a blow to the myth of racial supremacy and invincibility of the colonial overlords, a necessary first step in the development of political nationalism and one that encouraged Nigerians to have more confidence in themselves. During the war southern Nigeria, especially Lagos, became the stopping off place for over 100,000 white troops from Europe and the United States en route to the Orient. Nigerians could not help but learn from these troops about the political ideas of liberalism and nationalism expressed by the leaders of the United States and Britain. Thousands of Nigerians who served the British Empire abroad in Burma, India, and other theatres broke their traditional ties and returned home with new ideas, values, and aspirations. Nigerians were aware of the continuing struggle of Indian nationalists for independence throughout the war period. They knew about Gandhi and other Indian nationalist leaders and were duly impressed when India received her independence at the end of the war.

Finally, during and after the war there emerged a new group of Nigerians, many of them southerners, who were articulate, influential men like Nnamdi Azikiwe. These men championed a liberalization of the colonial administration and ultimately supported the drive for independence. Azikiwe was typical of the new Nigerian nationalist leadership. He was educated in the West and ultimately entered journalism. He succeeded in establishing a chain of newspapers in southern Nigeria on the eve of World War II. Azikiwe tried to stir pride in Nigerian accomplishments, encouraging his readers to voice grievances against the British regime. In the early 1930's Azikiwe had spoken of a race consciousness, but not until World War II, like many others who shared his feelings, was he caught up in Nigerian political affairs.

Azikiwe combined liberalism and nationalism in his thinking about the future of Nigeria. He favored nonviolent means to independence and in this connection he helped to establish a political party called the National Council of Nigeria and the Cameroon (NCNC) which was supported by literary groups, social clubs, professional organizations, labor unions, tribal associations including the Ibo Union, and other active political organizations in the country. The NCNC sought self-government for Nigeria within the British Empire.

Azikiwe had an opportunity to increase his influence and advance the cause of liberalism and socio-economic reform during the general strike in the summer of 1945. This strike had been called for higher wages to meet the rising costs of living that had resulted from the war and involved organized labor in the key service industries. The strike demonstrated to the British that Nigerian dissatisfaction could not be ignored. The British government investigated the complaint of the Nigerian workers and ultimately granted wage hikes in the service industries.

Azikiwe's role in all this was significant. He really did not take full advantage of the strike to weld together a truly national grouping that could demand extensive political and socio-economic change. Of course the British had moved quickly and shrewdly to deal with the strike in an effort to deprive him of an opportunity of mobilizing a popular anti-British movement. But then Azikiwe's personal behavior also was a factor. Instead of dramatizing his cause, he meekly submitted to an administrative ban on his newspapers. If he had defied the colonial authorities and been jailed, becoming a martyr, he could have become a truly national figure. But this never happened. Nigerian nationalism was thus deprived of a unity in policy and organization that would have been helpful in promoting political cohesion in the period of party development during the 1950's.

Political Parties and the Transition to Independence

In the 1950's the new political parties were very active in the development of self-government. Their strong local orientation and divergent policies foreshadowed the bitter political conflicts of the immediate post independence years.

Origins of Political Parties

The emergence of the Nigerian party system in the late 1940's and 1950's was influenced largely by the development of nationalist sentiment and activity during and immediately after World War II, especially the appearance of articulate and activist national leaders, like Azikiwe. But, of decisive influence on the growth of the political parties was the expansion of popular participation in colonial government, first on the regional level and, ultimately, at the center in Lagos.

Several factors account for the British decision to move Nigeria closer to self-rule and unity of which the most decisive, perhaps, was the growth of nationalist agitation in 1945 and 1946. But also of importance was the anti-colonialist attitude of Britain's new Labour government which had entered office in the summer of 1945. The Labour government was commited to devoting Britain's resources to internal socioeconomic reform rather than to expend them on campaigns to suppress nationalism in Nigeria and India.[11]

Devolution of substantial administrative authority to Nigerians in the postwar period began with the promulgation in 1947 by Sir Arthur Richard of a Constitution which provided for two major changes in the Nigerian colonial administration: (1) northerners were to be members of the legislative council at Lagos and (2) new legislative councils with native majorities were to be created in each of the Regions.[12] Appearance belied reality, however, in regard to unification and self-rule. The central legislative body at Lagos still lacked administrative power and authority, and remained ineffective. At the same time the regions became more autonomous; thus the process of centralization and unification were undermined and the tendency toward regional separatism was strengthened.

Also, the British allowed the regions to determine the manner in which members of the new regional legislative councils were to be selected, and thereby virtually assured the perpetuation of the power and influence of the unpopular and conservative chiefs who had been the instrument of indirect rule before 1947. Furthermore, the British deprived the regional legislative bodies of any real power and responsibility, and in so doing preserved the basically authoritarian character of the colonial government. In sum, Nigerians were still denied management of their affairs. They were simply given greater opportunities than before to discuss and to participate.

Nevertheless, a very positive consequence of the Richards Constitution was its catalyzing effect on the growth of the political parties which ultimately provided Nigerian nationalists with the single most important means by which they were able to lead their country toward self-rule, unity, and ultimately, independence. Yet, regional legislative councils rather than the national legislative council at Lagos were the focal points and constituencies of the new political parties. Because each region was dominated by one large ethnic group, the new political parties were for the most part ethnically and regionally oriented. Under these circumstances it was difficult if not impossible for a truly national party to develop. To that extent the party system was unable to foster tendencies toward political unification and integration.

Political party activity occurred earlier in the south than in the north because the European impact in the form of acculturation and socioeconomic change was strongest and had its most intensive effects in the south. Also, the center of colonial authority and thus the most important political focal point was located in the south, in Lagos. What is very interesting as well as significant about the early development of the first large party in the south, the National Council of Nigeria and the Cameroons (NCNC), as already suggested, is the role of Nnamdi Azikiwe. On the one hand Azikiwe and his followers in the NCNC were ambitious, aggressive, and cosmopolitan, and embarked upon a campaign calling for revision of the Richards Constitution. The persistent but relatively temperate and nonviolent efforts of the NCNC were in part responsible for inducing the British to grant further and more liberal change in colonial government in the form of a new Constitution which was established in 1951.

Several of Azikiwe's youthful Ibo followers, however, were impetuous and radical. They wanted liberalization of the Nigerian government overnight and were dissatisfied with the changes wrought by the Richards Constitution. These youthful militants launched a movement for rapid political change which they called the Zikist movement. But Azikiwe, their leader, disapproved of this impetuousity and radicalism and preferred to achieve further political liberalization by pressure on the local and national legislative bodies. He thus forfeited an opportunity to become a popular nationwide hero. It almost seems as if he were disinclined toward personality politics, preferring the impersonal professional style of politicians in England. Of course, what was uppermost in his mind was a respect for legality and a dislike of violence and lawlessness as a means of achieving political ends. Azikiwe's aversion to charismatic and demagogic behavior is one reason why the NCNC at least never did develop a large national constituency during the 1950's.[13] Azikiwe was certainly no Gandhi, Mao, or Cárdenas.

The Action Group was the other major southern political party and it was supported largely by the Yorubas. This was a much more ethno-centered party than the NCNC and its leader, Obafami Awolowo, a barrister, was much more concerned with tribal nationalism than Azikiwe. The Action Group was different from the NCNC in still other ways. The Action Group made no large bid for national support in contrast with the NCNC, which did try with some modest success to attract adherents in other parts of Nigeria. For example, the NCNC was supported by an increasing number of Ibo in northern cities who filled clerical and administrative jobs for which northerners had little talent and training. The Action Group's concentration on its own region made it a more narrow organization, not capable of developing a truly national philosophy, a liability for the party in the post-independence period.[14]

The development of political party activity in the north occurred later than in the south for several reasons. The north had no regional legislature and was not represented in the Nigerian Legislative Council in the period prior to 1945. Furthermore, the authoritarian political environment in the north discouraged the development of organizations committed to liberalism and nationalism. For some time the only channel for the expression of any political sentiment, conservative or otherwise, was through the traditional autocratic ruling elite—the chiefs and emirs. They, of course, were supporters of the existing conservative political system, and tolerated little criticism of and opposition to their society.

However, it is not surprising that reform-minded civil servants and other elements in favor of change formed the Northern People's Congress, which became a bona fide political party in 1951 ready to field candidates for seats in the newly created legislature of the Northern Region. In the early 1950's however, reactionary local authorities, who had little sympathy with the nationalist inspired movement for independence that was developing in the south, assumed control of the party. A clash between this parochial and conservative northern party and the progressive and cosmopolitan southern groups was inevitable.[15]

In 1948 the new governor, John Macpherson, convened a conference in Lagos to learn the views and sentiments of Nigerian political leaders. The conference recommended creation of a federal union with a strong central government in which all the regions would be represented and would enjoy substantial autonomy. There was deep division, however, on detail. The northerners wanted half the seats in the new federal legislature and when the conference voted to give them less, they threatened to leave and return home. Furthermore, the northerners, because of their superiority in population, were opposed to the southern proposal to distribute revenue according to derivation, which would have meant that the north would get considerably less than the other wealthier regions.

There were other divisions between the politicians. The northerners rejected various demands by Azikiwe and ethnic minorities to create additional regions in order to give more recognition and representation to smaller ethnic groups. The Hausa-Fulani political leaders of the NPC disliked the idea of creating new regions because the Northern Region was the most likely to lose power and influence in the new system were its minorities, like the Tiv and the Kanuri, to be given the political autonomy they were seeking. On this point the northern political leaders were supported by the British who also were opposed to the separatist tendencies of the ethnic minorities.

On the basis of recommendations submitted to the Governor in 1951, a new Constitution was promulgated by the Colonial Administration the following year. It went far toward leading the country toward unity and autonomy and to that extent it enjoyed a tentative consensus. The new Constitution, called the Macpherson Constitution, provided for the creation of new governmental machinery at Lagos to consist of a legislature in which the north was granted half the seats and an executive council of eighteen of which twelve were to be nominated by the regional assemblies. Federal tax revenue was ultimately to be redistributed according to need rather than derivation.

Southern politicians were disappointed by the provisions of the new instrument. It is obvious that the British had been very generous to the northerners, incorporating many of their preferences into the new Constitution. Southerners resented this British favoritism toward the north.[16] Furthermore, NCNC politicians and other southerners regretted that real executive power was not given to the Nigerians but continued to remain in the hands of the British.

But the NPC, as well, opposed the Macpherson Constitution. The north disliked any tendency toward a highly centralized system which they suspected might be dominated in the long run by the more politically sophisticated southerners. They were afraid that a highly centralized system would ultimately destroy their regional integrity and change their traditional way of life.

Because of general dissatisfaction within Nigeria with the Macpherson Constitution, the new instrument was replaced in 1953 by the Lyttelton Constitution, which endured until the achievement of independence in 1960. Under the Lyttelton Constitution Nigeria became a federation of three regions, one federal territory in which the national capital was located, and the quasi-federal territory of the Southern Cameroon which had been allowed to break away from the Eastern Region.[17]

This new Constitution, like its predecessors, tended to favor the Northern Region, again because the British wanted it that way. In consequence of the decision to give Lagos a separate administrative status, the Action Group and the Western Region were unable to exercise an undue influence over the capital. But, more importantly, the north benefited from a provision that the members of the regional legislatures were to be elected in a manner to be determined by the regional governments. The conservative Hausa-Fulani politicians were able to perpetuate their control over the Northern Region political system to the detriment of both liberal and minority interests in the north, something that obviously did not disturb the British.[18]

ETHNIC MINORITIES AND THE SMALL POLITICAL PARTIES

Another crucial variable affecting Nigerian political development in the 1950's was the growth of minority political groups. Like the larger parties, their behavior also affected the performance of parliamentary government and the achievement of national unity. And, also like the larger parties, the smaller groups had a strong ethnic orientation which in this instance helps to explain their preoccupation with minority rights and their ultimate demands for separatism. They periodically called for the creation of additional regions.

The Northern Region had several small political parties supported by ethnic minority groups. These small ethnic groups had at least one thing in common: resentment toward the NPC because of its authoritarian monopoly of the regional government. One of the larger minority party groups in the north was the Northern Elements Progressive Union (NEPU). The NEPU was supported by a variety of people with grievances against the Northern Regional Government such as ex-servicemen, teachers, and native administrative workers. Many of these people had been dismissed from their jobs in government ostensibly for inefficiency and insubordination, omnibus charges used by the emirs to get rid of political undesirables. Other sources of support were northerners who lived in the Middle Belt area, namely the Illorin Yoruba and the Tiv, and northerners living in southern cities.

Another minority political party in the north was the United Middle Belt Congress (UMBC) and the Bornu Youth Movement (BYM). The UMBC drew support from the non-Muslim people in the Middle Belt, notably the Tiv and the Illorin Yoruba and championed the creation of a separate middle belt region. The BYM was a radical group also critical of the Fulani dominated feudal administrative system in the north. It called for the creation of a separate region for Bornu.

There were several minority parties in the south and east. The most cohesive of the southern minority groups was the Benin Delta People's Party (BDPP) which represented the separatist interests of the Edo speaking people of Benin living in the area once known as the Kingdom of Benin in the Benin delta section of the Western Region. The largest minority party in the east was the United National Independence Party (UNIP) which wanted a separate region for the Efik and Calabar Ibo living in the Calabar and Ogoga areas of the Eastern Region.[19]

The major problem of these minority groups which helps to explain their persistent demand for the creation of new regions was discrimination against them by the large powerful ethno-based political parties which dominated the regional governments administering the local minorities. This domination was felt in both the executive and legislative branches of the regional governments, especially after 1954, when the leaders of each of the three major parties served as premiers of the region in which their parties were entrenched. Political dominance of the large ethnic groups was reinforced by cultural and educational factors. The Ibo and Yoruba, for example, the large ethnic groups in the Eastern and Western Regions, were westernized, progressive, ambitious, and eager for education which they knew was the basis of their privileged political and socio-economic position. In contrast many of the minority groups within these regions were backward, less progressive and ambitious. They were also less interested in education, and thus at a disadvantage in their relationship with the majority ethnic group. They were more easily discriminated against, while at the same time less able to articulate their cause and seek redress of grievances.

In the north there was still another kind of situation detrimental to the minority groups living there. There the minorities tended to be better educated and more progressive and articulate than the dominant Hausa-Fulani. The latter resented their dependence on these minority groups for the technical skills needed in government and business, and they used their position of political dominance to discriminate against the minorities.[20]

The large and small parties participated vigorously in the crucial federal elections of 1959—the last national election before the achievement of independence. This contest revealed quite clearly the depth of ethnic rivalry between and within the regions and in retrospect appears an inauspicious omen of Nigeria's post-independence political development. Because the results of this election would determine the leadership of the country in the post-independence period, the political contestants fought violently and desperately for victory. Their fighting left wounds on the whole country as well as on the losers. These wounds never healed and contributed to the political crises of the immediate post-independence years that led ultimately to the collapse of the parliamentary system.

The Action Group mounted an aggressive, organized, expensive, and flamboyant campaign which aroused the passion of the electorate and provoked the anger of the opposition. It proposed the establishment of no less than three new regions: an Eastern Region, a Northern Region to consist of the Middle Belt people, and a Western Region. The Action Group hoped that its dominance of the west together with the support of the minority groups whose separatist cause it championed would yield a majority in the Federal Government.

The NPC carried on a far less flamboyant, far more conservative campaign than the Action Group. The NPC cared little about developing support outside the north. The party realized that simply winning the 174 northern seats in the federal legislature would suffice to control the central government. The NPC therefore concentrated its campaign efforts on renewing the traditional ties between the Moslem tribesmen and the elites. In this respect the NPC did not campaign as a national party but rather as a regional one, virtually ignoring issues and problems in the south.

While the Action Group and NPC fought their battles alone, the NCNC tried to broaden its appeal and aligned itself with the NEPU in the north. It also pursued a strategy designed not to antogonize the NPC in the belief that the real enemy of both parties was the Action Group because of its stand on separatism and its flamboyant behavior. The NCNC, however, did make an appeal to the people of the Benin delta and urged the creation of a Midwest Region, an idea that the Ibo did not oppose provided it did not set a precedent for the Eastern Region. The NPC also approved of a Midwest Region because its creation would be at the expense of the territory, population, and political influence of the Western Region, thus weakening the latter's influence and that of the Action Group at Lagos. An electoral *entente* between the NPC and NCNC was in fact encouraged by the Action Group's vigorous support of minorities in the Northern and Eastern Regions.

How did the election turn out? The NPC won 148 constituencies, 9 short of the absolute majority needed to govern. What is significant is the fact that 134 constituencies won by the NPC were in the north, suggesting the overwhelmingly regional character of the party's electoral support. The NCNC-NEPU won 89 constituencies of which 59 came from the east, 21 from the west, and 2 from Lagos. Only 8 of the constituencies by by NCNC-NEPU candidates came from the north. The NEPU had not been very successful in helping the NCNC capture support in north. The Action Group enjoyed some success but obviously not enough of it. The party won the support of people in Bornu and in the Middle Belt area where the demand for creation of new regions had been strongest. In all, the Action Group and its allies obtained 75 constituencies of which 35 were in the west, 25 in the north, 14 in the east, and 1 in Lagos. It was paradoxical that the Action Group was the only major party to win the majority of its seats outside the region of its traditional strength.

The results of the election determined the political composition of the new government. Governor Robertson called Sir Abubakar Tafawa Balewa, leader of the parliamentary group of the NPC, to form a coalition. The NPC invited the NCNC to join the cabinet. The new coalition was dominated by the NPC though several important ministries such as Finance, Labor, and eventually Foreign Affairs went to members of the NCNC. Nnamdi Azikiwe, leader of the NCNC, was appointed Governor-General of the country in 1960, six weeks after independence. The Action Group was completely excluded from the coalition, a natural consequence of the animosity generated during the campaign.[21]

The British government was now ready to entertain favorably a formal request by this new government for independence which was duly made in the form of a motion passed by the Federal legislature in January, 1960. The British government consented to transfer power to the Nigerian government on October 1, 1960. Between January and October a number of changes in the governmental system were arranged and a new constitution was set up upon the transfer of power.

Nigeria on the Eve of Independence

While the British believed Nigeria was ready to govern itself, it was not yet a truly united community. As the 1959 election had shown, the view of Nigeria expressed by Governor Clifford in 1920 that the country was a ". . . collection of self-contained and mutually independent native states, separated . . . by great distances, by differences of history and traditions, by ethnological, racial, tribal, political, social, and religious barriers . . ." was a commentary on the national environment still not out of date on the eve of independence. Furthermore, the fact that the strongest political party in the Federal legislature and the source of national leadership, the NPC, was a regional party and not a national one, having won no meaningful support outside the north, was a bad omen on the political horizon. Worse than that, the NPC in representing the most conservative and particularistic of the ethnic groups in the federation, while also suspicious and hostile to the southerners, was the one political party least suited to convert the veneer of unity into the reality of a nation-state.

THE INDEPENDENT POLITICAL SYSTEM AFTER 1960: FAILURE TO ACHIEVE CONTROL

As suggested by Schmitt, the independent political system is more than a reflection of the environment which shaped it. It can be a positive force capable of altering that environment, though in Nigeria it never gained control. The following analysis of the post-independence Nigerian regime reveals the extent to which the formal institutions of government and the political parties, in enabling Nigerians to compete within a democratic framework , failed to establish national unity and to provide political stability.

The 1960 Constitution

The major governmental changes provided by the Constitution were in the area of federalism and parliamentary organization at the center. The new Constitution provided for a federal system based on separate jurisdictions for the national and regional governments similar in many ways to American federalism. The Federal Government was to consist of a figurehead Chief of State who would serve as a symbol of national leadership with real decision-making power vested in a Prime Minister and Cabinet drawn from and responsible to the popularly elected lower chamber of a bicameral legislature. An indirectly elected upper chamber was to represent the Regions.

FEDERALISM

The new federal system had both liabilities as well as assets.[22] On the one hand, the provisions for administrative decentralization, which involved assignment of the bulk of local police power to the Regions, tended to reinforce regionalism and the regional character of the political parties. To that extent it represented a step away from rather than toward national cohesion and unification. On the other hand, this tendency was somewhat checked by the assignment to the Federal Government of enormous authority to regulate and foster economic development.[23] In this way the Federal Government was provided with considerable means to promote national unity. In using national economic power to resolve outstanding socio-economic problems and to further national material progress, the Federal Government would be able to strengthen loyalties to the center and discourage regional particularism.

POWERS OF THE NATIONAL GOVERNMENT AT LAGOS

The wide range of economic powers vested in the Federal Government included control over mines, minerals and nuclear energy, and regulation of railways, aviation, and shipping. The Federal Government had concurrent power with the Regions over industrial development, labor, water power and electricity. The Federal Government was given extensive power over commerce. In addition to its power to control currency and foreign exchange, it had exclusive power to regulate banks and banking, as well as business corporations, corporate issues of securities, and insurance. It had concurrent power over commercial and industrial monopolies, and it alone could impose taxes upon corporate income. Here was an enormous capability to build an economic unity through systematic development of and control over important sectors of the national economy. At the very least the Federal Government had the wherewithal to promote an economic interdependence between the Regions that would make secession by one or more of them from the Federation costly or impractical, and therefore, improbable.

The ability of the Federal Government to use its vast regulatory authority over the economy to further national unity, however, depended upon the willingness of the Regions to support and cooperate with central authorities. As the years passed, because of inter-ethnic animosities, the Regions became less willing than at the beginning of independence to cooperate with each other and with the Federal Government. For example, there was suspicion in both the Eastern and Western Regions that the NPC leaders who controlled the Federal Cabinet were acting as agents of the Northern Regional government and for that reason favored the Northern at the expense of the Southern Regions. Also, the Eastern Region was bitter over preference given by the Federal Government to its own projects to the detriment of Regional projects. Inter-regional and inter-ethnic rivalry paralyzed the operation of many federal regulatory agencies created to promote economic development. Under these circumstances the purpose behind the creation of a strong central government was thwarted. This misuse of federal power to serve exclusively regional interests tended to weaken respect for the federation and to impede the development of national unity.

The Federal Government had a variety of other powers designed to enable it to promote unity and cohesion. The federal Government upon a majority vote of the Federal Parliament could declare an emergency and suspend the lawmaking authority of the Regions in its favor. The Federal Government was given control of the police in that police commissioners in each of the Regions were to be federal officials. This provision was designed to protect ethnic minority groups and relieve their fears that a Regional police controlled by a dominant ethnic group would be used to repress them. The Federal Government had exclusive power over marriage and divorce unless the marriage took place under Muslim law. It also had control over movement of persons between Regions, the legal and medical professions, and tele-communications.

POWERS OF THE REGIONAL GOVERNMMENTS

The Regions also had substantial power and authority. An important aspect of Regional authority derived from Regional representation in the Federal Senate, the second chamber of the national legislature, which was created expressly for the purpose of giving all the Regional governments a direct say in the operation of the Federal Government. The Senate consisted originally of 12 members selected by the Regional legislatures, by the Lagos government, and by the Federal Executive. The Senate, however, was not a very effective representative of Regional interests. The Federal Executive, namely the Prime Minister and Cabinet, was responsible only to the lower chamber, the House of Representatives, in which representation was apportioned by population. Because one Region, the Northern Region, had the largest population, it dominated the House of Representatives and, therefore, the Cabinet as well. As the Senate was not co-equal with the House of Representatives, it could provide little protection to the other less populated Regions. Indeed, the Senate had little power, except in one key area: its consent was necessary for the declaration of a state of emergency. The Senate also had to approve any amendment of the Constitution.

The Regions did enjoy police power in the areas that traditionally belonged to local government—namely local law and order, education, health, housing, and agriculture. The Constitution provided also that any powers not specifically delegated to the Federal Government were reserved to the Regions. Furthermore, the Regions did have some power, though not very much, to protect themselves against the Federal Government. Three out of the four Regions had to approve Constitutional amendments. Also, the Regional Prime Ministers had to be consulted by Federal police commissioners in the use of Federal police power in the Regions though this advice was not binding.

Quite important to the Regions was a guarantee of fiscal security under the new Constitution. The Regional governments were vested with the power to tax, though care was taken to assure the lucrativeness of the taxes collected by the Federal Government. Furthermore, the Constitution guaranteed the Regions a Federal subsidy from taxes collected by the Federal Government. The Regional governments received back Federal funds on the basis of both derivation and need. It was reckoned, however, that as the years went on, the Federal Government would become increasingly wealthy because the receipts from taxes it kept, notably on industry, would increase as the economy developed, while the receipts from taxes returned to the Regions, namely those on exports from and imports into them, would decrease as more of what was consumed was produced at home.

This fiscal system in assuring the Regions of income, while simultaneously strengthening the Federal Government in the performance of its unifying function, had certain political liabilities. Making the Regions depend for their effectiveness and survival on their share of the funds transferred to them by the Federal Government tended to accentuate inter-regional rivalry and tensions and to strengthen the regional character of the political parties.

Southern politicians, for example, always suspected northern politicians, like Sir Abubakar, the Federal Prime Minister, of using Federal wealth, accumulated largely from revenue collected in the Southern Regions, to favor the economy of the north. Since the economy of the north was far less developed than the economy of the south, and thus more dependent on Federal funds than the south for growth and development, it is not difficult to understand why the political parties vied so ferociously with one another in electoral contests to strengthen their influence in the Federal Government.

A final aspect of regional power was local control over education, a condition inherited from the colonial period when the British had fostered decentralization of school administration in deference to northern preferences and prejudices. Almost all educational agencies and functions were financed by the Regional governments although the Federal Government was empowered to provide funds for universities. By perpetuating this condition after 1960 in accordance with federal principles, practiced for example in the United States, the new Constitution prevented the primary and secondary school systems of Nigeria from making their contribution to the development of a truly Nigerian political culture. Indeed, decentralization stood in the way of Nigerianization of school curricula, which were still largely influenced by British goals and methods.[24]

In summary, the new Nigerian federal system was set up in such a way as to defeat the purposes for which it was established. The enormous powers given to the Federal Government were designed to enable it to build a unified national community in a sophisticated and subtle manner, namely through the fostering of national economic development and interdependence rather than by the more obvious method of political and administrative centralization.

The purpose of granting substantial economic power to the federation, however, was never fulfilled. Federal power became just another cause and focal point of inter-regional rivalry and animosity and to that extent retarded rather than fostered the development of national unity. Also, the Federal Government was handicapped in efforts to counteract the effects of these new stimuli of inter-ethnic animosities in consequence of the decentralization of control of the primary and secondary schools. Federal control of the school system could have been an important means of promoting a popular understanding and acceptance of the Nigerian national idea.

PARLIAMENTARY GOVERNMENT

Another major aspect of the 1960 Constitution is its parliamentary character, which was largely inherited from the earlier Constitutions of 1947, 1952, and 1954, and patterned after that of Great Britain.[25] There were several problems in the adoption of the British parliamentary model by Nigeria bound to undermine the efforts of the new government to promote national unity. The Northern Region, because it was the most populous of the three Regions and, therefore, assigned over one half the seats in the Federal House of Representatives, would control that body and thus be able to dominate the Federal Cabinet. This meant northern dominance of the national governmental system. It was a mistake to permit the Federal Cabinet, responsible for the governance of an ethnically heterogenous society, to be dominated by one particular ethnic group—and the most provincial and reactionary one at that. Furthermore, the Senate, where all the Regions had equal representation, could not provide the Southern Regions with an effective counterweight for the Northern predominance in the House of Representatives because it had no control over the Federal Executive. The latter was responsible to and could be overturned only by the House of Representatives. Here was a serious mechanical defect that would intensify inter-ethnic hostilities and antagonisms and to that extent undermine the functioning of the national government.

The liabilities of this mechanical defect were probably rendered more dangerous in consequence of the parliamentary inexperience of the politicians elected to the House of Representatives, especially northerners, who for too long had isolated themselves from the south and from European ideas on liberalism and democratic government. The party groups in Parliament, especially the NPC, were somewhat intolerant of opposition and in any event not sufficiently national in their perspective to permit compromise in controversial issues of national importance. Consequently, in the months and years that followed the promulgation of the 1960 Constitution, a truly responsible and constructive opposition in Parliament, similar in character to that in the British House of Commons, could not and did not develop at Lagos. Southern political groups, at first the Action Group but ultimately the NCNC, resented and became hostile to domination of the national system by the parochial, authoritarian, and intolerant NPC leaders.

This federal and parliamentary system, based on the principle of fusion of power, was ill-suited to a country that was as ethnically heterogeneous and conflict ridden as Nigeria. To have worked well in Nigeria the new parliamentary system should have been provided with an effective means by which the several ethnic groups collectively determined national decision-making, or at least were able to reconcile their political differences within the framework of existing governmental institutions and without recourse to violence. Perhaps, a strong Senate, endowed with authority at least equal to that of the House of Representatives in the legislative relationship with the executive, would have been preferable. Another alternative might have been a system of separation of powers in which a strong and independent executive, representative of the entire country could serve as an effective national symbol, inspire the confidence of the different ethnic groups, and thus encourage a national loyalty at the expense of Regional and tribal loyalties.

The New System Under Stress, 1: The Action Group Crisis 1962–1963

A very serious political and constitutional crisis involving the Action Group and the Western Regional government, which came to a head in 1962, although its roots went deeply into the pre-independence period, revealed difficulties in governing Nigeria that the new constitutional system had to overcome.[26]

ORIGINS: HOW THE ACTION GROUP PROVOKED THE GOVERNMENT PARTIES

The crisis developed almost immediately after the conclusion of the 1959 Federal election when the Action Group began a campaign to develop a large radical and nationalist constituency. The party's behavior was doubtless provoked by the decision of the NPC and NCNC to exclude it from holding office—a gesture on the part of the ruling groups that hardly encouraged the Action Group politicians in the legislature to be conciliatory, cooperative, or constructive.

Awolowo attacked the Federal Government in strong terms. He condemned the NPC leadership as pro-British and soft on colonialism. He proposed an increase of Nigerian trade with Communist countries in order to reduce economic dependence on the West. The Action Group charged that the country was growing weak and corrupt and that the government abounded in mediocrity.

These criticisms and charges aroused great resentment at Lagos. In a new nation eager to disprove the belief of some that it was not ready for independence or that black people could not govern themselves, Awolowo's attacks were considered disloyal. Especially offensive to the Federal Government was the fact that Awolowo had actually made one of his inflammatory speeches in London to a group of Nigerian students. To attack the country in the capital of its former master was considered tantamount to treason by the government at Lagos. In 1961 the Federal House of Representatives voted to censure Awolowo, who held a seat there.

Another source of irritation to the Federal Government was the Action Group's sponsorship of a program of nationalization designed to appeal to the young, radical, somewhat left-wing elements in the country. The conservative northerners and the business interests of the east vehemently opposed nationalization beyond the extent of public utilities and marketing boards. The NCNC also disapproved of nationalization, and a radical wing of that party, which originally had favored nationalization, was also antagonized by the Action Group's behavior, if only because of resentment over the fact that the latter had stolen its thunder.

Finally, and what probably caused most resentment, was the Action Group's continued support of minority separatism, viewed in Lagos as treasonable because it tended to undermine the cohesion and unity of the new state. But, the NPC and NCNC had other reasons for being opposed to minority separatism. The Northern and Eastern Regions stood to suffer the most in the event new states were created because they were the most ethnically heterogeneous. Furthermore, the Eastern Region and the NCNC were particularly sensitive to national unity because the Ibo lived everywhere in Nigeria and held important posts in many Federal agencies. Also, the Eastern Region relied heavily on the Federal Government for many services that the other Regions provided themselves. The Federal Government and the national idea were, therefore, at least in this period, more meaningful to the Easterners than to the other ethnic groups in the country.

One aspect of Action Group behavior on the minorities issue which offended the Federal Government involved the ultimate disposition of the people living in the British Cameroonian Trust. The Federal Government had to determine the fate of the Cameroons which had been a British mandate since the end of World War I. One alternative favored by the Action Group was continuation of the British administration of the Cameroonian Trust. To the NPC the Action Group's policy on this matter appeared as an unpatriotic effort to diminish the size of Nigeria, to say nothing of the north.

Ultimately the northern portion of the Cameroon Trust voted to join the Nigerian Federation and became a part of the Northern Region while the southern portion of the Trust voted to join the French-speaking Cameroon Republic. This turn of events was of decisive significance for the north, increasing its representation in the Federal House of Representatives by seven seats, thus giving it an absolute majority. The NPC politicians resented Action Group strategy on this issue and the Action Group's relations with the Federal Government further deteriorated.

Still another dimension of the conflict between the Action Group and the government parties involved the creation of the new Midwest Region in 1962. Determined to do something to counteract Action Group strategy on the minorities issue, the NCNC pressed forward with a plan to establish a new Midwest Region which, if carried through, would result in considerable decline in the political influence of the Western Region and, therefore, of the Action Group in the Federal House of Representatives. Although the Action Group had committed itself in the past to creation of new regions and specifically had endorsed the creation of a Midwest region in 1955, it opposed the NCNC plan. The party leaders did not want to lose the Benin Delta area in part because no other minority region would be created and only the Western Region would suffer loss of territory, population, and influence. Also Benin had become especially attractive because oil had been discovered there. Thus, to the dismay of its parliamentary leadership at Lagos, the Action Group had been outmaneuvered by the wily Ibo politicians who now sought the creation of that Midwestern Region.

The Action Group was obviously in a difficult dilemma when the final vote on the Midwest Region came up in the House of Representatives: if it supported the creation of the new region, the Western Region would most certainly be disadvantaged because the NPC-NCNC alignment opposed creation of additional regions. If the party did not support the creation of the new Midwest Region, however, it would alienate its minority allies in the east and north and thus end forever its hope of splitting those Regions. The Action Group resolved the dilemma by voting against the proposal to create the Midwest Region, thus further exacerbating interregional rivalry. In 1963 the Action Group's resistance to the creation of the Midwest Region was, of course, futile thanks to the NPC-NCNC alignment. In 1963 the Midwest Region was formally established.

The NPC-NCNC alignment launched a frontal assault against the Action Group by attacking Chief Awolowo, the party's leader. The Government parties took full advantage of a split within the Action Group between Chief Awolowo and a conservative faction led by the deputy leader, Chief Samuel S. Akintola, who was Premier of the Western Region and friendly to the Federal Government. The split had been encouraged by the fact that Awolowo, as head of the party, had gone to Lagos in 1960 to sit in the Federal House of Representatives while Akintola, his Regional lieutenant, had remained at Ibadan, free to develop his own personal following. Akintola opposed Awolowo's attacks on the Federal Government as serious liabilities for the well-being of both the party and the Western Region. In turn, Awolowo's followers tried to unseat Akintola and the two factions came to blows inside the regional legislature at the end of May, 1962.

Ostensibly to suppress the violence that had broken out in the Western Region's House of Assembly on May 25, the Federal Government declared a state of emergency on May 29, and proceeded to depose Action Group politicians loyal to Awolowo from their governmental positions. The Federal Government also placed the Western Region government under the authority of a Federal administrator for a nine-month period. Federal actions clearly benefited Akintola and his followers. Federal authorities proceeded next to prosecute Awolowo for treason on the ground that he was plotting to overthrow the government. The treason charge was a convenient means of separating Awolowo from the Action Group, thus helping the moderate Akintola to succeed to the leadership of the party.

The Federal Government also carried out a thorough investigation of the Action Group's financial activities to determine if there had been a misuse of Regional funds. A Federal Commission found indisputable cases of misuse of Regional funds for political purposes by Action Group people. At the same time a trial was held for Awolowo in which the cards were stacked against him by his political enemies, a situation which raised very serious questions about the legitimacy of the whole legal procedure. There seemed to be a real possibility that the indictment against him was based on a fabrication of evidence calculated to discredit him and provide the means to his enemies in Lagos to get him out of politics. Awolowo was denied counsel of his own choice; and witnesses who testified against him were suspected of being political opportunists. Awolowo ultimately was convicted of treason and sentenced in September, 1963. For the moment his enemies had succeeded in eliminating him from Nigerian politics.

In retrospect the most serious aspect of the Action Group crisis was the manner in which it so clearly revealed the impact of inter-ethnic and inter-regional rivalries on the functioning of the new federal and parliamentary system. The intervention of the Federal Government in the Western Region to destroy the Awolowo faction of the Action Group was motivated by political rather than constitutional considerations. The same might be said of Awolowo's treason trial. And behind Federal behavior was, of course, the interests and policies of the NPC and the NCNC politicians who were far more concerned with the well-being of their parties and their Regions than with either the Federation or the successful operation of parliamentary democracy. Furthermore, the political character of Awolowo's treason trial diminished confidence in and respect for the Federal courts which the NPC seemed to view as just another instrument of Federal power at the disposal of the NPC to use as it saw fit to further its own interests and those of the Northern Region.

The New System Under Stress, 2: The Federal Election of 1964 and its Aftermath

Changes in Party Alignments

In this election of 1964 there was a new alignment of political forces, very different than the one which had prevailed in 1959.[27] The nucleus of this new political alignment was an alliance between the Awolowo faction of the Action Group, led by Chief Adegbenro, and the NCNC. Minority groups from the north, notably the UMBC and the NEPU were also part of this new alignment. Here was a new coalition, called the United Progressive Grand Alliance (UPGA), that could conceivably defeat the NPC and deprive it of national power. The UPGA promised the creation of new Regions by a constituent assembly and urged a strengthening of the Federal Senate to give it power equal to the Federal House of Representatives in order to provide more equitable representation in the national government to all the Regions.

Behind the establishment of this new grand coalition was a determination on the part of the southern political parties to bury the political hatchet and to unite in an effort to halt the continued northern domination of the Federal Government. Creation of the UPGA doubtlessly had been encouraged if not actually prompted by publication of a new census in 1963 which revealed that while the population of the Northern Region had remained the same, the population of the Eastern Region had declined. At the same time the population of the Western Region, in spite of the loss of territory to the new Midwest Region, had increased. This information seemed to suggest that unless the southern parties collaborated, the NPC would continue indefinitely to dominate the government. Furthermore, given the increase in the population of the Western Region, there was a real possibility that such east-west collaboration could very well result in the defeat of the north.

Opposing this coalition was Chief Akintola and those in the Action Group who had never shared Awolowo's hostility to the political leadership at Lagos. Akintola and his followers had withdrawn from the Action Group following the 1962 crisis. They had established a new political party, the United People's Party (UPP), which was committed to good relations with the NPC and to cooperation with the Federal Government. Why did Akintola and his followers refuse to align with the NCNC? Akintola's Yoruba supporters, who had always constituted a sort of right wing of the Action Group, resented the fact that the Ibo in the Federal Government, especially, it was believed, in the Federal Army, engaged in an undisguised nepotism to the detriment of job-seeking Yorubas. This practice of personalism, not uncommon in Third World countries, was the result of lingering tribal values and loyalties not yet replaced by the national idea.

In March of 1964 Akintola's United People's Party, together with a small number of maverick members of the NCNC who held seats in the Western Region Assembly, met to form a new grouping called the Nigerian National Democratic Party (NNDP). The NNDP now aligned itself with the NPC in a grand coalition called the Nigerian National Alliance (NNA). The NNA enjoyed some minority support in the Benin Delta and Lagos as well as elsewhere in the north and west. By the summer of 1964 the battle lines were drawn for this last, most traumatic, and most decisive of elections in Nigeria since the establishment of parliamentary politics in the early 1950's.

THE CAMPAIGN AND ITS OUTCOME

The 1964 election was fought even harder than the one in 1959. Considerable violence and disorder occurred during the campaign. Opposition politicians were harassed in all Regions and curfews, arrests, street fights, and even party killings were not unusual. From the very beginning there was a sense of frustration in the south, particularly in the Eastern Region, over the fact that the results of the elections could really be predetermined because of the Northern Region's overwhelming superiority in population. Furthermore, specific features of the campaign added to its unpleasantness and revealed again how detrimental the inter-ethnic and inter-regional rivalries could be for the preservation of national unity and the successful functioning of parliamentary democracy. For example, there was much condemnation by northern politicians of the Ibo, as well as violence against the property and person of Ibo people living and working in the north. The NPC used the coercive power of the Regional government to harass opposition candidates. It became very difficult if not impossible for UPGA candidates to get on ballots in many northern constituencies.

The Eastern Region was provoked to threaten secession: a threat that was not carried out. Rather, the easterners did what they thought was the next best thing: they boycotted the election, making victory all the more certain for the northerners. When the election was over no one was surprised to learn that NPC candidates had won 162 seats in the Federal House of Representatives and thus commanded an absolute majority.

It was up to President Azikiwe to call upon Sir Abubakar to form another government. Azikiwe wavered. He resented the smear campaign of northern politicians against his fellow Ibo. For a moment he may have contemplated appointment of a minority or provisional government. He ultimately decided to summon Balewa because he had no other constitutional alternative. His hesitation, however, aroused the suspicions and anger of the NPC leadership who saw in his behavior another example of Ibo localism.

Balewa was confronted with a difficult political situation: how to heal the wounds of the election battle and promote political peace and harmony. It was obvious that he could not ignore the southern political groups, especially as the Eastern Region was again in early 1965 threatening secession. Balewa decided to form a very broad government which would include representatives of the NCNC. The Action Group, however, was not invited to join. Balewa also proposed a conference to consider changes in the Constitution and called for new elections in the Eastern Region to fill its seats in the Federal Legislature. This election was held in March at which time the NCNC strengthened its situation in the Cabinet.

These actions of the Federal Prime Minister, however conciliatory, had certain shortcomings and really did little to achieve political reconciliation. Packing the government with additional ministerial positions just to broaden the political spectrum upon which the Cabinet was based was not the real answer to the problem and, indeed, antagonized many Nigerians who saw the Prime Minister's actions as just another example of self-seeking political maneuverings of the NPC leadership at Lagos. Furthermore, the fact remained that the northerners dominated the governmental system and the southerners, both Ibo and

Yoruba, were very resentful. This resentment ran deep and was not merely political in character but ethnic, religious, and even ideological. In addition to dissatisfaction with the efforts of the Federal Prime Minister to mediate and conciliate, there was much Ibo resentment over the Western Region election on November, 1965, which may well have inspired the military coup against the Federal Cabinet in January 1966. The Western Region election offered the UPGA a last chance to challenge the political predominance of the NPC by defeating Akintola's NNDP government at Ibadan. Like the Federal election the preceding December, this election was a tough and nasty fight. One of the most offensive aspects of the contest was the NNDP use of the power and influence of the Western Region government to further its political cause against the UPGA. For example, at the last meeting of the Western Region House of Assembly before the election, the NNDP enacted into law a series of special electoral rules specifically designed to disadvantage the UPGA. Public meetings were banned for two months and polls were to close on election day at four in the afternoon rather than at the normal time of six o'clock, thus enabling employers, of which the government was the largest, to keep employees—many of whom had UPGA sympathies—from voting.

During the campaign the NNDP reminded the Yoruba of the benefits that had accrued to the Western Region in consequence of Awolowo's retirement from politics and the NNDP's alignment with the NPC at Lagos. For the first time in many years, the party declared, the Western Region was able to participate in the Federal Government and benefit accordingly, at least in terms of Yoruba people getting more jobs at Lagos than before.

The UPGA countered with revelations of the seamier side of Western Region politics, reminding the Yoruba of how Akintola's government had ruled ruthlessly and autocratically, favoring those who supported it, while discriminating against and injuring those who opposed it. The UPGA pointed out, further, how self-seeking the NNDP politicians actually were by revealing how Akintola rewarded his friends by giving them political jobs with the result that the Regional Cabinet was swollen with virtually every loyal NNDP member of parliament enjoying some kind of portfolio. The UPGA promised to secure the release of Awolowo, reduce the size of the Cabinet, and reorganize the public corporations "with a view to reducing the number of parasitic appendages now parading themselves as executive directors."

There were questionable irregularities in each of the three stages of the election, nominations, voting, and counting; so much so that each side was able to declare itself the winner. The so-called official result, which gave Akintola's NNDP an overwhelming majority, was broadcast from both Ibadan and Lagos and was the signal to the Western Regional

Governor, Sir Joseph Fadahunsi, to call upon Akintola to form a new government. On the other hand, the UPGA leader, Chief Adegbenro, complained to the Governor of open rigging by the NNDP and asked him not to invest Akintola. At the same time Adegbenro announced the creation of his own cabinet for which he was immediately arrested and charged with unlawful assumption of power.

Though Chief Adegbenro assured the Governor that he did not intend to assume office illegally and that his party would pursue its goals by constitutional means, it was plain that once again the Western Region was on the verge of anarchy and civil war. During December 1965 and January 1966 there was violence and disorder everywhere in the Region. Furthermore, both Akintola and Sir Abubakar, the Federal Prime Minister, had received warnings of assassination and of an imminent *coup d'état.* Some action to calm the Western Region would have to be taken by the Federal Government. The UPGA asked the Federal Prime Minister to declare a state of emergency in the Western Region, as had been done in 1962, and arrange for another election. In 1966, however, Sir Abubakar demurred, primarily because Federal intervention would result in the unseating of political friends, rather than enemies, as had been the case in 1962. This hesitation proved to be the Prime Minister's undoing. Before he knew what had happened, a group of disaffected Ibo officers of the Federal Army carried out a coup to unseat him.[28]

THE CONSEQUENCES OF POLITICS: MILITARY DICTATORSHIP AND CIVIL WAR

Violence

THE ARMY DESTROYS THE PARLIAMENTARY SYSTEM

Military officers in general and those of Ibo background in particular had become fed up with the performance of the civilian politicians. The Nigerian military never had had much respect for the strife-ridden, overly professional politicians and blamed all the problems of the post-independence Federal Government on their misdeeds. Behind this hostility toward the politicians was the belief that they talked too much, were deceitful, and tended to be motivated primarily by self-interest. Furthermore, the military had a deep-seated dislike of the democratic process, particularly elections in which the politicians consulted what the army officers believed were the uneducated and ignorant masses. The military believed, furthermore, that if the politicians were the experts in government they claimed to be, such consultation was unnecessary and even dangerous.

Ibo junior officers were particularly hostile to the government of the Federation. The political philosophy of these officers was very reminiscent of that of the short-lived, radical Zikist movement of the late 1940's. These Ibo officers were responsible for the coup in the north. They sought radical political change for the better without thoughts of tribal advantage. Ultimately, however, tribal interests intervened and to a degree perverted the coup, making it appear, at least in the eyes of northerners, as an Ibo offensive against Hausa-Fulani rule in both Lagos and the Northern Region.

Largely responsible for this arousal of Ibo tribal feelings were the fears of Ibo officers of widespread anti-Ibo sentiment based on the belief of the non-Ibo officers that their Ibo colleagues "packed their own" into military positions. Ibo fears of prejudices against them in the army went back as far as the colonial period when it had been perfectly plain to the Ibo officers that the British officers disliked them and preferred those of northern extraction. Furthermore, Ibo officers believed that they were discriminated against in salary and promotion within the army, although there is little evidence to prove that discrimination of this kind in fact existed. Finally, Ibo officers were afraid that in the event the Federal Government, dominated by northerners, settled on a policy of early retirement for officers, they would be the first to be asked to go. For these reasons the Ibo officers were suspicious, frustrated, and therefore extremely restive. Their feelings reflected in the army the same severe inter-ethnic tension that had undermined the civilian administration.

The Ibo also feared the future. They were well aware of the enormous hostility of NPC politicians toward Azikiwe because of the possibility that he might have used the presidential office to reverse northern political dominance after the NPC victory in the 1964 Federal elections. The Ibo feared that the NNA coalition, with its two-thirds majority in both the House of Representatives and the Senate, might attempt to intervene in the Eastern Region to give the NCNC the same treatment given to the Action Group in 1962 and, even worse, carve out of the Eastern Region a new separate Rivers Region which would include the oil-rich districts so important to the financial strength and security of the NCNC and the Enugu government. The military coup against the NNA leadership at Lagos could well be considered a timely move to forestall such events.

The coup began when Ibo officered army units abducted Federal Prime Minister Sir Abubakar in January, 1966. At the same time the Premiers of the Northern and Western Regions, Sir Ahmadu Bello and Chief Samuel Akintola, respectively, were assassinated. For the moment the civilian governments in most of the country were paralyzed. The Federal Cabinet now called the Ibo General, Aguiyi Ironsi, to head a provisional military government to restore order. Ironsi, a senior commanding officer, appeared to be neutral and willing to restore order within the military, though his sympathies obviously lay with the anti-regime activities of his brother officers. Ironsi accepted the Cabinet's bid and proceeded to suspend civil governmental machinery on the Federal and Regional levels in the middle of January. He then established a national military government at Lagos and military administrations in each of the four Regions. Politicians were effectively displaced by high ranking military personnel in the top decision-making positions on the national and regional levels.

Ironsi's ascendancy for the moment had broad national support. Radical elements critical of the policies and actions of the politically conservative NNA government were delighted over its fall and the prospect of change and reform. Many less radical elements in the south were equally delighted with the new turn of events if only because they signalled the end of the despised northern dominance of the national government at Lagos. Even politically conservative interests in the north itself went along for the time being with Ironsi, relieved that a more radical and tribal oriented figure had not emerged in the wake of the collapse of the civilian regimes. Ironsi encouraged this conservative acceptance by appointing subordinates who represented a cross-section of tribal interests. He appointed Lieutenant Colonel Yakubu Gowon, a senior officer from the north, as his Chief of Staff.

At the end of January Ironsi announced plans for sweeping reforms designed to end corruption, nepotism, and tribalism in civil appointments. He attacked the political parties for their excessive professionalism and greed and in May he decreed the dissolution of most of them. In his dismissal of prominent politicians from high positions in the Federal Government, notably those at the head of the public corporations, he effectively cleaned out NPC people from most of the influential positions in the Federal Government. His long-range goal was creation of a strong central government in which political parties would not play a dominant role and in which administrative power would be concentrated at the center and no longer in the hands of only NPC politicians and their allies. In a speech in January in support of Ironsi's policies the new military governor of the Eastern Region, Lieutenant Colonel Odumwegu Ojukuwu, attacked "ten wasted years of planlessness, incompetence, inefficiency, greed, corruption, avarice, and gross disregard for the interests of the common man."

THE NEW DICTATORSHIP UNDERMINED BY ETHNIC CLEAVAGE

The Hausa-Fulani political leaders did not like this turn of events. They were stunned by news that Sir Abubakar's body had been found in a roadway near Abeokuta in the Western Region. They did not like

Ironsi's plans for a strong central government, which they viewed as dangerous to their future condition in the country. They rightly recognized that the things Ironsi was seeking to accomplish would be detrimental to their influence on the government of the Northern Region and on the central government at Lagos. They suspected that everything Ironsi was doing in the months following his accession to power was motivated primarily by tribal considerations and that as a typical Ibo he was looking after the interests of his kinsmen at the expense of other groups. For example, northerners were alarmed by what struck them as an unduly large number of Ibo promotions in the army.

At the same time Ironsi's personal relations with the northerners were very poor. In his efforts to ingratiate his government with the north, he dealt primarily with the traditional conservative elite, the Sultan of Sokoto, the emirs, and chiefs, people who in the late 1960's had very little rapport with the masses. For example, his military governor of the north was Hassan Katsina, the son of the Emir of Katsina. Ironsi preferred Katsina because of his aristocratic background and greatly overestimated the man's real political influence among the people. Katsina turned out to be a liability for Ironsi in not having forewarned him of growing unrest in the north.

Northerners disliked Ironsi's regime and in fact began to seethe over its apparent Ibo orientation. In May Ibo residents in northern cities were selectively massacred. Local police and northern contingents of the Federal Army stood by and allowed this lawlessness to prevail. Northern dissatisfaction over the Ironsi government suddenly exploded in July, and the Ibo ascendancy was brought to an abrupt and violent end just as the country was beginning its political recovery. A clique of northern officers of the Federal Army abducted Ironsi. Ironsi's Chief of Staff, Lieutenant Colonel Yakabu Gowon, leader of these rebel officers, now emerged as head of state. Gowon disclaimed any involvement in the abduction of Ironsi and called upon the officers to support his program of political change for Nigeria. Clearly, this new military coup was the result of northern fears of southern domination of the Federal Government.

There were, however, other more specific considerations underlying the northern attack on the Ironsi government. The military government of General Ironsi had not promoted a national consensus on centralization, but rather had presented the country with an unpleasant *fait accompli* which had offended many of the smaller tribal groups especially in the north, which had hoped for Regional status. Ironsi for the moment had ruled out the possibility of creating additional Regions. Also, the army as a source of national leadership had been undermined by a continuing process of internal disintegration, primarily in consequence of latent inter-ethnic rivalry within its ranks over such issues as promotion, salary increases, and duty assignments. Although General Ironsi in January had enjoyed national support and was a real national leader, in the succeeding months he had lost his grip as officers of different tribal groups, especially from the north, became increasingly uncomfortable with his centralizing policies, which they viewed as Ibo inspired. The July coup, then, was caused also by deep-seated resentment of smaller ethnic groups over the political and economic consequences of "big tribe chauvinism," in general, and Ibo aggressiveness, in particular.

Still another factor that may account for the demise of the Ironsi regime was the weakness of its communication with the Regions which were in touch with the center only through membership of the Regional governors in the Supreme Military Council and the Federal Cabinet. In this instance, only one man was able to articulate Regional interests and grievances before the central government, and then quite inadequately in that the meetings of these bodies were more like a military briefing than a political caucus where differences are freely discussed and agreements reached on the basis of bargains and compromises. This situation, though it sharply contrasted with the opposite extreme under the civilian regime of the early 1960's, when there was too much opportunity for regional interests to express themselves at the center, was equally unsatisfactory.

The Ibo refused to accept the reversal of their ascendancy. The military governor of the Eastern Region, Lt. Colonel Odumwegu Ojukuwu, condemned Gowon and his military regime in August.[29] He accused Gowon of being an agent of northern political leaders and of the military conspirators who abducted Ironsi. Ojukuwu also charged Gowon with plans to divide the country into separate autonomous states and to compel minorities in these states to go home to their own Regions. The Ibo in the Northern Region stood to suffer most from such a step.

Ojukuwu was encouraged to boycott the new regime when he received news in August that Ironsi had been assassinated. At this point he began to take steps that led eventually to the secession of the Eastern Region and the establishment of the independent state of Biafra. After consultation with the staff of the Eastern Region's contingents of the Federal Army at Enugu, he told Gowon that the Eastern Region wanted its own army to protect it. At the same time, incidentally, there was a mass exodus of 300,000 Ibo from the north to the Eastern Region. Always having been the object of scorn and discrimination in the Northern Region, the Ibo living there were now subjected to a massacre that began at the end of September. There was a new determination in the northern cities to expel the easterners who had held jobs as clerks, civil servants, and artisans which were coveted by the northerners themselves. The northerners viewed these Ibo as arrogant and clannish aliens. In October, 300 Ibo were slain in Kano. Looting occurred everywhere, suggesting the intensity of northern prejudice against the Ibo. At first the killings had been sporadic, but in time they became systematic and inclusive of the entire Ibo community. The Ibo were terrified and their only alternative in October was to leave the north once and for all. Against this somber background the rift between the Eastern Region and the Federal Government widened in the latter part of 1966 and early 1967 as Gowon proceeded to consolidate his power at Lagos. In the beginning of September Gowon opened discussions with Regional leaders about the future organization of the Nigerian state. Though Gowon favored restoration of the federal system and decreed it on paper on September 1, he began to doubt the wisdom of the federalism his northern supporters wanted. In his discussions with the representatives of the Regions at Lagos he found to his dismay a general desire for Regional autonomy and separate military forces.

Gowon's efforts to preserve national unity and carry on a dialogue with the leaders of the other Regions were also decisively undermined by the northern massacre of the Ibo. The immediate consequence of the Ibo massacre in Kano was the strengthening of Ojukuwu's determination in September and October that the Eastern Region pursue a separate path. He told the Hausa people in the Eastern Region that for their own safety they must go home. He warned the rest of the country publicly that the Eastern Region may have to secede in consequence of the anti-Ibo riots and massacres in other parts of Nigeria. Ibo anger and hostility toward the northerners built up as Ibo refugees from the north returning home to the east told of northern outrages against them. In November Ojukuwu refused to participate any longer in the constitutional discussions at Lagos.

Gowon now warned the eastern leadership against secession and pledged to do everything possible to hold the country together. Furthermore, Gowon refused to consider a plan for a decentralized military organization. He opposed the idea of regional armies preferred by the east. In January 1967, at a meeting with senior military personnel, including Ojutuwu, held in Ghana, he affirmed the preservation of a national military force, though he was willing to permit subdivisions of the federal army into area commands which could be used for internal security purposes by local military governors.

At the Ghana meeting and immediately after, it was clear that Gowon was willing to be conciliatory to avoid a break-up of the Federation. His conciliatory approach, however, was undermined by northern civil servants in the Federal Government who placed obstacles in the way of implementing the agreements reached at Ghana. These people deplored the tendencies toward administrative decentralization which Gowon was willing to permit in the interests of preserving national unity.

At the same time, Ojukuwu remained defiant in the face of Gowon's efforts. He refused to heed Gowon's warnings and exhortations about separation and in March, 1967, he took steps to lead the Eastern Region out of the Federation. Ojukuwu then prepared for the inevitable clash with Gowon and the national government. Military personnel and civilians were mobilized for conflict. In April the Eastern Region ceased payment of Federal taxes and the Regional government at Enugu asked President Nasser of the United Arab Republic to mediate between the Eastern Region and the central government. Also at this time the Enugu government had assumed control of Federal utilities. At the end of May, in response to a partial economic blockade by the central government and stern warnings from Gowon, Ojukuwu asked the Eastern Region Legislature at Enugu to vote Biafra's independence. This was done on May 30. Ojukuwu's determination to secede was unaffected by a last minute change in the structure of the Nigerian Federation put through by Gowon, namely the creation out of the four Regions of twelve self-governing states based upon tribal differences. This reform split the Eastern Region into three parts: an Eastern state with its capital at Calabar, a Central-Eastern state with its capital at Enugu, and a Rivers state with its capital at Port Harcourt. Ojukuwu ignored this new arrangement.

In an attempt to reverse the secession, military forces of the central government invaded Biafra on July 7, 1967, inaugurating a long and bitter military conflict that finally came to an end in 1970 with the conquest of Biafra and the reimposition of national control over the area. The former state of Biafra was subsequently divided into the three self-governing states Gowon originally had intended to create in the Eastern Region on the eve of the secession.

In leading the Eastern Region to secede, Ojukuwu did not have the unanimous support of all the Eastern peoples. Minority groups such as the Calabar and River people had little enthusiasm for secession. They had long standing grievances against the majority Ibo and their dominance of the NCNC which had controlled the Regional government in Enugu. The latter had frequently frustrated the activities of the Federally-controlled Niger Delta Development Board which had been set up to deal with the socio-economic problems of the Delta people. Indeed, when the Ibo began to leave Lagos in the spring of 1967, Calabar and Rivers people were unwilling to return home. The irony in this situation lies in the unpleasant analogy between the relationship of Ibo to northerners on the one hand and that of the eastern minorities to the Ibo on the other.

REUNIFICATION AND RECONCILIATION: THE POLITICAL SYSTEM EMERGING AS AN INDEPENDENT VARIABLE

When the war came to an end in 1970 the most important concern of the military regime was restoration of national unity. The government of General Gowon did not gloat over the defeat of Biafra, refrained from victory celebration, and, rather, took positive steps to help promote inter-ethnic reconciliation. Ibo holders of Federal jobs in Lagos, which they had left when the civil conflict had broken out three years earlier, were invited to return for reinstatement. To the surprise of some Ibo, returning to their former homes in the north, abandoned property had been protected and kept in repair—clearly a conciliatory gesture on the part of some northerners eager to redress the wrong done to the Ibo on the eve of the conflict. Furthermore, General Gowon himself symbolizes reunification and reconciliation in that he has been accepted by all Nigerians. Because he is from the north, the Hausa and Fulani thus far accept him. And since he is not a Hausa but a member of the minority Angas tribe and a Methodist, he is also acceptable to the Yoruba, Ibo, and other Southern and Christian groups.

BUREAUCRACY AND ADMINISTRATIVE REFORM

Also significant in the restoration of inter-ethnic harmony and promotion of national unity was the administrative reorganization of the country into twelve new states based upon ethnic divisions carried through by Gowon's government at the end of May 1967. When the war was over the reform had already been in effect for three years and its beneficial results were beginning to show. For example, the creation of six new states out of the former Northern Region had contributed to the permanent dismantling of the Hausa-Fulani political empire that had exercised a decisive influence over national politics to the detriment of the other large and small ethnic groups in the country. In the future it would be very difficult if not impossible for Hausa-Fulani politicians, whose political base was now confined to the new Northwest State with its capital at Sokoto, and to the city of Kano, to regain their former influence on national affairs at Lagos. Furthermore, the other ethnic groups in the North such as the Tiv, Kanuri, and Nupe were relieved to be out from under the conservative and discriminatory Hausa-Fulani administration at Sokoto and to that extent inter-ethnic animosities—an important obstacle to the development of national unity—were reduced. At the same time and in the same way the Calabar Ibo and the Rivers people, who in 1970 had their own states, were happy to be out from under the control of the Enugu government of the former Eastern Region, especially as these small groups had had misgivings about the wisdom of secession when it had been carried by Ojukuwu in May, 1967.

Gowon has made it plain that a very important prerequisite for permanent inter-ethnic harmony and national unity in the future, when civilian rule presumably shall have been restored, is a new party system which, as he put it, will rest "on the widest possible national basis . . .". Gowon dismisses the possibility of a return to a party system based upon states, regions or tribes alone and warned against "the dangerous consequences of ethnic and clannish exclusiveness." and, certain that the time was not yet at hand to build the kind of truly national party system he believed Nigeria should have, he pointedly reminded the country in October, 1970, on the tenth anniversary of its independence, that political activity was still banned by a military decree of 1966.

ECONOMIC MODERNIZATION AS A POLICY TOOL

Still another way in which the military regime has endeavored to promote unity in the post-war period is furtherance of economic recovery and development. In the beginning of October, 1970, Gowon spoke of the need of the Federal Government "to wipe out the traces of the war," and referred to the reconstruction of bombed out towns, rebuilding of bridges and roads, and the resumption of normal educational and social services. Accordingly, physical recovery of the war-torn areas of the country, most of which were in the former Eastern Region, was given top priority. This recovery has proceeded with astonishing speed in consequence of not only Federal initiative but also the amazing physical and spiritual resiliency of the Ibo.

Gowon has also addressed himself to the more far-reaching goal of economic growth and development. In the beginning of November he announced a four-year development plan which, in addition to promising recovery of war-torn parts of the country, laid out a program to promote a "just and equalitarian society." One of the most conspicuous features of the plan is the reassignment of control and management of the national economy to the central government. The plan revealed also the military regime's intentions to promote "meaningful Nigerianization" of foreign companies by which certain businesses would be operated only by Nigerians and to provide the central government with control of the "commanding heights of the national economy." In this way Gowon intends to provide his government with the material wherewithal to strengthen the economic underpinnings of the national political community and to avoid the inter-ethnic and inter-regional competition of the pre-war period that resulted in wasteful duplication and haphazard development.

Furthermore, in calling for a "radical and militant program of social action" which he says is needed for "a just and equalitarian society," Gowon wishes to eliminate the economic and material inequalities that had fostered inter-ethnic animosity and inter-regional political friction before the war. To that end the plan envisages expansion of the public transport system, development and diversification of the educational system, and modernization and expansion of the agricultural sector which, incidentally, employs 70 percent of the labor force.

One conspicuous accomplishment of the Gowon government was the nationalization of all Nigerian universities in August, 1972. This action had three purposes: (1) to ensure a national direction of education, important for the creation of a much needed technical intelligentsia that has been affected by a "brain drain," namely emigration of highly trained citizens to foreign countries where there are high paying jobs; (2) to promote uniformity in content and standard of teaching, with a view to emphasizing value of and pride in citizenship, and finally (3) to relieve the state governments as far as possible of the financial burdens of maintaining an adequate school and university system so that they can devote their resources to other aspects of development. Furthermore, the regime doubtlessly wishes to continue the Nigerianization of the university curricula which for too long stressed European ideas, values, and learning. Gowon sees the universities as one of the best means of developing a national consciousness and unity.

Of particular importance with regard to encouraging inter-ethnic harmony and national political unity is the effort to promote national uniformity in primary and secondary education. The regime wants to diminish the wide variation in patterns and standards of teaching that prevailed in different parts of the country and to eliminate the discrimination in the educational system against the less wealthy people who send their children to schools that are inferior to those attended by the children of the well-to-do.

Prospects of a Return to Parliamentary Government and Democracy

Perhaps the next most important question about Nigeria's future when the war was over was whether or not Gowon's military regime should continue to administer the country. A return to civilian rule upon the successful conclusion of the effort to end the secession had never been foreclosed by the military government. Indeed, Gowon had released from prison a number of civilian political prisoners such as Chief Awolowo, who had been put away by the NPC government of Sir Abubakar in the mid 1960's. Furthermore, Gowon had instructed the military governors of the twelve states to appoint civilian commissioners as their administrative subalterns, people to whom local administrative power might conceivably be transferred at the proper time.

On the other hand, at the end of the war the military government realized the dimensions of the problem of restoring and strengthening both political and economic unity and a decision was made to remain in power. In October, 1970, Gowon listed a number of tasks the military regime must perform before a return to civilian rule. The most important of these tasks were elections, and the preparation of a new Constitution. Gowon further declared: "We must . . . proceed very carefully so that the final handover of the government to elected representatives of the people may usher in a period of lasting peace and political stability." He did not foresee a return to civilian government before 1976.

THE MILITARY AS AN INSTRUMENT OF CONTROL

There were, of course, other factors that explain the unwillingness of the military leaders to transfer power to civilians in 1970 and why, indeed, that transfer may not occur for some time. First, is the fact that the military leaders and their bureaucratic subordinates at Lagos have developed in the preceding years into a vested interest group unwilling to do anything to jeopardize the power position which they presently enjoy. The military at present is the only national institution that has the physical means of not only preserving control over the country but also of promoting national unity and political stability. In addition, the army itself, apart from its leaders, constitutes a vested interest committed to the perpetuation of military rule. The army today is a large, experienced, and confident military force in consequence of the three-year civil conflict. It is very different from the small, inexperienced, and uncertain military organization of 1960 inherited from the colonial period. Also this new army may not wish to abdicate its present central, powerful, and prestigious position in Nigerian national life, even if its top leadership, such as General Gowon, should prefer to do so. At the very least the date of a return to civilian rule in Nigeria is at this time an imponderable. Democratic government of the Western type, however, may not be a viable form of politics for ethnically-fragmented Nigeria.

There are, of course, certain obstacles to and dangers in the indefinite prolongation of military rule. The military administration of the country was imposed without popular consent—something to which the Nigerian people are very sensitive, regardless of the degree of personal political sophistication. At first the regime enjoyed some consensus of support if only because it brought to an end an unpopular and inefficient political system. But upon the conclusion of the war, popularity of the military governors of the states had begun to wane.

The military officers have been found to be often dishonest and inefficient administrators. What is worse, they are not removable except by decree of their commanding officer, General Gowon. Furthermore, Gowon has shown himself averse to rotating these administrators. He seems disinclined to do much to discourage the inevitable empire building which leads to partisanship, dishonesty, and inefficiency—characteristics that are becoming noticeable in upper levels of the state administrations, especially among governors and the civil commissioners they have appointed as administrative assistants.

It is on the very local levels of the present Nigerian governmental system that the military could conceivably begin a planned withdrawal. The most obvious way in which this could be done might be to hold elections for local office which could be followed by statewide elections of civil commissioners. The military could exercise a supervisory function in these electoral processes. In any event, the restoration of large-scale civilian participation in and control of local and state governments could be, as in the case of post-war West Germany, the beginning of the liquidation of military rule and the establishment of a democratic political system, if that is what the Nigerian elites choose.[30] Democratic politics because of its emphasis on compromise and conciliation, might, however, jeopardize other national goals such as economic development and modernization.

Causes of Political Failure in Retrospect

INTER-ETHNIC CONFLICT

One of the most important factors responsible for the collapse of the 1960 federal and parliamentary democracy, the establishment of a military dictatorship, and the outbreak of civil war was intensification of inter-ethnic rivalry and conflict in the post-independence years. Certain aspects of the post-independence political system intensified this inter-ethnic rivalry and conflict.

The very achievement of independence fostered ethnic rivalry. Each of the large ethno-centered regionally based political parties sought dominance of the new Federal Government not merely for the sake of leading the country but also to exercise control over the country's vast economic wealth for the benefit of the particular Regions which the parties represented and from which they derived their support. It is not difficult to understand the bitter resentment of an antagonism toward these so-called government parties felt by not only the Action Group and the political leaders of the Western Region but also the smaller ethnic groups. For example, NPC control of the Federal Cabinet in the early 1960's and the prospect that such control might continue indefinitely because of the population advantage enjoyed by the Northern Region aroused great resentment in the south if only because of the fact that the north was the poorest part of the country and therefore the Hausa-Fulani leaders of the NPC were the most likely of all politicians to use Federal power for Regional advantage.

The achievement of independence also intensified ethnic based inter-personal rivalry, especially between the southerners. More than ever before Yoruba and Ibo competed with one another for Federal jobs in the public corporations which had become tremendous centers of patronage. Here, on the personal as well as governmental level, tribal ties and orientation seemed to be much stronger than any commitment to nationhood.

Furthermore, this intense personalism was not appreciably diminished by education which was controlled and determined by the Regions—which is to say the large ethnic groups that dominated the Regional governments. Indeed, the decentralization of Nigerian education is largely responsible for the failure of the post-independence regime to socialize Nigerians in the national idea.

INADEQUACIES OF THE BRITISH PARLIAMENTARY MODEL

Ethnic rivalry and conflict produced a political divisiveness which proved too much for the Nigerian parliamentary system. Worse than that, it is now clear that the parliamentary system at Lagos, which was patterned after the British model, worsened inter-ethnic jealousies and antagonisms by allowing the NPC, a Regional and a very parochial and politically conservative party, to control the Federal Government and lead the nation, the NPC was never not really representative of the nation.

Nigeria is quite unlike England where the political majority the government enjoys in the Parliament represents a national constituency, the logical consequence of ethnic and cultural homogeneity. Furthermore, in the English House of Commons there is a large well-organized and disciplined political minority, ready to play a constructive role without malice or vindictiveness resulting from electoral defeat.

To have worked better than it did, the Nigerian parliamentary system should have provided for executive responsibility to both the Senate, which represented the Regions, as well as the House of Representatives; or there should have been a strong, truly national, cross-communal executive who enjoyed both the loyalty and confidence of many ethnic groups. Or, the Northern Region originally should have been broken up into several states based upon large tribal groups as was done in May, 1967. If this step had been taken in the early 1950's, it would have prevented an ethno-centered and regionally based party like the NPC from exercising an influence over Regional as well as Federal policies far out of proportion to the strength of its limited ethnic and geographic constituency.

Inter-ethnic and inter-regional jealousies and antagonisms fostered by the 1960 parliamentary system help to account also for the violent and divisive character of the political crises of the early 1960's, notably the dispute over disposition of the Cameroon Trust, the fight over the creation of the new Midwest Region, the suspension of the Western Region government, and the treason trial of Chief Awolowo. The Action Group and, ultimately, the NCNC bitterly resented the efforts of the NPC to use national power to further its own narrow political ends and those of the Northern Region, as was done in the suspension of the Western Region government and the treason trial of Awolowo. The NPC leadership had been determined to divide, weaken and possibly even destroy the Action Group if only because it had been one of the most aggressive and outspoken opponents of the NPC since the early 1950's.

These political conditions might have been different and the parliamentary system inherited from the British might have worked better than it did, had there been continuous and concerted efforts on the part of the Nigerian Federal Government in the post-independence years to socialize the masses in the national idea, through the primary and secondary schools. But education was decentralized and, like the regional and ethnic based parties, the school systems divided rather than unified the fragmented Nigerian society. Perhaps one of the most important reasons why the Federal Government failed to promote Nigerian unity from above has to do with its failure to reach the masses of Nigerians in the back country and especially in the north and to instruct them in the idea of a national political community.

POLITICAL BEHAVIOR AND THE FAILURE OF POLITICS

Behavior of the individual politicians also aggravated and worsened the effects of inter-ethnic rivalry and conflict and to that degree was a liability for the successful operation of the post-independence parliamentary system. The Nigerian politicians were not sufficiently experienced in parliamentary procedure to permit the British system to work effectively. In the crises of the early 1960's the political leaders showed no sense of fair play toward their opponents, no respect for opposition or belief that opposition could play a constructive role in the governmental process.

NPC and NCNC politicians were offended all too easily by the behavior of the Action Group people after the Federal election of 1959 and made no allowances for the discomfort losers always have after a hard fought contest. And the Action Group's behavior is also open to criticism in that Awolowo and others pursued a "sour grapes" policy after the election that raised doubts about their willingness to play the role of a loyal and constructive opposition. They needlessly antagonized the government parties, widening the gap between "outs" and "ins."

Most Nigerian politicians in these early post-independence years simply did not understand the spirit and values that underlay the smooth functioning of the parliamentary forms introduced to them by the British. Looking back at the events of the early 1960's it almost seems as if the parliamentary system was little more than a façade, another means available to ethnic groups to continue in new ways their endless rivalries and conflict.

The Federal elections of 1964 and the Western Regional election of 1965 marked a nadir in the parliamentary politics of the post independence period. They revealed the depth and severity of inter-ethnic jealousy and rivalry. The large and small ethno-centered parties fought these political contests with ruthless determination to win control of the power centers. The battle scars never really healed and it is not exaggeration to say that after both elections there was more division and uncertainty about who controlled what than before. That these elections in 1964 and 1965 were indeed fought so hard and with greater inter-ethnic animosity than earlier contests suggests the extent to which political disunity and disintegration had progressed since the achievement of independence in 1960.

Intrusion of the Army in Politics

The military coup and counter-coup in 1966 were both cause and consequence of political failure under the Republic. Army officers deplored the inability of the politicians to preserve unity and promote stable government. Ibo officers in particular resented the excessive ethnic orientation of the northern leadership at Lagos in the early 1960's. The Ibo inspired military coup in January, 1966, led by General Ironsi, was an attempt to displace these politicians and achieve the inter-ethnic balance that had eluded them.

Although the soldiers succeeded in removing the politicans, they were unable to preserve national unity. It turned out that they too were divided by ethnic jealousy and prejudice in spite of the veneer of unity and discipline within their ranks. The Ironsi government was undone by a northern counter-coup which had been based on a coalition of northern interests that had in common dislike of centralization and Ibo domination. Having lost control of the center and fearful of new northern outrages against them now that northern interests had regained control of Lagos, the Ibo of the Eastern Region decided that the only course left to them was to pursue a separate political path, to sever their political and administrative ties with the Federation. To the dismay of the new military regime of General Gowon, inter-ethnic antagonisms had now reached an all time high, threatening national anarchy and dissolution in spite of heroic eleventh hour efforts to reassure the Ibo and put off secession.

A final comment on the failure of parliamentary and democratic government and the development of dictatorship in Nigeria has to do with Eric Nordlinger's notion that stable, effective, and representative government is possible only if political development occurs in four stages with gradual rates of change: (1) formation of national identity; (2) institutionalization of a central authority subordinate to an executive and legislature; (3) establishment of mass parties based upon wide and varied constituencies and (4) mass suffrage.[31] It is clear that Nigerian political development did not proceed through these stages and that rates of change were not gradual. Nigeria was quite unlike India where men like Gandhi and Nehru as well as the Congress party developed a following amongst many sections of society and within different parts of the country and thus helped to promote a national identity. Its development was also unlike China's where Mao Tse Tung and the Chinese Communist Party used ideology and power to create a unified and disciplined society. Nigeria had no charismatic political leaders and no mass parties representing wide and varied segments of the population. Indeed, political institutionalization during the parliamentary period of the 1950's and 1960's occurred before many Nigerians, especially in the north, had begun to see themselves as part of a national political community.

Furthermore, insofar as rate of change was concerned, Nigeria was less fortunate than India, Chile, or Mexico. The period in which Nigerians had the opportunity to learn how to make their parliamentary system work well was far too short. Thus, political change to representative government and self-rule in the 1950's and early 1960's was anything but gradual when compared with India, where central government and local political participation as well as structural unity developed leisurely over a period of 150 years. In this time span Indians obtained a substantial experience in government and when they achieved independence in 1947, they were far better able to handle the cumbersome parliamentary machinery than the Nigerians when they achieved independence with only 56 years of experience in politics.

PROSPECTS FOR POLITICAL DEVELOPMENT

In the long run, the traumatic political disruptions of the 1960's may have done the Nigerian nation good in the sense of having brought the vicious inter-ethnic rivalry to its natural, inevitable, but unfortunately violent conclusion. As pointed out by Schmitt, violence can be a means of political development. The unity of the nation clearly has survived the secession crisis as evidenced by the success of the national government between 1967 and 1970 in returning the Eastern Region to the country and imposing on it the constitutional changes introduced in the other Regions in 1967.

The prospects that past ethno-centered rivalries will diminish in intensity and that Nigeria will endure as a national unity are very good. A military dictatorship like that of General Gowon can provide, albeit with coercion, a valuable opportunity for the development of inter-ethnic harmony and cooperation which the liberal democratic parliamentary system of the post-independence period manifestly was unable to do.

Gowon is fostering development of the essential preconditions for political stability and modernization in Nigeria. Possible avenues of development could emphasize local, tribal, or specifically African values in quite unique ways. In any case, the present government is generating consensus, toleration, and unity in the following ways: (1) by de-emphasizing party politics, which the recent past revealed as an all-too-convenient vehicle of inter-ethnic rivalry and competition and thus a source of divisiveness; (2) by obliging the country to preoccupy itself with internal economic development, particularly industrialization, expansion of food production for domestic consumption as well as for export, and achievement of full employment; and (3) by developing, albeit at the expense of the powers of the states, a strong central government that can effectively inspire confidence and provide leadership for the entire Nigerian community.

In strengthening at least economic unity, the military government hopefully can diminish the possibility of a return to the intense inter-ethnic conflict of the 1950's and 1960's. Ultimately, the habit of peaceful and cooperative coexistence between the large and small ethnic groups, encouraged by a self-imposed respite from divisive party politics and by cooperative efforts at economic growth and development, will make possible the re-establishment of a stable parliamentary government and political democracy, which the Nigerians may prefer to the tutelary military regime imposed upon them.

The only potential obstacle to a smooth transition in the future from military to civilian rule may be the development of a vested interest on the part of military bureaucrats who may be unwilling ever to relinquish power. The soldiers may always believe the country owes them a debt and that if they do depart there will be a return to the party anarchy of the early 1960's. Even if they do relinquish their power, the precedent of military interference may encourage another effort by soldiers to displace civilian rule. At the moment, prospects for the future are uncertain, but a potential foundation for political development and modernization may be emerging.

FOOTNOTES

1. Good general histories of Nigeria include Sir Arthur Burns, *History of Nigeria* (London: George Allen and Unwin, Ltd., 1955), Michael Crowder, *The Story of Nigeria* (London: Faber and Faber, 1962); on the coming of the British see Arthur Norton Cook, *British Enterprise in Nigeria* (Philadelphia: University of Pennsylvania Press, 1943), John E. Flint, *George Goldie and the Making of Modern Nigeria* (Oxford: Oxford University Press, 1960); several interpretive studies of the historical development of modern Nigeria include Frederick Schwartz, *Nigeria: The Tribes, the Nation, or the Race* (Cambridge, Massachusetts: M.I.T. Press, 1965), Henry L. Bretton, *Power and Stability in Nigeria* (New York: Praeger, 1962), James S. Coleman, *Nigeria: Background to Nationalism* (Berkeley: University of California Press, 1958).

2. The best work on the Nigerian republic before the military dictatorship is John P. Mackintosh, *Nigerian Government and Politics: Prelude to the Revolution* (Evanston, Illinois: Northwestern University Press, 1966); see also Robert O. Tilman and Taylor Cole, eds., *The Nigerian Political Scene* (Durham, North Carolina: Duke University Press, 1962), pp. 45–114; on the antecedents of the military dictatorship and secession crisis during the post-independence period see S. K. Panter-Brick, *Nigerian Politics and Military Rule: Prelude to the Civil War* (London: University of London Press, 1970), Robert Collis, *Nigeria in Conflict* (London: Secker and Warburg, 1970), pp. 137–206, Sir Rex Niven, *The War of Nigerian Unity* (Totawa, New Jersey: Rowman and Littlefield, 1970); an interesting explanation of the civil war from the Biafran point of view is Arthur A. Nwanko and Samuel U. Ifejika, *Biafra: The Making of a Nation* (New York: Praeger, 1969).

3. The whole question of ethnic conflict and political development in Third World countries is very thoroughly explored by Cynthia Enlohe in *Ethnic Conflict and Political Development* (Boston: Little, Brown, 1973); studies of ethnic groups living in the north appear in Laura Bohannan and Paul Bohannan, *The Tiv of Central Nigeria* (London: International African Institute, 1953), Harold D. Gunn, *Peoples of the Plateau Area of Northern Nigeria* (London: International African Institute, 1950), Charles Kingsley Meek, *The Northern Tribes of Nigeria: An Ethnographical Account of the Northern Provinces of Nigeria*, 2 Vols. (London: Oxford University Press, 1925), S. J. Hogben and A. H. M. Kirk-Greene, *The Emirates of Northern Nigeria* (London: Oxford University Press, 1966).

4. On the ethnography of the southern parts of Nigeria see Cyrill Daryll Ford and G. I. Jones, *The Ibos and Ibibio Speaking Peoples of Southeastern Nigeria* (London: International African Institute, 1950); Cyrill Daryll Ford, Paul Brown, and Robert Grenville Armstrong, *Peoples of the Niger Benue Confluence* (London: International African Institute, 1955); Cyrill Daryll Ford, *The Yoruba Speaking Peoples of Southwestern Nigeria* (London: International African Institute, 1951); R. E. Bradbury, *The Benin Kingdom and the Ibo-Speaking Peoples of Southwestern Nigeria* (London: International African Institute, 1957).

5. On the political, administrative, and socio-economic aspects of British colonial policy in Nigeria see Coleman, *Nigeria*, pp. 36–60; Burns, *History of Nigeria*, pp. 111–293; Crowder, *The Story of Nigeria*, pp. 155–224; Niven, *Nigeria*, pp. 29–82; Walter Schwarz, *Nigeria* (New York: Praeger, 1968), pp. 82–113; Tilman and Cole, eds., *The Nigerian Political Scene*, pp. 17–44; I. F. Nicolson, *The Administration of Nigeria 1900–1960: Men, Methods, and Myths* (Oxford: Clarendon Press, 1969), pp. 46–250.

6. Quoted in Coleman, *Nigeria*, p. 194.

7. The best study of the origins and development of Nigerian nationalism appears in Coleman, *Nigeria*, pp. 63–270; see also Sklar, *Nigerian Political Parties: Power in an Emergent African Nation* (Princeton: Princeton University Press, 1963), pp. 41–54; an important general study of nationalism in Africa helpful in analyzing nationalism in Nigeria is Gabriel Almond and James S. Coleman, eds., *The Politics of Developing Areas* (Princeton: Princeton University Press, 1960), pp. 247–368, and Thomas Hodgkin, *Nationalism in Colonial Africa* (New York: New York University Press, 1957); important in understanding the beginnings of Nigerian nationalist sentiment are works by Nigerian nationalists themselves such as Nnamdi Azikiwe, *Renascent Africa* (Accra, 1937) and Obafami Awolowo, *Path to Nigerian Freedom* (London: Faber and Faber, 1947).

8. Coleman, *Nigeria*, p. 72.

9. See especially Azikiwe, *Renascent Africa*, pp. 135, 140, and W. E. B. Du Bois. *The Souls of Black Folk* (Chicago: McClurg, 1903), p. 105. Both of these sources are cited by Coleman in *Nigeria*, ch. 5.

10. Schwarz, *Nigeria*, pp. 98–100; see also Meyer Fortes, "The Impact of the War on British West Africa." *International Affairs*, XXI (April, 1945), pp. 206–219; on the emergence of Azikiwe see Richard Sklar, *Nigerian Political Parties*, pp. 41–60, Nnamdi Azikiwe, *The Development of Political Parties* (London: Office of the Commissioner in the United Kingdom for the Eastern Region, 1957), pp. 8–12, Schwarz, *Nigeria*, pp. 95–98, Obuvole Idowu Odumosu, *The Nigerian Constitution: History and Development* (London: Sweet and Maxwell, 1963), pp. 32–40.

11. Coleman, *Nigeria*, pp. 271–272; see also Robert Strausz-Hupe and Harry Hazard, *The Idea of Colonialism* (New York: Praeger, 1958), pp. 50–53; Stewart Easton, *The Twilight of European Colonialism: A Political Analysis* (New York: Holt, Rinehart & Winston, 1960), pp. 29–32; Odumosu, *The Nigerian Constitution*, pp. 35–36.

12. Coleman, *Nigeria*, pp. 272–281; on the Richards Constitution see also Hatch, *Nigeria: The Seeds of Disaster* (Chicago: Henry Regnery, 1970), pp. 248–250; Schwartz, *Nigeria*, p. 99; Odumosu, *The Nigerian Constitution*, pp. 40–56, 70–77; Nicolson, *The Administration of Nigeria*, pp. 251–300.

13. Sklar, *Nigerian Political Parties*, pp. 41–86; Coleman, *Nigeria*, pp. 284–302, 332–343; K. W. J. Post, *The Nigerian Federal Election of 1959* (Oxford: Oxford University Press, 1963), pp. 27–31; Odumosu, *The Nigerian Constitution*, pp. 48–50, 53–56; after independence the NCNC stood for National Convention of Nigerian Citizens.

14. Sklar, *Nigerian Political Parties*, pp. 101–112 and 233–242; Coleman, *Nigeria*, pp. 343–352; Post, *The Nigerian Federal Election of 1959*, pp. 31–38; Audrey Smock, *Ibo Politics: The Role of Ethnic Unions in Eastern Nigeria* (Cambridge, Massachusetts: Harvard University Press, 1971), pp. 12–21.

15. Sklar, *Nigerian Political Parties*, pp. 87–101; Coleman, *Nigeria*, pp. 353–364; Post, *The Nigerian Federal Election of 1959*, pp. 38–43.

16. Crowder, *The Story of Nigeria*, pp. 249–252; Coleman, *Nigeria*, pp. 310–312, 348–349, 352, 369–371; Sklar, *Nigerian Political Parties*, p. 118; Odumosu, *The Nigerian Constitution*, pp. 56–66, 78–82.

17. Coleman, *Nigeria*, pp. 399–402; Sklar, *Nigerian Political Parties*, pp. 125–133; Crowder, *The Story of Nigeria*, pp. 253–254; Odumosu, *The Nigerian Constitution*, pp. 82–108.

18. Sklar, *Nigerian Political Parties*, pp. 133–140; Crowder, *The Story of Nigeria*, pp. 254–257; Odumosu, *The Nigerian Constitution*, pp. 92–110.

19. Sklar, *Nigerian Political Parties*, pp. 94–96, 136–138, 321–376, 339–344; Coleman, *Nigeria*, pp. 356–366, 395, 386; Post, *The Nigerian Federal Election of 1959*, pp. 68–110; a detailed study of the UMBC by J. M. Dent appears in Mackintosh, *Nigerian Government and Politics*, pp. 461–507.

20. Coleman, *Nigeria,* pp. 384–396; Post, *The Nigerian Federal Election of 1959,* pp. 16–20; Crowder, *The Story of Nigeria,* pp. 263–265; Odumosu, *The Nigerian Constitution,* pp. 111–132, 241–244.

21. Post, *The Nigerian Federal Election of 1959,* pp. 158–160, 284–436.

22. The text of the 1960 Constitution appears in the appendix of Odumosu, *The Nigerian Constitution,* pp. 309–397.

23. On Nigerian federalism see Odumosu, *The Nigerian Constitution,* pp. 227–275; Mackintosh, *Nigerian Government and Politics,* pp. 55–86; Cole, ed., *Nigerian Political Scene,* pp. 72–77; Schwarz, *Nigeria: The Tribes, the Nation, or the Race,* pp. 172–212.

24. On Nigerian education in the 1950's and 1960's consult L. J. Lewis, *Society, Schools and Progress in Nigeria* (London: Pergamon, 1965), Ayo Ogunsheye, "Nigeria" in James S. Coleman, ed., *Education and Political Development* (Princeton: Princeton University Press, 1965); see also Okoi Arikpo, *The Development of Modern Nigeria* (Baltimore: Penguin, 1967); two good books on the role of schools in political socialization are Herbert Hyman, *Political Socialization: A Study in the Psychology of Political Behavior* (New York: Free Press, 1959) and Kenneth P. Langton, *Political Socialization* (New York: Oxford University Press, 1969).

25. Mackintosh, *Nigerian Government and Politics,* pp. 87–123, 619–626.

26. On the origins, character and short-range consequences of the Action Group Crisis of 1962 and the treason trial of Chief Awolowo, see Odumosu, *The Nigerian Constitution,* pp. 276–305; Mackintosh, *Nigerian Government and Politics,* pp. 441–460; Schwarz, *Nigeria,* pp. 131–151; Nwankwo and Ifejika, *Biafra: The Making of a Nation,* pp. 40–45; Schwarz, *Nigeria: The Tribes, the Nation or the Race,* pp. 117–139.

27. A detailed analysis of the 1964 Federal Election and the November 1965 Western Regional election appears in Mackintosh, *Nigerian Government and Politics,* pp. 545–609; see also Schwarz, *Nigeria,* pp. 157–190; Nwankwo and Ifejika, *Biafra,* pp. 46–54, 72–88, 95–96; Schwarz, *Nigeria: The Tribes, the Nation or the Race,* pp. 140–148.

28. On the Ibo coup, the Ironsi regime, and the northern inspired counter-coup in the period January through July, 1966 see John Oyinbo, *Nigeria: Crisis and Beyond* (London: Charles Knight, 1971), pp. 36–61, Schwarz, *Nigeria,* pp. 191–212, Nwanko and Ifejika, *Biafra,* pp. 97–105, 123–170; Panter-Brick, ed., *Nigerian Politics and Military Rule,* pp. 14–27; Robert Luckam, *The Nigerian Military: A Sociological Analysis of Authority and Revolt: 1960–1967* (Cambridge: Cambridge University Press, 1971), pp. 17–82, 252–278; Robert Melson and Howard Wolpe, eds., *Nigeria: Modernization and the Politics of Communalism* (Lansing: Michigan State University Press, 1971), pp. 43–68, 367–390; A. H. M. Kirk-Greene, *Crisis and Conflict in Nigeria: A Documentary Sourcebook,* 2 Vols. (London: Oxford University Press, 1971), Vol. I.

29. On the conflict between Gowon and Ojukuwu and the events between July, 1966 and July, 1967 when the Eastern Region seceded and proclaimed itself the independent state of Biafra, see Oyinbo, *Nigeria,* pp. 61–80; Schwarz, *Nigeria,* pp. 212–231; Nwanko and Ifejika, *Biafra,* pp. 171–253; Panter-Brick, ed., *Nigerian Politics and Military Rule,* pp. 27–57, 78–93; Kirk-Greene, *Crisis and Conflict in Nigeria,* Vol. II.

30. Oyinbo, *Nigeria,* pp. 111–194; *The New York Times,* (May 5, October, 2, 4, November 12, 1970), (September 13, 1971), (August 27, 1972); for a detailed analysis of the structure of the present military government see John Ostheimer, *Nigerian Politics* (New York: Harper & Row, 1973), pp. 57–74.

31. See Eric A. Nordlinger, "Political Development: Time Sequences and Rates of Change," *World Politics,* 20; 3 (April, 1968), pp. 494–520.

SYRIA

A Case of Authoritarian Political Development Arising from Instability

ALAN R. BALBONI

The Syrian Arab Republic, a nation of approximately six million inhabitants, is situated in the northwest section of the Arab Middle East. It is bordered by Turkey to its north, Iraq to its east, Jordan and Israel to its south, and by Lebanon and the Mediterranean to its west.

From 1946, the year in which Syria became independent of France, Syria's political development has been characterized by frequent and occasionally violent changes of government, mostly engineered by the military. Where changes in the political institutions and ideology of Syria have occurred, these will be considered changes of regime. Where new participants assumed power, these will be referred to as changes of government.

In spite of the many alterations in the political system of Syria and the even greater number of changes among the individuals who have determined who gets what, where, when, and how; there appear to be indications that the Syrian Arab Republic may be moving toward the relative political stability exemplified by Mexico. That is, the Ba'th Party may well be playing a role in Syrian political development similar to the role played by the Institutional Revolutionary Party (PRI) of Mexico.

A study of Syria demonstrates that the basis for political development and economic modernization may be laid during periods of instability. During the first sixteen years of Syria's existence as an independent state, amid numerous changes of government and regime, a sense of national identity was being forged among Syrians belonging to different sects and classes. There also was growth in the agricultural and manufacturing sectors of the economy, and the Ba'th Party was growing in numbers and in influence.

POLITICS AS A DEPENDENT VARIABLE

The Arabs of Syria,[1] like the Indians and Chinese, take great pride in their long history, particularly in the fact that Greater Syria and its early inhabitants influenced the development of Judaism, Christianity, and Islam.[2] "Syria" for many centuries included the area now comprising the independent states of Lebanon, Israel, Jordan, and Iraq, as well as present-day Syria itself. The designation "Greater Syria" will be utilized in discussing events prior to the dismemberment of Syria following World War I.

The most significant single event in Greater Syria's long history, in terms of its influence on contemporary affairs, was the conquest of the area by Moslem Arab armies from the Arabian desert in the seventh century. Within the three or four decades following the Arab conquest, the great majority of the region's inhabitants converted to Islam and Moslems constitute about 75 percent of the population of the area today.[3] At the same time, the languages of Greater Syria were replaced by Arabic. Arabs today are very proud of the Arabic language and its literature. Indeed, an Arab is generally defined as one who speaks Arabic. So, in a very broad sense, the Arab conquest laid the basis of unity in Greater Syria.

Cultural Fragmentation

The unity of Islam was not long lasting, however, as disputes over doctrine and leadership erupted shortly after the death of Muhammed, the founder of Islam. While most of the Moslems of Greater Syria remained Orthodox (Sunni), several of the breakaway sects of Islam gained substantial followings. Between the eighth and twelfth centuries, adherents of the different sects flocked to the relatively inaccessible mountainous areas of what is now eastern Lebanon and southern Syria. The principal sects which were to find refuge in these areas were the Ismaelis, and in greater numbers, the Alawites and the Druse. Today the Ismaelis constitute 1 percent (60,000) of the population of the Syrian Arab Republic, Druse constitute 3 percent (175,000) and Alawites 11 percent (610,000).

The Christian population of Greater Syria was affected by the major schisms of Christianity as well as by a number of local schisms. Today adherents of Greek, Armenian and Syrian Orthodoxy, and Greek Catholicism each make up more than 10 percent of the population of the Syrian Arab Republic.

Particularly as centralized power deteriorated from the twelfth century onwards, the various Christian groups and heterodox Moslem sects sought to live in their own areas and to minimize their contact with the formal political authorities. Most often they chose their own leaders and managed their day-to-day affairs with a minimum of governmental intervention. The leaders had the responsibility of dealing with whomever exercised formal governing power in the area. They sought to protect their co-religionists and to minimize the taxation for which their respective communities were made accountable.

As time went on, leadership of the various communities remained within certain families and a patron-client relationship developed which lasted into the twentieth century. As we shall see later, members of these leading families dominated the first regime of independent Syria.

Thus, if we look back at Greater Syria just prior to the conquest of all the Middle East by the Ottoman Turks at the beginning of the sixteenth century, we see that the great mass of people, both Christians and Moslems, had become suspicious of political authority and sought to minimize their contact with government. Political authorities appeared to be rapacious, unjust, and inefficient. The populace retreated to sectarian communities for safety. The two major Moslem breakaway sects, the Druse and the Alawites, in particular, sought the most inaccessible mountainous areas in order to avoid persecution by the Ottoman Turks, who were more orthodox in their profession of Islam. Thus, loyalty to family, to sect, and to *patron* rather than to any larger concept such as Syria or the Arab nation characterized the populace of Greater Syria from the twelfth century until the twentieth century.

The Ottoman Turks, a non-Arab people who had embraced Islam, utilized a policy of divide and rule in Greater Syria as well as in the other parts of their immense empire in the Middle East and North Africa. That is, the Turkish authorities allowed the various sects of Greater Syria to conduct their own affairs provided that taxes were paid and that law-and-order prevailed. The Turkish governors generally would deal only with the leaders of the various sectarian communities. The average person, peasant or artisan, Christian or Moslem, could conduct his life without ever having contact with either political leaders or members of other sectarian communities. Oftentimes, there was minimal contact between members of the same sect who lived in different villages. All of this had the effect of further limiting the development of any general Arab consciousness among the inhabitants of Greater Syria.

Religion had always played a significant role in everyone's life, and the Ottoman system of divide and rule further enhanced the importance of religion in all aspects of life. An individual lived in a certain village because of his adherence to a particular sect, married another member of his sect, was loyal to the leader of his sect, and was taxed as a member of his particular sect.

As time went on, the Ottoman regime centered at Istanbul lost its early dynamism, and the quality of the personnel who were made governors of the various districts of the empire deteriorated. By the eighteenth century many of the Turkish authorities were rapacious, arbitrary and increasingly exploitative of the population in their districts of Greater Syria. There was a general economic decline in Greater Syria, and whole villages disappeared as the Turkish authorities made little effort to maintain irrigation systems. The amount of land being farmed decreased, the tax burden on the remaining peasants grew, and, in consequence many inhabitants of Greater Syria, particularly Christians, migrated to North and South America in the nineteenth century.

In addition to increasing the cultural fragmentation and personalism inherent in the society of Greater Syria, the period of Turkish domination had the effect of contributing to the development of a fatalistic attitude among the population. This was especially true of the Moslem peasantry who had neither the recourse to emigration, as did the Christians, nor the recourse to appeal for help to Christian European powers. The Moslem peasantry tended to regard the selfish and arbitrary rule of the political authorities as inevitable and tried to minimize their contact with such authorities.

The period of Turkish control has left a substantial effect on the contemporary society of Syria. The present-day inhabitants of the states carved out of this region cannot conceive of a person who does not belong to the same religion. So too, the suspicion of political authority remains so deeply ingrained that it is still difficult for governments to undertake a reliable census or to try to fairly tax the citizenry. Even many of the same Syrians who clamor for socialism are suspicious of the integrity of the political authorities in avowedly socialist regimes.

Imperialism

During the nineteenth century some of the Christian minorities sought deliverance from Turkish persecution by appealing to their co-religionists in Western Europe and in Russia. At this time Great Britain and France were quite interested in expanding their influence in the Middle East. Both of these nations were developing empires in South and East Asia, and the Middle East was a strategically important area. The construction of the Suez Canal sea route to the Far East was important to these imperialist nations. Britain and France viewed protection of the Christian minorities as a method of guaranteeing access to this area of strategic importance.

Great Britain and France made representations (and later demands, as the weakness of the Ottoman Turkish Sultanate became more apparent) to the Turkish authorities at Istanbul concerning discrimination against various Christian groups. They also established schools, colleges, and social welfare institutions throughout Greater Syria. Russian authorities made contact with Orthodox Christian groups and made representations in their behalf to the Turkish authorities, but did not develop social and educational institutions.[4]

Although the development of Western institutions contributed to sectarianism, the expansion of educational opportunities also had the effect of gradually reawakening a pride in the Syrians of their Arabic heritage. Many of these intellectuals undertook teaching careers and were able to import their concept of Arab consciousness to their students, along with knowledge of history, literature and science.

On balance, however, an Arab identity that transcended sectarian differences spread only very slowly and unevenly to the masses of people in Greater Syria. Even today, some Christians, notably Maronites, are reluctant to refer to themselves as Arabs. Thus, most contemporary Arab nationalists view the Western impact on the Arab Middle East as more detrimental than beneficial in bringing about a sense of Arab national consciousness.

During World War I, Turkey and Germany were aligned with one another. The Turkish authorities had watched Great Britain, France, and Italy take away various parts of their empire in North Africa and limit their control in the Arab Middle East. They hoped that the Germans could help them regain their empire and deter any Tsarist Russian territorial expansion at Turkey's expense. At the same time, Great Britain, France, Italy, and Russia were anxious to break completely Turkish power in the Middle East, especially as the value of oil had become recognized.

Great Britain was the power most concerned with the Arab Middle East because of its control over the Suez Canal and Egypt. Still, Europe was the main theatre of the war and the British did not want to have to commit too many of their armed forces to operations in the Middle East. The British recognized both how much an Arab revolt would weaken the Turkish position and how to spark such a revolt.

The Turks called for an Islamic holy war against the infidel Europeans, but few Arabs responded to the call. Christians had no reason to answer the call and most of the Moslem masses did not feel that they had anything to gain from the conflict. The Arab elite was split into pro- and anti-Ottoman groupings with the younger, more dynamic elements, particularly army officers and intellectuals, wishing to bring about the creation of a large Arab state in the Middle East.

The British made contact with the disaffected Arab elements and, more importantly, with the noble Hashemite family on the Arabian Peninsula. The Hashemites were the traditional guardians of the Islamic holy places in Mecca and Medina and the Turks needed their support if the call for an Islamic holy war was to have a meaningful effect. However, for a variety of reasons the Hashemites resented Turkish hegemony over a large segment of the Moslem world and they were anxious to become leaders of an independent Arab state.

The British, in urging the Hashemites to call for a revolt of Arabs made a number of promises to them. The Hashemites and other Arab leaders interpreted the British promises to mean that when Germany and Turkey were defeated, an Arab state embracing all of Greater Syria, as well as the area of the Arabian Peninsula, would be established and the Hashemites installed as the ruling family.

While the mass of Arabs remained apathetic, thousands of Arabs, ranging from nomadic Bedouin tribesmen to officers in the Turkish armed forces answered the call of the Hashemite family and aided the Allied war effort in the Middle East. They did not receive the rewards that they had envisaged.

While the Western powers succeeded in dividing Greater Syria into a number of separate entities, neither the British nor the French were able to repress the desire for a united Greater Syrian nation. This quest was led by a large part of the informed populace of the mandated territories of Syria, Lebanon, Iraq, and Palestine.[5] In the same fashion the leading members of the Hashemite family did not give up their goal of ruling over a united Greater Syrian nation. The British had made members of the Hashemite family rulers of Trans-Jordan and Iraq in the hope that this would be considered a reasonable compensation for services rendered to the Allied cause during the war.

The French moved quickly to establish control over their two mandated territories, Syria and Lebanon, in the Middle East. A small force of young men tried to stop the entry of the French authorities into Damascus in 1920. They were poorly armed and organized and they were quickly defeated by the French forces. More importantly, however, many of the young men who resisted the French were from Syria's leading families and they continued their nationalist activities during the twenty-six years of French rule over Syria. French rule was total as the League of Nations was virtually powerless to modify the nature of the administration of any of the territories taken from Germany and Turkey and placed under British and French control.[6]

The fact that there was some violent resistance to the French imperialists became a source of pride to many Syrian people and a basis for the further development of national consciousness. Meaningful resistance to imperialism would seem to be an important building stone of national cohesion. Certainly the Chinese Communist Party's guerrilla warfare against the numerically larger and technologically more advanced Japanese armed forces won the respect of many non-Communist elements in China, and helped the Communist regime acquire legitimacy in 1949.

Even the resistance of Mahatma Gandhi and other future leaders of the Indian Congress Party, while not violent, did involve sacrifice, and hence helped to develop some degree of Indian national consciousness. Conversely, the lack of meaningful resistance to British imperialism in Nigeria contributed to the lack of nationalist unity among the numerous ethnic groups.

The French initially tried to continue the divide and rule approach that the Turks had utilized during their governance of Syria. They tried to capitalize on the existing differences among the various religious groupings by establishing separate states. Fortunately, educated Syrians were well aware of what the French were trying to do and registered their disapproval. In all of the administrative states within Syria the French civil and military authorities played upon the tensions among the various sects. The French also tried to develop an indigenous elite who would be educated in the French language and tied to the French cultural tradition. The French in addition forbade all Arab nationalist agitation either in the press or through organizations. The French were much less successful in their efforts in Syria than they were in other parts of Asia and especially in Africa. There were numerous armed revolts and nationalist demonstrations throughout Syria from 1920 through 1925.

The French made some concessions to the nationalist demands. They allowed some of the moderate nationalists to form a political party—the People's Party—and reunited all of the separate administrative states into the Syrian Federation, except the Jabal al-Druse state. These concessions, however, were too little and too late. A major revolt erupted in the Druse area in 1925 and quickly spread to other areas of Syria including Damascus. In fact, the revolt was initiated by traditional Druse notables, but the notables cooperated with nationalist figures in Damascus. Elements of all classes and sects joined the year-long uprising; hence, the revolt became a symbol of Syrian, rather than merely Druse, resistance to French imperialism.

The French authorities utilized aerial bombing and heavy artillery in Damascus to quell this rebellion. This indiscriminate reliance on firepower had the effect of increasing the commitment to Arab nationalism among the population of Damascus.

The revolt was a positive step in Syria's political development. It served to lessen the cultural fragmentation among the differing sects and brought new, more modern leaders to the forefront of nationalist agitation. Most importantly, it served as a symbol of Syrian resistance to French imperialism in much the same way as the May 4th movement served as a symbol of Chinese resistance to Western and Japanese imperialism. Once the rebellion was finally suppressed, the French policymakers determined to try to come to terms with the moderate Arab nationalist figures of Syria; they realized that there was an irrepressible desire for a united Syria.

While the French allowed two main nationalist parties to function, they still refused to grant Syria self-government during the decade preceding World War II, in spite of continuing Syrian agitation for self-government and a promise of eventual independence. Due to cultural fragmentation, personalism, distrust, and an elite-mass gap, these two main Syrian parties were beset by factionalism and instability. Both parties were completely dominated by members of the wealthiest families, and separatist sentiment redeveloped among the Druse and Alawites, whose leaders resented the dominance of Sunni Moslems in the two parties. Syrian leaders wanted a united and independent Syria, but rivalries among various sects prevented the emergence of a single, strong nationalist party.

Thus, if the events surrounding World War II had not profoundly weakened the French position in the Middle East it is questionable whether Syria would have won its complete independence from France in 1946. Even as France itself tried to recover from the German occupation, the French colonial authorities endeavored to reassert their control over Syria. However, world opinion, and more importantly, British and American leaders, were opposed to this. They felt that the day of direct Western imperialism in the Arab Middle East had come to an end. The French capitulated, and Syria, which had been admitted to the United Nations in April, 1945, achieved sovereign independence on April 17, 1946.

National Identity in Independent Syria

It was noted by Schmitt that a prime requisite of political stability is a sense of national solidarity among the populace within the boundaries of the newly created state. A government may enhance national unity if it is legitimate. Initially, the parliamentary regime established in Syria in April, 1946 did have a reasonable degree of legitimacy, as it was based on the Western European model of government, which most of the best educated and politically powerful Syrians associated with liberty, equality, and social and economic progress.

Of course, most Moslem religious leaders, *ulemas* (and even some of the Christian clergy) rejected the achievement of modernity as a reasonable goal. However, they made no concerted effort to garner support for a different form of government as long as the political leaders of the parliamentary regime made certain concessions to them. For example, government leaders declared religious holidays to be national holidays and affirmed that the main inspiration for public law would be Islamic law. The power of the *ulemas* was checked by the fact that many of the Christian clergy, who were every bit as traditional in their attitudes as their Moslem counterparts, were more strongly opposed to Syria as an Islamic state than they were to Syria as a modern state. Thus, the legitimacy of the parliamentary regime was not immediately challenged. This was particularly important as Syria lacked any charismatic leaders and a challenge to the legitimacy of the first regime possibly could have plunged the nation into chaos and sectarian controversy.

In comparison with the modern industrialized nations of Europe and North America or with a Third World nation such as contemporary Mexico, a sense of national identity was underdeveloped in Syria at the time of independence. Many citizens of all classes still felt a primary loyalty to their family, patron, sect, or in the case of the Bedouins (about 7 percent of the Syrian population in 1946) to their tribe.

Another factor limiting national unity was the fact that many Syrians, especially the better-educated, felt a higher loyalty to a Greater Syria or to the whole Arab nation than to the newly created state of Syria itself. Some of these individuals favored a Greater Syria under one or another of the Hashemite family while a greater number sought a Greater Syria with a republican form of government. Thus, there were actually many citizens of Syria whose primary loyalty was to their family and sect and whose loyalty to the new Syrian state was minimal.

Yet the Syrian people were more unified at the time of independence than were the people of many other states of Asia and Africa which became independent in the two decades following the end of World War II. Certainly, for instance, the variety of sects in Syria provided a better basis for building national identity in 1946 than did the many ethnic and linguistic groups of Nigeria. Three factors—the Arabic language, the memory of a glorious Arab history, and the resistance to French imperialism—were a basis for developing national unity in Syria.

Differences in spoken Arabic among the sects of Syria were minimal and all educated individuals read and wrote the same language. The Syrians, like all Arabs, took great pride in their language and even the largely illiterate peasantry was aware of the great Arab writers and poets. In this respect Syria was more unified than India or even China, where the spoken dialects can be mutually unintelligible to people in different regions.

Similarly the memory of the great periods in Arab history served as a basis for building national identity. Like the Chinese people the Syrians could look with pride at those epochs where their ancestors led the world in many areas of learning. Such historical pride is somewhat less developed in India, where citizens look back at different periods with pride depending on whether they are of the Hindu or Moslem religions, or of Aryan or Dravidian background. In Nigeria the military regime must forge a national history out of the diverse traditions of the major ethnic (tribal) groupings.

Class Differences and the Agricultural System

At the time of independence there was a significant social and economic gap between the elite and the mass of citizens. More than 50 percent of the irrigated land and 30 percent of the dry land was owned by less than 3 percent of the total number of landowners. Most of these landowners actually resided in such urban centers as Aleppo, Homs, Hama, and Damascus and had minimal contact with over 70 percent of the rural inhabitants, who worked as sharecroppers or tenant farmers. As Professor Schmitt pointed out, this form of agricultural system may be unstable. As a traditional society begins to break down the peasants question their rewards for working the land. The peasantry may be attracted by radical political movements that promise an equitable redistribution of land. For instance, the promise of agricultural reform was the basis of the rise to power of the Chinese Communist Party between 1924 and 1949. However, traditional attitudes generally change slowly and the Syrian peasantry, with its fatalistic attitudes and subservience to wealthy landowners and sect leaders, did not initially challenge the status quo.

There also existed a substantial difference in life styles and attitudes between the urban dwellers and the rural inhabitants. The former were likely to value education, to be aware of developments in the Arab world, to be interested in Western culture, and to have rejected the traditional fatalism of the rural dwellers.

It must be pointed out once again that, in comparison with other developing nations, Syria's elite-mass gap was not as great as the gap in many other states. There was not as great an economic and cultural gulf between rich and poor as in India nor the broad differences between the gentry and the mass of peasants as in China prior to 1949. A middle class of artisans and merchants was developing in the cities and the larger towns.

The landowning elite of Syria was not united. It was divided into two factions—the National Party and the People's Party. This split actually was beneficial to Syria's political development in the long run, as each party was primarily concerned with gaining more support than its rival and each cared little about the activities of the small, but growing ideological parties. Had there been only one elite party its leadership would probably have acted to suppress any radical movement that appeared to offer a threat to the status quo. But the leaders of each of the major parties worried about advances by their major rival, not about the small ideological parties.

Bureaucracy and Armed Forces

Neither the bureaucracy nor the armed forces were well prepared for service in the new Syrian republic. The bureaucrats were literate and technically competent, but they were drawn almost exclusively from those members of the elite who had most completely immersed themselves in the French language and culture. Most of the bureaucrats looked upon their position as an opportunity to have a guaranteed annual salary in return for a minimum of work. Many bureaucrats had either full-time jobs in the private sector of the economy or were corrupt.

The armed forces personnel were not representative of the Syrian population. The French had created several infantry units, and a disproportionately large segment of the personnel came from semi-Arabized Kurdish and Circassian backgrounds and from the non-Sunni Moslem sects. Few of the officers in 1946 had taken part in nationalist activities and none of the officers had any extensive knowledge of modern warfare. The ranks of the officers corps and enlisted personnel were swollen within two years by young nationalists anxious to take part in the struggle between the Arabs and the Zionists over Palestine, but the degree of technical proficiency and professionalism within the armed forces remained low.

Many of the new nations of Asia and Africa inherited from their colonial overlords bureaucracies and armies which had goals not in accord with those of the political leadership. This significantly limited the capacity of the political system to respond to a variety of problems. Even in contemporary Chile—a state which has been independent for over one hundred and fifty years—the fact that most of the bureaucracy and armed forces leadership was opposed to the goals of President Allende limited the capacity of the Chilean political system to remold the Chilean economic and social system.

In short, Syria faced independence in 1946 with more of the seeming prerequisites of political stability than did many of the Asian and African states that achieved self-government during the next fifteen years: virtually all of Syria's population spoke the same dialect of Arabic; the level of distrust among religious groupings did not approach the hate that existed between Moslems and Hindus in India; the differences between people from various regions of Syria were not as great as the tensions among the inhabitants of the major regions of Nigeria. Indeed, many Syrians of all regions and sects had put aside their rivalries to unite behind their protest of the division of their nation by the French.

Some of the rivalry among the Syrian elites was lessened by a sense of having struggled against the French. In contrast, a true nationalist struggle was absent in Nigeria and in most other African nations, an absence which contributed to the lack of political stability in so many of these nations. The degree of unity among the Syrian elite was more analogous to the unity among the adherents of the PRI in Mexico and the Congress Party in India on the eve of Indian independence than to the ideologically based unity of the Chinese Communist Party in 1949 or even the unity of the Chilean Socialists and Chilean Communists, who supported ex-President Salvador Allende in Chile. But as has been previously pointed out, Syrian political development would not have been served had the political leadership been completely unified because the Syrian leadership was drawn from a narrow and nonprogressive elite.

One other factor which helped Syria achieve relative stability in its first few years of independence was the economic situation. Syria did not face independence with an economy disrupted by years of civil war, as was the case with the Chinese People's Republic. During World War II, Syrian merchants realized significant profits from purchases by the Allied Powers. Of course, virtually nothing of the profits gained filtered down to the peasantry, but the emerging middle class had a higher standard of living as well as capital to invest. Thus, the politically conscious middle class had no reason to challenge the first regime of independent Syria. In sum, the chances of stable, though not equitable, political and economic evolution seemed good.

Effect of Foreign Relations

RELATIONS WITH OTHER ARAB NATIONS. There were two elements which served to invalidate this evolution. As Professor Schmitt pointed out in the introduction, foreign relations can profoundly affect the politics of a developing nation. Certainly India's relations with Pakistan, and China's relations with the United States affected their social and economic policies. So too, the fact that Chilean leaders permitted the unfettered investment opportunities of United States business interests for decades is now having repercussions that will profoundly affect the course of political development and economic modernization in that nation. In few nations, modern or Third World, did foreign relations have such a profound effect on the course of politics as was evidenced in Syria for almost two decades following independence.

The first element in Syria's foreign relations which must be kept in mind is that the new nation's Arab neighbors—Iraq, Jordan, Saudi Arabia and Egypt—were substantially concerned about influencing the course of Syrian politics. The two monarchs of the Hashemite family, Abdullah, King of Jordan, and Faisal, King of Iraq, both wanted to incorporate Syria into their realms. At the same time, the ruling house of the Arabian Peninsula, the Sa'ud family, which had come to power by ousting the Hashemites, remained as traditional rivals to the Hashemites and opposed any union of Syria with either Iraq or Jordan. Egyptian leaders, too, were wary of the creation of a Greater Syria under the control of the pro-British Hashemite family. The Egyptians had experienced over half a century of British rule and were afraid that their former colonial overlords would attempt to dominate the Arab Middle East by helping pro-British leaders enhance their power.

The Iraqis, Jordanians, Saudi Arabians, and Egyptians all tried to influence the course of developments in Syria by a variety of overt or covert actions. Syrian politicians, armed forces officers, and newspaper editors were often handsomely financed by one (or more) of these interested powers. All of these subversive activities, quite naturally, introduced a destabilizing element into the Syrian political system.

The second, and most important element was the problem stemming from the establishment of the modern, dynamic state of Israel to the south of Syria.

RELATIONS WITH ISRAEL. The Arab-Israeli dispute has engendered a great deal of controversy. It is not necessary for the student of Syrian political development to have a detailed knowledge of the origins of the dispute or to make an assessment of the moral rights and wrongs involved. However, it is necessary to have some understanding of how the Syrian people viewed Israel.

European Jews, largely from Russia and Eastern Europe began settling in Palestine in large numbers during the last quarter of the nineteenth century. Some Jews were drawn to Palestine because of that area's central role in the Jewish faith while other Jews, of little or no religious belief, were drawn to Palestine because it seemed to be the only place for the Jewish people to build a national home. Religious or agnostic, the European Jews who emigrated to Palestine were known as Zionists. They were profoundly different from the surrounding Arab population in their way of life. The Zionist Jews were relatively well-educated and organized and they were able to apply Western technology to guarantee a better life for themselves in Palestine.

Not surprisingly, tension developed between the Arabs of a traditional culture and the Zionist Jews of European culture. The tensions were worsened by the fact that some Zionist leaders spoke and wrote openly about their desire to create a Jewish state which would embrace parts of what are now Lebanon, Syria, Jordan and Egypt as well as all of Palestine itself.

By the third decade of the twentieth century Syrians and Arabs had become increasingly fearful that the Zionists, whose ranks had been swelled by Western European Jews fleeing Nazi persecution, would create an alien and expansionist state in the midst of the Arab world. Their fears that the Zionists were cooperating with the Western imperialist powers seemed to be justified when the British suppressed a large-scale revolt of Palestinian Arabs in 1936.

After the conclusion of World War II the British decided to withdraw from Palestine and asked the United Nations to devise a settlement of the Zionist-Palestinian Arab dispute over the disposition of the territory. The United Nations recommended the partition of Palestine between Zionist Jews and Arabs, but the Arabs of Palestine and the governments of the several Arab states rejected the arrangement for two reasons. First, they felt the arrangement was morally wrong, because Arabs constituted the majority of the population of Palestine. Secondly, they felt that the establishment of a Zionist state would soon lead to further encroachment on Arab land.

The Zionist military forces defeated the Palestinian Arab forces and Syria, like many other Arab states, sent units of its armed forces into Palestine in the latter part of 1947. Virtually all of Syria's citizens expected an Arab victory. They did not properly estimate the strength and resources of the worldwide Zionist movement. When it became apparent, in the spring of 1948, that the Syrian forces had been thoroughly defeated by the well-organized and technologically superior Israeli forces, the Syrian people sought a simple reason to explain the debacle. This search for a scapegoat eventually sealed the fate of the elite-dominated parliamentary regime.

Had not the defeat in Palestine demonstrated to many Syrians the weakness and corruption of the government, the first parliamentary regime would have lasted, at best, only a few years. More and more younger, educated Syrian citizens were demanding a government which would modernize the nation. The landowning elite, who along with a handful of leading commercial figures dominated the parliamentary regime, lacked the capacity to increase political participation, undertake land reform, plan for economic growth, provide for a more equitable distribution of wealth, create a unifying ideology, or reform the bureaucracy and the armed forces. It was indeed fortunate for the long-range political and economic development of Syria that the debacle in Palestine brought about the collapse of this ineffectual regime in 1949.

The Rise of Internal Opposition

During the three years of the parliamentary regime several ideologically-based political movements were slowly gaining support among key elements of the Syrian populace. The three major parties which advocated substantial political, social, and economic reform were the

Ba'th Party, the Syrian Social Nationalist Party (SSNP) and the Arab Socialist Party (ASP).

The most tightly organized of these three parties was the Ba'th Party, which had the most fully developed ideology and had the greatest appeal to Syrian intellectuals. The Ba'th Party, which has been the dominant political force in the Syrian Arab Republic for the past decade, was formed by two Syrian intellectuals during World War II. Salah al-Din Bitar and Michael Aflaq had, in their studies in both France and Syria, acquainted themselves with a variety of political philosophies. They concluded that no contemporary ideology was adequate to unite the Arab people and to motivate them to throw off the legacy of centuries of foreign domination. Thus Bitar and Aflaq, the former a Moslem and the latter from a Greek Orthodox family, sought to create an ideology and a plan of action which would unite the Arabs and bring about a rebirth of Arab society.

The basic goals of the Ba'th Party—today the dominant political force in Syria—were to gradually achieve a socialist, egalitarian, and democratic society. Its goals were similar to the goals of other progressive, though non-Marxist, parties throughout the Third World.

Both the Syrian Social Nationalist Party (SSNP) and the Arab Socialist Party lacked the tight organizational structure of the Ba'th Party which was also the most selective in its admissions. These features, together with the sophisticated Ba'thist ideology, attracted the most progressive elements among educated Syrian youth. Because of its ideology and organization, the Ba'th Party was best able to limit the personal, regional, and sectarian rivalries that, sooner or later, surface in any major Syrian political movement.

Syria at the time of its independence had no charismatic political leader and no truly effective political party. We will see that the various leaders of the several regimes which appeared between 1946 and 1963 tried to build strong political parties, develop meaningful ideologies, and endeavored to reform the bureaucracy and the armed forces so that these two public agencies would be both effective and loyal. At best the leaders of these regimes achieved only partial successes. Yet, these partial successes were important in laying a basis for the Ba'th Party to transform the Syrian political system into a more viable entity.

As has been mentioned previously, the overwhelming defeat of the Syrian armed forces in the struggle over Palestine sealed the fate of the first parliamentary regime. As the magnitude of the disaster became known to the populace, the civilian leaders of the government tried to place the blame on one another or on the Syrian armed forces. Stories of graft and corruption among the governmental elite began to spread and protest demonstrations broke out in Damascus. It was easier for the general public to believe that corrupt politicians had sabotaged the

Syrian armed forces than to accept the fact that the Syrian forces were less technologically advanced and less disciplined than the Zionist forces. At the same time, the military leaders could not accept criticisms from politicians who all too often were corrupt and inefficient. Thus, it was not difficult for the military chief-of-staff, Colonel Husni al-Zaim, to organize and successfully carry out a bloodless change of regime on March 30, 1949.

Colonel al-Zaim's dominance lasted less than four months. However, even in that short space of time, he and his associates were able to make a contribution to Syrian political and economic development by rooting out some of the most blatantly corrupt individuals in the civil service of Syria. Unfortunately, too many of the top level Syrian bureaucrats were neither honest nor efficient—necessary prerequisites for modernization. The bureaucrats viewed a government job as an opportunity to have a guaranteed salary, and eventually a pension, while pursuing a private vocation. Colonel al-Zaim forced the bureaucrats to make a choice between their private careers and public service. Many chose their private careers and other administrators were dismissed from their positions after being charged with corruption.

While Colonel Husni al-Zaim and his supporters were able to take measures which made it easier for more progressive leaders later, they lacked the capacity to retain political power. This was fortunate as these individuals had no ideology to offer the Syrian people and no political party to help control the pressures from various groups in Syrian society.

This first military regime was beset by two problems which plagued subsequent regimes. The first arose from the pressure to do something about the growing Israeli nation; the second from the desire of other Arab states and Arab leaders to either bring about or to prevent the unification of Syria with neighboring states. These are problems which few new nations have faced. Perhaps the threat that the Chinese People's Republic perceived from the United States during the Korean War and for a decade thereafter is most similar to the threat that Syrians perceived from Israel. Of course Syrian leaders did not have either the political or the military resources possessed by the Chinese Communist leadership.

The first problem, Israel, was (and still seems) insoluble. The effects of the second problem would have been greatly reduced if the Syrian leaders had gradually fostered a sense of Syrian nationhood. This could have been accomplished (and eventually was after the Ba'th Party assumed full power) by the following means: development of an ideologically-based mass political party, institution of effective government by creation of an efficient and responsive bureaucracy, and promotion of economic growth.

Four months after achieving power Colonel Husni al-Zaim was over-thrown by a group of military officers headed by Colonel Sami Hinnawi. Colonel Hinnawi's activities were abetted by the Iraqi government whose leaders sought to join Syria to greater Iraq. Colonel Hinnawi was the leading figure in Syria for only several months as he, like his prede-cessor, lacked both an effective base of support and the personal quali-ties required of a national leader.

The Al-Shishakli Takeover

The next *coup d'état* took place in December, 1949. Once again the leader of the conspirators, who were primarily, but not solely, armed forces officers, was a Colonel named Adib al-Shishakli. This third top-pling of government with a year's time was brought about by individu-als who were drawn together by the goal of preventing the joining of Syria with the Hashemite Kingdom of Iraq; the regimes agreed on little else.

Colonel Shishakli had more of the personal qualities required of an effective national leader than did his predecessors, and he made a sub-stantial contribution to Syrian political development in the four years that he held power in Syria. He tried to create a nationalistic ideology which would be disseminated to the populace through a broadly based political party. He sought to eliminate the involvement of leading bu-reaucrats and high ranking armed forces officers in political decision-making. He was especially anxious to end the entanglement of other nations in Syria's domestic affairs.

Syria's Arab neighbors were vitally concerned about the course of political development. Foreign involvement in Syrian affairs increased after the overthrow of the parliamentary regime, as it appeared that any group which was relatively cohesive and had some backing of armed forces could seize power. The Egyptian and Saudi Arabian governments funnelled money into the hands of Syrians who were dissatisfied with the government led by al-Shishakli. Iraqi and Jordanian agents were as active in making contact with various dissident groups as they had been during the periods that Colonels al-Zaim and Hinnawi held power. It is not just modern nations that meddle in the internal affairs of Third World nations.

Colonel al-Shishakli was determined that Syria should remain a free state able to make its own foreign and domestic policy choices. He imprisoned any Syrians who were convicted of making contact with foreign agents and had the intelligence section of the armed forces keep a particularly close watch on those politicians, mostly associated with the People's Party, who favored unity with Iraq and/or the Hashemite Kingdom of Jordan.

In his efforts to end foreign intrigue within Syria, he was forced to rely on the military. During the first year of Colonel al-Shishakli's dominance there were numerous shiftings of cabinets, arrests of various politicians, and even the assassination of the commander of the air force.[7] As the situation deteriorated, a number of leading members of the People's Party refused to cooperate with Shishakli's wishes unless he promised to end their harassment. He refused to do so and instead, with the support of the armed forces, ended the façade of parliamentarianism and assumed plenary powers in November, 1951. Given the absence of a dominant and cohesive political party, the still extensive cultural fragmentation along sectarian lines in Syrian society, and the involvement of foreign powers in Syria's domestic affairs, it was fortunate that al-Shishakli relied on the armed forces to reaffirm his control.

Usually military takeovers are a short-term solution to the problems of political instability and lack of economic modernization. Long-term political stability and economic modernization can best be nurtured by the institutionalization of political organizations capable of sustaining the stresses of rapid social change. However, in Syria in 1951 the most pressing necessity was for a short-term solution to political and economic problems and the armed forces were, at this time, the most stable and cohesive institution in Syria.

Colonel al-Shishakli's greatest contribution to Syrian political development was his fostering of Syrian nationalism. For example, he closed the foreign missionary schools, which frequently taught subject matter in a language other than Arabic and where the study of Arab history and culture was relegated to a position secondary to the study of European history and culture. Students in these schools often developed an elitist attitude and sought to pursue their advanced studies in Europe. Equally important was the prohibition against the functioning of those sport and youth associations which were organized along sectarian lines. Such associations prevented young people of different religious persuasions from exchanging ideas and forming friendships with one another. This was a very wise decision as it is much easier to broaden the horizons of young people than to induce new ways of thinking among older citizens. At the same time the nature and extent of the contacts that Syrian business, educational, and cultural leaders and institutions were permitted with their counterparts in non-Arab nations was carefully limited by the government. There were two reasons for this: first, too many prominent Syrians looked upon Western culture and institutions with undue reverence. Secondly, the Western powers too often used these contacts for espionage purposes. In short, all of these measures were necessary to help cast off the legacy of Turkish and French imperialism.

Al-Shishakli also continued the policy of his predecessors by ensuring that the bureaucracy remained responsive to the policies set by the political authorities. In addition he limited the political activities of trade union leaders and newspaper publishers. These actions helped to lay the basis for increased governmental effectiveness and national unity. Later, when the Ba'th Party came to power, the relatively few trade union leaders and independent newspaper publishers were generally willing to accept the fact that there were boundaries on the nature of the criticism that they could level against the government. Once again, there is a tendency for United States students to view restrictions on criticisms of governments as a backward step along the road to political development. However, it should be remembered that whenever the United States was threatened by foreign powers or by internal division the government quickly limited the nature and degree of criticism which was acceptable. Syrian leaders, of course, have had to confront foreign threats and internal divisions since independence.

Gradually al-Shishakli's position began to deteriorate. Ba'th Party leaders began to suspect that his devotion to progressive reforms and to the nonalignment of Syria in international politics was tenuous. They and many other prominent figures, of a variety of political persuasions, suspected that Colonel al-Shishakli's main goal had become the achievement of vast personal power. The discontent surfaced in December, 1952 as dissident army officers and civilians associated with the Ba'th Party and the Arab Socialist Party made an unsuccessful effort to overthrow the government.[8]

Although the *coup d'état* failed, Colonel al-Shishakli lacked the power to reverse the undermining of his basis of support. Indeed, his position was further weakened by a rigged election in which few noteworthy Syrian personalities participated. This gave the Arab Liberation Movement, the party created by al-Shishakli, sixty of eighty-two seats in the national assembly. The fact that the agricultural sector was booming because of good weather, increased mechanization of cotton farming, and small-scale expansion of irrigated lands was probably the key factor in explaining why al-Shishakli continued to hold power, even though governmental policy had little effect on the increased farm production.[9]

By the end of 1953 al-Shishakli had alienated the radical social reformers of the Ba'th Party and, to a lesser degree, of the Arab Socialist Party because of his unwillingness to embark upon a meaningful large-scale land reform program and because of his increased desire to accumulate personal power. At the same time he had little support from the landowners of Syria because of his initial acceptance of peasant seizures of land. He had backed off from his support of such seizures but still wealthy landholders did not trust him. A final important contributing factor to the decline of al-Shishakli was the fact that he incurred the hostility of many armed forces officers by reducing the role of the military in the Syrian government. He created the Arab Liberation Movement and required a reasonable level of technical proficiency for appointment to command responsibilities.

Why did Colonel Adib al-Shishakli fail to establish a more viable political system in Syria? Because he was attempting to change too much of Syrian life rapidly: he had no grassroots organization; no cohesive dedicated group of followers; no revolutionary ideology to motivate individuals to sacrifice for the social, economic, and political goals which al-Shishakli sought for Syria. He did not head a well-organized political party, he was not informed about public opinion, the degree of discontent among various classes or sects, his relative popularity among armed forces officers, or the attitude of the radical reformist elements associated with the Ba'th Party and the Arab Socialist Party.

A well-organized, cohesive political party is a basic necessity if there is to be long-term political and economic development. There is no better illustration of this than the role of the Chinese Communist Party in the modernization of China from 1949 until the beginning of the Cultural Revolution. The Chinese Communist Party had the primary responsibility of carrying out the far-reaching social, economic, and political changes in China and, at the same time, the party transmitted to the top decision-makers the attitudes of Chinese of various backgrounds towards governmental policy.

Although Colonel Adib al-Shishakli ultimately failed he was more successful in promoting political development than his two predecessors. His contributions to Syrian political development are several. First, he gave the Syrian citizenry a respite from parliamentary instability. Had the *coups d'état* continued interspersed with periods of parliamentary instability the Syrian people might well have sought deliverance by joining with the Hashemite Kingdom of Iraq. Such a union, of course, would have eliminated the possibility of any substantial independent political or economic development. Secondly, al-Shishakli strengthened the efficiency and professionalism of the bureaucracy and of the armed forces. Much remained to be done, especially in the latter area, but Al-Shishakli at least made a start. Thirdly, he called attention to the problems of achieving land reform, ensuring equal educational opportunity, and limiting the cultural fragmentation brought about by excessive sectarian loyalties. Fourthly, al-Shishakli diminished the involvement of other Arab states, as well as that of France and the United States, in Syria's internal affairs.

His period of rule also saw the Ba'th Party and the Arab Socialist Party forge a working alliance and move forward in their recruitment among the new generation of educated Syrians, particularly university students and armed forces officers. Had al-Shishakli tried to eliminate the Ba'th Party as a force in Syrian politics by imprisoning its members, he certainly would have set back the growth of the party by many years and consequently would have impaired Syrian political development. Even in his downfall he contributed to the growth of the Syrian state, as he refused to allow the nation to be torn apart by civil war. Al-Shishakli abdicated even though a substantial portion of the armed forces were willing to support him.

Return to Parliamentarianism

The military, with civilian backing, restored the parliamentary regime. The next four years, culminating in Syria's union with Egypt to form the United Arab Republic, were characterized by a return to unstable parliamentary government. The government was dominated by politicians attached to the major landowning families, but unlike the first period of a parliamentary regime (1946–1949), the Ba'th (now united with the Arab Socialist Party of Akram al-Hawrani) had become a major force in Syrian politics. In the same fashion, the armed forces, politicized by virtue of its previous interventions, exercised a substantial effect on policies and personalities.

In the elections which the new leadership decided to conduct, the Ba'th Party won a substantial minority of seats in the legislative assembly.[10] Although the assembly was numerically dominated by members of the People's Party and by independents, the Ba'th Party was the most cohesive grouping in the assembly and had more dedicated supporters in the Syrian armed forces.

Throughout the four year period the informed segment of Syrian citizenry was divided by a variety of domestic and foreign policy issues. Land reform, the pace of cultural change, expansion of educational opportunities, and nationalization of large-scale enterprises were the major domestic issues. While these issues were discussed in the legislative assembly, little progressive social and economic reform was undertaken. This lack of action worked to the benefit of the Ba'th Party, as many educated young Syrians despaired of accomplishing reform through a parliament dominated by conservative parties. The Ba'th leadership was anxious to bring these discontented individuals into the party. But they also wanted to ensure that new members adopt the egalitarianism and socialism of the Ba'thist Party and become dedicated to the Ba'thist plan of eliminating sectarian and class differences.

The role of Jordan vis-à-vis the Western-oriented Baghdad Pact, unity Iraq and/or Jordan, and relations with Arab states were the foreign policy issues. The key issue was whether or not Syria should join the Baghdad Pact. The United States, Great Britain, and Turkey were anxious to involve the Arab states of the Middle East in a military alliance which would be directed against the expansion of the influence of the Soviet Union in that area. Those Arab states that joined would be expected to commit themselves to anti-Communism and to cooperation with Great Britain and the United States in their diplomatic and trade policies. In return they would receive economic and military assistance from the West.

The Egyptian government, led by Gamal Abdel Nasser, refused to join the Pact, while Iraq quickly joined. Thus the success of the Pact depended on whether or not the Syrian government could be persuaded to adhere to it. Pressures were exerted on the Syrian government from a variety of sources. The Egyptian and even the rather conservative Saudi Arabian government made certain that the Syrian leadership and populace knew that they opposed Syria's joining the Pact. On the other hand, the Iraqi regime did everything possible to bring Syria into it.

The Ba'th Party, the Arab Socialist Party, and the Syrian Communist Party were absolutely opposed to the Baghdad Pact. The two major conservative parties and the independents in the Syrian government were split over the issue. Great Britain, Turkey, and the United States were unwilling to allow the Arab people to make their own decision on this issue. These three powers utilized a variety of techniques, including mobilization of Turkish forces along Syria's borders, United States naval maneuvers off the Syrian coast, as well as encouragement of conspiracies in order to try to ensure that Syria would join the Baghdad Pact. These foreign powers apparently misunderstood the extent of Arab consciousness among the Syrian populace. The exertion of pressure by the Western powers had the effect of increasing the appeal of all the more radical parties and greatly enhanced the reputation of Gamal Abdel Nasser among all elements in the Syrian population. The Ba'th Party, in particular took advantage of the changed atmosphere and expanded its influence in Syrian high schools and universities, in the bureaucracy, and among armed forces officers.

Almost two decades later, United States decision-makers attempted to influence decisions of the Chilean government regarding American business interests. These attempts as in Syria, had the opposite effect, as many prominent Chileans who did not support the Left resented United States imperialism and were more willing to back President Allende's plans for nationalization.

The period of parliamentarianism during the mid-1950's in Syria reveals that a basis for political and economic development was laid amid governmental instability. That is, an ideologically-based, cohesive political party, the Ba'th grew in strength. A similar example of political development amid seeming political disintegration would be the growth of the Chinese Communist Party during the chaos of the 1930's. Both examples seem to point out that political development, as well as economic modernization, may not be a steady process.

Long periods of relative governmental stability such as that which prevailed in Mexico in the late nineteenth century, or even in India or Chile since independence, may occur amid economic stagnation, increasing inequities in the distribution of wealth, and lack of widespread participation in public affairs. Thus, stability does not necessarily lead to political development and economic modernization or development. However, when modernization takes place new groups, organizations, and classes arise which produce more complex patterns of conflict and mandate a need for technologically sophisticated methods of coordination and control. The political systems which had previously ensured stability will probably not be able to deal effectively with the rising level of demands. Oftentimes military takeovers occur and coercion is employed to deal with the new demands and to ensure stability. Such repressive regimes generally accomplish little in the way of political development or economic modernization. If, during this period, however, dissatisfied individuals are developing an ideology and a cohesive party organization which recruits elements of the middle and lower classes, then they may be able to seize power after a period of conflict and begin the task of institutionalizing new patterns of organizations and procedures. This can increase the ability of the political system to deal with rising demands, increasing groups, and the expanding tasks required of governments confronting modernization.

In India there does not as yet appear to be a political movement that will be able to really challenge the Indian political system which, dominated by the Congress Party, has sacrificed rapid social change upsetting the status quo in favor of gaining and maintaining the support of diverse groups and nurturing a system that stresses bargaining, accommodation and incremental change.

Union with Egypt

The second parliamentary regime in Syria came to an end in 1958 as Syria entered into union with Egypt to form the United Arab Republic. The factors leading to the union are complex and seemingly contradictory.[11] The most basic reason for the union of the two Arab states separated by Israel and by the Mediterranean was that the parliamentary regime was near the point of collapse by the end of 1957. No prime minister could muster the necessary support to put through substantive legislation. There were numerous personal rivalries among members of the same party. Frustration among politicians, bureaucrats, and informed citizens was growing about this state of affairs. Although most members of the military were dissatisfied, the officers belonged to different political groups and were too fragmented to achieve a military *coup d'état.*

Many Syrians of all classes looked favorably upon Nasser's regime in Egypt. The Egyptian people had a stable, honest, and relatively efficient government. Too often the Western press portrayed the Nasser regime as authoritarian. Actually, Nasser had to consult the leadership of Egyptian military, bureaucratic, intellectual, and religious circles before he could proceed with any major policies. He generally sought to develop a consensus before embarking upon any significant undertakings in domestic or foreign affairs. Nasser himself was immensely popular with the Syrian people. He had nationalized the Suez Canal and shown that an Arab government could effectively manage it. He gained enormous prestige by his defiance of Great Britain, France, and Israel during the Suez War and its aftermath. Many Syrians felt that the Egyptian president could give Syria the same type of leadership he had given his homeland. That many Syrian leaders of all political persuasions looked to leadership from Gamal Abdel Nasser was true partly because of Nasser's charismatic personality. Nasser appeared to the Syrian conservatives to be the man to halt the steady increase in influence of the radical Ba'th Party and of the Syrian Communist Party. At the same time, members of the more radical Syrian parties were impressed with the land reform and the regulation of commercial enterprises which had been undertaken in Egypt. These groups viewed Nasser as the man to take away political and economic power from the wealthy landowning elite.

As a result of the Syrian situation at the end of 1957, a group of Syrian military and civilian leaders of various political persuasions invited Nasser to end the political impasse in Syria by uniting the two Arab nations. Nasser reluctantly agreed to the union, under pressure from various Syrian groups. In January, 1958, amid much rejoicing, the United Arab Republic came into existence. Like the parliamentary and military regimes which preceded it, the regime during the period of union contributed to the growth of national unity and to both economic growth and modernization.

The base of the Syrian economy, like the base of the economies of most all developing nations, is agriculture. Most of the population works on the land. Increased and modernized agricultural production not only provides the Syrian people with a better diet, it also allows Syria to gain revenue to import industrial goods by exportation of its agricultural surplus of various types of grains.

During the first decade of Syria's independence, agricultural production increased rather significantly, as did small-scale commercial manufacturing. In both cases these advances occurred because of the actions taken by private individuals. Neither parliamentary nor military regimes adopted policies which had any substantial impact on the pace or direction of economic growth. Rather, wealthy landowners invested in land and opened up new areas to cultivation with the aid of small-scale irrigation systems. There was an increase in the use of farm machinery, especially in cotton farming. So too, Syrian entrepreneurs used profits made during World War II to invest in new machinery and factories.

By 1958, however, Syrian agricultural development had reached the point where large-scale state planning and financing was called for if increased production and diversification of crops were to continue. Developing nations which export raw materials and agricultural commodities are quite vulnerable to fluctuations in international trade. It is important that their exports be diversified. Such diversification is better undertaken by centralized government planning than by individual agricultural producers. In addition, further agricultural expansion in Syria depended upon the construction of large irrigation works, production and distribution of artificial fertilizers, dissemination of the principles of scientific farming to the peasantry, and quicker distribution of farm products to avoid loss through spoilage and to guarantee that the small producer would not become indebted to the wealthier landowners. The new regime of the United Arab Republic undertook to accomplish all of these necessary measures and planned for the construction and financing of a massive dam on the Euphrates River.[12]

Post-independence economic growth had the effect of raising many middle class families into the upper class, but the great majority of families, particularly in the rural areas, gained little from the economic advances. Thus, Syrian reformers, mostly members of the Ba'th Party, hoped that the new regime would undertake land reform and regulation of the economy. Their hopes were at least partially realized as President Nasser decided to undertake land reform on the Egyptian model. That is, the goal was to give all cultivators enough land to feed their families. Land was to be taken from the wealthy landowners, two-thirds of whom were absentee landlords. Unlike the land reform in China or in Mexico, the landowners were compensated on a very reasonable basis. The new landowners—generally illiterate peasants who had not had any experience in making decisions for themselves—were wisely urged by the government to join agricultural cooperatives which would help them irrigate their land and market their produce.[13] Syrian reformers associated with the Ba'th Party were disappointed that the land reform was not more radical or rapid; the landowners viewed the reforms as quite radical.

The period of union put a temporary stop to the internal struggle for power within the military. Syrian officers became united behind a common goal—to put an end to Egyptian domination of command positions in the armed forces. The Syrians resented the fact that Egyptian officers were put in charge of Syrian units while Syrians were not put in command of Egyptian troops. The Syrians refused to believe that the Egyptians were more highly skilled than they were.

The Union also ended the previously substantial involvement in Syrian domestic affairs of neighboring Arab states and personalities. Other Arab states and leaders realized that Syria was part of the most powerful state in the Arab world and did not make any efforts to subvert Syria. They also realized the futility of trying to organize or finance conspiracies against the centralized regime headed by Nasser.

The Egyptian-dominated regime also indirectly contributed to the development of Syrian national identity among leaders of the Syrian political parties and among Syrian bureaucrats. Politicians of all persuasions increasingly resented Nasser's ban on their functioning as members of specific parties. Reformist politicians in particular were not impressed with the quality of leadership and with the virtual absence of ideology in the Egyptian-dominated National Union Party. Like Syrian politicians and like their counterparts in the armed forces, Syrian bureaucrats resented being placed in less responsible positions in the formulation and implementation of policy than their Egyptian counterparts. They were probably correct in asserting that the Egyptian administrators had no greater expertise than did they and, indeed, that the Egyptians lacked the knowledge of Syrian customs which were a necessary prerequisite for effective administration.

By late 1960 the Nasser regime had lost the support of the greater part of the Ba'th Party (which included the Arab Socialist Party), the Syrian armed forces, and the Syrian bureaucracy. There was still a good deal of admiration for President Nasser as an Arab leader, but anti-Egyptian feeling was on the upswing. If Nasser had had a really well-organized, cohesive political party backing him and his regime, the union probably would have lasted. But the National Union Party was too weak to draw new support to the regime.

In spite of the fact that support for the regime by 1961—the year Syria withdrew from the United Arab Republic—was stronger among the moderately conservative politicians than among the reformers, Nasser proposed a series of laws which would have nationalized a substantial segment of Syrian commercial enterprises. President Nasser was being true to his principles by his proposals, but it cost him dearly in support. Many Syrian businessmen had originally favored union with Egypt in part because they felt that the union would rule out the future possibility of nationalization of their enterprises by the Ba'th Party. When the Egyptian-dominated legislative assembly enacted into law the nationalization proposals, the Syrian businessmen withdrew their support.

The regime thus was left without an organized basis of support within Syria. Ba'th Party members welcomed the nationalization decrees, but they still deeply resented the fact that their party, more disciplined and more ideologically developed, was made subservient to the National Union Party. Most Syrian citizens still admired President Nasser but they resented the domineering attitude of too many of the Egyptians who were sent to Syria.

Parliamentarianism Once Again

It was no surprise, then, when the armed forces revolted in September, 1961 and declared an end to the union of Syria and Egypt. A new parliamentary regime was established and an election was held. Most voters cast their ballot for the most widely known politicians, most of whom were rather conservative. The Ba'th Party, deprived of the opportunity to function effectively during the period of union, fared poorly in the election of the new legislative assembly.

The new government wasted no time in repealing the nationalization laws and in watering down the program of land reform which had been initiated during the period of union. These reactionary measures provoked a response from many elements in the military, particularly officers associated with the Ba'th Party who objected to the undoing of all of the progressive measures passed during the period of union.

Another group of military officers overthrew the parliamentary regime in March, 1963. These officers were united in their belief that the civilian regime should not be allowed to turn back the clock in Syria. However, they were divided on a number of basic domestic and foreign policy issues and were unable to establish an effective new regime. In particular, there was disagreement over how rapidly land reform should proceed, and, after a period of consultation, the pro-unionist officers involved in the *coup d'état* left Syria in order to avoid armed conflict within the Syrian armed forces. The remaining officers, still in disagreement on fundamental social, economic and foreign policy issues, released the civilian politicians who had been jailed and invited a respected figure with moderately progressive views, Dr. Bashir al-Azma, to form a new cabinet.

The assembly, not wishing to undergo another military intervention, accepted the proposal of the new cabinet that the amendments to the original reform law be repealed. The assembly also approved the nationalization of certain large-scale commercial enterprises. But most of the leading civilian and military figures in the Ba'th Party were not satisfied with the moderate economic and social reform measures contemplated by the government, and Ba'thist-led elements in the armed forces moved on Damascus and overthrew independent Syria's third parliamentary regime on March 8, 1963.

It is not easy to state the exact date that Syria's political system ceased to be primarily a reaction to the economic and social system. When a violent revolution occurs it is easier to fix a more exact date. For instance, when the Chinese Communists achieved victory over the Kuomintang in October 1949 after decades of fighting, the political system of China ceased merely to reflect the norms of a traditional society with a great gap between the landed elite and the mass of peasants. The Communists immediately began to remold the Chinese society and economy and, indeed, to remold Chinese ways of thinking. It would be much more difficult to say at what precise point the Mexican post-Revolutionary government achieved control. Rather, the process was more gradual than in China.

Since the Ba'th Party was not as revolutionary as the Chinese Communist Party, and since it achieved power without violence, the designation of March, 1963 as the beginning of the political system as a viable controlling agent over its environment is an arbitrary one. The basis of political development had been laid during previous regimes. Cultural fragmentation based upon sectarian divisions had been attacked and steps had been taken to lessen the divisions by various governments. The honesty and efficiency of the bureaucracy and the armed forces had been important during previous regimes. Similarly a sense of Syrian national identity had been promoted, especially during the military regime of Colonel al-Shishakli. President Nasser had helped to prepare the way for both economic reform and economic growth by instituting land reform measures and centralized state planning.

Throughout all of these previous regimes the Ba'th Party had been growing in power and support, and it was determined to substantially change Syrian social, economic, and political life when it seized power in March, 1963. The Ba'th Party in part reflected Syrian society, and it was not as cohesive as the Chinese Communist Party. Nevertheless the Ba'th Party has remained in power since 1963 and has made significant strides in political development and economic modernization.

The Military

The non-Ba'thist military officers were guaranteed a role in the formulation of domestic and foreign policy through the establishment of the National Council of the Revolutionary Command (NCRC). This institution, composed solely of armed forces officers, exercised an effective check on the powers and policies of the civilian officials. Salah al-Din Bitar, one of the founders of the Ba'th Party, became prime minister of the new Ba'thist regime, although he had to consult the NCRC before embarking upon any major policies.

Unity talks were quickly reopened with Egypt, as spokesmen for the new regime expressed a conviction that the problems which arose in the first attempt at union could be eliminated if a new federation was formed of the two Arab nations. Naturally, President Nasser was wary of the Ba'th Party's commitment to unity as it had wavered in its support for the first union. He became very critical of the Ba'thist leaders during the subsequent discussions. Pro-Nasserite armed forces officers, aware that the unity talks were deteriorating, attempted to oust the Ba'th Party. They were defeated after some fighting in Damascus, and the unity talks were terminated. The Ba'thist leaders needed the support of the army to quell the rebellion. General Amin al-Hafez, a leading member of the Ba'th Party, provided the armed forces support. The General, however, was not willing to return power to the civilian Ba'thists, and he became the dominant figure in Syrian politics for the next three years.

At first glance it would seem that the Ba'th Party failed to control the armed forces and that the military controlled the party and hence dominated Syria. However, such an analysis would be an oversimplification. The military officers were loyal to Ba'thist ideology and goals. They desired a greater equalization of wealth, expanded educational opportunities for children of all classes, state planned economic growth, an end to sectarian divisions, and a neutralist and Pan-Arab foreign policy. The Ba'thist armed forces officers did not rule solely on the basis of their own will. They consulted and took into account the wishes of the traditional Ba'th Party leaders as well as the Secretary-General of the party. It is true that these individuals resented the extent of the power which the Military Committee of the party had reserved for itself, but they were not totally deprived of influence as other civilian political leaders of Third World nations have been when a purely military dictatorship has been established.

Economic Development

The Ba'thist government led by General al-Hafez was limited in its accomplishments by internal differences among civilian and military policy-makers. Nonetheless the government was able to make significant advances in Syria's economic development. It carried out the basic goals of the five-year plan that the previous regime had instituted in

1960. Since two-thirds of Syria's 72,000 square miles are steppe and desert, land reclamation and irrigation were necessary to make such land cultivable. Much progress was made in these areas as the largest share of expenditure was allocated to irrigation and land reclamation. Funds were also utilized for improvement of techniques in agriculture, fishing and animal husbandry, as well as the dissemination of information about these new techniques.

Political leaders and top-level administrators were well aware that the development of power and fuel resources was essential to the country's development. Construction of an oil pipeline from the previously unexploited oilfields on the coast was begun and electric power facilities were constructed. Surveying for mineral deposits and research on the feasibility of developing mining and processing industries was initiated. A good deal of effort was expended on the improvement of road, rail, sea and airport facilities. Such improvements fostered national unity as well as economic growth.

Professor Schmitt has argued that economic development by itself does not necessarily lead to political stability. Indeed, economic growth which is not accompanied by economic modernization may contribute to the maldistribution of wealth that already exists in the society. The Ba'thist government was aware of this problem and was determined to continue the steps toward economic equality begun during the period of union with Egypt. It further limited the amount of cultivable land which could be held by any one family. Agricultural tenants were protected against arbitrary eviction and the share of produce that a landowner could take from share-cropper families was reduced.

Most importantly, in making certain that the land reform would be meaningful, the government decreed that all new landowners had to become members of farm cooperatives, which were eventually to become self-supporting and fully controlled by the membership. Government agencies replaced the former wealthy landowners as the source of whatever credit was necessary to ensure that the new owners were independently established. The process of giving land to the peasants and building cooperatives was slow. This was due partly to the traditional nature of peasant society. Nevertheless, during 1963 and 1964 over 10,000 previously landless peasant families were given their own land.

The government was more hesitant in undertaking reformist measures in regard to commercial enterprises. This was partly because General al-Hafez came to power with the support of Syrian businessmen, who feared the Nasserites more than the moderate elements in the Ba'th Party. Eventually, however, even the most moderate individuals in the Ba'thist government despaired of achieving close cooperation with the businessmen in their efforts to reform the Syrian economy, and in 1965 major industries were nationalized and plans to run the enterprises by self-management of the workers under government direction were formulated.

Nationalism

Most of the economic measures mentioned had the effect of increasing unity among the Syrian populace. The several hundred thousand peasant families who benefited from land reform became quite aware that the government in Damascus, previously viewed with suspicion, could bring them a better life. The cooperatives, established by the government, made them aware of the immediate benefits of common endeavor with many other peasant families and of contact with the centralized agencies of government. The peasants, who were given land, and the wealthy landowners, whose land was expropriated, were of every major sect in Syria. This had the effect of giving many Syrians a sense of class consciousness which tended to limit sectarian consciousness. As the political authorities achieved more and more things that had previously been the responsibility of individuals, families, and sect leaders, the government acquired more legitimacy and support. As a result, it could undertake to further increase the scope of its authority.

Another way in which the first Ba'thist government increased national unity was through its supervision of the Syrian educational system. The number of children from poor families who attended public schools was greatly increased by increasing the number of schools and by an expansion of the program to provide free textbooks for students from poor families. The government also sought to increase the number of school hours spent in the study of Arab history and culture and the teaching of Syrian patriotism was required in all schools, whether public or private. The requirement to instruct in Arabic was strictly enforced.

The government also sought to enhance national unity through the activities of the Ministry of Information and the Ministry of Cultural Affairs and National Guidance. The two ministries sought to develop pride in Arab history and culture, particularly the contributions of Syrians, through extensive use of radio, the government newspapers, and publication and distribution of numerous books and pamphlets. In all these efforts sectarian divisions were not mentioned and the government stressed that all citizens were Arabs and owed loyalty to a government constantly threatened by an expansionist Israel.

As a result, the first Ba'thist government made several significant contributions to Syria's political and economic development. Its efforts to achieve economic growth, a more equitable distribution of wealth, and a more united populace could not have taken place without the contributions of previous governments, particularly the governments led by Nasser and al-Shishakli. The land reform program was based on legislation passed during the period of Syrian-Egyptian unity and the five-year plan drawn up in 1964 was similar to the previous one begun in 1960. The propagation of nationalism by the Ba'thists would not have been nearly as successful as it was had Colonel al-Shishakli not endeavored to put at least one radio in every village.

Nonetheless, the Ba'th Party was not united. In addition to the tensions existing between civilians and military officers within the Ba'th Party, there were differences of opinion within the military committee of the party. Certain officers, predominantly of Alawite and Druse backgrounds, felt that the pace of reform in Syria was too slow. A number of younger civilian figures in the Ba'th Party agreed with the officers and challenged the older leadership. These more radical reformers also believed that the extent of Syrian support for the various Palestine liberation groups was too limited. There were over 100,000 Palestinian refugees in Syria and they, like Palestinians scattered throughout the Arab world, were becoming anxious to oppose Israel through guerrilla actions. The Syrian government, headed by General al-Hafez was well aware that the Israeli armed forces, particularly the air force, was far superior to Syria's and could inflict great damage on the Syrian economy should Syria become a sanctuary for the guerrillas. The more radical elements in the Ba'th Party felt that if Israel did take such action it would bring all the Arab states to Syria's aid and any damage done to Syria by the Israelis would be beneficial in the long run, as it would bring the Ba'thist ideal of Arab unity closer.

Dominance by the Radical Wing of the Ba'th Party

This more radical faction of the Ba'th Party moved successfully against the regime on February 23, 1966. The 1966 *coup d'état* was more violent than previous disorders. Several hundred armed forces personnel and civilians were killed in the fighting. The leading figure to emerge in the new Ba'thist government was Major General Salah al-Jedid.

The new government adopted a variety of socialist measures in an effort to increase rapidly the rate of transformation of Syrian society to an egalitarian ideal. The leaders of the new government were as vigorous in their denunciations of Western imperialism as they were in their praise of the Soviet Union. Syrian financial and diplomatic support of the Palestinian guerrillas was greatly expanded.

In order to understand the reasons behind the violent change of government in Syria in 1966 one must remember that the Ba'th Party had been moving toward a more leftist position regarding such matters as the social and economic policies of Syria, revolution in the Arab world, and opposition to Western imperialism. This trend was manifested in the decisions made and the resolutions passed during the party's Sixth National Congress meeting in October, 1963. While the basic belief in a distinctly Arab form of socialism was reaffirmed, there was recognition that the drive towards socialism must be stronger and that the ultimate achievement of socialism in the Arab world was closely linked to the anti-capitalist, anti-imperialist struggles elsewhere in the world. That is, more and more Ba'thists came to feel, for example, that any people struggling against Western imperialism were indirectly helping the Arab people to throw off imperialism and that they deserved the support of any progressive Arab regime.[14] Since Israel was perceived by the Ba'thists as a state in alliance with the Western imperialist nations of the United States, Great Britain, and France, the Palestinian guerrillas were seen to be fighting imperialism as well as Zionism and deserved extensive support from the Syrian Ba'thist regime.

The differences between the moderates and the more radical elements of the party were somewhat complicated by sectarian factors. However, too many Western commentators on Syrian politics have paid excessive attention to the sectarian factor. They have contended that the dominance of the al-Jedid faction of the Ba'th represented a conscious grasping of power by the two major Moslem religious minorities: the Druse and the Alawites. In view of what has been said about cultural fragmentation based on sectarianism in the past in Syria, the ethnic aspect of intra-Ba'th politics is not to be dismissed without explanation.

First, the Ba'th Party drew to its ranks the best educated and least tradition-bound individuals in Syria. The new members of the party were further drawn away from narrow sectarian loyalties by the Ba'thist ideology which stressed pan-Arabism. Secondly, the new government purged many Druse and Alawite armed forces officers as well as officers of Sunni Moslem and Christian background.[15] Had Major-General al-Jedid been narrowly sectarian in his outlook this would not have occurred.

The reason that such a large proportion of the individuals occupying positions of power in the new government were of Druse and Alawite background can also be explained. Adherents of the two major non-Sunni Moslem sects made up a greater proportion of the military personnel of Syria than did the Sunni Moslems or the Christians. Educated Sunni Moslem families looked down on the armed forces as a profession for their sons. However, for the poor but aspiring Alawite or Druse families, the military academies seemed to offer a golden opportunity for free education, financial security, and prestige for their offspring. Thus, the members of minority sects, particularly the Alawites, have made up a large proportion of career armed forces personnel.

Naturally many of these young officers of Alawite and Druse background were attracted to the socialist, egalitarian, and reformist positions of the Ba'th Party. Had they been narrowly sectarian in their views, they would have become clients of the traditional leaders among their respective sects rather than becoming adherents to the non-sectarian party which has endeavored to carry its message to all parts of the Arab world.

As these young men, originating among the have-nots of the Syrian population, came to positions of political power they carried with them memories of exploitations by the landlord and commercial classes. No doubt these individuals were disturbed by General al-Hafez and Prime Minister Salah al-Din Bitar's conciliatory gesture to the leaders of Syrian commerce following disturbances against socialistic decrees in June of 1964.[16] They, as well as many other members of both the civilian and military committees of the Ba'th Party, who were neither Druse nor Alawite, were anxious to proceed more rapidly with the building of a true socialist society in Syria.

The Continuing Effect of Foreign Relations

The foreign policy adopted by the second Ba'thist government was initially supported by the Syrian citizenry. Eventually, however, two central tenets of the government's foreign policy—almost unlimited support for the Palestinian guerrillas and very close relations with the Soviet Union—came to be questioned by many members of the Ba'th and by many informed citizens.

When Major General al-Jedid announced that Syrian financial, diplomatic, and military aid to the Palestine liberation movement would be greater than ever before, the public reaction was overwhelmingly favorable. Israel was perceived as an immoral and expansionist state and the Palestinians were viewed as a segment of the Arab people fighting to regain their homeland. Syrian support for guerrilla incursions into Israel brought about Israeli military action against Syria. Syrians who lived along the Syrian-Israeli border or who looked skyward during the air battles over Damascus, were quickly reminded of the enormous technological superiority of the Israelis. Nonetheless the government continued to openly proclaim its support of the Palestinian commandos. Partly as a result of the continued Syrian assistance to the growing Palestinian liberation movement, the June, 1967 war broke out between Israel and the Arab states of the United Arab Republic (Egypt), Jordan, and Syria.

All of the Arab states were thoroughly defeated within six days. Informed Arabs were dismayed by the capacity of the Israeli forces to virtually destroy the Egyptian armed forces while only sustaining a few hundred casualties. Syria's losses in men, equipment, and territory were small compared with the other two Arab states substantially involved in the war, but they were significant. The weaknesses of the Syrian army and air force were made evident as the Israelis seized the strategically important Golan Heights area of southern Syria. Naturally, the loss of valuable territory, the creation of almost 75,000 refugees (inhabitants of the Golan Heights) within Syria, and the military debacle weakened the public support for the government and even lessened Major General al-Jedid's position within the radical section of the Ba'th Party.

Another aspect of the government's foreign policy which also eventually contributed to its downfall was its increasing dependence on the Soviet Union. The government was critical of virtually all other Arab states because they were not truly socialist. It, of course, was hostile to the Western, capitalist powers. The government of Syria virtually isolated itself and was forced to rely on the Soviet Union for economic and military support. In return for Soviet assistance the government had to allow the Syrian Communist Party to expand its activities and, of course, the government-controlled radio and press had to refrain from criticism of Syria's one loyal ally. Many Ba'thists came to feel that the government was limiting Syria's independence by this policy. Many non-Ba'thists, holding the widespread Arab distrust of Communism because it is an atheistic philosophy, were even more disturbed by what seemed to be the subservience of this second Ba'thist government to the Soviet Union and the Syrian Communist Party.

Social and Economic Reform

Major General al-Jedid and his associates of the left wing of the Ba'th Party quickened the pace of the land reform and reduced compensation to the landlords. They proceeded with the self-management program for nationalized industries begun by the previous government. These measures increased support for the radical Ba'thists among all but the most reactionary elements in Syria. What cost the radical Ba'thists support among the middle class and urban intellectuals was not their economic modernization programs so much as the glorification of the workers and peasants. Because the radical Ba'thists were more Marxist than their predecessors, they critically examined the class background of Ba'th Party members and government officials. Hence, many reformers of middle class origins began to turn against Major General al-Jedid and his associates.

The attempt of the radical Ba'thists to completely separate church and state also led to widespread dissatisfaction even among progressive elements within the Party. In a new constitution drawn up in May, 1969 the clause present in all previous constitutions, which had declared that Islam must be the religion of the president of the Republic, was omitted. Religious Moslems and Christians feared that this was just the beginning of the radical attack on religion. While the influence of traditional religious leaders has waned considerably in Syria in the past two decades, the Syrian people still regard religion as fundamental to each person's life. Since the radical Ba'thists appeared to many to be irreligious and even pro-Communist, they lost support from segments of the Syrian citizenry who were otherwise in favor of their domestic reforms and support for the Palestinians. Not surprisingly, shortly after the June, 1967 war, an anti-al-Jedid faction developed within the military committee of the Ba'th Party. These officers were well aware of increasing discontent among various segments of the Syrian populace and were in contact with many civilian Ba'th Party figures critical of the radicals. The new coalition was led by Major General Hafez al-Assad. He and his associates were most critical of Syria's isolation from the rest of the Arab world. The radicals were strident in their attacks on other Arab regimes. Such isolation made it difficult for Syria to expand its trade in the Arab world or for it to get loans from such wealthy, conservative Arab states as Kuwait.

The Ba'thist opponents of the al-Jedid regime were not in fundamental disagreement with the domestic goals of the radicals. They correctly realized, however, that every reform could not be accomplished immediately. They also realized that it was still necessary for the leaders of any Syrian government to reaffirm their faith in God and in religion. Without such affirmations the government would lack the ligitimacy and the support to carry out effectively its program.

The developing tensions within the Ba'th Party, especially within the military committee came to a head in September, 1970. King Hussein, the Hashemite ruler of Jordan, became convinced that the Palestinian guerrilla groups in his nation were becoming too powerful and would soon challenge his authority. The United States urged him to crack down on the Palestinians and he ordered his Bedouin armed forces to move against the commando bases.[17]

The Palestinian commando groups had few heavy weapons and no air power. They called upon the Syrians for help. At the same time the United States and Israel made it clear to the Syrian government that it would tolerate no interference in Jordan. Major General al-Jedid wanted the Syrian armed forces to enter Jordan, but Major General al-Assad and his associates, realizing the overwhelming superiority of the Israeli air force, prevented any significant influx of Syrian troops into Jordan. This episode signalled the final downfall of the radical Ba'thist faction led by al-Jedid, as Major General al-Assad organized dissident Ba'thists and seized power.

The government of the radical Ba'thists contributed to Syria's political development and economic modernization. They continued the social and economic reforms instituted by their predecessors. They stressed the need for national unity in messages to the Syrian people.

Probably their most important contribution was to present to the youth of Syria a more highly developed ideology than had their Ba'thist predecessors. That is, they gave the youth of Syria guidelines concerning the reforms that future political authorities would have to undertake and the methods to achieve them.

The Ba'th Party Broadens Its Base Of Support

The new Ba'thist government led by Major General al-Assad was anxious to mend fences with Egypt and Iraq. Announcement of the desire to achieve better relations with Egypt brought the government in increased level of support from the still sizable number of pro-Nasser armed forces officers and from many pro-Nasser civilians. Better relations with Iraq meant heightened support for the new government from the more traditional elements in the Syrian section of the Ba'th Party as the Ba'th Party was then in power in Iraq. At the same time Major General al-Assad maintained close relations with the Soviet Union. He had, because Syria was no longer isolated, more leverage in gaining military aid and economic assistance without compromising his nation's independence than did his more radical predecessor. Thus, by wise foreign policies, the new Ba'thist government retained substantial support from the more radical Ba'thists while it garnered backing from the more traditional Ba'thists and even from non-Ba'thist elements.

The Ba'thist government, led by Major General Hafez al-Assad, wisely balanced its goals of continued social and economic reform and achievement of even greater unity with the realization that not all things could be accomplished at one and the same time. This does not mean that they wished to turn the clock back to the pre-1963 period, when the Syrian political system was more a reflection of Syrian society than a force committed to reform. Rather, the political leaders realized that if social and economic reforms are to be successful in the long run, individual attitudes must be changed. This change does not occur simply in response to governmental fiat, particularly if the legitimacy of the regime is substantially questioned. Similarly, such a change in basic attitude occurs gradually and must be reinforced over a period of time.

For instance, the Chinese Communist Party, a group which has changed the face of China in two and one-half decades, realized the nature of attitudinal change and proceeded in stages to modify the nature of landholding and business enterprise.[18] Particularly during the first seven years of the Chinese People's Republic, the Chinese Communist Party sought to include a variety of non-Communist, progressive elements in the legislative assembly, bureaucracy, educational institutions, and in the People's Liberation Army.

In short, no government can move ahead with equal effectiveness in improving the responsiveness of public institutions to the demands of the citizenry, redistributing wealth in more equitable fashion, providing for economic growth, and increasing national unit. For instance, too rapid a broadening of political participation might actually increase cultural fragmentation as each group in society presses its sectarian or ethnic leaders to make more demands on the political authorities. Or, a rapid and uncontrolled growth in certain sectors of a nation's economy may increase the disparity in wealth between urban and rural citizens, or between citizens of different sects or ethnic backgrounds. Both phenomena have occurred often in the newly independent states of Africa and Asia and have contributed to the political instability of these nations. Nigeria is a prime example.

Particular circumstances dictate that in certain developing nations one or another of the various aspects of political and economic modernization receive major attention first.[19] The Ba'thist government under the leadership of Major General al-Assad was more aware of these basic principles of political development and economic modernization than was the previous Ba'thist government. Since the Ba'th Party was not as hierarchically organized, as ideologically cohesive, or as legitimate in the minds of the citizenry as was the Chinese Communist Party, it was important that it kept these principles in mind.

Promoting National Identity

The new Ba'thist regime realized the importance of religion in the life of the Syrian people. Major General al-Assad stressed that he was a Moslem who observed the prayers and fasts of his faith. He and other leading public figures made a point of appearing at mosques and churches to take part in religious services[20] in an effort to erase the anti-religious stigma of the previous regime.

Shortly after achieving power in March 1971, Major General al-Assad decreed the formation of a People's Council which would have the power to formulate a constitution and, in general, the traditional prerogatives of a legislature. Membership in the council was to be allotted to a variety of progressive political parties—the Socialist Unionist Movement, the Arab Socialist Union, the Arab Socialists, and the Syrian Communist Party, as well as to a variety of labor unions and mass organizations. The Ba'thists kept members of the conservative parties from membership in the People's Council. This was necessary to ensure that there would be no lessening of Syria's commitment to socialism. The Ba'thists, however, did not take repressive measures against any members of the more conservative parties. Individuals of all political persuasions were invited to run for local government offices. In this manner the Ba'thists received the cooperation, if not the ardent support, of the most conservative political figures.

The Economy Minister of the third Ba'thist government made it clear that the new leadership recognized that trade constituted 45 percent of Syria's national income. He sought to give new confidence to the private sector of the economy. In addition, private investment from other Arab nations was encouraged by guarantees against seizure without compensation (and even against nationalization in some instances). Such policies not only contributed to economic growth but also permitted the government to continue the development of agricultural cooperatives and self-management in the large nationalized industries without substantial criticism from the middle class entrepreneurs, who had the memory of the period of radical Ba'thist dominance firmly in the mind.

General al-Assad (who was elected president in March, 1971) and his associates realized that aid from other nations was needed to develop more fully Syrian economy. The Soviet Union had been Syria's main source of foreign assistance for a decade. This aid continued as Soviet leaders were gratified at the new government's acceptance of members of the Syrian Communist Party in the People's Council. The most significant of all Soviet financed projects was the construction of the Euphrates River Dam. Its completion in 1975 will allow the Syrian government to double its area of irrigated land and to quintuple the amount of electrical power produced. The plans for the Euphrates River Dam had been drawn up during the period of Syrian-Egyptian union. The agreement which resulted in the actual beginning of construction was entered into by the al-Jedid-led Ba'thist government in 1968. The completion of this massive project will greatly aid both economic growth and socio-economic reform. Modern cooperative farms may be established on the newly irrigated land while new industries can utilize the electrical power output.[21]

Syria has received much less nonmilitary foreign assistance than many other Third World nations. The various Syrian governments have, however, utilized such assistance more wisely than has been the case in many Third World nations. Port facilities and airports have been improved, primary-processing industries have been established, and irrigation works expanded with Soviet economic and technical assistance.

Attainment of the Ba'thist government's goal of better relations with the variety of other Arab regimes has not only brought internal support to the government from many Syrian citizens; it has also made it possible for President al-Assad to secure over $30 million from the wealthy and conservative sheikdom of Kuwait.[22] The rulers of this oil-rich state had offered a similar aid package to the previous Ba'thist government but the radicals had spurned their assistance.

The third Ba'thist government has embarked upon a policy of administrative decentralization in an effort both to broaden the base of citizen participation in politics and to strengthen the effectiveness of the government. Under a Local Administration Law of May, 1971, Syria was divided into a number of governates with sub-districts of city, town, village, and rural administrative units. Each unit has a popularly elected People's Council that is responsible for the implementation of those policies formulated by the national People's Council which relate to agriculture, industry, housing, health, education, transportation, and communications. In elections held in March, 1972 a large minority of the 644 seats in the various People's Councils were won by non-Ba'thist candidates. Many of these non-Ba'thists were individuals backed by Moslem religious leaders. The Ba'th Party appeared to accept the results with equanimity.[23] This was wise because the dominant position of the Ba'th Party in top-level policy-making was guaranteed and more importantly in the long run, it had been decreed that only the Ba'th Party could undertake political activity among the armed forces and in the universities.[24] The contributions to Syrian political and economic development of the third Ba'thist government are best discussed in a review of the evolution of Syrian politics.

SIGNIFICANCE OF THE SYRIAN EXPERIENCE

As one looks back over the twenty-seven years of Syria's independence, it might appear at first glance that Syrian politics has been largely a response to Syrian society and culture. It would appear that the several different types of regimes, the many governments, and the numerous *coups d'état* all reflected the lack of national unity of modern Syria—a state created by the Western imperialist powers. But most of these changes in the political system eventually led to some degree of political development and economic growth and modernization.

The fact that three changes in leadership have occurred by means other than the orderly transition of power causes some Western commentators to posit greater instability to the Syrian political system than does the author. It is too often forgotten, however, that procedures involving the orderly transition of power acquire legitimacy only slowly and that there has been substantial continuity in the political, social and economic goals as well as the methods utilized for the achievement of these goals among the three Ba'thist governments. The political, social, and economic power of the wealthy landowning class is completely broken. The narrow sectarianism of the Syrian people has been largely eliminated, particularly among the younger generation. No longer do foreign states manipulate and conspire with Syrian politicians. All the Ba'thist governments have utilized the communications and educational system to stress national unity and to mobilize public support for their efforts in behalf of economic modernization.

The political system is now more in control of the economic and social systems than controlled by them. It must be remembered, however, that this is a relative judgment. The political authorities in Syria since 1963 have not had the capacity to radically change every aspect of society as the Chinese Communist Party has done in China. The Ba'th Party has not been as cohesive as the Chinese Communist Party, and its members did not adhere as absolutely to all-embracing revolutionary ideology as have the Chinese Communists. On the other hand, it is a more disciplined and ideologically-based party than the Congress Party of India or the coalition of parties which supported ex-President Salvador Allende of Chile. The Ba'th Party is somewhat like the Institutionalized Revolutionary Party of Mexico in that it reflects certain of the tensions existing among various groups in the society even as it works to eliminate the basis of these tensions, but the Ba'th Party is, of course, more radical and reform-minded.

The greatest contribution of the Ba'th Party has been to bring together the younger, dynamic, better-educated elements of the Syrian population to pursue the goals of progressive social and economic change. Sunni, Druse, Alawite, and Ismaeli Moslems as well as Christians of many sects have joined in this endeavor. They have gradually put aside their sectarian loyalties, fatalism, and acceptance of class distinctions and replaced them with loyalty to Ba'thist ideology, commitment to change, and advocacy of egalitarianism.

Like other political parties discussed in this book the Ba'th Party has evolved. A new generation of leaders has come to power. Some of these younger party members, Marxist in their worldview, constituted the radical faction of the Ba'th Party which held power for almost four years. However, they were unable to consolidate their power in the party and in Syria because they lacked the necessary minimum level of support from the politically conscious elements in Syrian society and within the armed forces.

Thus the Ba'th Party has come under the direction of younger, more progressive leaders and, at the same time, rejected leadership from a radical faction which incorrectly assessed the pace at which domestic reforms could be undertaken. The changes in the party and the subsequent changes in the government have been accomplished with a minimum of violence. The near absence of violence has been beneficial to Syria's political and economic development at least in the short run.

However, the long-range effects on any nation's political and economic development of violence are difficult to assess. Certainly the economy of China suffered during the long period of war between the Kuomintang and the Communists. Yet, during these years of conflict the Communists were able to develop hundreds of thousands of dedicated cadres whose devotion to Marxist socialism motivated them to transform and revitalize the Chinese economy after 1949. So too, Nigeria is a more cohesive entity today after a violent confrontation among ethnic groups than it would have been had the ineffectual parliamentary system continued. Thus, one cannot conclusively say that the absence of significant violence has been a mark of political maturity in Syria; rather, it may indicate, at least in part, insufficient commitment to ideology on the part of too many leading Syrian political figures. At any rate, the extent of deep commitment to ideology is greater among Ba'-thists than among members of any other Syrian political party.

The Ba'th Party has instituted substantial land reform in a society in which the overwhelming majority of peasants lived in abject poverty dominated by several hundred landlord families and by foreigners. It has increased the amount of arable land through large-scale irrigation projects and has laid the basis for cooperative agricultural efforts to free the peasants from being dependent for their survival on good weather. Through selective nationalization and large-scale planning the Ba'th Party has established the basis for economic modernization. These reforms also garnered support for the regime.

The Party, under the leadership of President Hafez al-Assad, has endeavored to bring government closer to the masses of people in order to end the attitude of resignation all too common among the illiterate. This has been done without sacrificing the dynamism of reform or the dominance of the most progressive elements of Syria. Membership in the highest policy-making body of government has been restricted to Socialists (both Marxist and non-Marxist) while non-Socialists have been allowed to hold positions in the administration of local affairs. Such an arrangement is similar to the one employed by the Chinese Communists of "new democracy" from 1949 to 1954. The Chinese Communists brought representatives of progressive parties, cultural, scientific associations, and mass organizations into the governmental structure, the Chinese People's Political Consultative Conference, in order to consolidate their power and to enhance their legitimacy among the large majority of Chinese citizens who were not Socialists. The Syrian Ba'thists also have recognized the necessity of such a maneuver.

In assessing the effectiveness of the Ba'th Party one cannot avoid discussing the issue of the party's relations with the Syrian armed forces. Constant involvement of the military in the government of a Third World nation often, though not always, is an indication of political instability. Generally, as has been the case in Mexico, the armed forces must refrain from intervention so that civilian political leaders may deal more effectively with a multitude of social and economic problems. However, there may be times when military intervention is necessary to prevent a new state from disintegrating.

In discussing Ba'th Party relations with the Syrian armed forces it is necessary to keep two facts in mind. First, the Syrian people correctly perceive a threat to their homeland from Israel. Naturally, they believe that a large and modernized military organization is the best deterrent to this threat. Therefore military expenditures will constitute a significant share of the Syrian budget and the need to have access to modern weaponry must be a factor in the formulation of foreign policy by any Syrian government. Secondly, the Syrian armed forces became active in Syrian politics before the Ba'th Party developed enough strength to seek to control Syria. The Ba'thists were forced to take the expectations and goals of the several factions in the armed forces into account when they achieved power.

When one takes all of these factors into consideration it is not surprising that the Ba'th Party has not been able to fully control the military in the same fashion that the Chinese Communist Party has controlled the People's Liberation Army. The Ba'thists chose to try to convert armed forces personnel to their party rather than to create their own army as the Chinese Communists did in the 1920's. Nonetheless, the Ba'th Party has brought the military into a position where it acts in conjunction with the progressive reform-oriented elements of the Syrian population rather than as an entity separate from the will of Syrian citizens.

Syria is an interesting case study of a Third World nation for two reasons. First, it is a good example of a state achieving political and economic goals even as there are changes of regime and government. Second, a study of Syria shows that the leaders of a Third World nation may choose to modernize with different methods and different goals than those of Western capitalist nations.

The history of independent Syria shows that the process of political development does not need to be either a smooth one with constant increments of modernization originating with a stable government or one arising from the success, through violence, of a revolutionary party or coalition. Rather, the process may be uneven, with progress sometimes grinding to a halt and even interspersed with short periods of regression. This was the case in Syria from 1961 through 1963, where political development was characterized by frequent changes of governmental leadership. If, throughout these periods of instability, a party is developing that is dedicated to social and economic modernization, the advancement of the general level of political consciousness and greater national unity, then political growth is occurring.

One also learns from a study of Syria that economic development and even the initial steps of economic modernization may take place during periods of political instability. Between 1946 and 1958 Syrian citizens witnessed several changes of regime and numerous cabinet shifts, yet the economy advanced because of the actions taken by individual interprises involving small-scale manufacture. Continuation of such economic growth unregulated by a reformist government probably would have contributed to greater political instability in Syria because the growth was widening the gap between the poor and the rich. Nonetheless the advances made during this period, particularly the expansion of agricultural land by use of irrigation techniques and the mechanization of cotton farming, helped the Ba'thist regime to achieve its goals of guaranteeing to every peasant an opportunity to support himself from the land. Similarly, the existence of small factories meant that the Ba'- thists had only to nationalize these enterprises to ensure profit-sharing. Nationalization is easier than finding scarce capital to invest in establishing industries.

The Ba'th Party of Syria has adopted a non-Marxist and noncapitalist road to political development and economic modernization. The trend of governmental economic policy has been to restrict the amassing of private capital. Also, economic policy has favored redistribution of land, even if such a policy temporarily interferes with the increase in levels of production. Political leaders have additionally favored large-scale governmental planning rather than individual decision-making.[25]

The Syrian Ba'thists seek to create a government which will play an expanding role in virtually all areas of the lives of the citizenry rather than a government of limited powers. The leaders of the Ba'th-directed government have undertaken to accomplish the following tasks: to expand educational institutions; to instruct the peasantry in modern agricultural techniques; to ensure that private capitalists utilize their resources in a manner that serves the public interest; to restrict the influence of narrowly sectarian religious leaders, and to redirect the cultural interests of the Syrian elite from Western cultures to Arab art and literature. In short, the Ba'thist believe that it is only the government, led by a cohesive party, which can provide the ideology and organization necessary to build a modern, unified Syrian nation.

They are correct. All of the studies in this book demonstrate that there can be no significant long-term modernization until the political system achieves some control of its destiny and is not merely a reaction to internal economic and social systems.

POSTSCRIPT

As this textbook goes to press, war has once again come to the Middle East. The precise outcome of the most recent manifestation of the decades-old tensions between Arabs and Zionist Jews is impossible to predict. It is possible to say, however, that Israel will not occupy Syria or Egypt and that the Arab states will not be able to eliminate Israel as a major power in the Middle East.

The fighting on the Syrian front has demonstrated that President al-Assad's policy of trying to improve Syria's relations with other Arab nations has paid dividends, as Iraqi, Saudi Arabian, and Jordanian units are aiding in the defense of Damascus. It appears that the vast majority of Syrians accept the legitimacy of the ruling coalition dominated by the Ba'th Party. The Syrian people are well aware of the military might of the Israeli armed forces and they are therefore proud that their forces have been able to protect most of Syria's territory in the weeks of fighting. The continuation of the creditable military performance of the Syrian military will further strengthen the unity of the Syrian people and will add credence to the Ba'thist claim that only through socialism will Syria become a strong, modern nation.

It is true that Israeli bombing of power facilities, oil refineries and port facilities in Tartus, Latakia, Homs, and Damascus have set back the Syrian economy. The Syrian leadership, however, remains convinced that the economy can be restored through mobilization of all of that nation's human and material resources and by foreign assistance from such socialist nations as the Soviet Union, the Chinese People's Republic, and the Democratic Republic of Korea.

FOOTNOTES

1. The Syrian Arab Republic is 99 percent Arab. There are small Armenian, Jewish and Circassian minorities.

2. Philip K. Hitti, *Syria: A Short History* (New York: Macmillan, 1959), pp. 1–2.

3. Approximately 86 percent of the Syrian Arab Republic's population professes Islam. Moslems constitute over 90 percent of Iraq's population, over 80 percent of Jordan's and over 50 percent of Lebanon's.

4. See Benjamin Rivlin and Joseph Szyliowicz, *The Contemporary Middle East* (New York: Random House, 1965), pp. 122–131 for a fuller discussion of the Western impact on the Middle East.

5. Lebanon and Syria were ruled by France with nominal League of Nations oversight; Palestine and Iraq were ruled by Great Britain with nominal League of Nations oversight.

6. Ernest Dawn, "The Rise of Arabism in Syria," *The Middle East Journal,* 16 (Spring, 1962), pp. 145–168.

7. Patrick Seale, *The Struggle for Syria* (New York: Oxford University Press, 1965), p. 98.

8. The Syrian Social Nationalist Party (SSNP), having lost influence and direction since the death of its leader, Antun Saadeh, by a Lebanese firing squad, aligned itself with the Arab Liberation Movement. This move eventually further limited the appeal of the SSNP.

9. See R.S. Porter, "The Growth of the Syrian Economy," *Middle East Forum* (November, 1963), pp. 17–22.

10. The Ba'th won 22 seats, the People's Party won 30, the National Party won 19, and the independent candidates won 64 in an assembly of 142 seats.

11. See Seale, *The Struggle for Syria,* chapter 22, for a more detailed discussion of these events.

12. Porter, "The Growth of the Syrian Economy."

13. See Eva Garzouzi, "Land Reform In Syria," *The Middle East Journal,* 17 (Winter-Spring, 1963), pp. 83–90 for a full discussion of changes in Syrian rural life.

14. Gordon Torrey, "The Ba'th—Ideology and Practice," *The Middle East Journal,* 23 (Autumn, 1964), pp. 463–464.

15. Martin Seymour, "The Dynamics of Power in Syria Since the Break With Egypt," *Middle Eastern Studies,* 6 (January, 1970), p. 40.

16. See Torrey, "The Ba'th Ideology," p. 467 and Kamel Abu Jaber, *The Arab Ba'th Socialist Party* (Syracuse, New York: Syracuse University Press, 1966), pp. 88–91.

17. See Rowland Evans and Robert D. Novak, *Nixon in the White House* (New York: Random House, 1971), pp. 262–265 for an account of this incident.

18. The rapid elimination of the landholdings of the gentry class in 1949–1950 would seem to be an exception as the subsequent goal of collectivization was undertaken in stages.

19. See Leonard Binder, "Crises of Political Development," in Binder *et al., Crises and Sequences in Political Development* (Princeton, N.J.: Princeton University Press, 1971), pp. 3–72, and Eric A. Nordlinger, "Political Development: Time Sequences and Rates of Change," *Politics and Society* (Englewood Cliffs: Prentice-Hall, Inc., 1970), pp. 329–347.

20. Moshe Ma'oz, "Attempts At Creating a Political Community in Modern Syria," *The Middle East Journal,* 16 (Autumn, 1972), pp. 389–404.

21. *Middle East Monitor,* I; 3 (March 1, 1971) and No. 6 (April 15, 1971).

22. *Ibid.,* II; 11 (June 1, 1972).

23. *Ibid.,* II; 7 (April 1, 1972).

24. *Ibid.*

25. See article by Samir A. Makdisi, "Syria: Rate of Economic Growth and Fixed Capital Formation, 1936–1968," *The Middle East Journal,* 25 (Spring, 1971), pp. 157–179.

CHINA

The Politics of Revolution and Mobilization

Victor C. Falkenheim

In January, 1949 Mao Tse-tung rode at the head of a
dusty column of People's Liberation Army soldiers into
the new capital city of Peking. That event marked both
a beginning and an end point in modern Chinese
history: an end in that it represented the culmination
of a long process of revolutionary change dating back
to the 1800's; a beginning in that it symbolized the
start of a new process of reintegration after a long
period of political fragmentation and foreign
domination. In 1949, Mao was justified in saying,
"Today, the Chinese people have stood up."[1]

Since 1949, China has been ruled by one party, the
Chinese Communist Party (CCP). As in India and
Mexico, one-party rule has resulted in basic political
stability. But unlike India and Mexico, political
stability in China has been accompanied by an intense
revolutionary dynamism. In pursuit of their
revolutionary goals, Mao Tse-Tung and the CCP have
launched a series of massive assaults on the problems
of poverty, backwardness, and social inequality. China
since 1949 has been little short of a revolutionary
society embodying Mao's view that the "true way (tao)
that governs the world of men is that of radical
change."[2]

The spectacle of the world's most populous nation
engaged in seemingly perpetual revolution has both
attracted and repelled observers. Some, struck by the
self-reliant discipline and vigor with which the Chinese
seemed to be facing the difficult problems of
modernization, have held the Chinese up as a model
for the rest of the Third World. Others, repelled by the

authoritarian nature of the regime, have deplored what they view as the human costs of a coercive solution to the problems of political unification and economic development. Still others have argued that the egalitarian values of contemporary China might well be emulated by even the advanced industrial nations.

Evaluating these conflicting assessments is no easy task. It requires both that we judge the effectiveness of Chinese institutions and policies in meeting China's needs and that we understand the conditions and constraints that generated a mobilization approach to development.

Such a judgment is not made easier by the faddism which governs images of China. As one recent visitor cautioned, Americans viewing China "have an extraordinary capacity to shape their picture of the country to fit their own mood and preconceptions of the moment." Not long ago images of China were largely negative. Now many Americans "in a mood of euphoric admiration of all things Chinese," see it as a country "surging ahead at breakneck pace towards a model 'new China'. . . ."[3]

The reality of China is clearly more complex. While China has been largely free of many of the political weaknesses of other modernizing nations in Asia and Africa, it has not been entirely free of them. The "Cultural Revolution" (1966–1969) was a period of considerable upheaval in Chinese domestic politics. Similarly, despite major achievements in economic modernization since 1949, the "Cultural Revolution" underscored the fact that even in the late 1960's and early 1970's Chinese leaders were still plagued by the problems of inequalities, the persistence of rural and adult illiteracy, and the lingering influence of traditional, cultural and social patterns.

Yet the success of the Chinese in building a powerful new social and political order since 1949 is undeniable. As one scholar has written:

> The relevance of the Leninist model of political development is perhaps most dramatically illustrated by China. Surely one of the most outstanding political achievements of the mid-twentieth century was the establishment in China in 1949 for the first time in a hundred years of a government really able to govern China.[4]

One of the aims of this chapter will be to describe the Chinese model of political development in some detail. But it is important first to understand why such a "Leninist" solution emerged in China. China's experience in the late nineteenth and early twentieth centuries resembled much of the later experience of the rest of the Third World. In a period of turbulent change, China passed rapidly from monarchical rule (the Revolution of 1911) through a disillusioning and abortive phase of constitutional democracy, to militarism, political fragmentation and single-party rule. The Chinese Communists came to power only after many years of war and revolutionary struggle.

The perspective of this volume enables us to pose some fascinating comparative questions about the nature and significance of Chinese political evolution. Both Syrian and Mexican politics, for example, were characterized by a similar party government. In Mexico (and less clearly in Syria), "moderate" forms of single-party rule have proved to be relatively effective in dealing with the problems of participation and integration. Yet similar rule by Chiang Kai-shek's Nationalist Party (KMT) was overtaken after 1927 by a deeper and more convulsive revolution which resulted in a far more intense form of single-party authoritarianism.

In all three cases, a lengthy post-revolutionary period of instability prevailed (China, after 1911; Mexico, after 1910; Syria, after 1946), marked by considerable political change but little political development. In all three, this period laid the foundations for new forms of institutionalization. How then do we explain the different outcomes in the three cases?

Are the roots of China's more thorough-going revolution to be found in the more profound nature of the modernization crisis in China or in the differing sequences and rates of change that confronted China's rulers in the nineteenth and twentieth centuries? During a recent visit to China, Mexican President Echeverría stressed the importance of national heritage in shaping the Mexican and Chinese revolutions. "The Mexican Revolution and its institutions," he said, are "the result of a unique historic process. It is easy for us to understand that the special characteristics of the Chinese revolutions are inseparable from a special culture and national past."[5]

What role in fact did traditional political patterns and culture play in shaping Chinese politics in the twentieth century? What was the impact of imperialism on Chinese political development in the nineteenth and twentieth centuries? What kinds of changes, social, economic and demographic, were occurring in the first half of this century and how did these affect the efforts of successive Chinese leaders to establish political order? How was the Chinese political system, formerly at the mercy of convulsive economic and social forces, given the capacity to shape social and political change? How, in short, did politics become an "independent variable" in the development of China?

CHINA IN REVOLUTION: POLITICS AS A DEPENDENT VARIABLE

China entered the modern world in revolution. Dynastic decline and Western invasion had already begun to undermine the traditional political order by 1850. Yet it is important to look briefly at China's imperial past, for the Confucian political legacies crucially affected China's transition to modernity.

The Traditional Political Order

Chinese leaders historically faced many problems in establishing viable and effective political institutions.[6] One of the most important was sheer territorial size. The vast expanse of China, at times well over 3 ½ million square miles, has posed enormous difficulties of integration and control—difficulties compounded by topography and the inadequacy of communication links.

China's enormous population, almost 600 million by the time of the Communist takeover in 1949, has posed even greater problems of control. With the bulk of the population clustering in hundreds of thousands of natural villages across the country, more loyal to clan and family than to Peking, the problems of political penetration were staggering.

Yet despite these difficulties and perhaps because of them, China developed a remarkably effective political order. One source of China's national unity and strength lay in its political institutions. The Emperor personified a tradition of strong central political authority. Confucian ideology both legitimized and tempered that authority by stressing norms of humane and benevolent rule. Imperial authority was made effective by a sophisticated and complex bureaucracy recruited by merit through a relatively open examination system.

The longevity and stability of these institutions were striking. Despite cyclical collapse, the imperial order persisted for well over 2,000 years until the revolution of 1911. Clearly the socio-cultural setting of these institutions was of prime importance.

Cultural Unity

Although China contains many nationalities, including Tibetans, Mongolians, Manchus, and a variety of smaller tribes, the bulk of the population is overwhelmingly (94 percent) Han Chinese. This ethnic homogeneity is reinforced by linguistic unity. Despite significant regional differences in spoken vernaculars, the written language is the same for all Chinese. On this basis of ethnic and linguistic unity, the Chinese built a very powerful cultural homogeneity.[7] All literate Chinese became heirs to the same traditional values. Taking great pride in the achievements of their civilization (which was unmatched in the region of East Asia), the Chinese developed a sense of pride and self-sufficiency which some scholars have labelled *ethnocentrism*—a premodern analogue to nationalism. These unifying factors contributed strongly to later efforts at political modernization. The scholar-gentry played a crucial role in inheriting and transmitting these traditions over the centuries. These values not only provided the normative underpinnings of joint imperial-gentry rule, but linked peasant households to the state by inculcating values of hierarchy and submission. These were formally enforced by local magistrates, but they reached right down into village China through informal mechanisms of gentry rule.

The family was the nucleus of the state. It schooled young Chinese into a pattern of obedience to all authority, beginning with obedience to one's parents and elders. Although there were potential dangers that the family might serve as an alternative focus of loyalty to the throne, normally, submission to family authority and political authority were mutually reinforcing. Confucian social and political institutions normally held Chinese society together despite the enormous size of the country, its striking topographic diversity, its pre-modern communications, and its tradition of localistic and clan loyalties.

The Dynastic Cycle

Much of Chinese history, however, was characterized by turmoil and fragmentation. In fact, the alternation between periods of strong and weak central rule was one of the characteristic rhythms of Chinese history and has been labelled by historians the "dynastic cycle."

At the root of cyclical dynastic collapse was the population problem. Years of peace swelled population pressure on the land. In the short run the government was able to cope with the political pressures generated by rural distress. Eventually these pressures led to increasing institutional weakness: decreasing central control over the bureaucracy, increased corruption, eroding fiscal base, and poor leadership. This shrinking governmental capacity intensified the agrarian crisis through neglect of transport, irrigation, and flood control facilities. Not only was the government increasingly unable to check arbitrary landlord exactions from the peasantry, but more fatefully, it was unable to check the peasant insurgencies that became more frequent as the dynasty declined.

With military impotence, central power disappeared, unleashing powerful separatist drives in the different provinces and regions. Regional power supplanted central authority, causing decades of warfare. Ultimately, after a long period of disunion the most able domestic (sometimes foreign) contender for the "mandate of heaven" would elbow his competitors aside, take over the "dragon throne" and reestablish central power, on much the same basis as before. During periods of disunion, many Chinese turned their loyalties and concerns to their localities and families—a regression that made later reintegration very difficult. When Sun Yat-sen in the 1900's likened the Chinese people to a "sheet of sand" he was describing a defensive response to political breakdown which had to be overcome before unification could take place.

This process of breakdown was apparent by the 1800's.[8] By the time of the British assault on China in the 1840's, the last ruling dynasty, the Manchus (who took the dynastic title of Ch'ing), had been in power for almost 200 years. By then many of the classic signs of dynastic decay were in evidence. The original Manchu garrison forces had lost their martial qualities and become a rentier class. Corruption was on the increase. An enormous population explosion, together with decaying water works had led to a rising incidence of peasant discontent and banditry. These agrarian problems erupted in a series of rebellions beginning in the 1790's, culminating in the massive Taiping Rebellion of 1851–64.

Colonialism in China: The Century of Unequal Treaties

Dynastic decline made China increasingly vulnerable to Western commercial and political pressure.[9] The British defeat of the Chinese in the first Anglo-Chinese war (the Opium War) of 1840–42 marked the real beginning of imperialist penetration of China. Continued central government weakness in the last half of the nineteenth century led to a steady increase in foreign encroachment, as the English, Germans, French, Americans, Russians, and later the Japanese, consolidated their political and commercial gains into local spheres of influence (the treaty ports). These privileges were conferred by treaties imposed on China by force (the unequal treaties), which deprived the Chinese government of legal jurisdiction over much of foreign activity in China. Within the treaty port framework, foreign entrepreneurs were able to organize commercial and industrial activities free of Chinese restrictions and free of high tarriff barriers, which were also limited by treaty.

The high tide of imperialist pressure came in the 1930's with the abortive Japanese effort physically to occupy and dismember China. Only during World War II, as an ally of the Great Powers, did China succeed formally in terminating the unequal treaties, 100 years after the Opium War.

Imperialism and Cultural Fragmentation

Before assessing the effects of imperialism on China's political evolution, certain features of colonial domination should be noted.[10] First, in contrast to India, China as a whole was never occupied and ruled by foreigners. China's sovereignty in a formal sense was thus left intact.

Second, China was never physically dismembered, despite the success of various powers in establishing spheres of influence. Third, China was never converted into an economic dependency like Nigeria. China's efficient domestic commercial integration, and the internecine struggle of the powers diffused the imperialist onslaught. Though China was thus a "semi-colony" in Marxist terms, these differences were scarcely comforting to Chinese nationalists. Sun Yat-sen, the "father" of the Chinese Republic, described China as a "hypo-colony," equally exploited by all, without the minimal protection afforded by a single colonial overlord.[11]

The political impact of imperialism was twofold: (1) It made real revolutionary change inevitable by undermining the ideological basis of the Confucian order, and (2) it intensified the process of revolution by adding a cultural dimension to the multiple social and economic changes already underway. Although the tenacity of the old traditions slowed down the process of cultural fragmentation, by the early 1900's the bankruptcy of the old values were obvious to most Chinese. Paradoxically, imperialist pressure also helped to forge the nationalist spirit animating almost all Chinese leaders during this period.

Chinese nationalism was the most important recipient of the Chinese political legacy. The contrast with India makes this clear. The development of Indian nationalism required centuries, with an all-Indian identity only emerging slowly in reaction to British rule. In China a culturally and geographically defined sense of identity already existed. Further, a class existed which was well aware of China's greatness and antiquity. Imperialism effectively transformed an essentially cultural sense of identity into a more narrowly national one. In this sense the colonial interlude resolved the issue of identity for politically aware Chinese by forging the basis for a potent anti-foreign nationalism.

While the question of identity may have thus been resolved, the issue of legitimacy was not. For those anxious to "save China," the political solutions ranged from revitalized monarchy to anarchism. Even within the context of reform, the values of nationalism were potentially revolutionary, for they required widespread structural renovation which rested uneasily on a Confucian basis. The sweeping imperial reforms of the early 1900's, including the abolition of the traditional examination system and the establishment of new Western-style schools, accelerated the revolutionary process, ultimately undermining the throne itself.

The Revolution of 1911

The collapse of the Manchus in 1911 signified the final failure of traditional political institutions to adapt to the accelerating social, cultural, and economic changes of the late nineteenth century or to absorb the new political forces generated by these changes.[12] The revolution of 1911 involved rapidly expanding popular participation in the context of institutional collapse.

Yet within a year after the revolution, the new republican institutions it had created had also been subverted and the party of revolution, Sun Yat-sen's Kuomintang (National People's Party), had gone underground to resume the struggle. Why did the revolution of 1911 succumb so rapidly after its initial triumph? Partly, the failure of the revolution of 1911 can be traced to the disintegration of the loose revolutionary coalition of students, regional merchants, overseas Chinese and secret societies, whose only common aim had been the overthrow of the Manchus. But, two other factors were involved.

In the first place the new political institutions rested on an inadequate social basis. Traditional forces were still powerful, with the local gentry remaining the dominant force in the countryside. The bourgeoisie was only slowly emerging in this period and was too weak to buttress the new republican order. Equally important, the new institutions lacked legitimacy. There was little basis in the traditional political culture for constitutional democratic government, particularly in the first decades of the twentieth century.

In this situation the fledgling institutions were vulnerable to counter-revolutionary pressures. As in Mexico, after 1910 military intervention in China undermined the new postrevolutionary institutions of rule. For a decade and a half the Peking government was a pawn of conflicting military forces during the period known as "warlordism"—a period directly comparable to the Huerta period in Mexican history.

Political Mobilization After 1911

While the period after 1911 was marked by turmoil and conflict, it was also a period of important political growth and mobilization. The growth of a mass national consciousness accelerated and deepened after World War I, primarily because of foreign intervention. A major political eruption occurred in May, 1919, after the Versailles conference awarded Germany's China holdings to Japan. The May 4 Movement, as it became known, represented a real broadening of the mass movement. Throughout the 1920's, numerous anti-foreign strikes and boycotts signalled a growing alliance of merchants, students, and workers in a classic anti-imperialist united front.

This period also featured a deepening cultural fragmentation. The May 4 Movement had called for a rejection of Confucian values and for the discovery of new beliefs to guide nationalist movement.[13] In response, great numbers of students enrolled in Western schools began studying abroad. The movement deepened as the shift to vernacular language led in turn to the proliferation of popular newspapers and journals.

The growth of the student movement and the parallel expansions of the proletariat and bourgeoisie during and after World War I was of decisive importance in preparing the ground for the rise of both the KMT and the CCP in later years. The decade after 1911 laid the ideological and social foundations for the emergence of a movement capable of challenging the narrow legitimacy of regional military gentry coalitions.

Partial Institutionalization of the Revolution: The Rise of the KMT

Revolutions, as Huntington has noted, tend to lead either "to the restoration of traditional structures of authority, or to military dictatorship and the rule of force, or to the creation of new authority structures."[14] To yield stable results they must lead to the growth of institutions more flexible and with greater capacity than those displaced. The emergence of the PRI in Mexico marked a crucial benchmark in stabilizing the gains of the Mexican revolution. By broadening the appeal of the revolution, by integrating new groups into the political process and by helping to reduce the military role in politics, the PRI played a crucial role in the success of the Mexican Revolution. In striking contrast to Mexico, the emergence of the KMT in the 1920's proved to be only a halfway house to full institutionalization of the revolution.

The Kuomintang before 1911 was a loose coalition of revolutionaries loyal primarily to Sun Yat-sen. Although the party reorganized after 1911 to participate as a parliamentary party, Yuan Shih-kai's counterrevolution forced it underground and cut short efforts to broaden the party's popular base of support.[15] During the warlord period, Sun Yat-sen vainly sought warlord or foreign support for a military campaign to reunify China. Only in 1923 did the party gain a sponsor, the Soviet Comintern, which saw the KMT as a potential vehicle for Russian national and revolutionary interests in China. With Soviet support, the KMT acquired a semblance of a tight-knit organization, and a broad revolutionary program. The merger of Sun's charismatic appeal with Bolshevik organizational talent and money gave the KMT real momentum. In particular, the radical student movement, among them many Communists, joined the KMT and supplied it with a mass base in the labor movement and the peasant movement which helped make possible the successful Northern Expedition to reunify the country in 1926.

The reorganization of the KMT as a revolutionary party under Soviet sponsorship seemed to offer real opportunities for political growth. Sun Yat-sen had envisaged a three-stage political program for China. The first stage, "military unification," was to be followed by a second phase, "democratic tutelage," which was inaugurated in 1928 with the establishment of the new government in Nanking. Like Sukarno's "guided democracy," it was to be a preparatory phase of limited democracy designed to usher in the third phase—full constitutional democracy. During the period of "democratic tutelage," political power was to be monopolized by one party, the KMT. Guided by Sun Yat-sen's Three People's Principles (nationalism, democracy, people's livelihood), the proclaimed aims of the party included representative government, social and economic equality, and the recovery of China's sovereignty.

Though some of these aims were partially achieved, the promise of the 1920's was not fulfilled. External pressures were in part responsible for this failure, but more important was the changing character of the KMT.[16] Many of the strengths of the early KMT were forfeited after 1925. Sun Yat-sen's death in March of that year led to the splintering of the party. Sun's successor Chiang Kai-shek, with the support of the more conservative groups within the party, turned to the business community and the gentry for support. The party repudiated its left wing and Communist supporters and eliminated them in 1927. The abandonment of its reformist commitment alienated the committed youth who had flocked to its support just a few years earlier.

Gradually the KMT became increasingly factionalized and corrupt, preoccupied with its own rule and internal challenges to it, and decreasingly responsive to domestic economic crisis or foreign pressure. Its failure in particular to deal forcefully with Japanese military, diplomatic and commercial pressure in the 1930's, led to the alienation of nationalistic youth throughout China. The shrinking basis of KMT support was clearly visible in the 1930's. Power became centralized more and more narrowly in the person of Chiang Kai-shek. The ideological basis of the party became more traditional as the KMT leaders invoked Confucian values in the hope of propping up their declining movement. The war against Japan (1937–1945) which drove the National Government inland, deprived the KMT of the support of the more progressive coastal bourgeoisie, and the subsequent inflation which destroyed middle-class support were final blows to a weakening party.

The KMT's record was not a total failure. It achieved some progress in administrative modernization despite problems of corruption and personalism. It made substantial gains in reducing the military power of warlord and regional military forces which had pledged only nominal loyalty to Nanking in 1927.[17] But its failures to deal adequately with rural discontent and its inability to integrate new groups into the political process proved fatal. Perhaps the most important failure of the Nanking (KMT) government was the failure to achieve meaningful social and economic reform. One scholar has argued that the problem of the KMT was that it created new organizations but staffed them with old elites.[18] This was only part of the problem. In both Mexico and Japan, sections of the elites were sufficiently innovative and forward looking to provide the leadership necessary to propel modernization and reform. Chiang Kai-shek, unfortunately for China, was no Cárdenas!

The Rise of the Chinese Communist Party

The emergence of the Chinese Communist Party (CCP) as a major force in Chinese politics dates from the war against Japan (1937–1945).[19] Its initial support after World War I was largely limited to radical intelligentsia on the left wing of the nationalist movement. The appeal of Marxism to these men was not primarily theoretical. What gave the doctrine relevance and thrust was the borrowed prestige of a successful revolution in Russia. The party made major gains under the Soviet Comintern tutelage which, after helping to organize the party in 1921, urged it to concentrate on organizing a trade union movement in the cities and peasant associations in the countryside. The Comintern also urged the CCP to work within the KMT.

This high-risk policy proved successful in the short run. The party grew from a handful of members in 1921 to over 50,000 by 1927. Under the KMT aegis it made major gains in acquiring a mass base. Its rapid growth however, made it vulnerable to the hostility of the right wing of the KMT. When Chiang Kai-shek decided unilaterally in 1927 to destroy the "united front," the CCP was without the means to defend itself and as a consequence was devastated.

Forced into the countryside, the party gradually shifted to a primary reliance on the peasantry, with Mao Tse-tung emerging as one of the early leaders of the Communist rural insurgency. This ultimately became the chief mode of Communist activity. Equally important, the party concluded that the key to political power was military force. The resolve to create its own strong military force based on remote regional strongholds proved successful initially. Between 1928 and 1934, the Communists were able at times to field and supply an army of almost 100,000 men.

However, Nanking, previously preoccupied with warlord foes, gradually became determined to dislodge the Communist threat in southeast China and did so in five successive "annihilation" campaigns. In the last of these, the Communist armies were decisively defeated and driven to the west and north. Ultimately they reestablished themselves in Yenan in northwest China after an epic retreat, known as the "Long March." In 1935 when the Communists reached Yenan with less than 20,000 troops, it seemed unlikely that a comeback would be possible.

Yenan Communism

It was during the Yenan Period (1936–47) that CCP fortunes took a decisive turn for the better. The coincidence of the improvement in their position with the onset of the Japanese invasion has led scholars actively to debate the importance of the Sino-Japanese War to ultimate CCP victory.[20] The question has been whether the expansion of Chinese Communist strength in this period should be attributed to their ability to exploit anti-Japanese nationalism or to their radical agrarian program. Clearly both ingredients were crucial to CCP success. More importantly, the Communists "brought nationalism to the countryside, they did not reflect it."[21] The comparative records of the CCP and the KMT underscore this latter point. Both were in a position to exploit anti-Japanese nationalism, but only the Communists really succeeded in creating a modern mass movement.

Important as the issues were, the organizational skills which formed the basis of this mass movement are equally worth considering. The unique methods of leadership developed by the CCP during this period not only were crucial to wartime success but were important in shaping the way in which political power was organized and exercised after the war. If one views the CCP as essentially an alternative government during this period, then the system and forms of leadership they developed were a major institutional breakthrough which provided the basis for institutionalization of authority after 1949. Political development occurred in the context of revolution.

While these techniques and institutions will be the subject of the next section, their origins are worth examining. The requirements of people's war led the CCP to discover new approaches to leadership. The CCP learned to reach down to the village to integrate the peasant into the political process.[22]

Eight years of war permitted the enormous expansion of Communist strength in both military and political terms. By 1945 they had almost one million men under arms, and a party organization whose membership was over one million, passing a crucial threshold in size and strength. Although they were at a serious disadvantage in terms of number of troops and quality and quantity of materiel, compared to Nanking they had a more powerful organization, a more able and cohesive leadership, and strong mass support. These advantages in terms of morale and fighting spirit paid off in a series of military triumphs in 1947 and 1948 which led to victory by 1949.

With CCP victory, China gained a cohesive, skilled and experienced group of leaders who had stood the test of 28 years of struggle and warfare. More importantly, it gained a resolution of the authority crisis that had followed the collapse of the dynasty in 1911. Power passed to a new revolutionary leadership with genuine legitimacy. The revolutionary break in Chinese history gave the CCP enough room to make real changes.

MOBILIZATION AND DEVELOPMENT: POLITICS AS AN INDEPENDENT VARIABLE

The revolution of 1949 was a massive peasant-based revolution led by intellectuals on a platform of nationalism and reform. The success of the Communists in leading this revolution depended on their ability to mobilize an effective mass movement in a highly fluid social and political context. But the ability to make a revolution under one set of conditions does not guarantee a similar ability to govern under others. Mao's assertion in 1949 that the Chinese Communist Party was "not only good at destroying the old world . . . but also good at building the new" was a prediction, not a guarantee.[23]

Many of the same factors that had undermined the KMT were still present in Chinese society after the CCP victory. The problem of cultural fragmentation was even more severe, having been intensified by the twelve years of international and civil war. Wartime destruction of economic infrastructure and plant capacity aggravated economic discontent. The CCP, in taking over the administration of the economy and the large industrial and treaty-port cities, was hampered by the lack of experience and trained personnel.

A number of factors, however, helped facilitate their assumption of power. First, they were no strangers to the tasks of civil government. The CCP had governed large areas of China for many years. Second, they enjoyed considerable legitimacy and support as a result of their leadership of the national revolutionary movement. Third, the decades of political struggle had created a constituency for change and a desire for unity and order. Presumably, such traditional antecedents in Chinese political culture as national pride and a sense of the rightness of a unified political order, also helped the initial consolidation of power by the CCP in 1949 and 1950.

While these advantages may have contributed to stable rule in the short run, they do not explain long-term stability. The CCP's goals were not merely to govern China but to transform it. The introduction suggested that modernization tends to undermine political stability. This assumption is borne out by the cases of Mexico and Chile, and clearly by the experience of China after 1927. The ordinary stresses of modernization, moreover, would be intensified by the CCP's revolutionary program.

Consider some of the changes set in motion by the CCP since 1949.[24] As a consequence of peace and the provision of basic public health services, China has experienced a demographic explosion, resulting in a population growth from less than 600 million in 1953 to over 800 million in the early 1970's. This growth has been accompanied by rapid urbanization and industrialization. The expansion of educational services has reduced illiteracy from 80 percent of the population to less than 30 percent. New elites have emerged to direct and administer society and old elites have been displaced. Traditional village social and work patterns have been altered as the state has extended organizational roots into the countryside. The peasantry has been dramatically politicized by a party bent on a radical reordering of society.

In many societies, such a drastic alteration in the socio-economic fabric would generate explosive tensions. Increasing levels of literacy, urbanization, and political awareness are precisely the forces identified by scholars as most disruptive to the political order. How then has the CCP managed simultaneously to initiate and to contain rapid social change?

In one of the earliest examples of rapid, directed modernization, namely Japan, traditional values of hierarchy and discipline helped maintain integration and absorb the tensions of early industrialization. Modernizing elites can profit from a selective reliance on traditional values, institutions, and behavior patterns as the cases of India and Mexico clearly show. The Chinese leaders chose to forfeit these advantages and to mount an immediate assault on traditional social structure and values. They approached modernization through "mobilization" and revolution.

Mobilization systems are defined generically in terms of certain common traits. They are "oriented towards the future," stressing communal rather than private values, and characterized by "full politicization of social and political life."[25] Their strength is seen to lie in their ability to increase the power of the state by eliciting mass support. The mobilization label has been applied to a variety of actual systems including Ghana, Egypt, and China.

While these countries vary in the form and style of mobilization adopted, they share certain common institutional patterns and emphases. All stress the primacy of political values and organization and all are marked by the presence of a strong centralizing party, an official ideology and a strong government.

It is useful for comparative purposes to think of China since 1949 as a mobilization system with certain distinctive features deriving from the guerrilla struggle and the Yenan experience. In the next few pages I will try to summarize the main features of the Chinese mobilization model, both in institutional terms and in terms of the philosophy and approach to development which underlies them. It should be noted that the Chinese leadership has been divided over many questions affecting the speed of social and economic transformation, as well as over methods for resolving conflicts that arise, and that the idea of a unified Chinese approach to political development involves some simplification.

Ideology, Legitimacy and Participation

The main feature of present-day politics in China is the pervasiveness of political values. The prominence of ideology is visible in the omnipresent slogans, posters, and loudspeakers far more pervasively than was the case in Allende's Chile or in Syria today under the Ba'th Party. What explains this distinctive emphasis? In part the explanation is historical. The CCP came to power as a revolutionary movement and the ideology of insurgency became a natural legitimating force in the postrevolutionary order. But the striking emphasis on ideology in China suggests that more than just legitimacy is involved.

It is important to consider the role of ideology in historical context. If much of modern Chinese political and intellectual history can be seen as a search for a new set of values to guide China into modernity, then the political and military victory of the CCP in 1949 foreclosed the issue in favor of Marxism-Leninism on the battle fields and in the villages of China. The necessity in 1949 was to put an end to the cultural fragmentation of the previous decades by reshaping the values and loyalties of Chinese around the new ideology.

The necessity was twofold. First, shared values, even implicit ones, help hold a society together. In the aftermath of a long-term social revolution, effective reintegration requires the development of a conscious, articulated set of values (ideology).[26] Second, such an ideology is all the more necessary in a political system in which the leaders are determined to continue the process of revolutionary change.[27] In China where the bulk of the population remained strongly traditional in their values, the need to generate popular support for the regime's new goals was clear.

Ideology is also needed to help formulate and rationalize the goals and priorities of the regime. In practice the application of ideology to the formulation of policy has been highly flexible. This flexibility is evident in the description of Chinese ideology as the application of "universal" Marxist-Leninist principles to the "practice" of revolution and building socialism in China, an application which results in a changing synthesis of theory and practice known as "Marxism-Leninism—Mao Tse-tung Thought." Ideology is not fixed and by no means rules out debate over how to build socialism. It is a framework within which that debate is conducted. Moreover, the formulation of policy in China has been marked by vigorous debate since 1949[28] over such issues as the speed of collectivization and the need for mechanization, which involve basic questions of development strategy. Chinese ideology has, in fact, proved flexible enough to justify varying strategies of economic and social development.

While the grounds of policy debate often seem to shift, there are certain recurring emphases in Chinese ideology which reflect continuing efforts to create a disciplined political community. These emphases are often labelled the "Yenan spirit," for they derive in large part from Mao's views of China's long revolutionary struggle.[29] These values stress the limitless potential of people imbued with the values of service, self-sacrifice, and struggle. They are seen not only as instrumental in speeding economic and social development, but as good in their own right, and as preconditions in the long run for the creation of the "new socialist man."

These populist and voluntarist strains in Mao's thought have led some to question his Marxist orthodoxy,[30] but the relevance of his insights to the problems of development seems undeniable. Maoist values form the basis of an effort to reshape the Chinese people. They are intended not only to build a new sense of community and commitment, but to discourage such negative traits as excessive loyalty to family, clan or region or opportunist orientations towards jobs, schooling, or personal success. To the extent that these values take hold, they can enhance political stability by maximizing links between leaders and the people and by reducing the tensions generated by the modernization effort.

Political Education and Participation

All political systems teach civic values. Revolutionary systems which embrace new values must do so in a conscious and purposeful way, not only because of the limited public familiarity with the new official political culture, but because the older values continue to permeate society, undercutting the new system. The process by which citizens acquire political values (political socialization), is a learning process in which the "agents" of socialization may include the family, schools, peer groups, work place, and political or social organizations. In China, efforts have been made to harness these agencies of socialization in a way that will create new patterns of loyalties and identification.

This process is greatly facilitated by state control of the public media. Unlike the KMT which tended to rely on the negative instrument of censorship, the CCP since 1949 made the public media an important mechanism for fostering value change.[31] All newspapers, journals and publishing houses are supervised by Party departments to ensure that publications transmit official policy and values. Art, literature, movies, television, plays, and opera are subject to similar political direction.

Traditional and popular art forms are given revolutionary content and are widely used to reach mass audiences. Travelling dance and opera and film companies pack their screen, cameras and equipment into the rural hinterland to reach as many people as possible. The educational system also plays an important role in shaping political attitudes. Political education is an important part of school curricula at every level.

While the public media and the school system help expose most Chinese to new orientations towards authority, they do not assure their acceptance. Supplementary learning techniques are used to reinforce these lessons, utilizing face-to-face channels of communication. One of these devices is the "study group." To ensure that learning is active and not passive, all citizens of China are members of small study groups. Each group meets approximately once a week for two hours to discuss political and social questions, under the direction of an appointed group leader. Each participant must play an active role, and must articulate his views. There is no right to silence. Dissenting views must be set forth for the purpose of clarifying their erroneous nature. The dynamics of group pressure and "criticism–self-criticism" are effective, in the view of participants, in molding opinions and values.

Similarly, all citizens must participate in politics.[32] Virtually everyone is enrolled in one organization or another, ranging from youth federations to trade unions. In the context of these "mass organizations" citizens will perform a variety of civic tasks such as giving blood, carrying placards in demonstrations, voting, and helping dig public shelters. Participation in these tasks is highly structured and institutionalized, yet their effects are politically significant. Aside from contributing to the implementation of specific programs, they reinforce political education by inculcating a more active sense of community. Since all modernizing political systems must deal with participation explosions, and do so in ways which range from accomodation to direct suppression, the Chinese solution is an interesting one. It provides for, and requires, a pattern of action which affirms the importance of the collectivity, without building an individual sense of political autonomy. Political activity thus builds citizens, not lobbyists.

One form of activism particularly stressed by Chinese leaders is the importance of physical labor. Labor, they hold is crucial to prevent subtle forms of elitism and status differentiation from corroding the sense of community. This is particularly necessary in China where a traditional contempt for manual labor runs deep. Mao Tse-tung himself confessed to an early feeling that labor was degrading and said that only decades of rubbing shoulders with peasants and workers in the revolutionary movement eradicated that deep-seated prejudice.[33] Students, teachers, professionals, and particularly party and state cadres spend much of their time at the "basic level" in physical labor on the farms or factory floor. These efforts to "send down" bureaucrats and intellectuals began in the mid-1950's and were institutionalized in the 1960's. They are now the basis of a new institution, the "May 7th Cadre School," which was developed during the Cultural Revolution for the purpose of re-educating cadres to the traditions of struggle and service.

Particularly strong efforts are made to minimize student elitism. From kindergarten on, students do practical work which helps to build a sense of community service. Efforts are made to break down the artificial separation between the student and his community. Afternoons, weekends, and vacations are often spent in some form of public service. Moreover students are explicitly taught that they are educated not to "become officials", but to "serve the people." Access to higher education is in part contingent on demonstrating these qualities of service and responsibility. The millions of youths now in the countryside working in the villages are evidence of the determination of the regime that education should help to bridge the rural-urban gap, not widen it. The introduction to this book pointed out that education can be a two-edged sword, often disrupting political stability by politicizing previously passive youth. The Chinese solution to this potential problem is to shape the *form* of politicization so that it serves the community.

It should be emphasized that an extraordinary commitment of energy and manpower is devoted to these efforts at political education, distinguishing China from virtually all other mobilization systems. The emphasis on moral suasion and its corollary that men *can* be educated and changed, suggests important continuities with the Confucian tradition. In an interview with Edgar Snow Mao said that though he was known variously as the "great helmsman," the "great leader," the "supreme commander" and the "great teacher," soon all those honorifics would be dispensed with and he would be remembered only as "a school teacher."[34]

It is clear that not all Chinese accept these values. Émigrés continue to flow out of China, and the press continues to report dissension and debate. During the "hundred flowers" campaign in 1957, strong criticism was directed at the Party by students and teachers. Reports of peasant unhappiness with work point systems and student discontent with life on the farms are not uncommon. In the absence of public opinion polls it is impossible to get a feeling for the views of the man in the street. In fact it would be surprising if, in an era of rapid directed change, there were unanimous support for all party policies.

Mao Tse-tung, analyzing the reaction of the peasants to communization in 1958, said that 30 percent supported the program, 30 percent were pessimists or bad elements and opposed it and the remaining 40 percent followed the mainstream and would go along with the party.[35] This assessment reveals a pragmatic view of the problems of legitimacy.

Chinese emphasis on changing attitudes is neither cynical nor utopian. By communicating its political expectations and attitudes to the people, the leadership elicits the support of many, neutralizes the criticism of others, and sets out the limits of acceptable debate.

The relative success of the regime in defusing potential antagonisms rests on several things. It recognizes the importance of maintaining communication between the leadership and the people. It responds to opposition or discontent by stressing values of unity and community, avoiding where possible a repressive response which might polarize groups. Most importantly, real effort is made to narrow the gap between elites and masses, and to make bureaucracy responsive. The credibility of the new value system can be maintained in a vital way only so long as the leaders behave in accord with their own ideology. The efforts by Mao Tse-tung and other leaders to ensure an egalitarian "working style" on the part of bureaucrats, and a genuine respect for the masses, seems the heart of the system.

In the event that persuasion fails, the leadership has ample police powers to deal with opposition. Many studies of mobilization systems begin with a discussion of coercion and terror. I have reversed the order of discussion because of the striking emphasis in China on nonviolent methods. But recurrent doses of repression have been used against enemies of the regime since 1949. Many political campaigns end with the detention or execution of those identified as deviants. Lesser penalties, including labor re-education in penal settlements, are part of the process. These instruments serve as a backdrop to efforts at reeducation and reform, and confront Chinese citizens with some of the unpalatable consequences of improper behavior.

It is impossible to discuss the uses of ideology in China without recognizing the manipulative aspects of political education. What is important to stress however, is that the active emphasis on equality and community seems to reduce the saliency of this manipulative dimension and to make the new values more attractive.

Organization

The energetic and unremitting stress on political attitudes and values is perhaps the single most important dimension of Chinese politics. But to stress values to the exclusion of structural and institutional factors is to neglect an important part of politics. Ideas and values are embodied in organization. Organization in turn is a vehicle for transmitting and actualizing values.

One analyst, writing of the Leninist model of political development, has argued that "the stress on organization has been the crucial characteristic differentiating Communist from other nationalist movements."[36]

If one examines, for example, the Chinese village today, there is ample evidence of a major organizational breakthrough. New organizations have grown up displacing clan, lineage, and religious associations. Communes, production brigades and teams now manage agricultural work. Poor and lower-middle peasant associations, militia groups and youth groups play important supporting roles. Party members, demobilized soldiers, and local peasant activists dominate local leadership organs. Study groups, literacy training classes, and technical training classes abound. New marketing, distribution and transportation ties link the villages to the wider economy. Similar organizational growth has taken place in the cities as well. In a political system which stresses mass mobilization and structured participation, organization supplies the framework, the discipline, and the control that makes cohesive group effort possible.

THE COMMUNIST PARTY OF CHINA (CCP). When one thinks of organization in a socialist system, one thinks first of the party. One writer has observed that if the party did not exist, it would have to be invented.[37] To establish effective leadership in a country the size and complexity of China required rapid party expansion after 1949.[38] At the time of takeover in 1949, the CCP was a party of 4 ½ million members, 80 percent of whom were peasants largely drawn from North China. It had little strength in the southern or western regions of China, few roots in most villages, and negligible strength in the industrial cities. In 1950 there was barely one party member for every hundred or so citizens. By the early 1960's the party had over 17 million members, with one party member for every 39 citizens, and by 1973, 28 million members.[39] Rough uniformity in regional representation had thus been achieved. During the programs of land reform and collectivization, large numbers of cadres were recruited in the villages, giving the Party a "backbone" force in most rural areas. Rapid enrollment of ethnic minority members also gave the party a foothold in the autonomous regions on China's periphery. In 1961 the percentage of party members in the total population was 2.5 percent. This proportion was much smaller than that found in many socialist countries (for example, the equivalent ratio in Cuba was 3.9 percent; in the USSR, 4.5 percent). The smaller numbers in China may reflect tighter standards, but may also reflect their success in attracting broad mass support. The party relies on mass organizations such as the Communist Youth League or recruited activists and cadres to assist in fulfilling objectives. The party has further amplified its support by converting all institutional associational groups such as women's organizations or trade union organizations into extensions of party power. In the rural areas, groups such as the demobilized People's Liberation Army soldiers or poor and lower-middle peasant associations play important leadership roles despite their non-party status. Thus the party since 1949 has embraced virtually all potentially competitive elites through a process of co-optation.

The guidelines governing recruitment and expansion during the 1950's and early 1960's aimed at comprehensive regional and institutional representation. To maintain its vanguard role, the party, through its Organization Department, maintains job lists for every organization which identifies those posts that must be filled by party members.

While expansion was easy, maintaining revolutionary standards was not. In the revolutionary period, joining the party required dedication and courage. In the post-revolutionary period it also attracted opportunists and careerists. Opportunism aside, the party often admitted those with little background in Marxism-Leninism, especially in the rural areas. Similarly, the recruitment of professionals introduced problems of role conflict in which party members were torn between loyalty to their sense of professionalism and the political demands of the party. As the party increasingly came to embrace all of society within its ranks, it confronted the problem of how to avoid degenerating into an adaptive party, in which the label "Party" was only a cover for competing interests bargaining over policy behind a facade of party discipline.

The evolution of a revolutionary party into a power broker for coalescing interests is a common weakness of mobilization systems. This pattern is reflected, for example, in the steadily shrinking commitment of both the Indian Congress Party and the Mexican PRI to reform. It is a problem, however, which is not confined to relatively pluralist societies, but reflects a basic dilemma facing all mobilization parties that are responsible both for administering and transforming society. On the one hand, the mobilization party must serve as the energizing core of the society, defining societal goals and priorities. On the other, to make itself effective, it must be large and far flung enough to blanket and penetrate the society thoroughly. Yet size and numbers create problems of management and coordination which lead to the proliferation of rigid managerial bureaucracies. Territorial or institutional penetration leads to the growth of competing perspectives and interests which threaten the party's directing role.

The Chinese have attempted to solve this problem by establishing quality controls and balance into the recruitment and training process. While all Chinese citizens who accept the party constitution are eligible for membership, strong efforts have been made through the use of preferential eligibility quotas to maintain the proportion of poorer peasants and workers whose loyalty is regarded as more certain. Second, the recruitment process has been selective, designed to ensure that new members, whatever their class background, will have already demonstrated qualities of revolutionary activism. To qualify for consideration for membership, most applicants must have passed through a rigorous apprenticeship as activists in political campaigns or as members of a feeder organization like the Communist Youth League or the People's Liberation Army (PLA). The necessity of recommendations and a period of probation also are intended to discourage opportunism. Further, the party vocation is clearly a difficult one in which the rewards in status and opportunity are offset by various sacrifices. Those who join the party are made aware that it often involves submitting to a virtual military discipline, to a reduction in one's privacy, and to heavy demands on time and leisure. The contrast with the PRI in Mexico could not be sharper.

Once in the party, a new member is engaged in constant and intensive education. This process, known as "party life," involves study, criticism and self-criticism and is crucial for socializing new members into the organization and maintaining élan. The initial selection and training are supplemented by periodic "rectification" campaigns to weed out undesirables. These purges supplement a variety of more routine checks on membership behavior which are carried out by specialized party control organs.

At times, the measures taken to guarantee revolutionary standards have gone even further. Though the vanguard role of the party has been recognized in all party constitutions, the party has never been held to have exclusive possession of revolutionary virtue. In 1956 and 1957, China's intellectuals were encouraged to criticize the party. In the 1960's the People's Liberation Army came to play an important role as a complementary, if not competing, political model. During the Cultural Revolution, the party came under attack for elitism and many of its functions were assumed by the PLA and the mass organizations. This subordination of the party was so unusual in a socialist country that Soviet leaders labelled it a violation of Leninist principles.[40]

The recent restoration of the party to its former leading role seems to confirm its organizational importance. But that it was not restored until it had regained a vitalized revolutionary ideology equally indicates the importance Chinese leaders have accorded to revolutionary values.

State Administration

Political development, as the introduction noted, often depends on rapid growth in the administrative capacity of the state. In China, as in India, the growth of the state sector partly resulted from its assumption of responsibility for modernization and for the provision of new services. In China this growth became particularly striking after the economy was brought under direct state control. The scale of this growth may be indicated by noting that in 1949 there were only 700,000 state workers in administrative and other posts, whereas by 1958 there were over 7 million.[41]

Administrative growth, as the introduction also pointed out, creates problems of its own for developing countries. It often carries with it new problems of red tape, inefficiency, and worse—corruption. In countries where jobs are scarce, bureaucracies may expand for the purpose of securing employment and security for relatives and friends and in the process consume vital funds rather than spending them for developmental purposes. This sort of administration is an obstacle to development.

The Chinese leaders have in fact had to confront many of these difficulties. They have complained often of bureaucratic growth and red tape and even corruption impeding effective administration. The solutions they have adopted are similar to those used to manage party bureaucracy. First, they have provided for party direction of administration to assure the overall subordination of the state to revolutionary goals. More importantly they have worked to achieve full politicization of the bureaucracy in order to assure a loyal, efficient, and frugal public service. Periodically, they have attempted to reduce the bureaucracy and the red tape accompanying administrative growth. Several retrenchment campaigns have been mounted since 1949, notably in 1957, 1959, and 1968–70, which have cut back the number of administrative employees. Of great interest is that bureaucrats are periodically rotated down to the basic level to remind them of the needs of the constituency they serve. As in the case of the party, these do not offer a perfect or a permanent solution, for the problems recur. But they, too, illustrate the party's strong commitment to integration and community.

The People's Liberation Army

The Chinese have had similar success in developing a loyal and responsive military, solving a problem that plagued KMT China as well as much of the Third World.[42] Unlike Mexico and Chile prior to Allende (which dealt with the military presence by limiting its political involvement, stressing values of the civilian supremacy, and somewhat segregating the military society from at large), the Chinese have integrated the military into the political community. The army has been thoroughly politicized and the guerrilla tradition of a "people's army," has been deliberately cultivated and extended.

In China, despite the importance of the military in the rise of the CCP to power, the supremacy of civil power in the hands of the party has been firmly maintained. As early as the 1920's the principle was enunciated that while "political power grew out of the barrel of a gun," it was the "party that commanded the gun; not the gun the party." To ensure the primacy of party command, a parallel structure of political commissars was established. Potential tensions between commander and political commissar were minimized, since approximately three-fourths of the army's military officers were party members as well. In addition to these institutional safeguards, the army's education program taught values of civilian supremacy and a tradition of military service which stressed respect for the people, avoidance of conflict with them, and more positively service to them. The People's Liberation Army (PLA) plays an important role in the civilian economy, raising its own food where possible and helping peasants out during peak agricultural seasons or during emergencies or special construction campaigns.[43] Units of the army are further responsible for directing and maintaining the vast militia system with its membership in the hundreds of millions.

After the Korean War there was some movement away from these traditions. The PLA was re-equipped and modernized along Soviet lines. With professionalization came the establishment of ranks and insignia, and the growth of a professional perspective among some top-ranking officers. There were some military leaders who felt, for example, that the PLA defensive needs required a reduction of its civilian functions, including militia building and economic work, and particularly a de-emphasizing of political training. After the dismissal of the Minister of Defense, Peng Te-huai, in 1959 over these and other issues, the more traditional PLA values were reasserted, with a return to a stress on political controls and civilian service. In 1965 rank and insignia designations were removed, restoring many of the pre-1955 traditions.

In the 1960's the PLA played an increasingly prominent political role. The nationwide "learn from the PLA" campaign in 1963 reflected Mao's view that the army under Lin Piao exemplified many revolutionary virtues. When his dissatisfaction with the party reached its peak in the Cultural Revolution, he called on the PLA to intervene in "support of the left." The PLA's entry, in January, 1967 into politics and the simultaneous decline of the party made it both political vanguard and crucial arbiter of power from 1967 to early 1969. Students of the Third World saw an ominous similarity between events in China and the pattern of military takeover common in Latin America and Africa. The fall of Lin Piao in 1971 and the firm efforts to restore the Party's leading role since 1969 have largely removed this prospect.

The Chinese effort to combat elitism and bureaucracy stresses the close links between organization and legitimacy. The Chinese leaders have recognized that directing the process of revolutionary change both requires strong leadership and control from above, as well as active mass support. To achieve the latter they have stressed the accountability of the leadership to the people and the subordination of the organizational interests of the elite to the values of the revolution.[44]

Party and Leader: The Limits of Charisma

The altering balance of power between party and army, between elite and masses, between values and organization, owes much to the thinking and periodic intervention of Mao Tse-tung.[45] Many of the emphases described above reflect his insights into the process of modernization and revolution. His central role raises two questions about the nature of mobilization politics in China. First, to what extent does the form of mobilization depend on Mao's leadership? Second, is this form of charismatic mobilization likely in the long run to prove a source of weakness and fragility?

In Marxist-Leninist theory, ideology, not charisma, is the primary source of legitimacy.[46] Individual leadership status within the party flows from demonstrated ideological wisdom affirmed through party support. The leader becomes leader by acclamation, but he is subject to party discipline no less than any other member. There is, however, a potential conflict between the party and its leader. To the extent that the leader finds it necessary to work within the party for his goals, the party both limits and extends his autonomous power. In many socialist countries including China, Cuba, and the USSR, the result has been conflict between the leader and party and the growth of a socialist variant of "personalism," or the cult of the personality.

Mao's leadership is clearly an enormous asset to the CCP. His prestige as a national leader in war and revolution is important to the party. His image as a wise, omniscient leader has been deliberately cultivated. This manipulation of his charismatic appeal, while clearly pragmatic, has a basis in fact. Mao *is* the stuff of which legends are made.[47] He was born in 1893 in Hunan province in central China, the son of an increasingly prosperous peasant farmer. By temperment he was a rebel nonconformist and a passionate nationalist. As he acquired education he joined the swelling ranks of student revolutionaries. Through skill, ruthlessness, and talent he bulldozed his way to the top of the faltering Communist movement in the later 1920's and early 1930's—becoming first among equals by early 1935. His rise to power within the party coincided with the beginning of a period of the dramatic expansion of party power. His leadership of the party during that period and after is the concrete basis of his prestige. Since 1949 that prestige has been consciously inflated.

Although some critics have attributed the growth of Mao's "personality cult" to his vanity, Mao himself has been ambivalent. He has remarked that the need of the Chinese for an emperor figure is not easily eliminated and will take time. He has further commented pointedly that all leaders need support and had Krushchev spent more time creating a cult of his own he might not have been so easily overthrown.[48]

Despite Mao's own ambivalence and even distaste, the result of the cult is striking. Mao has become the symbol of the revolution. Songs, poems, and statues celebrate his role. These tributes to Mao's leadership are not hollow. Mao has been the single towering figure in the Chinese political landscape for over a generation. His vision has been the dominant one at almost every crucial policy juncture. His vision of the Chinese revolution has helped shape every institution in Chinese society. In particular, his views on issues of distribution, on social revolution, and on bureaucracy have been most important to Chinese political development. Is he then an indispensable part of that approach? More important, what are the likely consequences of his death?

Mao, when questioned on his indispensability, remarked cryptically that as long as he lived he was indispensable and that after he passed from the scene his indispensability would pass[49]—a point that seems partially confirmed by stability of North Vietnamese politics after the death of Ho Chi Minh. Without minimizing Mao's critical transitional role, even now his leadership seems to me ancillary to the processes and techniques of human organization which have been the foundations of Chinese rule since 1949.

Though Maoist charisma has been important in Chinese political development, the real base has been the organizations staffed by people loyal to and linked by the party and its revolutionary values which have reached down to the remotest village. Traditionally, formal government stopped at the county level where village and informal government reaches each individual. The creation of new collective goals and vital organizational forms has greatly increased the capacity of government to reshape its human and material environment.

Political Development in China: Summary and Assessment

The Chinese have recognized that a political system which requires massive mobilization and strong leadership will generate antagonisms. Mao Tse-tung identified these potential cleavages explicitly in 1957 specifying a number of "contradictions" between "leaders and led," between "center and locality," and between "coast and interior."[50] The Chinese try to manage these tensions within the context of strong leadership and discipline by narrowing the gap between conflicting groups and interests, stressing their shared values and interests. The insistent stress on community is an important avenue for achieving cooperation among party, state, army, and the people. The efforts to realize the values implicit in the idea of community is the basis for a self-renewing legitimacy. This approach is a far cry form the adaptive pluralism of Mexican party politics, not to speak of the failures of Nigerian leaders.

How effective has this strategy been in the past two decades? One writer describes the Chinese experience as a "great success" resulting in the "creation of a modern nation state," and in "organizing a poor backwards country, holding it together, preventing bureaucratization, and achieving basic social change."[51] Another credits the Chinese with achieving a "fundamental institutional breakthrough," developing "for the first time . . . a political system strong enough to control and transform society."[52] Both concede the existence of weaknesses and shortcomings, but emphasize the crucial growth in political capacity since 1949.

Other scholars find such judgments premature. A prominent development expert, though struck by the intensity of Chinese efforts at modernization, concluded that "one has to attach as much probability to the prospect of breakdown and disintegration as one does to the creative and innovative solutions of the problems of Chinese political development."[53]

What accounts for these different assessments of the Chinese political system? One source of disagreement is a failure to distinguish between the *ultimate* revolutionary goals of the regime and its *instrumental* policy goals. For example, the behavior of many Chinese is still affected by traditional cultural patterns and values. Regional and family loyalties persist. Many traditional religious and social practices have defied efforts to change them. Problems of bureaucratism and factionalism still exist at all levels of society and government. While these behavior patterns indicate a failure of many Chinese to internalize fully the collectivist values of the official political culture, such a failure can scarcely be taken as an indictment of the regime's capability. To change people is something that few systems have accomplished on a national scale. Moreover, the Chinese revolution is only 2 ½ decades old.

A second source of confusion lies in the mobilization model itself. Most scholars see mobilization politics as a transitional form of rule. But the model itself contains few criteria for judging whether any given modification in the system involves growth and maturation or deterioration and breakdown.

The most profound source of disagreement is the lack of a consistent view of what constitutes political development. Often it is defined in terms of national stability, or capacity; at other times in terms of socioeconomic equality or institutional differentiation and specialization.[54] If the standard is *stability*, then China is developed, the cultural revolution notwithstanding. If it is *equality*, then China is well developed. If it is *capacity*, defined as *mobilization potential*, China is also developed. However, if capacity includes the rationality of the decision-making process, then scholars would disagree in their evaluation of China's record. If *differentiation* or *specialization* is an important aspect of development, then the powerful efforts of the Chinese to blur lines of differentiation might seem to be distorted development.

The criteria are not only difficult to apply but often seem flawed by a pluralist bias. Many analysts seem to measure the degree of political development in terms of the "responsiveness" of the system to individual or group demands. While the Chinese government in fact meets many of the most pressing needs of the majority of citizens, analysts deny its responsiveness on the grounds that it controls "demands." A political system which limits demands by controlling associational groups, it is argued, cannot by definition be described as responsive.

While the standards are arbitrary to some extent, "stability" and "capacity" seem to be meaningful standards. These criteria, of course, fit the definition of political development offered in the introductory chapter. Huntington's judgment (which rests on these standards) is worth repeating—that in 1949 a government was established in China which was "really capable of governing."[55] In the next section we shall examine the social and economic consequences of the 1949 victory.

Economic Development and Modernization: Goals and Strategies

China's major developmental goals can be summed up in part in the traditional Confucian phrase, "wealth and power,"[56] Her long-term aims from the start were to create a modern industrial economy as rapidly as possible. These aims reflected a commitment to restore China's greatness and international prestige, and to build a better, more productive society at home. Ideology and nationalism converged from the outset to set goals of rapid industrial growth.

The introduction to this volume stressed the importance of economic development to long-term political development. The Chinese leaders recognized this need early. Mao Tse-tung for example, acknowledged in 1957 that the successful "consolidation of the Chinese state" was due in part to the fact that "our economic measures are basically sound, that the people's livelihood is secure and steadily progressing."[57]

China's leaders approached the task of economic development with confidence. Admitting their lack of technical qualifications, Mao said in 1949:

> The serious task of economic construction lies before us. We shall soon put aside some of the things we know well and be compelled to do things we don't know well. This means difficulties. The imperialists reckon that we will not be able to manage our economy. They are standing by and looking on awaiting our failure.
>
> We must overcome difficulties, we must learn what we do not know. If we dig into a subject for several months, for a year or two, for three or five years we shall eventually master it.[58]

Despite this initial confidence, there were certain conditions which set limits on the possibilities for rapid development. The most important was China's low level of development at the time of the CCP takeover. Most of the population (85 percent) was employed primarily in agriculture, and the limits of intensive cultivation had been virtually reached. Agricultural output was barely sufficient to sustain a growing population, with little surplus for investment. The CCP began its industrialization drive with a per capita income base of about $50.00 (U S), considerably lower than Great Britain, for example, at a comparable period ($200 current dollars per capita in 1801). Further, China in 1949 had lower literacy rates and higher birth rates than Japan at the equivalent period (1870's).[59]

Despite these handicaps, in four Five Year Plans (1953–57; 1958–62; 1966–1970; 1971–1975) China has mobilized its resources and manpower in a concerted and largely successful development effort. First adopting the Soviet industrialization model and then a variant, Chinese development has been distinguished by its emphasis on broad mass participation and on national self-reliance. For ideological as well as political reasons (the Korean War; the Sino-Soviet Conflict) Chinese development has been largely domestic. In contrast with India and Pakistan, which absorbed a net capital inflow of over $8 billion between 1954 and 1964, China strikingly has been a net capital *exporter* in every year since 1955, exporting a total of $1.3 billion dollars during 1950–1964.[60]

In China's push towards self-reliant and rapid growth over the past 24 years, several phases and several shifts in strategy are discernible.

CONSOLIDATION. Between 1949 and 1952 Chinese leaders were primarily concerned with restoring the economy and consolidating their power —two tasks that were closely interrelated. In 1949 industrial production was less than two-thirds of the pre-war high. This was partly a function of dislocation, partly a function of damaged economic infrastructure and partly a product of spiralling inflation. Fiscal and monetary measures had brought inflation under control by the end of 1950. By 1952 industrial production had been restored to pre-war peaks in most industries. This was a substantial achievement, especially since it occurred at the same time as major political and social changes were taking place in the cities and the countryside. During the period 1949–52 a Land Reform campaign was completed with the result that by 1952 over 110 million acres (45 percent) of the land had been redistributed to 300 million peasants.[61] In the process not only was landlord power destroyed in the countryside, but considerable resources had been accumulated in the form of "reparations." A variety of tax devices and forced loans, similarly secured considerable resources from the urban middle class. During this period, the new leadership began to acquire the experience, the trained personnel, and the information necessary to direct economic change.

THE FIRST FIVE YEAR PLAN. With the restoration of production and the completion of land reform, the Chinese leadership began to plan more vigorously. The First Five Year Plan (FFYP) was introduced in 1953. It stressed priority for heavy industry over agriculture, and producers goods over consumer goods, emulating the Soviet FFYP of 1928–1932. The FFYP projected a total investment of about $17 billion over the plan period, actually spending over $20 billion. Most of this investment was in industry or transport with only 8 percent of the total going to the agricultural sector. Economists have estimated that this represented a remarkable gross investment rate 20 to 25 percent of domestic product. The industrial growth rate which resulted was over 14 percent per year, with the result that by 1957 the proportion of industrial production to total agricultural and industrial production by value had been raised from 26.2 percent to 36 percent.[62]

This picture of progress in industry was not mirrored in agriculture. The agricultural sector had to supply labor for the industrialization effort and raw materials to light industry (e.g., cotton for textiles); most important, it had to feed a growing population. Initially China's planners assumed that structural reforms in agriculture would generate a sufficient surplus to accommodate all these needs. Land reform had been uneconomic particularly in intensifying the fragmentation of farm holdings. It was also politically undesirable creating a class of private peasant proprietors on the land. For a number of related economic and political reasons, therefore, the leadership was intent on agricultural reorganization, leading ultimately to collectivization. They were aware of the costs of the brutal Stalinist collectivization in the USSR, and rather than allow a pattern of private production to freeze, they moved successively to larger and more permanent units of production, moving from the seasonal mutual aid team to the fixed mutual aid team, to the lower level Agricultural Producer's Cooperative (APC), to the higher stage of the APC—all between 1952 and 1957. That they did so without real loss of economic momentum is a tribute to their skill.

Yet the results in terms of increasing production were disappointing. Agricultural growth barely exceeded population growth; further, it was subject to seasonal and weather fluctuations that made planning difficult. Even though the APC gave planners the mechanism to extract surpluses from agriculture, they could not enlarge surpluses where they fell short of expectations. Neither could they increase the extraction rates at the expense of peasant consumption—as they learned from the peasant unrest of 1956.

By 1957 agriculture had become a distinct bottleneck to rapid growth. The harvest of 1956–1957 was no higher than in 1953–1954. Yet population was continuing to grow and increasingly and ominously the cities were beginning to draw unplanned migrants from the countryside. Further, many of the defects of the new economic administration, including overcentralization, bureaucratic rigidity, and red tape were becoming apparent. In short, in late 1956 and 1957, the new leaders really confronted the basic dilemmas and constraints of poverty for the first time.

THE GREAT LEAP FORWARD. The "Great Leap Forward" (GLF), (1958–1960) was an attempt to break out of this impasse.[63] Rather than accept the cutbacks and constraints with which they were faced, the Chinese designed a strategy to accelerate growth. Chou En-lai defined "Great Leap" growth rates at 25 percent per year or more. It was not intended that the GLF supplant the Second Five Year Plan (FYP) already in existence (1958–1962). It was intended to speed up its implementation, reaching FYP targets in three years. There were several dimensions to the strategy of the Great Leap. The most important was the decision to mobilize labor to create new resources for local development squarely on the provinces and localities. A new agricultural organization, *the commune,* was created as the basic unit of development. It was to be large enough to plan and sustain its own industrialization program. By merging local government and economic organs it would yield more trained manpower for the development effort. In addition, it would have a large pool of labor so that allocation between industrial and agricultural tasks could be rationally accomplished. The focus of the effort was to be on the development of local industry, which would adopt small-scale labor intensive techniques and low quality, local resources not required by the modern centrally controlled sector of the economy. Not only was the program intended to mobilize the masses but to create new employment in the countryside, cut down on urban migration, and, above all, supply the inputs to agriculture so desperately needed. The watchword of the GLF was local self-reliance.

Although initially the movement was reported a glowing success in 1958 and 1959, by the end of 1959 the euphoria had dissipated as it became clear that the GLF had backfired. While many of the problems of the GLF were officially attributed to natural disasters on an unprecedented scale, it is clear that weather apart, human error was also a factor. Many of the local projects were ill conceived and their output useless. Many normal economic functions were dislocated by the diversion of labor to the new projects. The subsequent economic decline was compounded by the withdrawal of Soviet advisers in 1959 and 1960.

The failure of the GLF resulted in a major economic crisis, marked by a fall in agricultural production and industrial output. In response to the crisis (which clearly had its political implications as well), the Chinese developed a pragmatic recovery policy which integrated the lessons of GLF and the previous FYP into a policy that is still in effect. Although domestic policy after 1958 was a matter of active dispute between a technocratic wing and more populist wing of the party (the so-called "struggle between the two lines"), there was a stability and a continuity in policy which reveals a basic consensus on economic questions.

ECONOMIC POLICY SINCE THE GREAT LEAP FORWARD. Much of the initial conception of the Great Leap Forward was retained, and some administrative decentralization had persisted.[64] The commune organization was also retained, with modification. Since 1961 the *production team*—the basis of the commune unit (approximately the size of a natural village)—has become the crucial accounting and management unit for most agricultural purposes. Smaller than the old Agricultural Producer's Cooperative, it is probably the optimal size farming unit at the present level of technology.[65] The production brigade at the next level plays a role in planning expenditures which go beyond the scope of the production teams, in irrigation, electrification, education, and so on. The commune level finally comes into play when the activities of several brigades need coordinating. At the individual level some scope is given to private plots, where produce is either consumed by the individual or family, or sold at open rural markets. In the modified commune the PRC has discovered a workable balance in the agricultural needs of the individual, the collective, and the state.

In policy terms the recognition of agriculture as a bottleneck resulted in increased priority to agriculture. Many industries were converted to agricultural purposes, supplying tractors, pumps, generators, and fertilizer during the 1960's. However, there has been a continued emphasis on small-scale rural labor-intensive industry using more traditional techniques. This economic "walking on two legs" reflects the Chinese commitment to local investment which makes growth possible despite the scarcity of capital. This is the message of the *Tachai model,* a self-reliant production brigade in North China much praised by Mao Tse-tung.[66]

ECONOMIC PERFORMANCE. How have these strategies paid off in terms of economic performance over the past 24 years? China's economy grew according to one source, at an estimated average annual rate of between 5.2 percent and 7.2 percent during the period 1950–1966—a rate of growth exceeding India's for the corresponding period, and comparable to Soviet economic growth during the period 1928–1938.[67] (An alternate estimate of annual average growth in China's net domestic product is 5.1 percent for the period 1952–1971.)[68] Even taking only the years

1957–71 and excluding the FFYP, the annual growth rate was still 4.7 percent. The long-run growth patterns indicate substantial progress despite losses during the Greap Leap Forward. Average per capita income in US dollars rose from a little over $50 per capita in 1952 to over $80 in 1970, a rate of growth of about 2 percent per year, somewhat higher than in India.[69] This is slow but steady progress. As a point of comparison one might note that long-run US growth rates per capita have been about 2.5 percent historically, though higher in the last 15 or 20 years.

Much of the growth took place in the industrial sector, which grew at an average annual rate of 12 percent or more between 1952 and 1971. As a consequence of this rapid growth, industry accounted for over half the aggregate national product by 1965.[70] This structural change was important because it insulated the economy from the impact of fluctuations of the farm economy. The performance of the agricultural sector has been less impressive. Between 1952 and 1967, according to one estimate, the average annual agricultural growth in foodgrain production was 1.9 percent (as compared to 1.8 percent for India).[71] The basic sources of this increase resulted from the intensive use of land, increased irrigation, better seeds and the reclamation of marginal lands. Agricultural growth in the period 1965–71, has been even more rapid, estimated by one writer at 3.4 percent per annum.[72] This recent dramatic success reflects the massive inputs of fertilizer, machinery, rural electrification, as well as the more relaxed incentive policy since the GLF.

SUMMARY. There has been substantial growth, modernization, and diversification in the Chinese economy since 1949. How effective China's modernization has been in comparative terms is a judgment for professional economists. One such judgment holds that though the growth of both China and India has been modest compared to Japan or the Soviet Union or Germany since World War II it has been quite impressive by long-term historical standards, falling within "the range of long-term rates for the most rapidly growing economies, such as the United States, Sweden, and Japan."[73] Another scholar has concluded after comparing China with the USSR and other countries that "in general, very few poor or developing countries have done as well as China in terms of growth and development since 1950."[74]

Despite its growth, however, China is still poor. As Mao wrote in 1957:

> We must spread the idea of building our country through diligence and frugality. We must help our young people to understand that ours is still a very poor country, that we cannot change this situation radically in a short time, and that only through the united efforts of our younger generation and all our people, working with their own hands, can China be made strong and prosperous *within a period of several decades.* The

establishment of our socialist system has opened the road leading to the ideal society of the future, but to translate this ideal into reality needs hard work. Some of our young people think that everything ought to be perfect once a socialist society is established and that they should be able to enjoy a happy life ready-made, without working for it. This is unrealistic.[75] (emphasis added)

While the economic record speaks for itself, it leaves certain questions unanswered. How was this level of development achieved, and at what cost? Critics of Chinese economic and social policy often argue that the only moral justification for high levels of political mobilization is rapid economic development. That other countries have done almost as well or better than China, (e.g.: India, Mexico, South Korea, Brazil) without resorting to mobilization seems to negate this justification. However, as the introduction argued, economic development *without* modernization often results in instability and conflict. One of the main achievements of the Chinese government has been to combine both economic development and modernization simultaneously. This suggests that the real costs of development for the large majority of Chinese may be less than the costs of capitalist development for the majority of Indians.

Certainly the mobilization system has weaknesses and inefficiencies, as critics have charged. Irrationalities in policy do develop on occasion as a consequence of ideological zeal. The excesses of the Great Leap Forward are a case in point. There are costs as well as benefits attached to the continuous rotation of experienced administrators to the basic levels. The distrust of professional and technical personnel, while in part valid, occasionally results in underutilization of scarce technical manpower. The frequent resort to mobilization campaigns disrupts routine functions, and creates imbalances.

On the other hand mobilization has important economic strengths which should be noted. Some of the contributions of mobilization politics to development are noneconomic in nature. For example to the extent that mobilization systems are effective in absorbing the strains of modernization, they provide a productive environment for growth. Second, many of the emphases characteristic of mobilization, such as the stress on mass literacy, and mass participation involve what the economist would call investment in "human capital." The affirmation of the creativity of the masses in a labor-rich developing country is as much a reflection of the economic facts of life as it is a tenet of Marxist faith. The potential contribution of China's ideology to economic development has been noted in the following terms:

It is likely that Maoist ideology discourages consumption and encourages saving and investment, and so promotes the growth of the capital stock. It does this by preventing the rise of a high-consuming "middle class," by fostering the Maoist virtues of plain and simple living and devoting one's life to helping others rather than to accumulating "pots and pans."[76]

A mobilization system has the capacity to extract and marshall resources for use by the leadership. Organizational controls allow Chinese leaders to set consumption rates, either through pricing or rationing systems. They thus provide central planners with a reliable basis for planning resource use. Mobilization promotes capital growth in other ways, too. The use of large pools of labor in road-building projects or dams or in the collection of organic fertilizers can generate new overhead capital. The campaigns for mass innovation, soliciting suggestions from workers and peasants have had some striking successes.

Every economic system has its own weaknesses and strengths and the Chinese system is no exception. Increasingly, however, development economists have begun to agree that many of the Maoist innovations are economically valid and worthy of wider application.

Economic Modernization

While aggregate national growth figures are an important indicator of overall development, they tell us little about the impact of growth on the lives of the average Chinese citizen. On whom does the burden of growth fall, and how are its benefits distributed? Though observers disagree over the question of how fast the Chinese economy has grown, few would dispute that major progress has been made in achieving a more equitable pattern of distribution. One study noted that while there are few statistics on income distribution available, there is "overwhelming . . . evidence indicating that the extremes of poverty and wealth have been eliminated."[77] After a recent trip to China John Kenneth Galbraith has reported his impression of "great continued movement— new housing, new industrial plants, new building at old plants . . . supply of staples in markets and shops, the people thronging through to buy them."[78]

The changing pattern of economic standards has both qualitative and quantitative dimensions. The most important qualitative change has been the new degree of security and stability for the average citizen. While political campaigns may create temporary uncertainties and anxieties, the basic issues of life—survival, food, and shelter—have been resolved for most Chinese. Careful distribution of food has assured an adequate diet. Huge public health campaigns have greatly reduced the epidemic diseases that formerly ravaged China. Infant mortality has been sharply reduced. A variety of welfare programs, including famine relief, old age care, unemployment insurance, dependent care, have set a living level below which no one is permitted to fall. In short, people can now plan their lives with new certainty.

We lack the specific data to trace changes in the standard of living, since most of the available information is limited to the 1950's. The evidence we do have suggests that even during the First Five Year Plan, at a time in which investment rates were very high, real consumption per capita increased.[79] Social purchasing power increased from an index of 100 in 1952 to 166 by 1956. Rural per capita food consumption went up from 227 kilograms of grain per capita to 258 kilograms in those same years, while urban consumption remained constant. Cloth consumption went up by about 60 percent during the FFYP period as well. The fall in production in the 1960's certainly reduced consumption of all goods, and it is unclear how China's recovery and growth in the 1960's has affected consumption. However, one might infer, both from the visual evidence of recent years, and from the commitment of China's leaders to improve living standards, that this economic growth has brought an increase in the general welfare. While per capita income has grown from about $50.00 (US) in 1949 to about $100.00 today, China is still poor.[80] But the doubling of per capita income, coupled with moderate distribution policies, has meant a very considerable change for most Chinese.

This is not to say however, that all Chinese fare equally well under this system. Inequalities continue to exist. While committed to broad egalitarian goals, the Chinese leaders believe that only economic growth will permit a fully egalitarian distribution system, and consequently oppose any premature income levelling schemes. Inequalities must continue to exist—not only because resources are scarce but because people are not fully socialized to the idea of selfless labor for the collective. Thus Chinese enterprise or government employees are paid according to level of skill, type of work, and length of service. The civil servant thinks in terms of rank, scale and in-grade promotion. The worker in a factory faces eight graded steps in his ladder of wages and promotion. Not only do wages vary within factories from about 30 Yuan to over 70 Yuan per month, but wages vary according to industrial sector and employer.[81] There is also a clear difference in status and rewards between the unskilled temporary laborer and the highly skilled worker in an automated centrally run plant in Shanghai.

Some of the greatest disparities exist between the urban and rural areas of China. The preference in China for urban life reflects the recognition that wage scales and opportunities, both in terms of jobs and welfare and health services are better in the cities. Mao Tse-tung in 1957 commented:

Many people say that the peasants lead a hard life. Is this true? In one sense it is. . . . In another sense it is not. . . . no one can say that there has been no improvement in the life of the peasants. [But] it is not right simply to compare a peasant's annual income with a worker's and conclude that one is too low and the other too high. The productivity of the worker is higher . . . [the peasant's] cost of living lower. However, the wages of a small number of workers and some government personnel are a bit too high, and the peasants have reason to be dissatisfied with this. . . .[82]

During the Cultural Revolution, supporters of Mao charged Chinese leaders with inadequate efforts to reduce these disparities and since the Cultural Revolution some attention has been paid to this question. However, the charges of elitism and neglect are scarcely supported by the record. For example, Chinese efforts from the beginning to put a floor under peasant income contrasts sharply to the exploitative policies of Stalinist agrarian policy.[83] Even during the period 1952–1957, when the agricultural sector bore the brunt of efforts at capital accumulation, with small direct return, the leadership attempted to assure peasant families a reasonable income. State purchase prices for agricultural products were set low enough so that the peasants had enough to eat and could see a return for their labor. The prices of goods used by the peasants were reduced so that on the whole, the terms of trade favored the rural sector.

A similar sensitivity to the divisive potential of unequal wage scales has governed Chinese policy on incentives. One official article suggested the following principles:

The system of high salaries for a small number of people should never be applied. The gap between the income of the working personnel of the Party, the government, the enterprises, and the people's communes on the one hand and the incomes of the mass of the people on the other, should be *rationally and gradually* narrowed, not widened.[84] (emphasis added)

The Chinese have been relatively successful in this aim. Galbraith wrote of a "truly astonishing approach to the equality of income" in China, adding that, if, somewhere in China, there is a privileged hierarchy, it is "the least visible ruling class in history."[85]

Nowhere are the achievements more spectacular or the imbalances more obvious than in the expanded public services, particularly health and education. In 1949 China had fewer than 70,000 hospital beds, and fewer than 10,000 fully trained Western-style doctors.[86] Undeterred by these shortcomings, the new leadership launched a major program of preventive medicine, pressing into service available paramedical personnel, a pool of 30,000 three-year medical graduates serving with the army, and over 300,000 traditional doctors.

Public health programs emphasizing sanitation, pest control, and cleanliness were mounted all over China. Local health clinics were set up to coordinate these efforts, including programs of innoculation and emergency epidemic control. At the same time a major effort was made to expand the number of available medical personnel. By 1953 over

70,000 paramedical personnel ("intermediate doctors") had been trained for public health work. The number of students enrolled in institutions of higher education in the fields of medicine and public health increased from 15,000 in 1949 to about 49,000 in 1957.[87] A simultaneous expansion of the number of hospital beds took place as well. China's efforts to develop an effective if rudimentary medical network throughout the country won wide praise from many foreign medical observers.

By 1965 medical help, however improved, was still in limited supply. On the eve of the Cultural Revolution urban-rural disparities in medicine were still severe. This disparity provoked Mao Tse-tung to criticize the Ministry of Health, calling it the "Urban" Ministry of Health.[88] The medical reforms that emerged during and after the Cultural Revolution involved a heightened emphasis on the development of paramedical personnel. The "barefoot doctor" is now the hero of Chinese rural medicine. Many are trained for periods from six weeks to a year and are able to dispense medicines, diagnose common ailments, and treat simple complaints and refer others to the nearest local clinics. Similarly, shortages of modern drugs have resulted in renewed interest in the traditional pharmacopeia and the development of new sources of medicine with good results.

The achievements of the PRC in extending educational benefits were marked by a similar pattern of progress and imbalance. On the whole, one of the most noteworthy successes of the regime has been the expansion of educational opportunities. Article 94 of the Constitution of the PRC guarantees the right of an education to every citizen.[89] Although this goal has not been met, the growth in educational programs has been remarkable. Between 1949 and 1957 for example, the number of children enrolled in primary schools increased 2 ½ times.[90] Similarly, the number of students enrolled in middle schools increased from 1 million to 4 million between 1952 and 1957.[91] Undergraduate enrollments in higher education went up from 116,000 in 1949 to 441,000 by 1957.[92] While these achievements were substantial, they fell far short of ideal. Many students were still without regular educational opportunities. For example, while 4 million students of middle school age (12–17) were enrolled in middle schools, 59 million youths in that same age bracket were not.[93] Of the 4 million enrolled in middle school only about 10 percent could hope to go on to university study. Thus not only were educational opportunities relatively restricted but they became increasingly so as one went up the educational ladder. Further, educational facilities were so distributed as to favor the youth of the cities and towns.

During the Great Leap Forward, a major effort was made to expand educational services through the creation of informal, local schools with the stress on part-time attendance. Although the so-called "people-sponsored" schools had been in existence earlier, they were vigorously promoted after 1958. These schools offered multiple advantages over the regular schools. On one hand, they were locally funded, thus saving the state heavy investment. They made available a broader program of rural education than would otherwise be possible. This program had the virtue of serving the locality directly so that the curriculum could be made relevant to local needs. On the other hand, they were inferior in terms of facilities, staff, and materials, and enjoyed lower status than the regular schools. The program of locally sponsored education made possible the doubling and tripling of primary, secondary and higher educational enrollments between 1958 and 1960.

Unfortunately, problems of quality, and the overall contraction of the economy between 1958 and 1960 squeezed many of these schools out of existence by the mid-1960's. For example, undergraduate enrollments in higher education went from 441,000 in 1957 to 955,000 by 1960 but declined to 695,000 by 1965.[94] A similar process of contraction took place in secondary and primary education during the early 1960's. Despite this shrinkage, educational growth continued thereafter. By 1966, 15 million youngsters of middle school age were enrolled in schools, but the middle school age population was by then 73 million, leaving 58 million youngsters still without opportunity for higher schooling.[95] The number of places were so few compared to the total student population that competition was very fierce, with the advantage to those areas with good educational endowments.

During the Cultural Revolution many of the same issues in education that had cropped up after 1957 were raised again: rural-urban disparities, and the failure to extend benefits to more than a fraction of the population. Two additional issues also became prominent in 1966. The first was elitism. Even the scarce number of openings were filled in a way that critics viewed as discriminatory. The system of competitive exams favored urban intellectual families, where better educational facilities and a more positive home academic environment conferred a joint competitive advantage. This competitive system seemed unhealthy, partly because it neglected political criteria in recruitment, partly because it resulted in elitist attitudes, and partly because it intensified the urban-rural gap. The reforms of the Cultural Revolution abolished the examination system, substituting a system of political recommendations.[96]

A further defect of the educational system lay in the perceived irrelevance of much of the curriculum to China's manpower needs. The course of study was too long, too formal, and too abstract. The recommendations made during the Cultural Revolution by Mao and others proposed a shorter, more practical course of study which combined classroom and on-the-job training. If the future of China were in the countryside, then the skills they needed were practical and mechanical. Even the more advanced courses of study were reorganized to embody some of these pedagogical principles, which were seen as educationally valid whatever the future role of the individual student.

The issue of distribution both in terms of income and in terms of health and education, has clearly been a divisive one. The approach of Mao Tse-tung and his supporters has been strongly egalitarian. It affirms the right of all Chinese to similar benefits and opportunities, irrespective of economic constraints. It demands not quantity instead of quality, but both—simultaneously. The commitment to equality is seen as a responsibility of the party and the government which must be redeemed by imaginative and innovative planning. What is vital is that the priorities be established to achieve more equal social benefits. The difference between Mao and his opponents, however, is only a matter of degree. The strongly redistributive commitment evident from the early 1950's mades it clear that most Chinese leaders shared similar goals. What divided them in the 1960's were divergent views over how to reconcile the needs of growth and distribution in a period of scarcity.

ASSESSMENT OF THE CHINESE APPROACH TO POLITICAL DEVELOPMENT

That it took a lengthy period of strife, the Cultural Revolution, to resolve these economic and social issues, raises a few questions about the stability and effectiveness of China's political institutions. Before the Cultural Revolution scholars and observers agreed on the general effectiveness and stability of the People's Republic of China. A similar consensus existed over the roots of that effectiveness: powerful organization, general leadership cohesion, and unity. That there were also weaknesses was clear, but they seemed adequately controlled by techniques long perfected by China's leaders. Top leadership clashes seemed to be resolved more or less by consensus; few open dismissals were necessary. Problems of bureaucratic growth and rigidity, while obvious to all, seemed to be managed through reliance on rectification campaigns, purges, retrenchment, and "down-to-the-countryside" movements. In short, China's very organizational strengths meant an endemic problem of bureaucratism, but it seemed under control in the mid-1960's.

The Cultural Revolution of 1966 caught most observers by surprise. While there was much that was familiar in the thronging groups of red guards who travelled to Peking to be reviewed by Chairman Mao the very framework of political mobilization was altered. The mandate for revolution —the "sixteen points" passed at the 11th Plenum of the CCP

8th Central Committee —called for freewheeling grassroots rebellion, not controlled, focused mass effort.[97] Rather than being precisely defined, targets were left vague and ultimately came to encompass the entire party, state, and military bureaucracy. Further initial attacks on party leaders in early 1967 paralyzed the party's control function, and the army began to provide the direction for these fluid political currents. Almost two-thirds of the pre–Cultural Revolution CCP Central Committee and Politburo members were removed between 1966 and Mao's "Congress of Victors" in April, 1969.[98]

The tumultuous events of 1966–1969, including the devastation of party organization, the rise of the army to a central political role, the widespread civil disorder, and the massive purges stimulated a rapid reassessment of the Chinese system. Its apparent weakness and instability seemed to imperil its long-term survival, particularly given the assertion that there would "inevitably be many more cultural revolutions" in the future.[99]

From the perspective of the 1970's however, with the gloomy predictions of "warlordism" and decay dispelled by time, the Cultural Revolution seems a more natural and less aberrant event. It was an event, however, that revealed a great deal about the strengths and weaknesses of the Chinese political order.

A complex event like the Cultural Revolution inevitably is interpreted in widely different ways. There is, however, an emerging consensus shared both by Western scholars as well as by the Chinese leaders that the Cultural Revolution was a response to a crisis in the Chinese revolutionary order. According to the interpretation, the Chinese revolution was losing momentum by the mid-1960's. The loss was reflected in declining élan and ideological vitality. It was reflected equally in problems of bureaucratic stagnation and routine and was linked to a process of social and economic restratification, resulting from industrialization and modernization. Western observers interpreted these phenomena as part of the natural decay of such revolutions. Mao Tse-tung similarly saw the issue as the survival of the revolution. In either case, the Cultural Revolution was a remedy designed to revitalize the system.[100]

An alternate interpretation (and one which I prefer) would trace the roots of the Cultural Revolution to a dispute between Mao and other party leaders over issues of ideology and policy, particularly issues of distribution. Since Mao's opponents were well entrenched in the party and state bureaucracies, it became necessary and expedient to attack those structures frontally. In this view the political system and its capacity for mobilization had not been seriously eroded by time. The issues, between Mao and Liu Shao-ch'i and others, were over the uses to which political mobilization should be put.

Either interpretation leads to an optimistic view of China's future stability. If the Cultural Revolution were a response to bureaucratic degeneration, then as the Chinese claim, they have found the key to the problem of continuing the revolution "under the dictatorship of the proletariat." If the weaknesses of the political order were exaggerated for political purposes during the Cultural Revolution, then perhaps the mobilization system was not really in danger.

For a time analysts felt that whatever the causes of the Cultural Revolution, its consequences would be profoundly destabilizing. The authority of the party had been questioned and seemed unlikely to be ever fully restored. The military had been invited into politics and appeared unlikely to withdraw. Many youngsters had been asked to play active political roles, and would probably not relinquish authority easily.

While it is still early to make a final judgment on these questions, this view of the remedy as more fatal than the disease seems exaggerated. For one thing, while the People's Liberation Army representation on the CCP Central Committee went up from 27 percent in 1956 to 41 percent in 1969, its active political role has been steadily *contracting* since that date.[101] The shrinking PLA presence has moreover been accelerated since the fall of Lin Piao in 1971. The strong commitment to restoring the party has been evident in the efforts to reconstruct party organizations at all levels. These efforts bore fruit in the Tenth CCP Congress, in August 1973, which restored many civilian party leaders to power, and further reduced the political role of the PLA.[102] Many of the young political activists who helped topple the establishment in 1967 and 1968 have passed from prominence to obscurity. Many have not taken their eclipse with grace, as the increased outflow of youngsters to Hong Kong indicates, but the return to controlled patterns of participation seems to have been achieved without real difficulty. The ability of the political leadership to launch, control, and terminate a movement of this sort without sustained damage seems in retrospect even more striking testimony to the capacity of the mobilization model.

The Cultural Revolution did highlight one major source of potential disruption—the succession to Mao Tse-tung. Mao has in the past 15 years selected and then turned on his two nominees for the succession —Liu Shao-ch'i and Lin Piao. It is unlikely that he will try again to designate a successor. It is probable therefore that he will be succeeded not by an individual but by a collective leadership. Conflict within the collective leadership will have to be resolved in the absence of Mao's authoritative intervention. Such a change may not necessarily prove debilitating to the political system. It might, however, mean that the mobilization system is beginning to become more pluralistic and adaptive.

The Quality of Politics

It is difficult to comment on the quality of political life in China. Too many subjective factors intervene. The implicit comparison is always with one's own life situation, and the yardstick is inevitably personal. While one may pose such a question in the abstract, it is not a meaningful one for the average Chinese citizen for whom the only valid comparison is the past.

For the average Westerner, Chinese political life seems too uniform, too austere, excessively moral in tone. By Western standards the Chinese system makes too many demands and offers too few rewards. Even sympathetic observers are prone to comment condescendingly that while the style of political life in China might suit China's needs, they themselves wouldn't want to live there.

Refugee testimony allows a limited glimpse at politics in China as perceived by participants. Their comments indicate that the Chinese have become accustomed to the high levels of politicization achieved by the PRC. They have learned to live with the demands of the system, sometimes responding seriously, sometimes cynically, and sometimes affectionately to its calls. While refugee testimony has it biases, at least their direction is clear.

It is interesting that many refugees are unhappy in the new settings to which they have moved. They frequently allude to a loss of a sense of purpose, or identity. They condemn the amoral competitiveness and materialism of Hong Kong or Taiwan or the United States. While their alienation may be rooted in personal difficulties or in the expatriate situation, it suggests that political life in China supplies a sense of commitment, belonging, and purpose that is generally missing in Western societies. This may well compensate Chinese for the loss of alternatives (which they really never had). What this amounts to is more than stating the old saw that the Chinese are comfortable in an authoritarian setting. It suggests that perhaps the mobilization system might be a vehicle for genuine fulfillment in many cases.

Costs and Benefits of the Chinese Approach

The very notion of a developmental "strategy" implies multiple goals. A political leadership will be concerned with maximizing many things, including perhaps political control, political stability, growth, equality, cohesiveness, social change, and so on. Some strategies aim for maximum economic growth, sacrificing equality and cohesiveness, as in South Korea or the Phillipines. Others have sacrificed equality as well as some growth for stability and democracy, as with India and Chile prior to Allende. In Mexico the stability of the political order rests in part on a foundation of inequality. The Chinese have clearly pursued many of these goals, accepting tradeoffs where necessary. They have clearly sacrificed Western-style democracy for the sake of revolutionary and egalitarian objectives. They have occasionally sacrificed maximum growth rates for that same end.

In all these cases some social groups are benefited and others victimized. Ultimately only a broad societal yardstick can measure the costs and benefits of a particular strategy. For many of the countries studied here, it is difficult to render a judgment on the comparative advantages of developmental strategies which are barely a generation old. The costs and benefits of Indian democratic development or Chinese mobilization will be more fully tested only in the coming generations.

FOOTNOTES

1. Stuart Schram, *The Political Thought of Mao Tse-tung,* rev. ed., (New York: Praeger, 1969), p. 167.

2. _____, *Mao Tse-tung* (Baltimore: Penguin, 1967), p. 244.

3. A. Doak Barnett, "There are Warts there, too," *The New York Times Magazine* (April 8, 1973), pp. 36–37.

4. Samuel P. Huntington, *Political Order in Changing Societies* (New Haven: Yale University Press, 1968), p. 342.

5. *Peking Review,* 17 (April 27, 1973), p. 9.

6. An excellent general introduction to the traditional political order is John K. Fairbank and Edwin O. Reischauer, *East Asia: The Great Tradition* (Boston: Houghton Mifflin Co., 1960), chs. 3–9

7. Ho Ping-ti, "Salient Aspects of China's Heritage", in Ho Ping-ti and Tang Tsou, *China in Crisis* (Chicago: University of Chicago Press, 1968), Vol. I, Bk. I, pp. 7–37.

8. An excellent introduction to the setting of revolution in China during this period can be found in John K. Fairbank, Edwin O. Reischauer and Albert M. Craig, *East Asia: The Modern Transformation* (Boston: Houghton Mifflin Co., 1965).

9. For an introduction to the debate over the consequences of imperialism in China, see the exchange between Andrew Nathan and Joseph Esherick in the *Bulletin of Concerned Asian Scholars* (December, 1972).

10. Rhoads Murphey, "The Treaty Ports in China's Modernization: What went Wrong?", Michigan Papers in Chinese Studies, No. 7 (1970).

11. Sun Yat-sen, *San Min Chu I* (Taipei: China Publishing Co., 1952), p. 10.

12. For an interesting discussion of this period see Ernest P. Young, "Nationalism, Reform and Republican Revolution: China in the Early Twentieth Century," in James B. Crowley, *Modern East Asia: Essays in Interpretation* (New York: Harcourt, Brace and World, 1970), pp. 151–179.

13. Chow Tse-Tsung, *The May Fourth Movement* (Cambridge, Mass.: Harvard University Press, 1960).

14. Samuel P. Huntington, *Political Order,* p. 313.

15. For an interpretation of this period and bibliography see Jerome B. Grieder, "Communism, Nationalism, and Democracy: The Chinese Intelligentsia and the Chinese Revolution in the 1920's and 1930's," in James B. Crowley, *Modern East Asia,* pp. 207–234.

16. Lucian Bianco, *The Origins of the Chinese Revolution: 1915–1949* (Stanford: Stanford University Press, 1971), pp. 108–139.

17. C. Martin Wilbur, "Military Separatism and the Process of Reunification under the Nationalist Regime, 1927–1937," in Ho and Tsou, *China in Crisis*, pp. 206–263.

18. Franz Schurmann, *Ideology and Organization in Communist China*, rev. ed., (Berkeley: University of California Press, 1968), Prologue, p. XX.

19. A good concise introduction to the history of the CCP can be found in Stuart Schram, *Mao Tse-tung.* For an analysis of various interpretations of CCP success see Roy Hofheinz, "The Ecology of Chinese Communist Success: Rural Influence Patterns, 1923–1945," in A. Doak Barnett, ed., *Chinese Communist Politics in Action* (Seattle, Washington: University of Washington Press, 1969), pp. 3–77.

20. For an interpretation of the impact of the war on CCP fortunes see Chalmers Johnson, *Peasant Nationalism and Communist Power: The Emergence of Revolutionary China, 1937–1945* (Stanford: Stanford University Press, 1962).

21. Maurice Meissner, *"Yenan Communism and Chinese People's Republic,"* in James B. Crowley, *Modern East Asia*, pp. 279–280.

22. Mark Selden, *The Yenan Way in Revolutionary China* (Cambridge, Mass.: Harvard University Press, 1971) pp. 276.

23. *Selected Works of Mao Tse-tung*, Vol. IV (Peking: Foreign Language Press, 1961) p. 374.

24. For an overview of the post-1949 period, see Harold Hinton, *An Introduction to Chinese Politics* (New York: Praeger, 1973).

25. David E. Apter, *The Politics of Modernization* (Chicago: University of Chicago Press, 1965), pp. 357–360.

26. Franz Schurmann, *Ideology and Organization*, ch. 1.

27. Chalmers Johnson, "The Changing Nature and Locus of Authority in Communist China," in John M. H. Lindbeck, ed., *China: Management of a Revolutionary Society* (Seattle: University of Washington Press, 1971), pp. 34–76.

28. "Outline of the Struggle between the Two Lines," Shanghai, *Chieh-Fang Jih-pao*, undated translated in *Current Background*, No. 884, (July 18, 1969).

29. Maurice Meissner, "Yenan Communism."

30. Arthur Cohen, *The Communism of Mao Tse-tung* (Chicago: University of Chicago Press, 1964).

31. Frederick T. C. Yu, *Mass Persuasion in Communist China* (New York: Praeger, 1964).

32. James Townsend, *Political Participation in Communist China* (Berkeley: University of California Press, 1967).

33. Mao Tse-tung, "Talks at the Yenan Forum on Literature and Art," in *Selected Readings from the Works of Mao Tse-tung* (Peking: Foreign Language Press, 1971), p. 255.

34. Edgar Snow, " A Conversation with Mao Tse-tung", *Life* (April 30, 1971), p. 46.

35. Mao Tse-Tung, "Speech at the 8th Plenary Session of the CCP 8th Central Committee," in *The Case of Peng Te-huai: 1959–1968* (Kowloon: Union Research Institute, 1968), p. 16.

36. Samuel P. Huntington, *Political Order in Changing Societies*, p. 339.

37. Franz Schurmann, *Ideology and Organization*, ch. 2.

38. John M. H. Lindbeck, "Transformation of the Chinese Communist Party," in Donald W. Treadgold, *Soviet and Chinese Communism: Similarities and Differences* (Seattle: University of Washington Press, 1965).

39. The material in this paragraph is drawn largely from Franz Schurmann, *Ideology and Organization in Communist China* (Berkeley: University of California Press, 1968), ch. 2. Party membership figures for 1973 can be found in *Peking Review* Nos. 35–36 (Sept. 1, 1973), p. 6.

40. V.I. Krivtsov, ed., *Maoism Through the Eyes of Communists* (Moscow: Progress Publication, 1970).

41. Ying-mao Kao, "Patterns of Recruitment and Mobility of Urban Cadres," in John W. Lewis, ed., *The City in Communist China* (Stanford: Stanford University Press, 1972), p. 706.

42. See Ellis Joffe, *Party and Army: Professionalism and Political Control in the Chinese Officer Corps: 1949–1964* (Harvard, East Asian Monographs, 1965). Also see Loffe, "The Chinese Army under Lin Piao; prelude to Political Intervention," in John M. H. Lindbeck, ed., *China: Management of a Revolutionary Society*, pp. 343–376.

43. John Gittings, *The Role of the Chinese Army* (New York: Oxford University Press, 1967).

44. Richard M. Pfeffer, "Serving the People and Continuing the Revolution," *China Quarterly*, 52 (October/December, 1972), pp. 620–621.

45. Michel Oksenberg, "Policy-Making under Mao, 1949–1968: An Overview," in John M. H. Lindbeck, ed., *China: Management of a Revolutionary Society*, pp. 79–115.

46. See Benjamin Schwarz, "The Reign of Virtue: Some Broad Perspectives in Leader and Party in the Cultural Revolution," in John W. Lewis, ed., *Party Leadership and Revolutionary Power in China*, (Cambridge: Cambridge University Press, 1970), pp. 140–169. Also in the same volume see, Leonard Shapiro and John Wilson Lewis, "The Roles of the Monolithic Party under the Totalitarian Leader," and Stuart R. Schram, "The Party in Chinese Communist Ideology."

47. See Jerome Chen, *Mao and the Chinese Revolution* (New York: Oxford University Press, 1967).

48. Edgar Snow, *The Long Revolution* (New York: Random House, 1972), p. 70.

49. *Ibid.*, p. 71.

50. Mao Tse-tung, "On the Correct Handling of Contradictions Among the People," *Selected Readings*, p. 448.

51. Franz Schurmann, *Ideology and Organization*, Prologue.

52. Ezra Vogel, *Canton Under Communism* (Cambridge Mass.: Harvard University Press, 1969), p. 351.

53. Gabriel A. Almond, "Some Thoughts on Chinese Political Studies," in John M. H. Lindbeck, ed., *China: Management of a Revolutionary Society*, p. 384.

54. James S. Coleman, "The Development Syndrome: Differentiation-Equality-Capacity, " in Binder *et al., Crises and Sequences in Political Development* (Princeton: Princeton University Press, 1971), ch. 2.

55. Samuel P. Huntington, *Political Order in Changing Societies*, p. 342.

56. Benjamin Schwarz, *In Search of Wealth and Power: Yen Fu and the West* (Cambridge, Mass.: Harvard University Press, 1964).

57. Mao Tse-tung, "On the Correct Handling of Contradictions Among the People," *Selected Readings*, p. 448.

58. "On People's Democratic Dictatorship," *Selected Readings*, pp. 385–386.

59. Alexander Eckstein, "Economic Development Prospects and Problems in China," *The Annals*, 402 (July, 1972), p. 108.

60. Thomas G. Rawski, "Foreign Contacts and Industrialization, *International Journal,* 26; 3 (Summer, 1971), pp. 526–527.

61. Pranab Bardhan, "Recent Development in Chinese and Indian Agriculture," in Kuan-I Chen, and J. S. Uppal, eds., *Comparative Development of India and China* (New York: The Free Press, 1971), p. 54.

62. K. C. Yeh, "Soviet and Chinese Industrialization Strategies," in Donald W. Treadgold, ed., *Chinese and Soviet Communism,* ch. 3.

63. *Ibid.* Also see Ezra Vogel, *Canton Under Communism,* ch. 6.

64. *Ibid.,* chs. 7, 8.

65. R. J. Birrel, "The Centralized Control of the Commune in the Post "Great Leap" Period," in A. Doak Barnett, ed., *Chinese Communist Politics in Action,* pp. 400–446.

66. "The Road Forward for China's Socialist Agriculture," *Peking Review,* 7 (February 13, 1970), pp. 3–9.

67. Barry M. Richman, "Quantitative Dimension of Communist China's Aggregate Economic and Industrial Performance," in Chen and Uppal, eds. *India and China,* p. 87.

68. Thomas G. Rawski, "Recent Trends in the Chinese Economy," *China Quarterly,* 53 (January/March, 1973), p. 21.

69. Barry M. Richman, "Quantitative Dimension."

70. Thomas G. Rawski, "Recent Trends," p. 20.

71. Pranab Bardhan, "Recent Development," p. 46.

72. Thomas G. Rawski, "Recent Trends," p. 27.

73. Alexander Eckstein, "Economic Development Prospects," pp. 113–114.

74. Barry M. Richman, "Quantitative Dimension," p. 92.

75. "On the Correct Handling of Contradictions," p. 859.

76. John G. Gurley, "Capitalist and Maoist Economic Development," in Edward Friedman and Mark Selden, *America's Asia* (New York: Vintage, 1971), p. 349.

77. Alexander Eckstein, "Economic Development Prospects, " p. 114.

78. John Kenneth Galbraith, "Galbraith has seen China's Future and it Works," *The New York Times Magazine* (Nov. 26, 1972), p. 38.

79. The data in this section is drawn from tables 9.1; 9.5; 9.6; and 9.13 in Chen Nai-ruenn, *Chinese Economic Statistics* (Edinburgh: Edinburgh University Press, 1967), pp. 428–437.

80. Alexander Eckstein, "Economic Development Prospects," p. 113.

81. For a good discussion of wage systems see Audrey Donnithorne, *China's Economic System* (London: Allen and Unwin, 1967), pp. 204–218.

82. Mao Tse-tung, "On the Correct Handling," pp. 453–454.

83. Pranab Bardhan, "Recent Development," in Chen and Uppal, *India and China,* p. 50.

84. "On Khruschev's Phoney Communism and its Historical Lessons for the World," in *On the General Line for the International Communist Movement* (Peking: Foreign Language Press, 1964), p. 475.

85. Galbraith, "China's Future," p. 101.

86. Chang-tu Hu, *China* (London: Mayflower Press, 1960), ch. 19.

87. John Philip Emerson, "Manpower Training and Utilization of Specialized Cadres, 1949–1968," in Jon Wilson Lewis, ed., *The City in Communist China,* p. 200.

88. *Current Background,* 892 (October 21, 1969), p. 20. See also Bruce J. Esposito, "The Politics of Medicine in China," *Bulletin of the Atomic Scientists* (December, 1972).

89. Chang-tu Hu, *China*, ch. 20.

90. *The Ten Great Years* (Peking: Foreign Language Press, 1960), p. 193.

91. Donald J. Munro, "Egalitarian Ideal and Educational Fact in Communist China," in John M. H. Lindbeck, ed., *China, Management of a Revolutionary Society*, p. 286.

92. John Philip Emerson, "Manpower Training," p. 200.

93. Donald J. Munro, "Egalitarian Ideal," p. 286.

94. John Philip Emerson, "Manpower Training," p. 200.

95. Donald J. Munro, "Egalitarian Ideal," p. 286.

96. See Marianne Bastid, "Economic Necessity and Political Ideals in Educational Reform during the Cultural Revolution," *China Quarterly*, 42 (April-June, 1970), pp. 16–45.

97. *CCP Documents of the Great Proletarian Cultural Revolution* (Kowloon: Union Research Institute, 1968), pp. 42–54.

98. Gordon A. Bennet, "China's Continuing Revolution: Will It Be Permanent?" *Asian Survey* (January, 1970), p. 3.

99. *Peking Review* (May 20, 1967), p. 47.

100. For an inventory of approaches to the Cultural Revolution, see Richard Baum, ed., *China in Ferment* (Englewood Cliffs, N.J.: Prentice-Hall, Inc., 1970).

101. Gordon Bennet, "China's Continuing Revolution." See also Harry Harding, "China: The Fragmentation of Power," *Asian Survey* (January, 1972), pp. 1–15.

102. *Peking Review*, 35–36 (September 7, 1973), pp. 9–10.

Conclusion

DAVID E. SCHMITT

You have just finished an overview of the dynamics of six interesting and important Third World nations. These countries have undertaken a variety of approaches toward political development and represent various major problems faced by the emerging nations. Because of the importance of developing effective political tools and sound leadership strategies in Third World nations, we have included some relatively successful countries. From the standpoint of learning useful techniques and strategies, successful examples may be the most helpful. Most Third World countries, however, have not yet developed effective, proven institutions and some face seemingly hopeless problems.

It is apparent from these case studies that sequences can be crucial. Institutionalization, that is, the creation of effective political and administrative organizations, occurred in India partly under British Colonial rule. The British had made a conscious effort to create an effective administrative elite. The Congress Party emerged as a vehicle for channeling mass participation prior to independence. Moreover, political leaders were eventually able to generate positive feelings of national identity partly as a result of the struggle against the British. Thus, some of the key problems of political development were resolved prior to independence.

In Syria, and especially in Nigeria, the development of effective political and administrative institutions did not precede independence and mass political participation. The British role in Nigeria contributed little toward the establishment of institutions capable of governing. Nor did British policies or the actions of Nigerian elites help foster a common sense of national identity. Syria was more fortunate from the standpoint of national identity and the legitimacy of the state; its struggle against the French, for example, had helped weld together its diverse cultural groups. Though key phases of Chilean development occurred sequentially rather than all at once, Chile had obviously not developed institutions capable of meeting the needs and demands of its masses.

The Mexican and Chinese revolutions created multiple crises for those nations. Institutions capable of extracting resources and regulating economic and political life had to be created from scratch, although in China's case partial institutionalization of the party occurred prior to Mao's victory march into Peking. However, revolutions themselves can help forge national identity and accord governments with legitimacy. Certainly in Mexico and China the mobilization of the masses under the revolutions helped solve the problem of mass participation by providing new leaders with a strong reserve of support. The new governments of these countries also faced less resistance than the new Nigerian and Syrian governments, because opposition had been largely emasculated during the violent phase of the revolutions.

The Chinese and Mexican cases also suggest that struggle and violence can be a unifying force for new nations. In both countries the revolutions produced heroes and traditions that helped provide an ideological and cultural underpinning for the new governments. India and Syria were both more fortunate than Nigeria in this sense. Though neither underwent the violence that wracked China and Mexico during their revolutions, their struggles against Britain and France certainly helped produce a unifying and legitimizing popular sentiment. Furthermore, the Arab-Israeli conflict in the Middle East has contributed to a popular sense of common nationhood in Syria. For Nigeria, on the other hand, independence came practically by decree of the colonial power, and Nigeria's experience with violence during the Biafran War was divisive rather than unifying. Of course, violence produces great human suffering and clearly is not necessary as a foundation for political development in all systems. Indeed, the struggle against colonial rule was a comparatively peaceful process in India. But there is no denying the potentially unifying or supportive power of violent struggle.

The experiences of the countries in this volume clearly demonstrate the profound significance of cultural conflict or its absence. The chaotic experience of Nigeria can be largely explained by its divergent tribes with different languages, religions, traditions, and levels of modernization. Though India, Syria, Mexico, and China were not culturally unified, none was so radically fractured as Nigeria. The cases of China, Syria, and India, moreover, suggest that one overwhelmingly dominant culture can more easily absorb and deal with various subcultures, particularly when there are historical and cultural unifying forces. India benefited from partitioning at independence; it lost most of its hostile Moslem subculture when the subcontinent was split up into India and Pakistan. Chile's problems, however, suggest that even with a rather unified culture, other problems of Third World political change may produce chaos.

All of the six countries have confronted the problems of rapid technological and economic change and resultant social and political pressures. Chile and Mexico seemingly have had fewer difficulties because these political systems were established much earlier than the others. The mass media, for example, had not yet emerged as a significant force in the early part of this century. With respect to the amount of time for national identity to emerge and institutions to be built, Chile and India appear to have been particularly fortunate. However, the rapidity of recent social change seems to have affected Chile about as seriously as it has many other Third World nations.

All of the six cases demonstrate that there are a number of key variables helping to determine Third World political change. We have just reviewed some of the most significant ones. Yet the case studies also illustrate a variety of techniques and strategies that present leaders can employ in coping with their environment and in the quest to achieve their goals.

TECHNIQUES AND STRATEGIES OF POLITICAL DEVELOPMENT

Both before and after these six political systems were established, charismatic and unifying leaders, or their absence, have affected political development. As Professor Goldman pointed out, unifying leaders in Nigeria were conspicuous by their absence, largely due to the tribal rivalries sustained and fostered by British colonialism. For Syria, charismatic leaders were not a primary factor in the institutionalization of that system. However, Mao in China, Gandhi in India, and to a lesser extent, men such as Cárdenas in Mexico constituted an important symbolic and instrumental force for molding political structures capable of penetrating and guiding social and economic change. The memory of Allende could be an important symbol in mobilizing future violence and change in Chile. Normally such leaders seem to emerge from revolutions, struggles for independence, or internal violence. Also, leaders with charismatic personalities cannot be created at will. This potent political force, therefore, is not directly subject to political manipulation; it is partly a matter of chance.

Political parties represent a crucial tool of political development. India, China, Mexico, and, more recently, Syria, have evolved effective parties for linking government with the masses and thus for controlling public participation in a way that strengthens the political legitimacy of these systems. The importance of effective parties in controlling public participation and bringing together the diverse groups is apparent for all types of Third World (and modern) political systems, whether they be of the democratic, limited-democracy, authoritarian, or mobilization types. Moreover, the effectiveness of party organization has had direct bearing on the capacity of these countries to extract and control resources for the purposes of economic development and modernization.

The development of effective parties depends partly on historical and environmental circumstances such as past revolutions or conflict with foreign powers as in the case of Syria, but this vital tool of political development is also subject to the organization skills of present leaders and thus constitutes both a necessary and possible vehicle for control by Third World elites. Whatever approach toward development is taken by Third World nations, the organizational techniques of India, China, Mexico, and Syria are quite instructive. However, Chile's failure to evolve a broad-based multi-class party reminds us that political party activity can also have a divisive effect.

If parties represent the most important means of linking elites and masses and of integrating various interests, public bureaucracy represents the crucial instrument by which government policies are carried out. Because administrators inevitably help mold major policy decisions and make important decisions in their day-to-day affairs, a professionalized bureaucracy, committed at least in part to public goals, is essential for political development. Multiple pressures often hinder effective administrative development in Third World nations. Corruption, loyalty to tribe or caste over nation, and excessive size can stymie even the best intentioned leaders. Even modern nations may suffer from some of these difficulties though usually to a lesser degree and with lesser consequences, in part because of their higher economic development.

Britain facilitated the evolution of viable public administration in India but did little to foster it in Nigeria, with disastrous consequences. Both Mexico and Chile evolved comparatively effective administrative systems, in Mexico's case through interpenetration of party, bureaucracy, and the presidency. The Communist Party and ideology constitute the principal means of administrative control in China, but the scope of activities undertaken by that mobilization system has given Chinese leaders continuing difficulties. Compared with most Third World countries, however, it has been quite successful. Syrian administrative development is occurring in conjunction with the development of an effective party organization under military influence.

The six country studies clearly indicate the significance of ideology. Of course, ideology was partly determined or at least constrained by the various international and historical forces. To build public support, Mexico and China could play upon their revolutions and the threat of foreign powers, India upon its struggle for independence, and the Ba'thist Party in Syria upon conflict with Israel. Yet, all Third World ideologies can emphasize such themes as national sovereignty, economic growth, and social reform. The ideological penetration of society and of government institutions has made ideology a central force for political control in China. The other countries, being more pragmatic, have employed ideology primarily as a force for legitimizing government. Of course, Nigeria has yet to develop a truly national ideology. If it can evolve a popularly accepted ideology based upon and acceptable to its divergent cultural groups, it will have taken an important step toward creating effective political institutions.

Education can be a prime instrument by which national ideologies help legitimize political systems; it can also facilitate economic development. Most of these six countries have employed education for these purposes. But from an ideological perspective, none have utilized it with such thoroughgoing fervor as China, where schools, work groups, and various organizations have attempted to mold the political beliefs and values of its citizens. However, as was pointed out in the introductory chapter and illustrated in several of the cases, education is not always a unifying force. Student riots in Mexico, for example, have been that country's major source of recent instability. From a long-term perspective, however, that unrest could help produce beneficial reforms. In any event, this book has shown that educational policies are of great importance to Third World nations, but that they can be a source of stress as well as a means of control and economic growth.

Economic development is a vital component of government strategy in nearly all Third World nations. Urbanization, for example, produces the need for greatly expanded government services and a more complex or advanced system of agriculture in which the basic needs of city dwellers can be met. Technological and social changes radically alter consumption patterns. Demands for consumer goods and even luxury items increase, especially where mass media employ modern advertising to stimulate demand. Because at least some of these needs must be met if governments are to retain their legitimacy, economic growth is a paramount need for most Third World nations. Even governments such as those of Mexico and China, which derive significant legitimacy from their revolutions, must meet the basic needs of substantial sectors of society. Land reform programs may produce greater legitimacy and sometimes greater productivity, but Mexico's difficulty with many small, unproductive farms suggests that agricultural output remains an essential ingredient of reform. Both the socialistic and capitalistic avenues toward economic development have proved effective, and often ineffective. China and Mexico have both experienced economic growth. Naturally substantial government intervention in the economy is necessary even in the more capitalistic systems in order to stimulate and control growth.

Foreign trade and investment as well as direct aid from foreign countries and international organizations offer a source of funds as well as technological expertise. But we have noted that foreign meddling can weaken support for governments. Certainly excessive US involvement in Chile and, at one point, Soviet involvement in Syria strained the legitimacy of those governments. Where nations play off one modern state against another or otherwise control investment and trade patterns, these difficulties can be mitigated.

Economic modernization seems essential for long term legitimacy and therefore political development. It will be recalled that economic modernization refers not merely to growth but also to relatively equal opportunities, stable and balanced growth, and a genuine improvement in the standard of living of most citizens. Economic development does not necessarily lead to economic modernization; it may even lead to greater inequalities and a decline in the quality of life.

Governments must consciously direct efforts toward economic modernization even more than they do efforts toward economic growth, which can be partially a result of private investments. It should not be assumed that socialist regimes automatically represent more viable paths toward economic modernization. For example, they might squander their resources in military adventures or emphasize quantity of production over quality of life as much as a capitalistic regime. Whatever the type of political system, leaders must certainly give serious thought to solving the problems of the masses. All of the nations studied in this book have made some strides. Their comparative levels of success in modernizing economically are a function of many forces, including ideology, economic resources, economic growth, and of paramount importance—political development. Without effective and adaptable political and administrative organizations and public support, even the most reform-minded government will have difficulty modernizing economically. Syria experienced economic growth under weak governments, but comparatively little economic modernization.

The military can be a curse or a blessing. Military leaders may become effective political leaders to the extent that they acquire political skills and seek policies of benefit to their nations rather than merely to themselves and to their followers. Certainly armed forces represent a potent force for ensuring compliance with government policies. In Syria military officers are reform-minded and represent a major force for reform. In Mexico and India the armed forces are subservient to political leaders and have not seriously impeded political development. India's and Chile's long period of constitutional evolution contributed to the military's reluctance to intervene. Chile, of course, witnessed a military takeover in 1973 produced by the leftist nature of Allende's programs, the chronic nature of Chile's economic problems, and various other factors. Early indications suggest that the policies of the military government in that nation may seriously impede long-term political development as well as economic modernization.

China has been the most aggressive in using the military not only as a means of political control, but also as a labor force and an educational forum. Control of the military has required strong party organization and effective ideological indoctrination. As Professor Falkenheim demonstrated, however, tension among military, party and administrative elites in China illustrates the potential problems as well as advantages of a strong military establishment.

AVENUES OF CHANGE: COSTS AND BENEFITS

India's experience illustrates that traditional structures such as caste systems are not necessarily incompatible with democratic parliamentary institutions. More importantly, Indian political development shows that political democracy can be a vehicle for previously dispossessed groups. Moreover, through its federal system, Indian political institutions even help mitigate cultural conflict and provide for local representation, although "President's Rule" has been necessary as a check to excessive federalism and the strains of modernization in that multi-cultural state. India is not quite a one-party or limited democratic system because of the genuine party competition that even allows opposition control of state governments.

Chile reflects some of the weaknesses of the democratic avenue toward development. Prior to the election of Allende, reforms had benefited primarily the middle classes, while the urban and rural masses remained impoverished and, for practical purposes, nearly disenfranchised. One of the disadvantages of the democratic approach is that it may allow, or even facilitate in some cases, dominance by the privileged sectors of society.

India reflects another problem with the democratic approach—the need for compromise and conciliation and sometimes the incapacity for decisive action. Certainly, India has less capacity to redistribute income among regions and among citizens than has communist China. Yet this limitation must be weighed against the potential capacity for representation and responsiveness in democratic systems such as that of India.

In any case, unlike India, most Third World countries did not institutionalize viable political and administrative structures and some did not forge a common national identity prior to independence or the rapid influx of new participants into their political systems. And few have had experience with democratic processes. Many groups in these countries will not follow democratic procedures, which are not a part of their cultural and political heritage. For these and other reasons the democratic road to political development is probably not a realistic short run alternative for most Third World nations.

Limited democracy provides a possible alternative, for authoritarian or mobilization governments may never change over to democratic institutions after substantial economic development has taken place, in part due to the vested interests of existing power structures. Mexico's experience indicates a possible alternative route, where the political culture may not admit of successful competitive party politics, but where the ruling party operates through conciliation and compromise and where significant political freedoms are allowed. Yet Professor Poitras warned that ". . . the Mexican path of one-party development . . . has gained political stability at the price of democracy and social justice." For those who may value the freedoms of democratic politics, however, the operation of democratic structures, even in a paternalistic fashion, offers greater possibility of future liberalism than do the authoritarian and mobilization avenues.

What the authoritarian systems lack in conciliation through democratic processes they may compensate for by resolute action that achieves a higher degree of social democracy. The Ba'thist governments in Syria not only deprived the landed and business aristocracies of much of their power but also provided the basis for redistribution of land and social benefits to the poorer elements of society. Moreover, despite its authoritarianism, the Syrian government has attempted to govern by acquiring the support of major social groups. In a sense, authoritarian structures are operating in a somewhat democratic manner. In any case, the failure of democratic institutions became apparent at an early stage, as they did in Nigeria.

Hopefully, reform-minded authoritarian leaders can help forge a sense of national purpose in Nigeria and bring about economic modernization with a minimum of bloodshed and a maximum of respect for Nigeria's various tribal entities. The cultural fragmentation of that nation is so severe, however, that this will be a difficult task. For those favoring democratic politics, there is also the possibility that Nigerian leaders may acquire such a stake in centralized government that they might be unwilling to relinquish control at a later date.

Despite the apparent necessity for authoritarian rule in many Third World countries, we should not forget that these systems may exhibit leanings that impede necessary economic and political change. Further, like governments following other approaches, they may reflect little more than self-serving, self-perpetuating power structures of a narrow, unrepresentative elite.

China exhibits both the enormous benefits and the enormous costs of a radical mobilization pattern of political development. There is no question that the Chinese "mobilization" approach has greatly increased the material well-being of China's masses and produced substantial economic modernization. The exploitation by former landowners has been eradicated, starvation seems to have been eliminated, and there is certainly greater equality of opportunity. China's successes are reflected not only by the radical improvements in the material well-being of its citizens, but also by the ultimate establishment of a fairly stable political order, and, above all, the capacity of government to exert substantial control over its environment. The Chinese government is a prime determinant of social and economic change.

China's failures and limitations are reflected by its recurrent leadership crises and persistent administrative problems. A chronic problem for mobilization systems is the transfer of power when a charismatic leader dies, retires, or is ousted, though collective leadership may partially alleviate this difficulty. Moreover, as Professor Falkenheim demonstrated, there are facets of economic growth and modernization that seem to respond only slowly to centralized planning and control. No political system is very likely to control completely its environment.

For those who value individual freedoms, mobilization systems present a drastic and unacceptable alternative. Yet there is no denying China's spectacular successes. What may seem surprising is the failure of greater numbers of Communist mobilization systems to emerge in the Third World, in view of Communism's goal of worldwide revolution. As we saw in the introduction, a distinct coming together of events is necessary for a true revolution to occur, and such a revolution need not necessarily lead to the Communist or other mobilization patterns, as the example of Mexico indicates. The case of Chile suggests the difficulty of achieving a Marxist society in a democratic setting. In the introduction, moreover, it was shown that most Third World leaders are far more concerned with nation building and economic growth than with following a particular philosophy such as Marxism. The opposition of Western powers and the cultural restraints within Third World nations are also among the factors explaining the failure of Communist efforts to achieve worldwide revolution or of Third World leaders to adopt the Communist mobilization approach.

The problems and outside pressures on Third World nations often seem overwhelming. Short-term political development is likely to be the exception rather than the rule. The example of Syria, however, demonstrates that stable evolution is not the only means of developing effective institutions. Instability can in fact be a useful and sometimes necessary vehicle for change. Today's violence may help produce tomorrow's viability. Citizens from Western countries are far too likely to overrate the virtues of stability and to forget their own chaotic national pasts. Even though countries such as the United States faced less rapid and certainly less simultaneous crises, they often have had shaky and sometimes violent histories. The US civil war was one of the bloodiest of all time, and United States history is littered with rebellion and discord.

In fact, while the modern economic nations seem more fortunate than their Third World cousins and sometimes cause them great misery, there is little reason for a complacent assumption that modern states are all that secure. The introductory chapter showed that political development is a process, not a final ultimate reality. Crises come and go, and there is no guarantee that modern nations can meet them all. The interplay between government and its environment is continual.

Thus, Third World and modern nations confront certain similar difficulties. Rapid change is a central reality of contemporary life, and the amazing pace of technological advances burdens modern as well as Third World countries. In the United States, for example, computers and mammoth bureaucracies contribute to a depersonalization that alienates young and old alike. The most profound issue for modern states, of course, is their need to avoid nuclear war. For technological advances have made possible the total destruction of these nations through the use of sophisticated weapons.

We have seen that without specialized, effective organizations, Third World nations are unable to deal with the complex political and social issues created by modernization. Yet modern states face a related problem. Though they have complex bureaucracies and highly-trained experts, they confront such difficult problems that solutions often seem beyond reach. Pollution, housing shortages, and especially cultural difficulties such as discrimination against Jews in Russia, blacks in America, and Catholics in Northern Ireland, illustrates not only the limited power of modern governments but also remaining injustice toward some citizens. From the standpoints of responsible foresight and justice, humanitarian development seems to have eluded the advanced nations. Third World countries may therefore have at least one advantage over their more advanced neighbors. They have the opportunity to avoid some of the errors and evils of modern nations while adopting their good features. How effective they will be in this endeavor, however, must remain an open question.